REGIONAL ORDERS

University of California

IGCC

Institute on Global Conflict and Cooperation

A project of the
University of California Institute
on Global Conflict and Cooperation

REGIONAL ORDERS

Building Security in a New World

Edited by
David A. Lake
and
Patrick M. Morgan

The Pennsylvania State University Press
University Park, Pennsylvania

Library of Congress Cataloging-in-Publication Data

Regional orders : building security in a new world / edited by David A. Lake and Patrick M. Morgan.
p. cm.
Includes bibliographical references and index.
ISBN 0-271-01703-1 (cloth : alk. paper)
ISBN 0-271-01704-X (pbk. : alk. paper)
1. Regionalism (International organization) 2. Security, International. I. Lake, David A. II. Morgan, Patrick M., 1940– .
JX1979.R3919 1997
327.1'72—dc21 96-50186
CIP

Printed in the United States of America
Published by The Pennsylvania State University Press,
University Park, PA 16802-1003

It is the policy of The Pennsylvania State University Press to use acid-free paper for the first printing of all clothbound books. Publications on uncoated stock satisfy the minimum requirements of American National Standard for Information Sciences—Permanence of Paper for Printed Library Materials, ANSI Z39.48-1992.

Contents

PART IV: BUILDING REGIONAL ORDERS

PART V: CONCLUSION

Figures and Tables

Acknowledgments

This volume was sponsored by the University of California's Institute on Global Conflict and Cooperation. We are grateful to IGCC and especially its director, Susan Shirk, for stimulating our interest in regional relations and generously supporting our efforts.

The Global Peace and Conflict Studies Program at the University of California, Irvine, organized three conferences over two years for this project. We are also grateful to GPACS, and especially Ira Gluck, for their administrative support.

This volume would not have been possible without the efforts of many individual scholars. The authors of the various chapters below are exemplary scholars who took seriously and sought to learn from the comments and criticisms of the editors, their fellow contributors, and other invited participants in our meetings. We are indebted to all for their outstanding efforts. In addition to the authors, we would like to thank Vinod Aggarwal, Richard Anderson, Michael Desch, Scott Gartner, Deborah Larson, Steven Spiegel,

Steve Weber, and Fred Wehling for sharing with us their insights and wisdom in one or more project meetings.

We would also like to thank Jennifer Pournelle at IGCC, Lynne Bush of Seaside Publishing, and Joni Harlan for helping to make this collection of chapters a book. Barbara Butterton at IGCC provided administrative support large and small; her efforts are acknowledged with considerable pleasure. Sandy Thatcher at Penn State Press saw the value in this undertaking early on and has been a constant source of support. Cherene Holland managed the production of the manuscript, and Keith Monley did the copyediting. We are deeply grateful to all.

Finally, we are indebted to our families for their encouragement and, most of all, their understanding when we had to spend yet another weekend in Laguna Beach working on regional order.

Part I

Introduction

1

The New Regionalism in Security Affairs

David A. Lake and Patrick M. Morgan

During the Persian Gulf War, George Bush sought to evoke a "new world order." The president was right in seeing a new potential for the international management of interstate and intrastate conflicts, but he was wrong in his horizons. Rather than a single *world* order, we are witnessing today the emergence of a variety of new *regional* orders.

For much of this tumultuous century international politics were clearly global in focus and scale. Great-power rivalries, and the resulting hot and cold wars, were conducted worldwide by states with global interests and global reach. These contests, in turn, had important effects and implications for nearly all other states and societies.[1]

The Cold War had a dual effect on regional conflicts. On the one hand, it internationalized many otherwise local conflicts. In Africa, Southeast Asia, the Middle East, and elsewhere, local conflicts were subsumed within the superpower competition. In dispute after dispute, local combatants appealed

1. Struggles for empire before World War I were also global in scale and possessed the same implications for regional conflict. We confine analysis here to the period after 1945.

for assistance from outside powers. Each superpower, fearing the other might provide decisive aid and thereby gain political advantage, was driven to assist one or the other party. This competition for influence expanded conflicts, as well, driving the superpowers (and their key allies) to provide ever greater resources to opposing clients. Despite their potentially independent dynamics, local conflicts—like lighter masses of matter near a black hole—were inexorably pulled into and lost within the Cold War.

On the other hand, the superpowers also restrained local conflicts out of a fear of escalation. In their spheres of influence, each superpower suppressed conflicts, concerned that open dispute would create opportunities for the other to intervene in its politically sensitive backyard. In areas of competition and struggle, the superpowers circled one another in a dangerous dance of mutual restraint, cautiously regarding the moves of both the other and their own clients—with the latter allowed neither to succeed nor to fail for fear of the consequences. Some analysts have cited the balance-of-power character of such management; others have pointed to the "regimes" the superpowers used to manage peace and conflict (Breslauer and Tetlock 1991; Kanet and Kolodziej 1991; S. Weber 1991). By whatever means, the superpowers did exercise a degree of management to counteract increased regional tensions, keep conflicts within bounds, and occasionally even impose settlements.[2]

Today, though tensions have receded between the great powers, they have exploded in various parts of the world. There is a continuing need for the international management of conflict and the promotion of cooperation. What is to replace the superpower management that, for all its faults and limitations, evolved and operated during the Cold War? Many analysts emphasize the possibilities and necessity for management at the global level, undertaken through a refurbished United Nations Security Council or some other variant of a great-power concert: a new world order with the great powers, one way or another, at the helm.[3] This vision is, at best, premature. It anticipates developments that appear unlikely for the foreseeable future.

Strong norms that dictate a forceful global-level response to aggression are emerging only slowly, if at all. The response to Iraq's seizure of Kuwait will not be readily and regularly duplicated. The multinational force that

2. On regional variations in patterns of foreign military intervention even during the Cold War, see Pickering and Thompson (n.d.).

3. For one example, see Dewitt, Haglund, and Kirton 1993. Although acknowledging trends toward the regionalization of security (5), the focus of that volume, like many others, is on the origins, forms, and threats to global order.

defeated Iraq was called into existence by the extraordinarily blatant violation of the norm of territorial integrity and by continuing concern over access to the oil resources of the Persian Gulf. The confluence of key great-power interests with those of so many other states, and within such congenial circumstances for action, is not likely to be repeated. This is particularly true for severe internal conflicts, the most widespread and lethal form of organized fighting in the world today. While evolving toward a more expansive conception, international norms governing intervention in internal conflicts remain highly contested (Deng et al. 1996; Damrosch 1993; Kaysen, Pastor, and Reed 1994). Apart from mounting its traditional humanitarian and peacekeeping activities, the United Nations is unlikely to impose itself in a forceful, consistent, and effective way in such conflicts. By themselves, regional conflicts are unlikely to force the further development of global management capabilities.

In addition, the great powers are now unwilling to accept the heavy burdens of conflict management in distant areas of the globe, sometimes rejecting even limited costs and burdens in areas where they have traditional ties. The desire in Washington, Bonn, Moscow, or Tokyo to avoid major engagement even in "their" parts of the world is palpable. The long-delayed response to the collapse of Yugoslavia is a vivid case in point. Reluctance to bear substantial costs leaves little scope for management through either a global organization or informal cooperation among the great powers.

Countries cannot, however, ignore threats from the territorial ambitions of others, unrest at home, or even strife between other states. Often they must do something. Increasingly, that something is likely to take form at the regional level. In the foreseeable future, violent conflicts will mostly arise out of regional concerns and will be viewed by political actors through a regional, rather than global, lens. Efforts to cope with violent conflicts, as well as to achieve order and security, will primarily involve arrangements and actions devised and implemented at the regional level.[4]

4. Also stressing the increasing regionalization of world politics, but focusing somewhat more on economic trends, see Hurrell and Fawcett 1995. For an alternative view of the forces making for the regionalization of international politics, see Katzenstein 1993. Although we do not discuss economic regionalism in this volume, this topic has recently received significant attention. See Yarbrough and Yarbrough 1992 and Mansfield and Milner 1997. The trend toward economic regionalism is perhaps more mixed than the trend toward security regionalism: in the international economy, globalization and regionalization appear to be pushing states in conflicting directions, but there is today, in our view, no major impetus toward globalization in the security arena. The effects of economic interdependence on regional security orders are discussed in the chapters by Solingen (4), Papayoanou (6), and Rosecrance and Schott (7), this volume.

The regionalization of security is not a universal trend. There are exceptions, such as the continuing global-level concern with nuclear proliferation. The overall direction and pace of the trend is also conditioned by varying domestic, regional, and global-level factors. However, as states focus increasingly on regional conflict and conflict management, analysts of the changing security environment must also delve into the nature and sources of regional order.

At one time there was strong interest in the regional level, both in system-subsystem studies and the analysis of regional integration.[5] Both languished when attention shifted to the global level with the study of system dynamics (neorealism) and cooperation and interdependence (neoliberalism). With no consistent trend toward subsystem dominance, attention shifted away from regional politics. Likewise, integration studies declined as the processes involved were explored instead at the global level, particularly in the subfield of international political economy.

The world has now changed. The regional level stands more clearly on its own as the locus of conflict and cooperation for states and as the level of analysis for scholars seeking to explore contemporary security affairs. With this volume we seek to understand better the emergence and variation of regional security orders and to identify when and how great powers, like the United States, can best contribute to regional stability in the years ahead. Both individually and collectively, we make four primary arguments.

First, regions are now more salient features of international politics. With the end of the Cold War, regional conflicts are more likely to stay regional, responding to their individual circumstances and developments. The ability of the great powers, and especially the United States, to intervene around the globe has not diminished. Their interest in supporting local clients and regulating regional conflicts has, however, significantly declined. Less competitive global relations free regions to develop along their own paths. While the role and importance of global relations have shrunk in analytic and practical importance, regional relations have grown.

As long as great powers retain the capacity to intervene, international

5. The major contributors to the literature on regional subsystems include Binder (1958), Brecher (1963), Zartman (1967), and Cantori and Spiegel (1970b). Boals (1973) and Thompson (1973) provide useful reviews. For some of the classic works on regional integration, see Deutsch et al. 1957, Haas 1958, Lindberg and Scheingold 1971, and Nye 1968. Regional integration studies have, of course, undergone a renaissance with the creation of the European Union. For a review of recent works in this area, see Anderson 1995.

politics will continue to be a complex interplay between domestic, global, and, increasingly, regional factors. Our argument is not that regions are now autonomous. We claim only that the importance of regional relations have expanded with the end of the Cold War, and that regions are a substantially more important venue of conflict and cooperation than in the past. Accordingly, regions are more important objects of study than ever before.

Second, the end of the Cold War has opened new possibilities for more cooperative regional orders. Greater responsibility now falls on local states to manage their own conflicts. In some regions, states are beginning to take up this challenge. In the Middle East, Israel and the Arab states are moving toward peace; and in Africa, the Organization of Africa Unity is taking the first, tentative steps toward collective security. While there is no guarantee that states will take advantage of these opportunities, there are encouraging signs on the horizon, and in several regions the possibilities are already beginning to take root. New regional orders of varying form are taking shape, with important consequences for the future of international conflict.

Third, regions are not simply "little" international systems that behave in ways identical to their "larger" counterparts. Nor are they sui generis, understandable only through unique theories. We need general theories that incorporate regional relations. The politics and dynamics associated with great powers—the focus of most analysis both in the academy and policy community—are not played out in miniature within regions. Theories, concepts, and analogies based on the analysis of great-power politics cannot, in most cases, be applied to the regional level without significant amendment or even wholesale revision. On the other hand, the politics of regions are not necessarily unique. We do not need a different theory for every region. As discussed in this volume, the task is to incorporate regional politics into our existing approaches and theories. This provides an important challenge to analysts and opens up new avenues for the comparative study of regions. This book takes the first steps toward meeting this challenge.

Fourth, as argued in several essays and, especially, our concluding chapter to this volume, *the foreign policies of the great powers must be tailored to the individual circumstances of different regions.* By definition, great powers possess a global reach and are involved in the politics of more than one region. In the new world of regional orders, the quest for universal principles of foreign policy in great powers like the United States is dangerous. Regional orders differ. Policy must accommodate these differences if it is to succeed within the varied circumstances of the post–Cold War world.

Understanding Regions

International politics within regions have traditionally been studied in three ways, with important implications for international relations theory. For some analysts, international politics are understood to be everywhere and always the same. In this view, certain behaviors hold at whatever level states cluster; regions are smaller but otherwise identical to global systems. "Region" is a diminutive term, but otherwise carries no analytic content. It follows that theories developed to explain global conflict and cooperation can be applied without modification in regional settings. One can generalize from the regional to the global, or vice versa. Basing their studies on the Middle East, for example, Stephen Walt (1987) examines the pattern of regional alliances to test a general theory of balancing, while John Mearsheimer (1983), in explaining why deterrence worked or failed in the region, applies an analysis intended to pertain to states everywhere. Similarly, the literature on strategic surprise offers a general explanation on the basis of case studies drawn from numerous regions, but especially the Middle East (e.g., Knorr and Morgan 1983). While often enlightening, this view denies the analytic importance of regions, however much they may have recently risen in significance as arenas of international activity.

A contrasting approach treats each region as unique. In this view, the Middle East, or any other region, is like nowhere else. What works (or fails) there has only limited implications for understanding other regions. The area-studies literature has often reflected this approach. For years, studies of the relations among Communist nations, for example, emphasized their distinctive ideology and political system (e.g., Brzezinski 1967). This approach can also be found implicitly in many theories of international relations. Kalevi J. Holsti (1992) has suggested that much of our theoretical equipment reflects a preoccupation with the distinctive international politics of just one region: the Western interstate system. Some analysts fear that nuclear deterrence is regionally specific in its dynamics and effects and will not work in the same fashion (i.e., not as well) elsewhere as it did in East-West relations.[6] In this view, explanations must be tailored to distinct regions. Assumptions, variables, and propositions appropriate in one region are irrelevant or wrong when applied to another. Each region requires it own theory.

The third alternative, endorsed here, falls roughly between the others. In this *comparative* approach, regions affect behavior and constitute a separate

6. For opposing points of view on this question, see Sagan and Waltz 1995.

level of analysis. As a result, we would not expect regional and global politics to be the same. Within this level, regions also differ in their characteristics, not in terms of the variables but in the values attached to those variables. Thus, while the Middle East, South Asia, or Latin America can be analyzed in the same terms, they may differ considerably in their relevant traits. One region might be bipolar in structure, another unipolar, a third multipolar. The variable of regional system structure, presumably, would be important for understanding politics in each region, even if it took different forms or levels in each case. Such a view deems it possible, and necessary, to generalize about regions while predicting different patterns of behavior from their individual traits.

While recognizing that regions differ in their characteristics or levels of common variables, this comparative approach—and this volume—rejects the call for a different theory for each region. Regions vary widely in their approaches to security management, but comparative analysis still requires a common typology and set of causal variables. Our desire is to construct theories of regional order. Taking the mode of conflict management—the regional order—as the common dependent variable, we seek to explain these patterns as a function of such factors as the regional system structure, the domestic politics of states in the region, and the interaction between the region and the global system.

At the same time, the volume rejects the view that regions necessarily operate according to the same laws and processes as the global system. Global systems are closed or can be safely treated for some purposes as if they are closed: all of the actors who can affect outcomes in consequential ways are included.[7] As a result, behavior is determined, and can be explained, by the constraints and processes of that system. Two closed systems from different levels of analysis but otherwise possessing identical properties (i.e., a bipolar global and a bipolar regional system) would be expected to display identical behaviors. However, regional systems are inherently open. The global system, other regional systems, and even "outside" states can have a

7. The defense of this position rests on the value of problem-solving theory (Waltz 1986). This discussion suggests an important implication for the study of the global system as well. Instead of being closed, this system may also be open. Treating it as closed implies strongly that regional systems are analytically and practically autonomous or, less strongly, that the global system is dominant and influences regional systems without being influenced significantly in return. If we take regional systems seriously, however, both positions are called into question. States make choices in one system that may affect other systems, and actions within one may be contingent on actions in the other. Thus, we will not be able to understand patterns of international affairs without "opening" the global system and explicitly including this interaction in our theories.

major impact on a region. In open systems, the constraints and processes of the system are only partial explanations of behavior. Thus two open systems with identical properties would not necessarily produce the same behaviors. "Outside" factors must be incorporated into theories of regional relations, and, equivalently, regional relations must be incorporated into other theories.

It follows that we may not be able to transfer extant theories of international relations to the regional level, at least not without substantial modification. Consider two examples. Waltz (1979) hypothesizes that bipolar systems will be more stable, defined in terms of great-power war, than multipolar systems. Central here is the proposition that superpowers rely on their own resources, not alliances, and that this internal balancing strategy is more transparent; miscalculations of the balance of capabilities are therefore less likely. An open regional system, however, can draw resources from outside; in such a bipolar system, the poles will be especially active in soliciting outside support—pursuing, in essence, external balancing strategies. Thus, whereas bipolarity produces internal balancing and stability in a global system, it logically stimulates external balancing and potential instability at the regional level. The same theoretical logic produces different behavioral predictions. Similarly, the theory of hegemonic stability hypothesizes that unipolar global systems are most likely to produce an open, liberal international economy.[8] It has been suggested that Comecon constituted an autonomous economic bloc, that the Soviet Union was hegemonic within it, and that the mercantilist nature of this bloc therefore disconfirms the theory.[9] Yet, Comecon was surrounded by more economically competitive states. Does it necessarily follow that the Soviet Union should have built a free trade system within the bloc? Or should it have attempted, as it did, to develop its industrial capabilities through a mercantilist strategy? Does a hegemon in an open system possess the same interests as one in a closed system? The answers are not obvious. Current theory offers no real guide.

Imposing a global theory on regions may raise interesting questions, but we should not assume the answers will be the same. It is not that theories of global politics never apply. Indeed, we expect such theories to be progressive guides in building theories of regional relations. Rather, the application of global-level theories must be pursued with sensitivity to the openness of regional settings.

8. For a review of this now voluminous literature, see Lake 1993.

9. On the concept of the Soviet Union as a regional hegemon, see Bunce 1985 and 1987. On an equally problematic conception of regional hegemons, see Myers 1991b.

Our approach does not dismiss the other options. Aspects of regional politics will resemble global politics, and studying one may inform us about the other. And global-level components, many in the contemporary world economy, will continue to affect regional security affairs in significant ways. In turn, there is no reason to expect that the unique features of regions will never play an important role. Ours is not a plea to include everything, but rather a call to start with regions and employ a comparative approach. In the years ahead, this is where the major progress is likely to be made in the management of order and security and, in turn, in the study of conflict and cooperation.

Regional Security Complexes and Regional Orders

To this point, we have been using the term "region" rather loosely. To outline the central analytic structure of this volume, it is now necessary to be more precise. In this collection, the basic unit of analysis is the regional security complex, a concept devised by Barry Buzan (1991) to describe a specific kind of region united by common security problems. A regional security complex defines the set of states that constitutes a "region" in ordinary language. In turn, all of the chapters seek to explain a common dependent variable: the regional order, or the mode of conflict management within the regional security complex. Along with other factors, the characteristics of a regional security complex can also serve as independent variables that influence the regional order.

"Region," of course, has many different meanings (see Thompson 1973). In one common definition, region refers to a set of countries linked by geography and one or more common traits, such as level of development, culture, or political institutions. Defined in this way, regions differ not on any fixed criteria but according to the purposes of the researcher—and they can be as broad as the Third World or as narrow as North America. In a second definition, a region is a set of countries that are or perceive themselves to be politically interdependent. Regional systems theories, most generally, conceive of regions as patterns of relations or interactions within a geographic area that "exhibit a particular degree of regularity and intensity to the extent that a change at one point in the [system] affects other points" (Thompson 1973, 101). Constructivist theories, using essentially the same definition but in a very different theoretical context, treat regions as socially created entities that take on meaning and importance because states perceive themselves as cohabiting a common area and sharing a common future.[10]

Regional security complexes are closely related to the second of these common definitions, but focus exclusively on the security interdependencies of states. Adjusting the concept to fit contemporary international politics, we define a regional security complex as a set of states continually affected by one or more security externalities that emanate from a distinct geographic area. In such a complex, the members are so interrelated in terms of their security that actions by any member, and significant security-related developments inside any member, have a major impact on the others. While geography may bind most members of a regional security complex together, geographic proximity is not a necessary condition for a state to be a member of a complex. Existing regional security complexes often have one or more significant members, typically great powers able to project force over distance, that are not physically located in the geographical area that is the locus of the complex. The United States clearly belongs in the regional security complexes of Europe and the Middle East, for instance, even though it is not geographically a part of either. In our view, geography defines the physical area from which security externalities radiate, not the set of states that may be members of a regional security complex. Patrick M. Morgan explicates this conception of regional security complexes in Chapter 2.

Regional security complexes, in turn, are distinct from regional orders. The existence of security externalities linking states together does not itself define the way in which those states seek to manage their security relations. Also in Chapter 2, Morgan presents a typology of alternative regional orders, discusses the attributes of each type, and illustrates the alternatives with examples from European history. Regional orders, Morgan proposes, range from a very traditional arrangement, in which security is sought via a "suitable" distribution (or "balance") of power, to various cooperative efforts at security management—a great-power concert, collective security, a pluralistic security community, or a modest level of integration. While a security complex normally has elements of more than one of these ideal types of orders, one tends to be dominant in terms of states' preferences, perceptions, and strategies. Analysis, then, turns on how and why the members have opted for that particular approach to security management, and what fac-

10. For the most part, these two approaches pose a "chicken-and-egg" problem that cannot be unraveled. Common conceptions absent interactions are not likely to be sustained, and dense interactions are likely to produce a perception of common destiny or "regionness."

tors affect the likelihood it will be retained or displaced. Both regional security complexes and regional orders, we believe, are useful analytic concepts for organizing inquiry into regional relations. These concepts are employed throughout the volume.

Understanding Regional Orders

The chapters in Part II of this book examine how regional systems, domestic political coalitions, and the changing international environment affect the type of regional order likely to be found in various security complexes. A serious focus on regions necessarily involves reopening the question of what constitutes a regional system, once a subject of considerable debate. In Chapter 3, David A. Lake builds upon the concept of an externality, as it is commonly used in economics, and poses a new approach. In his view, a regional system is the product of one or more security externalities or "spillovers." Normally these externalities originate in, but are not necessarily limited to, a specific geographic area. This set of linkages, in turn, produces the strategic interactions central to a regional system. From this point of departure, Lake examines how the number, magnitude, and distribution of security externalities, nonsecurity externalities, transactions costs, regional system structures, and the global system structure influence prospects for varying regional orders.

Etel Solingen, in Chapter 4, examines how domestic political and economic interests influence the pattern of regional conflict and cooperation and choice of regional order, and offers a domestic explanation of how and why members of a regional security complex may adopt more cooperative approaches to security management. In brief, if a coalition in power opts for vigorous participation in the liberal international economic order, it will be amenable to cooperative regional security arrangements as well. As Solingen demonstrates with reference to numerous examples, regional orders are strongly influenced by domestic politics.

In Chapter 5, Arthur A. Stein and Steven E. Lobell review the varied ways in which the collapse of the Cold War has shaped peace and security in the contemporary world. Arguing that there were always regional variations in the degree of superpower penetration, they demonstrate how the end of bipolarity—as well as some of the unique features of its demise—has created new patterns of regional relations. In some areas the end of the Cold War has led to a reduction in regional-level conflict, opening the door to a degree of regional cooperation not previously possible. In other regions it has eroded the existing arrangements that helped contain conflicts. In all cases, Stein and Lobell conclude, it has led to a greater regionalization of security.

While we are aware that regional systems, domestic politics, and international systems interact, these three essays focus primarily on discrete levels of analysis. Scholars are increasingly uneasy with the artificial divide between international and domestic politics and, by extension, with the distinction between global, regional, and domestic politics. There are many reasons for this dissatisfaction. Perhaps most important is the renewed recognition that the levels of analysis not only coexist, they interact. States create regional and international systems through domestically motivated actions, and these actions, in turn, are constrained by the regional and international systems. To capture this interaction requires that we move away from our current understanding of the levels-of-analysis problem to what are now often called, metaphorically, "two-level games" (Evans, Jacobson, and Putnam 1993). The levels-of-analysis "problem," as explicated by Waltz (1959) and others, pursues a logic of isolation, in which knowledge comes from identifying the independent effect of causal variables located in autonomous levels. The two- or, in our case, three-level-game alternative posits a synergism between domestic, regional, and international politics that, when it exists, can be missed by more traditional theories. The multilevel game alternative is still in its infancy, with only modest accomplishments to date, but it is a promising agenda for research. However, integrating regional politics into nascent models of multilevel games will likely produce theories of staggering complexity. We lack the analytic notions and methodological tools to create the kinds of models required. Consequently, we should not expect complete multilevel theories any time soon. Our theories and insights will remain partial. This has two implications for the present volume. First, the problem of understanding regional orders must be broken down into manageable parts. Second, even if the goal proves elusive, work on regional orders should move in the direction of multilevel games. Theories should be assessed not only by their empirical accuracy but also by the extent to which they produce progress toward this goal. The essays beyond Chapter 5 reflect our collective concern with both of these implications and will, we hope, spur additional research.

Problems of Regional Security Management

Two issues are central to regional conflict management after the Cold War and are addressed in Part III. First, although the superpowers, to one extent or another, previously globalized conflicts, undercutting the importance of regions analytically and practically, what is likely to be the role of the great powers in regional conflicts now? Will they continue to intervene? If so, will they compete or cooperate? While the essays in Part II suggest that the role of the great powers will be more limited, the questions of how, when, and why they intervene in regional affairs remain important. Placing greater emphasis on politics between the great powers than most others in this volume, Paul A. Papayoanou and Richard Rosecrance and Peter Schott address these questions and reach somewhat different conclusions.

In Chapter 6, Papayoanou argues that whether great powers intervene will be a function of (1) the regional balance of power, and the efficacy of regional management more generally; (2) the interests of the great powers in the region, especially the extent to which they are affected by the externalities that define the regional security complex; and (3) the ability of the great powers to make credible commitments. Papayoanou predicts a variegated response by great powers across regional security complexes, with only some areas displaying the conditions necessary for the great powers to cooperate in the effective management of regional conflict.

Rosecrance and Schott, in Chapter 7, examine whether concerts of great powers are possible solutions to regional conflicts. They identify the necessary conditions for a successful concert at both the global and regional levels, derive lessons from past practice, and address issues of current conduct—including cost-effectiveness, regional self-sufficiency in security, the presence of regional protégés, and the timing and phases of intervention. They generally take a more positive view of the prospects for and implications of great-power intervention, seeing concerts as a means of ensuring regional stability and order.

Second, what role can multilateral organizations and regional multilateralism play in managing regional conflict? Much attention has recently been devoted to this question, and in current policy debates some form of multilateral management is the most frequently offered alternative to great-power intervention. Indeed, as the essays in Part IV indicate, when states attempt to organize themselves to improve regional security management, they frequently select multilateral methods. In Chapter 8, Brian L. Job examines the concept of multilateralism, the operation of multilateralist forms of security management in regional settings, and expectations for multilateral regional orders after the Cold War. He argues that regional collective security arrangements tend either to perpetuate political divisions between countries or to fail to overcome problems of collective action. For these reasons, multilateral alternatives are not likely to be effective—at least in the short run. Taking a more constructivist view of regionalism, however, Job concludes that multilateralism supports the evolution of common identities and norms of intraregional relations that may enhance cooperation in the longer run.

Building Regional Orders

Part IV turns to the politics of building regional order in six different regional security complexes. The chapters on Latin America, the states of the former Soviet Union, the Asia-Pacific, the Middle East, Africa, and Southeast Asia identify each regional security complex, explore the forces that have shaped the policies of the relevant actors, and assess the direction in which the regional order is now evolving. Each essay brings together historical and practical knowledge while drawing on the analytic insights of Parts II and III. These six chapters are designed as examinations of regional security complexes that reflect on the variables above, but they also raise issues and trends specific to each region. The security complexes examined here, of course, are not exhaustive. We have made no effort to cover every piece of real estate, and have instead selected cases to illustrate different emerging regional orders.[11] Similarly, the regions are not exclusive. Susan L. Shirk takes up the Asia-Pacific complex as a whole, while Yuen Foong Khong analyzes ASEAN (the Association of Southeast Asian Nations), a regional security complex that is both distinct from and embedded in the larger Asia-Pacific complex. In each case, the appropriate level of aggregation is defined by the security complex under examination.

In both Latin America and the successor states to the Soviet Union, using

11. Although we select on basis of the dependent variable here, there is variation across the six cases in the type of regional order involved, thereby allowing some valid inferences to be drawn (see King, Keohane, and Verba 1994, 141–49).

power to restrain the ambitions of others remains the primary basis of regional order. In Chapter 9, David R. Mares demonstrates that the hegemony of the United States within Latin America is a force for both stability and instability. The United States helps stabilize the region by excluding outside forces, mediating conflicts, and providing public goods. On the other hand, its predominance and ability to intervene also make it the primary security threat to states within the regional security complex. With the end of the Cold War, efforts are being undertaken by the members of the complex to devise a new order that would reduce the role of military force in the region and restrain the overweening power of the United States—albeit within limits acceptable to the regional hegemon.

Despite the breakup of the Soviet Union, Russia remains the dominant power within the new regional security complex. As in Latin America, Philip G. Roeder argues, Russia helps stabilize the region by containing and resolving conflicts among the successor states, providing border defenses and bolstering domestic regimes, yet it simultaneously forms, in many cases, the most salient threat to the security of member states. Examining the central role of political leaders in the various successor states as they seek to retain office under threat from opponents at home and abroad, Roeder traces and explains the pattern of relations emerging in the nascent regional order. Although some successor states are seeking to balance against Russia, in others Russian hegemony is being embraced to bolster the local elite's chances for political survival.

In the other regional security complexes considered in this volume, the end of the Cold War has stimulated and, in a few cases, reinforced continuing efforts to build more cooperative regional orders. In different ways, the Middle East and East Asia security complexes appear to be moving gingerly toward regional concerts. In the Middle East, states are exhausted by decades of deep division, Cold War competition, and war. As David J. Pervin shows in Chapter 12, selected local powers—no longer able to play the superpowers against one another—as well as the United States, are trying to lay a foundation for a more cooperative regional order. Pervin concludes that the preconditions necessary for an autonomous concert of regional powers may now exist.

In a similar vein, Shirk argues that a concert may be about to emerge in the Asia-Pacific complex, largely because this is the one regional order that can successfully enhance the national interests of the major powers there. Interestingly, this is the only case examined in the volume in which several global powers are simultaneously full members of the regional security complex. Where Latin America and the former Soviet Union are dominated by one country, the Asia-Pacific has four—the United States, China, Japan, and Russia. Arguing that a regional balance of power will prove deficient for maintaining good relations among these states, Shirk draws upon their collective efforts to manage the problem of North Korea's nuclear weapons program and suggests that this may be a model of future collaboration in the regional order.

In Africa and Southeast Asia, even more extensive forms of regional security cooperation are being pursued. Today, Africa faces widespread domestic political instability, which can readily spread across borders through flows of refugees and armed rebels and other potential conduits of disruption. In Chapter 13, Edmond J. Keller shows that, as a result, political leaders in Africa have begun to reconsider norms restricting intervention in one another's internal affairs. Under the auspices of the Organization of African Unity and other subregional organizations, African leaders are creating the basis for what they hope will be a new, multilateral, regional collective security order.

In the Southeast Asia complex, Yuen Foong Khong argues that the growing "ASEAN spirit" animates efforts at building a more secure and cooperative regional order, one that may be evolving into a pluralistic security community. In 1967, several states in Southeast Asia created a regional multilateral organization (ASEAN) to escape from the local and superpower conflicts that plagued the area. In Chapter 14, Khong details the central political purpose and pattern of cooperation that has dominated this organization from its inception, and examines how it has slowly expanded to encompass most of the other states in the regional security complex.

The last chapter in this volume develops cross-regional comparisons, and returns to the analytic issues raised in Parts II and III. It also outlines the implications of this analysis for current U.S. foreign policy.

Conclusion

This volume highlights the increasing importance in the contemporary world of regional security complexes as the loci of both violent conflict and efforts to manage such conflict more effectively. The contributors agree that the regional level offers a separate and significant focal point for analysis, that regional security complexes are worthy of greater attention in the wake of the

Cold War, and that the comparative analysis of regional orders has considerable appeal. Nonetheless, their individual assessments as well as their analytic and substantive concerns differ. Thus we hope readers will appreciate the central themes in this volume, but at the same time note the variations offered by individual contributors.

In the end, we hope that the volume helps move the field of international relations away from the contrasting but, in our view, inadequate notions that international politics are always and everywhere the same and that regions are unique entities beyond the scope of general theory. We also hope it is a useful guide for understanding the process of building security in the new world of regional orders.

2

Regional Security Complexes and Regional Orders

Patrick M. Morgan

The subjects of "regional" conflict and what might be done about it now generate great interest. It is widely assumed that regional conflicts will remain important concerns of policy makers, offering serious threats to peace and to security arrangements while posing awkward and complex problems in security management.

"Regional" conflict calls to mind the general subject of regions and regionalism, which was once pursued with vigor (for examples, see Falk and Mendlovitz 1973), but then languished, due to a decline in the study of regional integration, a neorealist-induced preoccupation with the global system, and uneasiness about whether regions were meaningful entities in international politics.

This chapter has several objectives. First, it downplays the *region* in a traditional geographical sense as a focal point, and does not treat it as an important independent variable. The lesson from earlier regional system studies is that there is no way to identify regions, through geography, that enhances analysis in international politics. Second, it suggests focusing on "regional security complexes" and doing comparative analysis of such complexes in studying security today. Here it draws on the valuable works of Barry Buzan, where the concept of regional security complex was first developed and applied, but adjusts it to better fit contemporary international politics. Third, it offers a typology of regional security orders as a basis for comparative study of regional security complexes.

The discussion opens by considering how to define security,[1] a contested concept today. Then it takes up the question of how to define and identify regional security complexes and suggests why they deserve more attention now. The chapter concludes by laying out the typology of regional security orders.

The Concept of Security

In security studies the normal focus is on the safety of the state, its society, and its core values from physical harm and military coercion by external sources. There is now interest in broadening this along two lines.

First, desire to broaden our view of security arises from concern about drawbacks in the traditional conception of security itself. For instance, pursuing security via military strength has yielded a security that has seemed tenuous, a kind of controlled insecurity. An alternative is to focus on underlying causes of conflict and treat mitigation of them as an important contribution to security (a typical perspective in peace studies). Further, because deprivation (actual or potential) of any important value often induces fear, a sense of threat, and unhappiness, one word for which is "insecurity," the contention is made that security pertains to the enjoyment of any value of great importance, that threats to economic welfare or from a deformed environment are security issues. Along these lines Buzan (Buzan, Kelstrup, et al. 1990, 4) distinguishes military, political, economic, environmental, and societal security. The question is whether these matters should fall under the rubric of security or relate to it only through their impact on the threat and use of force.

Clearly, any issue over which fighting occurs is related to security. The

1. Our concern in this volume is with security via regional management arrangements, which makes it important that we indicate what we mean by security, what regional management is expected to provide.

same is true of anything states deem vital for military power. These things readily qualify as security matters. However, should the same designation apply to concerns about economic competition among states and its impact on jobs and welfare or to a threat to some other value considered vital (like the ozone layer) when there is no significant chance of fighting and any connection to military power is remote?

I assume that security ought to be defined fairly precisely if it is to mean anything. There is no benefit to lumping everything under that heading. I take security to be about being free from deliberate man-made violence. Security affairs principally concern the maintenance, use, and management of capacities either to inflict or to defend against man-made violence, especially war and, by extension, the conduct of political relationships that can readily lead to war. Many things can contribute to security either by affecting those capacities or the likelihood of their use, and thus many things have an impact on security affairs, and security concerns can intrude into lots of other matters. Tracing these interactions is easier with this conception than it is when they are all labeled security matters indiscriminately. It is better to treat security as one important value of many, among which trade-offs have to be made, than to throw the mantle of security over all of them.

The limitations of safety via military-related measures (wars, arms, arms reductions, etc.) do not justify watering down the concept. Certainly, such measures can produce insecurity instead, but that is a comment on their inadequacies under some circumstances, not grounds for placing any means that may have a beneficial effect on security under the same heading.

An emphasis on *physical safety* narrows considerably the threats, and the key resources (military and political) needed to cope with them, on which to focus. This has been of assistance in developing powerful bodies of theory on the security dilemma—deterrence, alliances, arms control, the balance of power—and this advantage we should not lightly discard.

This emphasis also permits the degree of insecurity—in the threat and use of force—to serve as a crude index of the condition of an international system or subsystem or as a measure of its change over time. (The same applies to assessing any state's security within the system.) This is of considerable value for analysis of security arrangements as well. When "threats" arise from more sources, take a great variety of forms, and involve change along many dimensions, measurement and analysis become much more difficult.

Also relevant is that states continue to operate as if physical safety is the core of security. Though they have broadened their list of security strategies and rhetorically applied "security" to more matters, they start with physical threats and military responses. Since this is the case, analysts should not lightly abandon the traditional conception of security either.

A second approach to broadening our view of security questions the traditional preoccupation with the state. This approach is on firmer ground. We can specify at least three levels of analysis as components of security: the individual, the state, and the (relevant) international system (Buzan [1991, 1992] offers extended discussion). Others have suggested a societal level as either a substitute for the individual (Morgan 1988) or as an additional level (Job 1992a).

Employing multiple levels highlights at least two security dilemmas beyond the one in which states, in seeking military strength to be secure, become threats to each other and thereby weaken their security. An additional dilemma results when systemic security requires marked restrictions on or intrusions into national autonomy, which states deeply value as a cornerstone of security. In such situations order and security on one level can be attained, beyond a certain point, only at their expense on the other. (The European Union is currently wrestling with this.) Another dilemma arises when a state's security effort in international politics threatens the security of its citizens. (Iraq's security efforts have imposed very severe burdens on its citizens.)

Employing multiple levels helps highlight the fact that in many countries the threats to states, societies, and individuals arise from *within* national boundaries. Most militarized conflicts today are internal (Wallensteen and Sollenberg 1995), not interstate wars. For many "weak states," those that lack legitimacy, cohesion, and a sound community, security is Janus-faced: external threats are of concern, but national security consists primarily in containing threats from within (Ayoob 1986, 1989, 1992; Paribatra and Samudavanya 1986; Azar and Moon 1988; Acharya 1992a). And if outsiders offer support to the government or the opposition or seek directly to contain or suppress the violence, the conflict becomes part of international politics.

It is apparent that true security requires some progress in easing all three of the security dilemmas noted above: progress on ways to keep the relevant international system safe from states, states safe from the system, and societies safe from both. It also requires coping with severe internal conflicts. This is a tangled area because it means treating human rights vis-à-vis governments, and other internal security matters, as important security problems in *international politics,* a considerable departure from tradition.

There have always been circumstances when "domestic" affairs incited intervention, including collective intervention for common purposes (Trachtenberg 1993; Krasner 1995–96). States refuse to erase completely the foreign-domestic distinction, partially because of self-interest and partially because it is a basic norm of international politics, but recent cases suggest that new norms of intervention may be emerging (Reed and Kaysen 1993). Some intervention has been managed through international organizations (Cambodia). Other efforts to dictate domestic changes (Haiti) have been undertaken by individual states. Political instability and ethnic conflict in various states are now treated by others as impinging directly on their interests in more ways than before.

The implications are striking. For instance, it is now plausible to suggest that a state's national security primacy can be displaced to accommodate the needs of a regional security complex. Precedents include the way Germany has been treated in Europe since 1945 and the way Iraq has been treated since the Gulf War. For reasons outlined below, the sense of interdependence needed for similar actions seems more likely these days to emerge and flourish at the regional than at the global level. In this context internal conflicts become salient for regional security complexes. For instance, other states may insist that domestic developments in A are a grave concern if they cripple A's ability to carry out its responsibilities in a regional security arrangement of great importance to them. This is how a vigorous Western response to the emergence of a right-wing government in Russia would be justified. Such a conception of the interplay between domestic developments and a state's external relationships underpins much of Europe's OSCE (Organization for Security and Cooperation in Europe) process.

Thus my concern here is with forceful, deliberate, organized threats to individuals, societies, regimes, and states, whether from within or outside national borders. The next question is, at what level will we find states and societies most powerfully arranged for dealing with threats of this sort?

Regional Security Complexes

Regions can be designated on the basis of conditions or factors that are constant or ones that vary. Geography or major ethnic or cultural groups are often used for the first. For the second almost anything can apply: level of economic development, nature of political systems, degree of interdependence.

How does one define a "region"? Judging by the literature, this cannot be resolved to everyone's satisfaction. Extensive consideration of the question years ago (see Yalem 1973) resulted in a variety of overlapping definitions (Feld and Boyd 1980, 3; Kaiser 1968, 86; Brecher 1963, 220; Zartman 1967, 546–48; Vayrynen 1984, 340; Myers 1991b, 9–10; Cantori and Spiegel 1970a, 6–7; 1970b; Boals 1973). A review some years ago identified eight different labels for region and twenty-one different attributes of it in use (Thompson 1973; on defining regions and regional security complexes, see Lake's chapter in this volume).

My concern is with *regional security complexes* (RSCs) as opposed to regions. I want to review Barry Buzan's conception of RSCs, indicate how it is related to the concept of a region, and suggest revisions. Along the way, I will make reference to David Lake's innovative approach to detecting a regional grouping, built on the concept of an "externality."

Buzan (1991) describes a regional security complex as a set of states with a significant and distinctive network of security relations that ensure that the members have a high level of interdependence on security: a "group of states whose primary security concerns link together sufficiently closely that their national securities cannot realistically be considered apart from one another" (190).[2] Thus the central element in an RSC is its security relationships and the elements of interdependence that concern security. Buzan also identifies these clusters by geography, such as the South Asian and Southeast Asian regional security complexes. RSC members, in his view, are located within a specified area, though the borders can be fuzzy.

Finally, the conception is intended to emphasize that regional security processes may have considerable life apart from the global system and may refract the impact of the global system. Buzan's is a system-subsystem approach, reflecting the Cold War context within which it was developed. When created, it presupposed the existence of a powerful global system dominated by a conflict between superpowers that drove them frequently to penetrate regional systems, and sought to revive appreciation of regional conflict dynamics within this larger pattern. Superpower rivalry penetrating

2. Buzan distinguishes between global-level complexes (mainly the superpower conflict during the Cold War), RSCs, supercomplexes (which consist of clusters of RSCs), and precomplexes (in which states that have almost no external reach and impact coexist). See Buzan 1983, 1986, 1988. The ones of interest here are the RSCs.

into an RSC was defined as an "overlay," driven by the global-level conflicts and concerns behind superpower foreign policies (Buzan 1983, 1986, 1988; Buzan and Waever 1992).

We can compare this conception of an RSC with other efforts to identify regions. In attempting the latter, analysts have most frequently cited the following criteria:

1. Self-consciousness of members that they constitute a region, and perceptions by others that one exists[3]
2. Geographical propinquity of members
3. Evidence of some autonomy and distinctiveness from the global system, so that it "refracts" the power of that system
4. Regular and intense interactions among members—notable interdependence
5. A high level of political, economic, and cultural affinities

The Buzan conception gives some weight to the first of these but emphasizes the second and third. He notes that members usually perceive themselves, and are perceived by others, as being in a particular security complex, but he allows for complexes to exist, or have consequences, that members may not clearly perceive or understand (Buzan 1986). With regard to the fourth criterion, the interdependence of significance pertains to security. States can have intense conflicts, with resulting high interdependence on security, yet have few other interactions. One thinks of divided Europe during the Cold War. While the fifth criterion might have some impact on relations among a cluster of states, it is not intrinsic to the concept of an RSC. For instance, conflicts might arise because states are members of a regional security complex but lack cultural and other affinities. Thus RSCs involve some self-consciousness, intense security interactions, a geographical location of the members, and a relationship with the global system.

We can see that Buzan views an RSC as a particular kind of geographical region, delimited by a specific pattern of security relationships. His objective

3. This includes the possibility that regions can be consciously created, in part, by actors. Waever (1992) discusses the Baltic "region" this way, and Hurrell (1995, 122) defines regionalism as "a set of policies by one or more states designed to promote the emergence of a cohesive regional unit, which dominates the pattern of relations between the states of that region and the rest of the world, and which forms the organizing basis for policy within the region across a range of issues." The idea that a regional identity can, and ought to be, constructed is found in contemporary discussions about East Asia.

has been to distinguish those relationships from the global system (itself a security complex) while allowing for the powerful ways that the global system can readily impose itself.

Further refinement of the concept might characterize an RSC in terms of its autonomy and distinctiveness from the global system. The Cold War produced so much "overlay" that the utility of focusing on regions eventually was dismissed, and Buzan asserted that this had been carried too far. The end of the Cold War invites additional revision.

Its expiry has ushered in expectations that there will be far less penetration now from the global system.[4] Some analysts take this to mean that new conflicts of a "regional" sort are now emerging, others that we can now better appreciate that the serious wars and insecurity of the past fifty years have been predominantly regional, with the Cold War just a thin overlay (Brecher and Wilkenfeld 1991). From either view, we can expect regional security complexes to be major arenas of conflict and security affairs.

However, it is not just that great powers are less poised to interfere with regional security developments. We think of the Cold War as a conflict *within* the global system; it is more accurate to see it as also having been a considerable part *of* the system. Take away the conflict and the system shrinks; there is less to it. What makes it shrink or grow, to a considerable extent, is the security situation among its major members. When conflict and insecurity among them is rife, the system shapes nearly everyone's security postures and policies, and penetration of lower-level systems out of global-level security considerations becomes common. When the dynamics of the global system seem, especially to great powers, crucial for security,

- the major security issues become global-level in nature;
- security issues even at lower levels are approached by great powers primarily with an eye to global-level concerns;
- hence states in a regional security complex can anticipate (and even seek) penetration from the global system.

Without this situation, as after the Cold War, governments put much less emphasis on global considerations, using the global system and their perceived relationship to it much less as a starting point for analysis, policy, and

4. There were suggestions even before the eclipse of the Cold War that the superpowers' grip was slipping and that regional actors were eager for greater autonomy (Vayrynen 1979; Miller 1973).

action. States' conceptualizations of their interests and security, therefore, are now more regional in character. Regional security complexes and regional conflicts have much greater relative salience.

This could readily be reversed by renewed and intense political conflict among the great powers. For instance, if huge trade blocs emerged, trailed by serious security rivalries, this multibloc system would cancel much of the distinction between the regional level and the global system, and analysis based on the former would not look very rewarding.

The same would occur if great powers agreed to global cooperative management of security (such as via a great-power concert), regional and otherwise. As a result there would be regular penetration of regional security complexes in pursuit of global-level goals.

What seems most plausible is a continuation of the present situation. The great powers are not likely to develop intense security-driven global rivalries for power and influence of the traditional sort any time soon. Meanwhile, cooperation by great powers or the global community to manage regional conflicts is apt to be selective, with only a handful of security problems treated as truly global concerns. Elements of more direct management exist—the increased use of the Security Council, the pursuit of nonproliferation, the possibility of more collective interventions like the Gulf War—but these are not highly developed. Collective management remains confined and uneven. Often, Security Council action is merely authorization, a global-level fig leaf, for regional responses, whether to North Korea's nuclear weapons program, Bosnia, or Haiti.

If no superpower conflict drives superpower penetration into regional complexes, then overlay loses much of its relevance. With no burgeoning of global-level management throughout the system, there is no alternative basis for overlay.

It is no longer suitable to talk about RSCs as embedded within a strong, penetrating global system. We can stop automatically identifying participation by a superpower or other great power in an RSC as "overlay." It most likely is driven now by considerations other than this conception supposed.

We can also question defining the members of RSCs entirely geographically. If a geographically distant great power consistently plays a powerful role in an RSC, with no global-system conflict and related incentives driving it to do so, and if this powerful role is unlikely to disappear, then the previous interpretation of what this participation means is no longer applicable. If the involvement is (*a*) central to the great power's foreign policy and its conception of its security and (*b*) central to the dynamics of the RSC, then it cannot be considered "outside." The system-subsystem framework no longer captures the rationale and nature of this participation. States playing such roles must be considered members of the RSCs with which they are intimately engaged.

For instance, the Buzan approach treats Russia and the United States as global powers whose conflict was such a powerful overlay on the European regional security complex as to repress it.[5] The end of the Cold War means that the European RSC can emerge from under that overlay (Buzan et al. 1990). The trouble is that Russia and the United States remain integral to Europe's security complex. To use "overlay" to explain this is now rather awkward. Instead, the United States and Russia always were and are now working members of that security complex because their security interests and those of the other members are intimately connected. To suggest they are "outside" the security system in Europe is untenable.

We can better appreciate this point via David Lake's approach to detecting regional security complexes. He emphasizes that a complex results from security-related externalities, important conditions related to security that are imposed on some states by developments in or actions of other states. Externalities spill over boundaries. Applying this to RSCs, we can say that the security externalities are far more extensive, compelling, and durable among members of an RSC than they are between those members and other states.

What about geographical contiguity? For investigating regional conflicts, geography is important. Military strength is a central ingredient of conflicts—in the insecurity felt, in any fighting that results, and in ways for coping with threats—and for most states military strength falls off sharply with distance. As a result, states mostly fret about and confront military threats nearby (or even within). Their most feared opponents are usually in the neighborhood.[6] The issues in serious conflicts are often rooted in territory, ethnicity (often linked to territory), or religion and involve states/peoples next to each other or intermingled (Vasquez 1993; Holsti 1991). Finally, competing claims for relative status or influence that lead to fighting are normally pursued within and with reference to a geographical neighborhood.

However, provision must be made for possible *members of a regional security complex not located in that neighborhood*. This situation arises

5. This treatment is highly problematic, since the Cold War was, both conceptually and geographically, centered in and about Europe and not something imposed from "outside."

6. This may not be true once longer-range ballistic missiles proliferate, particularly if linked to nuclear proliferation.

when the web of security relations and externalities embraces such a state in a clear and obvious fashion. The notion of externalities allows us to dispense with geographical membership criteria where they distort perception of the relationships that embody the complex. This does not arise if the outside actor is only temporarily "penetrating" the complex—the distinctiveness of the complex itself remains.[7] But what if the "outside" state has the greatest military strength (or nearly so) regularly deployed in the area for years, is a party to important alliances there, participates in nearly all important negotiations about conflict and security there, fights major wars there, is even regarded by some members as the greatest military threat they face? For all intents and purposes, when it comes to security and conflict, the "outside" state is inside. Thus, for detecting the members of any RSC we must use the active durable presence of important military forces, major security commitments, and profound security involvements over a lengthy period (something like two or more decades) to supplement a geographical criterion.

Pulling these considerations together suggests the following. A regional security complex has a geographical location, but this is not necessarily an exact guide to its members. The location is where the security relationships of consequence exist; the members are states that participate profoundly in those relationships. The participants see their security as much more closely bound up with some or all of the other members, and with their interactions *in that geographical area*, than with states that are not participants in those interactions. This set of perceptions defines the relevant "geography," as well as the membership of the complex, and allows us to treat the United States as a member of a European security complex but not to consider European states members of the RSC in the Americas. It also allows us to distinguish between, say, East Asia and South Asia as RSCs, which is one of Buzan's original goals; the states involved in each see their security linkages as far more substantial among themselves than with those in the other. It enables us to explain why the United States is a member of the East Asian, but not the South Asian, RSC.

This means tolerating gray areas. Identified complexes will overlap, or vary somewhat, with issues, events, and related perceptions of what actors and analysts deem to be relevant externalities. And perceptions also change, often within a short time. Hence identification will always be problematic; the perceptions are not guaranteed to match up and may fluctuate.

7. In fact, only if a region or a regional security complex is readily recognizable does the notion of penetration make any sense.

Thus far, then, we would say that perceptions and self-consciousness can make for a regional security complex when they arise out of intensive security interrelationships. The interdependence of note constitutes a shared security externality (or externalities)—what each member does, as well as what happens to it, with respect to security sharply affects the security of the others.

The Pursuit of Regional Security

A regional conflict can now be defined as one taking place within a regional security complex and seen by the members as having considerable relevance to their security and associated relationships, as having a significant externality. This allows us to distinguish between a minor interstate or limited intrastate conflict and a "regional" conflict. Within a complex, security is a matter of physical safety, but safety can be threatened or strengthened on any of several levels outside each state and inside it.

These complexes will likely be of much greater importance for coping with security issues and problems than in the past, and the management of order and security will increasingly be found there, especially if regional conflicts continue to flourish. There are numerous dimensions on which RSCs can be seen to differ and which might be of theoretical interest: degree of isolation from the global system, members' level of development, nature of members' political systems, and so forth. It is also possible to characterize regional conflicts by issues, as has been done for the global system (Luard 1986; Holsti 1991).

Buzan has proposed instead that RSCs be characterized in terms of their patterns of amity and enmity. While he thinks most RSCs are generated primarily by patterns of conflictual relations, he (like others) believes RSCs can vary in terms of degree of conflict. This use of patterns of amity/enmity in describing RSCs seems sound. In seeing each other as relevant to their national securities, the members must respond to perceived or actual threats and conflicts among themselves and, in the same fashion, to perceived or actual security relations that are indifferent, friendly, or highly cooperative.

Buzan has tried to identify relevant complexes and then to describe their patterns of security interactions. His particular concern has been to single out these features so as to suggest whether they are changing or likely to change in the future.

I am more interested in trying to identify dominant patterns of security management within RSCs, patterns termed regional security orders. It is these patterns of management, or "regional orders," that we should seek to explain. For this purpose it seems more promising to set aside other dimensions of difference and start instead with a conception of the management options open to RSCs, using this as a basis for comparative analysis. Then the above factors and others can be investigated to detect their impact on the choice among these options made in different RSCs and the success achieved in security management.

In doing this, it will probably be necessary to distinguish interstate from intrastate struggles. The impressive theoretical equipment on interstate conflict cannot easily be employed for intrastate struggles. (For a contrary view, see Wagner 1993.) Also, a conflict between states is different from a struggle over control of the state or its fragmentation: the stakes are different; the nature of the "legitimacy" sought and the "power" gained or lost is not the same. There is also the lingering foreign-domestic distinction. Interstate conflicts are automatically in international politics; intrastate conflicts only sometimes are. With the latter there is less legitimacy—or legitimacy is more difficult to generate—for interference by outsiders even just to quell violence and save lives, and this can affect conflict-management options.

The typology offered below rests on the following assumptions: first, that we can identify discrete security complexes; second, that the most feasible route to description and then generalization is to focus not just on the origins, nature, and dimensions of conflicts but on patterns of management that can provide a modicum of security, treating these patterns as options for RSCs; third, that in international politics *interstate* conflict remains of primary importance, the location of the gravest threats. Regional orders will therefore be designed initially with interstate conflicts in mind and should be analyzed accordingly. Whether and how they relate to internal conflicts is a different matter and depends on the circumstances.

Recently suggestions have proliferated about how states can best pursue the management of international politics to achieve order and security. Pulled together they form a catalog of ideal types, which appear to be applicable to RSCs (whether they are applicable at the global level is not relevant here):

integration
pluralistic security community
collective security

great-power concert
power restraining power

The discussion that follows treats these security orders as rungs on a ladder up which regional security complexes may climb as they pursue security management. Various examples are cited, but Europe is used in illustrating each alternative because it has gone furthest in exploring them. (For another view of Europe's security-order options, see Buzan and Waever 1992.)

SECURITY VIA THE USE OF POWER TO RESTRAIN POWER

The use of power to restrain power is traditional international politics, often referred to as security via the balance of power. Buzan emphasizes that an RSC should initially be characterized in terms of its power distribution. In a region where this pattern is dominant, states pursue security *primarily* via establishment and maintenance of what they consider a "suitable" or "stable" distribution of power. This may be unipolar/hegemonic, bipolar, or multipolar in nature. Interstate conflicts are analyzed accordingly (e.g., on hegemonic patterns, Myers 1991a, 1991b; Zimmerman 1972; Vayrynen 1979). The Middle East complex is a prime example. So is the Far East (Kahler 1991). Since we are talking about regional orders deliberately chosen and implemented, this means treating the distribution of power as consciously pursued, not as something that automatically or unconsciously emerges.

Where the members pursue security in this fashion, intrastate conflicts are of concern primarily in terms of their impact on the distribution of power. The members put great emphasis on autonomy and manipulate their relationships primarily on the basis of relative power capabilities, with intrastate conflicts of significance only in this context. We would not expect members to give them much attention otherwise.

To illustrate possible patterns, hegemony can either be clearly domineering or exercised more to provide security as a public good. South Asia has long had a hegemonic distribution of power. Pakistan greatly resents this, but its efforts to adjust the complex have involved trying to make it more bipolar (via nuclear weapons), and not to move to another security order. East Asia has been shifting away from a hegemonic structure (the United States as hegemon) toward a more multipolar one. Efforts to assess this shift now dominate literature about the region, and members of this complex are debating the options for a regional security order.

Europe has just passed from a bipolar distribution to a quite different category. Europeans wish to avoid returning to power balancing as the prime route to security. The classic realist view treats this as futile, predicting that Europe will slip back into power balancing, probably within a multipolar pattern (Mearsheimer 1990). Thus far the major states seem satisfied with avoiding this. Many smaller states are not. In Eastern Europe there is strong reluctance to trust other forms of security management in view of Russia's past behavior and uncertainties about its political future. Poland, the Baltic states, and others have been eager to join NATO *as an alliance against Russia,* seeking security in a traditional power-balancing way.

SECURITY VIA A CONCERT

In a concert, regional security is the collective responsibility of the most powerful states in that complex, whose actions derive legitimacy by providing order and security as a common good (see Schroeder 1986, 1989, 1992; Elrod 1976; Jervis 1986, 1992; Rosecrance 1992b). While these states may make the distribution of power among themselves a consideration, this is not the fundamental basis of security and does not drive their collective decisions and actions. They do not subject every decision to the test of how their relative power would be affected. Instead, they allow for each other's vital interests and right to participate in the concert, curbing their own foreign policies accordingly. Thus a concert contributes to regional security in two ways. First, it embodies the determination of the major powers to mute and manage their own conflicts. Second, it provides a vehicle for them to cooperate to deal with other security issues.

A concert operated successfully after the Napoleonic Wars, and analysts have proposed that it be the basis for security in contemporary Europe (Kupchan and Kupchan 1991; Mueller 1989–90). The clear preference there is for more collective approaches. However, the Russian government is not averse to the idea of a concert. Russia seeks "special responsibility" for security in and among the former republics of the Soviet Union (Roeder, this volume). It also seeks to be perceived, within Europe's security order, as having exceptional capabilities and responsibilities. A concert is an attractive way to institutionalize Western approval of both. Under a broader, and more collective, security management, Russia would face much greater restraints on its behavior.

SECURITY THROUGH MULTILATERAL COLLECTIVE MANAGEMENT

When RSC members constitute themselves as a collective to manage peace and security, management is not solely the prerogative of major states; their actions are to have collective endorsement. At less ambitious levels such management is common, in the form of regional organizations to promote or provide fact-finding, mediation, conciliation, and peacekeeping, as well as regimes to monitor dangerous developments or to promote arms control and other restraints. It is also not consistently effective. Such efforts are often combined with another approach that is, in fact, the *primary* one. For instance, in the Middle East the Arab League did little to displace power balancing as the primary recourse for security.

A low-level collective approach to security can also be coupled more evenly with either of the two security orders discussed above. For instance, elements of a concert may operate in conjunction with a collective security arrangement—decisions involve all of the members, but it is clear that a consensus among the strongest is the dominant factor. One could also find a hegemon seeking to ease its burdens and responsibilities by promoting a more collective approach to sustaining security.

The ultimate in collective security is Wilsonian, wherein peace is collectively enforced via a punitive response when necessary. All members accept the responsibility of contributing to a massive deterrence threat and, when necessary, implementing it. Wilsonian collective security has the difficulties of any deterrence-based approach, most notably a serious credibility problem. It is also difficult to keep truly collective if the main punitive capabilities belong to only a few states—they are apt to insist on a dominant voice in what is done to manage regional security and how. The Russians, as noted above, would like to be designated as having special responsibilities in their neighborhood. They have pressed to have their peacekeeping activities in Georgia, Tajikistan, and elsewhere designated as UN or OSCE actions, but have failed in their efforts because of fear such approval would legitimize not collective management but hegemony. Similarly, Francis Gannon (1982) treats the OAS as a highly successful collective arrangement, but many others see it as far more hegemonic in character. David Mares (this volume) demonstrates the threatening nature of the United States to other OAS members irrespective of American intentions.

For Europe, various collective security proposals have been offered (e.g., Flynn and Scheffer 1990). NATO is now inching toward conversion to a regional collective security system. NATO would be used to *enforce* the peace, and its membership would be broadened accordingly. Initial steps in this direction included the formation of the North Atlantic Cooperation Council (NACC), consisting of NATO and former Warsaw Pact members. In these and other ways NATO began demonstrating "interest" in security for Eastern Europe, as embodied in collective discussions that embraced most of Europe. Then, in connection with the situation in the Balkans, NATO made itself "available" for peacekeeping or peace enforcing under UN or OSCE authorization. Eventually, NATO was used to enforce UN sanctions on Serbia, to carry out military strikes against the Bosnian Serbs, and to help install an interim settlement.

The "Partnership for Peace" introduced in 1994 is another step down this road. It associates a large number of states with NATO, involving them in joint training exercises (and related activities) for potential peacekeeping and peacemaking operations. This partnership is to lead to some of the associates joining NATO. Since virtually everyone in Europe is participating, the result is movement toward a Wilsonian system. The capabilities required of the prospective members have little to do with collective defense against external attack, illustrating the anticipated change in the character of NATO.

Why is this necessary? As discussed below, Europeans would like to do without peace enforcement, but many governments lack confidence that this is possible, at least now. Eastern Europeans would like membership in NATO as an alliance against Russia; in their view the Partnership for Peace offers too little. They have not achieved what they want, however, because the members of the European security complex are, on the whole, committed to escaping from traditional power balancing.

SECURITY IN A PLURALISTIC SECURITY COMMUNITY (PSC)

In a pluralistic security community the members give no thought to using violence in their relations with one another (Deutsch et al. 1957). Hence enforcement of peace is unnecessary, and there is no organized collective capability for it. What makes it "pluralistic" is that the members retain national autonomy. North America constitutes a pluralistic security community, and the North Atlantic area has become one also (Greece and Turkey excepted). South America may have as well (Mares, this volume, disagrees).[8] ASEAN

8. He is obviously correct in that war is sometimes contemplated among Latin American states today. He is wrong in that this contemplation is so limited. In terms of the level of military

now seeks to become one (Acharya 1992a; Khong, this volume, partly disagrees). While available evidence strongly suggests that such an arrangement requires similar political (and probably economic) systems as well as high interaction and interdependence, it is hard to be certain whether such conditions are necessary, because ASEAN has come far toward a PSC without displaying them.

The foremost contemporary attempt to construct a PSC is in the RSC focused on Europe (Adler 1992), where it has now become the preferred European security order. Virtually everyone in the complex is officially committed to:

the nonuse of force or threats
the inviolability of borders
marked reductions in arms
clearly defensive military postures
elimination of large forces in central Europe
rising flows—economic, informational, and so forth—across borders

In domestic affairs they are committed to market economies and democratic political systems. On this basis, eventually they are to have nothing to fight about.

The problem with a PSC is that every member must rely on every other member's good behavior. This is a tall order, and governments in Europe have doubts it can be filled. This is why the developments in Yugoslavia were so disturbing. Here was a collection of peoples and governments who did not behave. What if this spread?

Thus states have retained forms of insurance for the time being. Nuclear weapons have not been renounced, and NATO is still in business as an alliance. Deterrence is not the first recourse for keeping safe, but it has not been abandoned. Another form of insurance is giving NATO a peace enforcement capability. A successful PSC would not need this.

SECURITY VIA INTEGRATION

This is a relevant category only in the early stages of integration and when the primary objective is security. Many steps toward integration in various

spending and the number of real wars and casualties since 1945, Latin America is simply not a serious arena of traditional international politics in comparison with other security complexes.

places do not qualify—their point is not enhancement of security. ASEAN's announced effort to create a free trade area is awkward to classify, since ASEAN has always had an unstated security purpose and greatly heightening member interdependence might be seen as an extension of it.

Unlike a PSC, integration involves transnational institutions to handle important interactions. It also involves commitment to far broader norms bearing on many more sectors. Carried far enough, the participants shift their relations out of international politics and create an amalgamated security community where even the use of force for members' internal security would be subject to some collective supervision.

European integration was initiated to enhance security by eliminating key national rivalries and creating an extreme interdependence that would cripple national capacities for modern war. It continues to be used for this purpose today. The immediate response to a unified Germany, and thus to fears of German domination and the insecurity this would induce, was a drive to deepen integration and then to broaden the EU by adding new members. Many governments in Eastern Europe regard membership in the EU as the ultimate guarantee of security. Thus integration is more than insurance against the possible weaknesses of the OSCE. It reflects a belief that a PSC is not enough, or not sustainable, in Europe, making it too weak an arrangement on which to rest the regional security complex.

A typology of this sort is vital for analysis of the security arrangements within a regional security complex and for comparative analysis of RSCs. For instance, it should provide an analytical grip on the relationship to security of the varied associations that have aroused analysts' curiosity (Sneider and Borthwick 1983; Acharya 1992a, 1992b; Haas 1989; Simon 1982; Alagappa 1991). The impact of international organizations should be assessed within the security order in which they operate. The typology could also be useful for denoting the conditions under which conflict-management processes are likely to succeed (see Hampson and Mandell 1990; *Annals* 1991).

The categories vary in the degree to which security arrangements are collective and cooperative. Where states look to keep safe by attending to their relative power and the distribution of power in the system, cooperation normally takes only two forms. States can agree that power balancing is vital and arrive at rules of the game to shape their behavior, and they can cooperate via alliances to adjust that distribution.

In a concert the major states cooperate to a far greater extent. Collective security extends cooperation further; more members are involved, with a richer array of norms and more elaborate decision making and implementation. In a pluralistic security community the norms are very powerful and cooperative behavior is very high. Technically this needs no organizational form, but in practice a dense cluster of agreements and institutions is likely. Finally, with integration states erode their autonomy, threatening their independent existence as political communities.

In any RSC there will be elements of several orders, with different states often espousing different ones. Participants in the European complex have not forgotten how to seek security by tending to the distribution of power. At times there are signs of a great-power concert at work or envisioned. The Bosnian situation pushed the members toward a form of collective security. The key to characterizing an RSC lies in detecting the *dominant* pattern, especially if it has the wide endorsement of the members. The European-complex members are aiming at a pluralistic security community in the short run and elaborate integration of most members for the long run.

Each arrangement can be stable and effective, or fail and disintegrate. Success is probably more likely and disintegration less so, the higher an RSC is on the list. The incidence of major warfare should decline as one moves up the list. In any RSC in which the threat of outright conflict rises, there should be a strong tendency for security management to revert to a lower place in the typology. Levels of military spending, the frequency and intensity of arms competitions, and the salience of security considerations in members' relations should all decline for RSCs moving up, and rise when they are moving down.

The higher an RSC security order, the less vulnerable it should be to external penetration, because it has fewer conflicts that invite intervention (see Rosecrance and Schott, this volume). This should also be true of the degree of success attained in managing conflict—the greater the success, the less vulnerability to outside penetration. Evading penetration has been an important selling point for regional security management (Vayrynen 1984). One motivation behind ASEAN was more autonomy from the East-West dispute (Ispahani 1984).

The typology downplays extraregional resources. The focus is on the complex itself and its resources. However, some analysts see regional conflicts as often so intractable that control or resolution requires significant contributions from outside (Kolodziej and Zartman 1996). Thus the possibility of significant intervention from the global system cannot be dismissed.

However, this need not diminish the utility of the typology. First, external actors may be primarily concerned with conflict containment, not regional security management. They may seek containment precisely so that the RSC can get on with effective management. If so, then the external actors are adjuncts to the workings of the regional security order.

Second, external actors may intrude via the existing security-management arrangements or in an effort to help install a new one. If so, their actions would not cancel the utility of the typology as a guide to what is taking place.

Finally, the possibility of intrusion from the global level raises questions about available resources for this intrusion. Many contemporary discussions explore the strengths and weaknesses of the UN (Lorenz 1992; Weiss and Kessler 1991) or the available will and capabilities of the great powers (Henkin et al. 1989). As suggested earlier, it would be better to look at the incentives for penetration (as in Papayoanou, this volume), and these incentives may depend in part on the capacity of an RSC for security management.

A larger theoretical question is whether there is a more fundamental link between levels. If the global level is developing into a great-power concert, does this *necessarily* shift the character, structure, or dynamics of regional complexes? Would it make a difference to RSCs and regional conflicts if the global concert was composed of liberal democracies? This volume anticipates that RSCs are going to be more important and more autonomous, but just how this works out is a matter for investigation.

The typology is clearly oriented toward management of interstate conflicts. But intrastate conflicts are far more common these days. Nevertheless, any security order can also be used to cope with intrastate conflict. The key, as David Lake points out, is whether internal conflicts seriously spill over into the regional security complex. European concert and then power-distribution considerations led to years of efforts to contain or repress conflicts in the Ottoman Empire, lest its collapse set off a destabilizing struggle over the corpse. The Concert of Europe was willing to intervene in several internal disputes to prevent the "wrong" sort of regime from coming to power. Collective peacekeeping efforts are regularly aimed at internal conflicts, and this target could be extended to peace-enforcement efforts; the operation against Haiti was a step in this direction. The most obvious responses of a PSC to an internal conflict are (1) to have every other member avoid involvement (as the West has done during the conflict in Northern Ireland) or (2) to exclude those who violate the norms of the PSC from the community (which happened to Serbia). Finally, integration cannot proceed very far without eliminating the worst forms of internal conflict; otherwise it will founder.

Several security orders have a strong appeal because they can legitimize intervention in internal disputes. Power balancing, however, is distinctly awkward in this respect; the competitive motivations of the members and their fear of unfavorable shifts in the status quo can block serious efforts to deal with an internal conflict. Concert, collective security, and integration provide not only legitimacy but machinery for the necessary decisions.

Finally, if RSCs will be of growing importance, regional security considerations should play a larger role in responses to intrastate conflicts, with a larger share of the burdens being handed on to regional security arrangements. It is likely that the members of many RSCs will prefer it that way.

As to the reasons a complex settles into a specific security arrangement, competing explanations are readily available and comparative analysis is the most rewarding way to proceed.

The Lowest Common Denominator

The arrangement that results is the highest on the list supported by all major actors. If realists are correct, regional systems will always end up on the lowest level because defections from cooperation are inevitable. There is also the potent problem of securing agreement among many actors, noted by Job (this volume).

Fear of Unbridled Power Balancing

The OSCE and European integration have been spurred by a widespread desire to avoid traditional international politics. A similar motivation shaped the development of ASEAN.

The Impact of the Global System

As noted earlier, the global system may exert a powerful influence or provide a permissive context (see Papayoanou, and Stein and Lobell, this volume). For instance, a global concert might decisively intervene to halt any outright interstate warfare (Rosecrance and Schott, this volume), pushing the regional system toward more cooperative security management.

Regional System Factors

A good example of regional system factors would be the preferences of regional system hegemons (Roeder, this volume). Hegemonic stability theory may explain the presence or absence of cooperative security management. There are also plausible structural explanations (Lake, this volume).

Domestic Political and Economic Factors

Some liberalist, domestically oriented explanations for collective retreats from anarchy are good candidates for examination in the comparative analysis of regional security (see Solingen, this volume).

Conclusion

This chapter has presented a review of relevant considerations for devising a better analytical grip on regional conflict. Earlier efforts at comprehensive approaches to regional conflict were strongly influenced either by the progress toward integration or by the impact of the East-West dispute on our image of international politics. Now the latter has disappeared and the former is confined to a single region. The topic can now be taken up under different conditions, perhaps with more satisfactory results.

Part II

Understanding Regional Orders

3

Regional Security Complexes: A Systems Approach

David A. Lake

Since the end of the Cold War, political analysts and policy makers alike have turned their attention to regional conflicts. Against the backdrop of diminishing tensions between the United States and Russia, conflicts in the so-called periphery of the global system—Northeast Asia, Africa, the Middle East, and elsewhere—appear to be the primary threats to international and national security. Yet, despite their increased priority, regional conflicts and how they are best managed remain poorly understood.

This volume focuses on conflict and cooperation within regions, both analytically and substantively. In Chapter 2, Patrick Morgan, beginning with the concept of regional security complexes, develops a typology of regional orders. In this chapter, after reviewing the existing literature on regional systems, I focus on two questions. First, what defines and bounds the set of

In addition to the other authors in this volume, I would like to thank Vinod Aggarwal, James Caporaso, Scott Garner, Peter Katzenstein, and Steve Weber for comments, and Risa Brooks for research assistance.

states that constitutes a regional security complex? I define such a complex as the states affected by at least one transborder but local security externality. Second, how do regional security complexes vary, and how do these variations affect the type of regional order that emerges in a given area? In the core of the chapter, I identify five sets of variables and examine their likely affects on regional order: the characteristics of the security externalities themselves, the characteristics of other, nonsecurity externalities, the transactions costs of cooperation, the regional system structure, and the global system structure. Finally, I extend the theoretical analysis to questions of great-power intervention in regional conflicts.

Regional Systems

The literature on regional systems, or "subsystems" as they were often called, flowered in the 1960s and then wilted in the 1970s.[1] Although regional systems continued to attract some interest over the intervening decades, only recently have they recaptured scholarly attention. The waning interest of academics, of course, was partly a function of the Cold War. For much of the last fifty years, regional systems were commonly overwhelmed and subsumed within the global system. As Barry Buzan (1991, 208) suggests, the global overlay of the Cold War masked regional variations.

The decline of the regional-systems literature, however, was also related to terminological and conceptual chaos. In his exhaustive review, William R. Thompson (1973) identifies twenty-two definitions of regional systems, containing twenty-one separate conceptual attributes. Some definitions are so broad that they fail to delimit regional relations as a distinct object of study. Others are too narrow, treating as defining characteristics much that can be understood better as dimensions across which regions vary. At least four analysts, for example, include "explicit institutional relations or subsystem organization" as part of their definition, positing that regional systems are coterminous with limited-membership international organizations. This characteristic isolates the phenomenon of "region," but circumscribes it too narrowly, closing off discussion rather than opening up inquiry. It also assumes too much. Some regional systems may possess a formal treaty organi-

1. The major contributions to this literature include Binder 1958, Brecher 1963, Zartman 1967, Cantori and Spiegel 1970a. Boals (1973) provides a useful review.

zation; others may not. Rather than build institutions into the definition of a regional system, it is preferable to treat the degree of institutionalization as a dimension of possible variation for further analysis. Likewise, some analysts limit regions to groups of small powers or states exhibiting a common developmental status. Again, these characteristics are overly restrictive and are better understood as dimensions of possible variation.

Thompson (1973, 101) distills the various definitions and conceptual attributes into four necessary and sufficient conditions for the existence of regional subsystems:

1. The actors' pattern of relations or interactions exhibit a particular degree of regularity and intensity to the extent that a change at one point in the subsystem affects other points.
2. The actors are generally proximate.
3. Internal and external observers and actors recognize the subsystem as a distinctive area or "theatre of operation."
4. The subsystem logically consists of at least two and quite probably more actors.

These conditions form the best definition to date of regional systems, and provide a solid foundation for further discussion. This definition is also closely related to Buzan's concept of a regional security complex, summarized by Morgan in Chapter 2.

Thompson's definition, however, blurs two distinct theories of regional relations, noted in Chapter 1. Constructivist theories, emphasizing Thompson's third condition, begin with a view of regional systems as collectively produced self-understandings (Boals 1973).[2] In this approach, adopted in part by Brian Job in Chapter 8 and David Pervin in Chapter 12, a region exists if the states themselves and outside parties believe that the states constitute a region. In short, to paraphrase Alex Wendt (1992), regions are what states make of them. It is this self-understanding, moreover, that influences or produces observable behaviors. Although to date there have been few attempts to deduce falsifiable hypotheses about regions from a constructivist approach, it might follow that, under some conditions, countries that understand themselves to be in a region will cooperate more easily; it might

2. See Haas 1990, Adler 1991 and 1992, and Wendt 1987. The processes associated with the constructivist approach are most obvious in Australia's successful efforts to create an "Asia-Pacific" region and the somewhat less successful attempt by the former "northern-tier" states of the Warsaw Pact to redefine themselves as "Central Europe."

also follow that, under different conditions, regional self-identification will raise political stakes in areas of disagreement and increase the probability of conflict.

Alternatively, a systems approach posits that regions are composed of states in an at least partly autonomous network of interactions that constrain and shape their behavior, found in Thompson's condition 1 and Buzan's emphasis on intense interdependence. The interactions may take many forms, but they produce effects that are independent of the actor's intentions. In this way, a strategic environment is created in which states influence one another's behavior. While actors may be cognizant of their interdependence, such self-understanding is not a necessary condition (Buzan 1991, 192). Just as Waltz (1979) argues that the intention to produce an equal distribution of power is not necessary for such a balance to arise (and may, in fact, be counterproductive), an understanding of "regionness" is not necessary for interactions to constrain the behavior of the members of that localized system. It is this approach that informs this chapter.

Thompson's definition, as well as Buzan's conception, also fails to distinguish adequately how regional interactions are distinct from global interactions. In the next section, I develop a systems definition of regional security complexes based on local externalities. This definition differs from others in its class by stepping back from the level of interactions and attempting to identify the source of the strategic environment that underlies regional security systems. As suggested in the conclusion to this chapter, this exercise at the level of the regional system helps reveal an additional dimension of variation in international systems as well.

Regional Systems as Local Externalities

I define a regional system as a set of states affected by at least one transborder but local externality that emanates from a particular geographic area.[3] If the

3. This definition parallels Thompson's in number (condition 4), but emphasizes externalities in lieu of interactions (condition 1). Early readers of this essay have argued that regions may require more than one externality, and I have considered a definition that focuses on regions as clusters of externalities. Unfortunately, the minimum number of externalities necessary to create a cluster is quite arbitrary. "Spillovers" can also be aggregated and disaggregated, within limits, according to the purposes of the analyst, suggesting that the number of externalities present in a geographic area may differ somewhat according to the questions being asked. For both of these reasons, I prefer a minimalist definition of region.

local externality poses an actual or potential threat to the physical safety of individuals or governments in other states, it produces a regional security system or complex. Not all local externalities pose such threats to physical security, and there may be many different types of regional systems, a point I return to below. Local externalities that produce threats to physical safety bound the sets of interacting states that constitute regional security systems.

Externalities are costs (negative externalities) and benefits (positive externalities) that do not accrue only to the actors that create them. They are also known as spillover or neighborhood effects (Fusfield 1988, 17; Cornes and Sandler 1986).[4] The classic example of an externality is a manufacturer who releases pollutants into a river and thereby imposes costs on downstream users of that common resource, who must either pay to purify the water or forgo its otherwise valuable use. Although not typically understood in these terms, the security dilemma is also an externality. The classic formulation of the dilemma postulates a state, under anarchy, that is dependent upon self-help and cannot be certain of the intentions of others. To ensure its own safety against the possibility of attack, the state procures weapons and other armaments, which in turn pose a threat to other states equally uncertain about the intentions of the first. In order to provide for their own safety, these states are then forced to arm at some cost to themselves. The net result is a spiral of costly arms racing, increasing hostility, and possibly war (Jervis 1978). In short, the actions of each party impose costs upon the others, creating a negative externality that binds the relevant states together as a set of interacting units. Virtually all salient security actions taken by one state and not solely intended to reduce the welfare of a second can be understood as externalities.[5] The containment of aggressive states, whether through deterrence or war, can produce positive externalities for other states, depending

4. Externalities are closely related to and subsume the better-known phenomenon of public goods. Public goods are nonexcludable and nonrival in consumption. That is, others cannot be prevented from enjoying the good, once produced, and the consumption of one party does not diminish the quantity available to others. Like public goods, externalities are nonexcludable. Costs are imposed or benefits conferred upon others who were not party to the decision to produce the good in the first place. Unlike consumers of public goods, however, who all consume the same good, consumers of externalities may consume different goods—thus implying that externalities are not necessarily nonrival in consumption (Mueller 1989, 25). In short, all public goods are externalities, but not all externalities are public goods.

5. The qualifier "not solely intended to reduce the welfare of a second" is important. If the sole purpose of the action is to impose costs on another, this would more properly be regarded as an act of aggression, not an externality. Even so, most acts of aggression, such as the seizure of the territory of one state by another, simultaneously impose costs on third states, producing an externality as well. In most cases, it is the latter effect that matters more to the definition of a region, both by the relevant states themselves and by the broader international community.

on local circumstances; just as defense is a public good within countries, it may also be a public good between countries. Internal state weakness may also create negative security externalities for neighboring states, if that weakness creates havens for insurgents or incentives for embattled leaders to initiate diversionary wars. Security externalities are ubiquitous in international relations.

Many externalities are global in their effects, imposing, or potentially imposing, costs on all states. Anthropogenic climate change is a much-discussed example of such a global externality. Security dilemmas between the great powers, who by definition possess the ability to project force to all corners of the globe, also tend to be general in their effects. These global externalities create global systems. Other externalities are very limited in scope and, as such, are "internalized" in the nation-state. Some river basins are wholly within the boundaries of a single country, and in some states the primary security threats to individuals come from other domestic factions or even the state itself. While often quite important on their own terms, and central to domestic political systems, these "internal" externalities have few implications for interstate relations.

Local transborder externalities create costs and benefits that affect only a limited number of states. Pollution in international straits mostly affects littoral states. "Regional" powers can only project force over limited distances, threatening their neighbors or perhaps their neighbors once removed, but not others who lie beyond their reach. It is these local externalities that create the set of interacting states that constitutes a regional system, and such local security externalities that create a regional security complex. It is the limited scope of such externalities that differentiates regional systems from the global system and regional security complexes from the global security complex.

Geography is central to the concept of a regional system. Nearly all of the definitions identified by Thompson include geographic proximity as one of the defining criteria of a regional system, and common usage implies this trait as well. As I define them here, however, regional systems comprise local externalities that radiate outward from a distinct, geographic locus, but these externalities are not necessarily limited in their effects to states within a particular geographic neighborhood. As Morgan suggests in Chapter 2, if states are affected in important ways by an externality over some extended period of time, they can be considered part of the regional security complex even though they are not located within the immediate area from which the externality originates. Thus, the United States is part of the Middle East regional security complex, but China—whose involvement in the region is episodic at best—is not. Externalities that affect countries but lack a geographic center, in turn, may create issue areas—such as money or trade (Keohane and Nye 1977)—but they do not form the basis for regional systems.[6] As Morgan also notes, this definition differs from that employed by others (even Buzan 1991, 190), but we believe it is more useful in understanding contemporary international politics.

It follows from the definition offered here that systems may be created even when there is no manifest or measurable "interaction" between states, such as the exchange of goods and services. As in the classic security dilemma, when one state prepares to defend itself, it produces a threat, or negative externality, for others even though no physical product crosses the borders. Differing from the transactions definition of Russett (1967), the definition here requires no actual exchange of products or material for an externality and, in turn, a regional system to exist. By the same token, dense interactions are not necessarily evidence of large externalities. If the interactions are purely voluntary and all parties are fully compensated, no externalities are created. Externalities occur only when one state is not a fully consenting party to actions initiated by another (or the mechanism of compensation is imperfect); in this case, the welfare of the first state is improved or damaged by the actions of the second without its consent.[7]

This distinction between interactions and externalities suggests, finally, that externalities are a form of "market" or bargaining failure (Cornes and Sandler 1986, 30). As Ronald Coase's (1960) famous insight suggests, in a world of costless bargaining and contracting, externalities would be effectively negotiated away. Only when bargaining is costly, when actors possess private information with incentives to misrepresent, or when actors cannot commit credibly to contracts do externalities arise (Fearon 1995). This recognition, in turn, has important implications for regional order, a topic I return to in the next section.

Transborder externalities affect, by definition, more than one state and are, therefore, inherently political and strategic. In coping with negative externalities or producing positive externalities, states must consider the actions and reactions of others. It is this interdependence that creates a system;

6. Vinod Aggarwal raised this possibility in the first IGCC workshop, "Reconceptualizing Regional Relations," 27–28 February 1993, Laguna Beach, Calif. Some analysts refer to the states of the G-7 as a "region," but this is not a universally accepted use of the term.

7. It is this nonvoluntary nature of externalities that makes them politically contentious and, thus, the foundation of *political* systems.

it is the localized nature of many externalities that creates regional systems; and it is local security externalities that define regional security complexes. A focus on externalities helps clarify what it is about the network of interactions central to previous definitions of regions that creates systems.

Regional Systems and Regional Order

Local security externalities bound the set of states in a regional security complex. Such complexes, in turn, vary in at least five ways, each of which has important effects on regional order.

SECURITY EXTERNALITIES

By definition, states do not receive the full cost or benefit when producing negative or positive security externalities, respectively. With externalities, the regional or "social" costs or benefits are greater than the national costs or benefits. It is the desire to reduce these greater social costs or capture the larger social benefits that motivates efforts at regional cooperation, but it is the national or private returns that guide state policy. Individual states will undertake to manage their relations only to the point where the private marginal cost of one less unit of a negative externality or one more unit of a positive externality is equal to the private marginal benefit of obtaining that unit. In the absence of an effective agreement between the relevant states, negative security externalities will always be overproduced, since the producing state does not absorb the social costs of its actions but does confront the private costs of modifying its behavior, and positive security externalities will be underproduced, since the state must pay the private cost of production but does not receive the full social benefit.

Security externalities nonetheless vary along three dimensions that are likely to affect regional order.[8] First, they differ in magnitude, defined in terms of the costs imposed on other states. The larger the externality, *ceteris paribus*, the more likely states will be to alter their behavior, organizing either to capture the positive or eliminate the negative effect. This relationship

8. For a related but more general discussion, see Cornes and Sandler 1986 and Sandler 1992.

is continuous: the larger the security externality, the more it will influence state action. The more costly it is to eliminate a negative externality or produce a positive externality, on the other hand, the less likely it is that states will successfully modify their individual or collective behavior in the desired way. In the end, it is the net benefits of mitigating a negative externality or providing a positive externality that shape the actions of states.

Second, security externalities differ by how their effects are distributed across the relevant states; inevitably, they affect some countries more and others less. These distributional effects may be the result of geography, especially proximity; preferences, since countries can have more or less intense desires for security; or other factors, including risk propensities and technology. Concentrated effects or intense preferences will increase the absolute value some states place on the externality. Intensely affected states, in turn, are more likely to produce privileged groups, or *k*-groups, willing and able to solve collective-action problems (Olson 1965; Schelling 1978; Snidal 1985).[9]

Finally, states face varying numbers of security externalities. For instance, a state may confront a traditional, interstate security dilemma with one neighbor, while simultaneously fearing that a second may be seized by a faction allied with its own internal rebels. Regional security complexes composed of a single externality will differ from those possessing several externalities. "Dense" regional systems of multiple security externalities possess greater scope for strategies of tactical linkage and conditional cooperation; in the absence of long time horizons, *ceteris paribus,* "thin" regions will tend to find cooperation problematic (Axelrod 1984; Oye 1986; Lohmann 1997). States in dense regional security complexes are also more likely to form institutions or regimes to manage their relations, spreading the fixed costs of institutional construction across a greater number of spillovers, while states in thin regional systems will tend to negotiate more ad hoc agreements (Krasner 1983; Keohane 1984). Multiple security externalities, of course, do not by themselves guarantee successful cooperation or the creation of effective regional regimes, as demonstrated by continuing problems of peacemaking in the Middle East. They do increase the potential aggregate gains from coop-

9. Alternative means of eliminating or producing an externality may also have distributional effects (both across and within states). As a result, states may have different preferences over both the externality itself and the means for managing it. As Krasner (1991) has recently suggested, bargaining on the Pareto frontier may be just as vigorous as negotiating over how to get there.

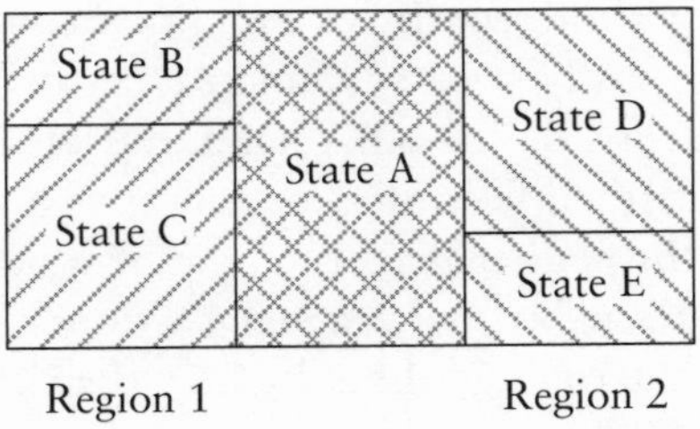

A. Interlocking Regions
State A belongs to regions 1 and 2

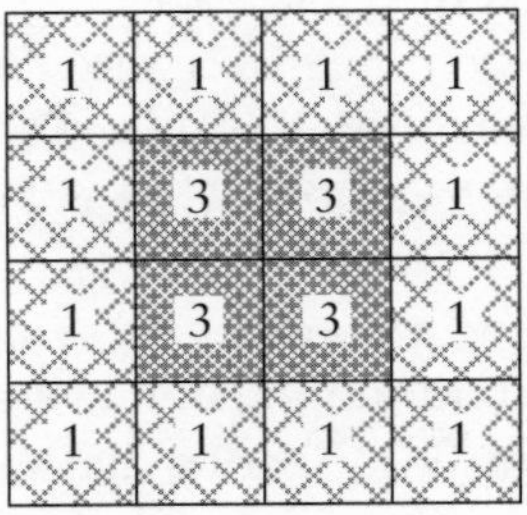

B. Nested Regions
Each cell is a state; entry in cell refers to number of shared externalities

Fig. 3.1. Mixed regions with multiple externalities: two possible types

eration and create opportunities for strategies of linkage and reciprocity, but they do not necessarily lead states to the more cooperative or higher regional orders in Morgan's typology.

When two or more security externalities exist, it is possible—indeed, it may be likely—that their effects will not be confined to identical sets of states. In this case, at least two mixed types of regional security complexes can arise, each with unique properties. If a state shares the same security externality with two (or more) mutually exclusive sets of states, an interlocking regional security system is formed.[10] This is depicted in Figure 3.1A; in this example, state A belongs to two different regional security complexes. Belonging to both the Middle Eastern and Northeast African regional secu-

10. Note: only if the *same* externality exists is an interlocking region formed; if the externalities are different, two distinct regional security systems are created.

rity systems, Egypt is but one of many possible examples (Keller, this volume). Here, the state influences and is influenced by the actions of other states in both regional security complexes simultaneously; actions taken by the state to mitigate the security dilemma in one area, for example, may also reduce the security dilemma in the other. This creates problems of coordination (of both substance and timing) between regional security systems, and, especially, for the state itself. These additional coordination problems are likely to impede, rather than facilitate, regional cooperation.

When two (or more) distinct security externalities coincide, in part, but extend over different sets of states, a dense regional system will be created among the subset of states affected by both, and a thin regional system will be formed among all. In other words, the denser system will be nested within its thinner counterpart.[11] Such a nested regional system is depicted in Figure 3.1B and illustrated by the examples of ASEAN, which is nested within the larger Asia-Pacific regional security complex (Khong, this volume), and Africa, where denser subregions are nested within a continent-wide regional security system (Keller, this volume). The more numerous externalities may facilitate cooperation within the denser nest; whether this cooperation will spill over into or influence the thinner regional system will depend on the economies of scope in the agreement, discussed shortly.

NONSECURITY EXTERNALITIES

States may also confront one or more nonsecurity local externalities, and thereby be embedded in several different types of regional systems. Although not necessarily exhaustive, it is possible to identify four categories of nonsecurity externalities—illustrated in Pervin's discussion of the Middle East (this volume).[12] First, policies that stimulate movements of goods and factors of production or impede such movements create what might be called *economic externalities*. A bilateral economic agreement may be trade creating, for instance, forming a positive externality for others, or trade diverting, creating a negative externality. Second, *environmental externalities,* created either in the process of producing goods and services (transborder air pollution) or

11. On nested regimes, see Aggarwal 1985.

12. These categories grew out of the list of externalities generated in the discussion at the first IGCC workshop, "Reconceptualizing Regional Relations," 27–28 February 1993, Laguna Beach, Calif. Most of the possibilities were suggested by other participants. The categories reflect my attempt to impose some intellectual order on the diverse externalities identified by the group.

through the joint use of common-pool resources (groundwater basins), are also frequently limited in their geographic scope and create important regional interactions. Third, *information* can easily cross national borders and, if publicly available to a limited number of states, can create a local externality. Through such information, states may be able to avoid costly conflicts and negotiate Pareto-improving agreements (Keohane 1984; Fearon 1995).[13] Finally, *national values* can create the bases for externalities produced by the actions of other states. For instance, ethnic persecution in one state can create negative spillovers for kin abroad who identify with the victims—the so-called kin-country effect. Likewise, the welfare of foreigners concerned with human life and political freedom may be reduced when governments repress their own people.[14]

Nonsecurity externalities may also vary in number, magnitude, and the distribution of their effects, creating incentives for regional cooperation similar to those produced by security externalities. If these externalities coincide with local security externalities, the incentives for some form of cooperation are magnified. Just as more than one security externality can create a dense regional security complex, so too can nonsecurity externalities aggregate with security externalities to increase the potential gains from cooperation and create greater scope for strategies of conditional cooperation.

If these additional externalities are not coterminous with the security externalities, on the other hand, interlocking and nested regional security and nonsecurity systems will be created. These mixed systems will again

13. Information acquired by one state about another or provided by the second to the first does not necessarily produce an externality; the extent of the externality depends upon how easy it is to exclude others from the information. If a state must make a substantial investment to acquire information about a second, and can then prevent this information from being disclosed to others, no externality is created; the information is "private" to the first state. On the other hand, if the information is necessarily revealed by any state (by reporting to international organizations or leaking to the local press) or can be acquired at very low cost by others (by monitoring public behavior or reading local newspapers), it is in the "public domain," potentially available to all, and therefore nonexcludable. Informational externalities are often important in creating "demonstration" effects or in diffusing behaviors across national borders. Public information tends to be a global, rather than local, externality. Given its nonexcludable nature and ease of transport, furthered by the continuing communications revolution, it is difficult to restrict information to a limited number of states. Nonetheless, under some circumstances it may be restricted; the costs of acquiring information may increase with distance, or regional states may act as an information cartel. When this occurs, informational externalities will remain local and relevant to regional systems.

14. In both of these examples, it is not that the countries in question share the same values that create the externality; it is that the behavior of one country alters the utility of individuals in another because of the values they hold. Although it is often difficult to establish the presence and influence of values independently of the behavior we wish to explain, they can, conceptually at least, create important transborder externalities.

be similar in their dynamics to those created only by security externalities. Whether these additional externalities reinforce regional order depends upon the transactions costs of cooperation and economies of scope (see below).

The regions most commonly identified by analysts of international politics, some of which are examined later in this volume, are typically characterized by numerous externalities; it is the large number of generally coterminous and overlapping externalities that make these geographic groups, rather than others, salient and important units in world politics. Nonetheless, the magnitude, distribution, and number of security and nonsecurity externalities in these regions are important analytic distinctions with significant behavioral implications. The greater the magnitude, concentration, and number of externalities, the larger the potential gains from cooperation and the more likely states are to engage in the higher forms of conflict management identified by Morgan (this volume).

TRANSACTIONS COSTS

Given the disparity between the national and social returns for all externalities, there must exist, according to the Coase theorem, some joint solution to the problem of overproduction of negative externalities or underproduction of positive externalities that makes at least one state better off without making any other state worse off (i.e., the solution is Pareto improving).[15] Yet, outside the rarefied conditions of the theorem—an existing legal liability framework, perfect and complete information, and zero transactions costs of negotiating, monitoring, and enforcing contracts between states—not all Pareto-improving solutions are practically possible. Indeed, when any of the conditions of the theorem are violated, as all must be in the real world, collectively suboptimal outcomes will result. As implied in the Coase theorem, however, the tendencies toward over- and underproduction of externalities can be mitigated through international cooperation. Nonetheless, states always incur positive transactions costs for negotiating, monitoring, and enforcing agreements to cooperate, and these costs influence their behavior in important and interesting ways.[16]

15. Coase 1960, Cornes and Sandler 1986.

16. Anarchy, functionally equivalent to the absence of a legal liability framework, and informational asymmetries are examined in Keohane 1984. I focus here on the structure of transactions costs, a relatively neglected subject in international relations. On the role of transactions costs in shaping economic and political behavior, see the now extensive literature on the economics of institutions, including North 1981 and Williamson 1985, much of which is reviewed in Eggertsson 1990.

Transactions costs typically rise with the number of participating countries: the more actors, the greater the tendency for free riding, the more difficult it is to monitor behavior, and the harder it is to write an effective contract modifying incentives. Rising transactions costs set a practical limit to the number of potential contributors to the regional order. It follows that the most efficient group of contributors may be smaller than the group of potential beneficiaries. States only marginally affected by the externality, but otherwise willing to participate, may increase transactions costs by more than their contributions; in this case, other states are better off excluding the potential contributors from the agreement. Efficient agreements need not include all the states in the regional security complex. By the same logic, efficient agreements will tend to include the states most intensely affected by the externality; in this way, states minimize their individual and collective transactions costs. Transactions costs that rise with the number of participating parties may explain why concerts of regional powers—larger and more intensely affected states—appear to be more common than multilateral regional management schemes (see Job, this volume).

Transactions costs that rise with the number of participating countries will also tend to inhibit the quantity of management observed in the regional security complex. If the transactions costs of cooperation are sufficiently high, no agreement may be possible even though states foresee large potential benefits from mitigating or producing the externality. Similarly, if an externality is subject to a threshold effect, in which a fixed contribution is required to produce any improvement, the efficient group may be too small to undertake the required action. Not every regional security problem contains a regional solution. Finally, the more rapidly transactions costs rise with respect to the number of participating countries, the more difficult it will be to reach agreements between states in interlocking regional systems.

The transactions costs of cooperation may also be subject to economies of scope, and thus may tend to decline as additional issues are included in agreements.[17] An agreement to manage one externality may facilitate others, especially if the costs of negotiating, monitoring, and enforcing agreements are fixed and, once in place, the necessary infrastructure can be extended to

17. Economies of scale refer to declining marginal costs for producing additional units of the same product (i.e., each unit of soap is progressively cheaper to produce); economies of scope refer to declining marginal costs for producing units of a related but distinct product (producing soap lowers the marginal costs of producing toothpaste). The latter underlie many of the multiproduct conglomerates observed today.

additional subjects. As noted, numerous externalities may also facilitate linkage strategies. To the extent that such economies of scope are present, zones of cooperation may emerge through virtuous circles of progressively lower marginal transactions costs as additional externalities are brought under the umbrella. Thus, "pluralistic security communities" and other higher forms of regional order may rest on economies of scope, rather than social or cognitive constructs as sometimes averred (Deutsch et al. 1957; Adler 1991, 1992). Similarly, economies of scope supporting cooperation in dense nested regional systems may also facilitate cooperation in thin regional systems; once cultivated in the nest, cooperation may spill over into surrounding areas that lack sufficient incentives to sustain effective management on their own. To be clear, this is not a functionalist argument such as that found in the early literature on regional integration (Haas 1958). Rather, the proposition follows from economies of scope in the negotiating, monitoring, and enforcement of international cooperation.

With disparities between the private and social benefits and costs of security externalities, and positive transactions costs, negative security externalities will always be greater, and positive security externalities smaller, than the states of a regional security system desire.[18] Regional order is never complete. States cannot regulate conflict or produce cooperation at the socially desired levels. Successful management must be measured by the direction and degree of change, not by some noble but impossible goal. In the pursuit of success, moreover, effective international leadership will and should come from the most intensely affected states of the regional security complex.

All of this suggests that building effective regional orders is difficult. We should expect states to rely upon the balance-of-power mechanism—the least costly mode of management, especially as the number of countries increases—and recognize that this minimalist form of regional order will occasionally fail to keep the peace within regions. We should also expect states to move up the ladder of regional order described by Morgan (this volume) when the benefits from managing the relevant security externalities are concentrated in a few states, the basis for a regional concert, or are diffuse

18. This conclusion is not simply a function of international anarchy, since externalities are not provided at socially optimal levels even within states. Under popular sovereignty, individuals have strategic incentives to misrepresent their preferences for public goods, creating a second-order problem of free riding. Under a leviathan, any state that can coerce "true" information from its citizens can also act monopolistically and earn rents for itself. Suboptimal results are a fact of political life.

and especially large, the foundation for a broad-based multilateral or collective solution to regional conflict. Finally, even when states succeed in building higher forms of regional order, the suboptimal levels of provision imply that conflict will still be a continuing and important part of regional relations.

REGIONAL SYSTEMS STRUCTURE

Regional security systems will be influenced by their structure (Buzan 1991, 211). Like the global system (Waltz 1979), regional structures can be defined by two dimensions: the ordering principle—anarchy—and the distribution of capabilities—multipolar, bipolar, and, in the regional case, unipolar. Like all systems effects, theories of regional structure are probabilistic. Structural constraints only influence the expected range of behavior; they seldom dictate a particular response. The range of behavior can be quite large. Policies can also fall outside the expected range if countries choose to ignore the constraints of the system. Like their global counterparts, theories of regional structure provide only a "first-cut" prediction. Nonetheless, as revealed in the region-specific essays elsewhere in this volume, regional structures exert an important influence on regional orders.

Even with this usual qualifier, however, predictions based on the structure of regional systems must be very tentative at this stage. Regional security complexes are themselves embedded in the larger global security complex. Where the latter is a closed system, or reasonably treated as such in "problem-solving theory," the former are inherently open systems.[19] In other words, whereas all of the relevant actors are included within or endogenous to the closed global system, important actors may be outside or exogenous to open regional systems. From a regional systems perspective, such exogenous actors are beyond the scope of the theory and, thus, inherently "unpredictable," rendering hypotheses based solely on regional systems structure more problematic.

Nonetheless, it seems plausible to suggest that unipolar regional security systems (on the Western Hemisphere, see Mares, this volume; on Soviet successor states, see Roeder, this volume) will be relatively autonomous and, according to the theory of hegemonic stability, will most easily manage negative security externalities and produce positive security externalities; the single pole is likely to reap a large absolute gain from managing the exter-

19. On problem-solving theory, see Cox 1986 and Waltz 1986.

nality, and is most likely to form an effective *k*-group.[20] Multipolar regional systems (on the Asia-Pacific, see Shirk, this volume; on the Middle East, see Pervin, this volume), where competition among the poles is attenuated and free riding most acute, will also be relatively autonomous but plagued by problems of conflict management. Cooperation, when it occurs, will most likely be found among the small number of highly affected powers in the region—producing concerts rather than collective security arrangements. Finally, bipolar regional systems will be relatively competitive, and while free riding may not be a significant hindrance, security concerns may thwart cooperation.[21] The poles will also be more likely to appeal to outside powers for assistance, thereby inciting intervention and reducing the autonomy of the regional system.

GLOBAL SYSTEMS STRUCTURE

Although distinct from regional security systems, the global system can also be expected to affect regional order. Not only are global system theories a useful supplement to regional systems theories, helping to lend some predictability to great powers outside the regional security complex, but the global system itself is likely to exert important effects on regional outcomes. Different global structures produce varying degrees of competition between the great powers: as in regional systems, this competition is greatest in bipolar, less severe in multipolar, and least intense in unipolar structures. While a constant across regions, the global system and the degree of competition within it does change over time, with two implications for regional relations.

As discussed by Arthur Stein and Steven Lobell (this volume), bipolar international systems tend to globalize regional conflicts. Because of the intense competition, and induced concerns for reputation and resolve, the superpowers' minor interests in a region are transformed into major interests.[22]

20. On the theory of hegemonic stability, see Kindleberger 1986 and my recent review (Lake 1993). While Kindleberger and I agree that externalities are most likely to be managed effectively under a single leader, I argue that this is neither a necessary nor a sufficient condition. Mares and Roeder (both in this volume) note that hegemony is a double-edged sword; the dominant country may provide certain public goods, but it also poses the largest threat to others in the region.

21. On the effects of reducing the number of poles in a system on the prospects for cooperation, see Snidal 1991.

22. To emphasize the point, both superpowers must possess some minor interest in the region to initiate this spiral. If the superpowers are not affected by the externality, the process of globalization will not occur.

Local externalities thus get transformed into global externalities—and the salience of the regional security complex per se is correspondingly diminished. As outside powers become more deeply involved, they are also likely to funnel greater resources to the regional actors, feeding and potentially expanding conflicts beyond their strictly local levels. The Vietnam War exemplifies this bipolar spiral. Since multipolar and unipolar systems are less competitive, reputation and resolve will be less central for the great powers. With the end of bipolarity and the Cold War, local externalities are more likely to remain local.

The more competitive the global system, the tighter are the constraints on the great powers. The range of expected behavior is narrower, and the penalties for policies that violate the constraints are larger. The looser the constraints of the global system, the more likely it is that great powers will act in the absence of any interest in the regional security externality and in the self-aggrandizing or personal interests of national political leaders. Thus, in bipolar global systems the policies of the great powers are most constrained, driven by national interests, and "predictable" (from a systems perspective). The constraints become less binding as we move to multipolar and, finally, unipolar systems.[23] This suggests that great powers in multipolar and unipolar global systems may be more prone to intervene in regions in which they lack substantial security interests. America's intervention in Somalia appears to fit this prediction: in the absence of any compelling regional interest, President Bush, a lame-duck executive, unilaterally initiated an American military operation for apparently humanitarian reasons.[24] Since these interventions will be primarily motivated by idiosyncratic concerns, their frequency and number are impossible to predict from a systems perspective; all we can conclude, at this point, is that global unipolarity and multipolarity create greater scope for domestically motivated great-power interventions. There is no particular reason to expect these "unconstrained" and idiosyncratic actions to help stabilize either the regional or global security systems.

These two implications produce partially offsetting effects. While bipolarity will tend to globalize and possibly expand regional conflicts, the in-

23. This parallels Krasner's (1978, 340) argument that hegemons are more likely to act ideologically than other, lesser powers. For an alternative view that great-power interventions are predictable during and after the Cold War, see Miller 1995a and 1995b.

24. On the limited American interests in Somalia, see Wolfowitz 1994, 32. On American policy in the Persian Gulf, and the lack of any public consensus on the need to intervene, see Mueller 1994.

tense competition is also likely to constrain the superpowers to act responsibly, prevent inadvertent escalation, and maintain global, if not regional, stability. Although regional security systems are more likely to remain autonomous under multipolar and unipolar global systems, those great-power interventions that do occur are more likely to be driven by idiosyncratic political motivations—with at present unknown implications for regional order. Whether these offsetting effects combine to produce greater regional and global order in bipolar, multipolar, or unipolar systems requires attention to particular circumstances; like most propositions, it probably "depends." The current concern with regional security in academic and policy circles reflects an intuition that possibly regional order and probably global order are likely to decrease as we move away from global bipolarity.[25] In my view, this should remain an open question.

Finally, regional and global system structures interact in determining the regional order and the level of conflict that flows from it. The most conflict-prone pairing is likely to be a bipolar regional structure embedded within a bipolar global structure: the intense regional competition will prompt each regional pole to seek outside assistance, and the intense global competition will compel each global pole to provide it. South Asia is a telling example; during the Cold War, this bipolar regional system witnessed three wars between India and Pakistan and a continuing standoff over Kashmir. The Arab-Israeli conflict is a second example (Pervin, this volume). Conversely, multipolarity at either level is likely to dampen bipolar conflicts in the other.

Great-Power Intervention

The issue of great-power intervention in regional conflicts is central both to current policy debates and to the broader themes of this volume. In this chapter, I have focused on the nature and characteristics of regional security complexes and their effects on regional orders, but the analysis is easily extended to questions of great-power intervention. In contrast to Paul Papayoanou (this volume) and Richard Rosecrance and Peter Schott (this volume), who generally see the great powers taking an active and productive role in managing regional relations in the future, my analysis leads me to a more skepti-

25. On the stabilizing effect of global bipolarity, see Mearsheimer 1990.

cal conclusion. In my view, great-power interventions, at least in the foreseeable future, will be mercurial and often motivated by extraregional and domestic political factors rather than regional security concerns. To the extent that great powers do contribute to regional order, the contribution will largely be a by-product of actions taken toward other ends.

Great powers possess global military reach. They have the ability to project force around the globe, and as a result, they can intervene in any regional security complex whenever it suits their interests. The willingness of great powers to manage regional conflicts and contribute to the creation of regional order, in turn, is contingent upon how deeply they are affected by the security externality that emanates from the area.

For deeply affected great powers that are full members of a regional security complex, the predictions in the previous section hold in their essentials. They will be affected by the character of the security and nonsecurity externalities, transactions costs, and regional and global systems structures in ways nearly identical to those of nongreat powers. Such great powers, however, may also be embedded in more than one regional security complex and, therefore, concerned even after bipolarity and the Cold War with questions of precedent and reputation. Although such concerns will be less intense now, they will still constrain the great powers in important, if somewhat unpredictable, ways. The great powers may be even more interventionist, in order to deter conflicts in other areas of interest, or less interventionist, for fear that acting in one instance will set precedents for action in other areas of less concern. In the final chapter, Pat Morgan and I argue that such concerns are overblown and that the United States, and other great powers, must now learn to think in regional rather than global terms, but reputation and precedent still matter in international affairs.

Great powers that are "outside" the regional security complex, on the other hand, will be unlikely to intervene in the region, except when prompted by internal and idiosyncratic factors.[26] This is, at one level, a near tautology, yet its implications are important. Such states will devote few, if any, resources to ameliorating negative or producing positive regional security externalities. Especially under global unipolarity or multipolarity, these rela-

26. Even when nonsecurity regional externalities affect great powers in important ways and economies of scope in agreements exist, great powers that are unaffected by the regional security externalities will still not have any incentive to pay the costs of mitigating these externalities. The arguments, developed above, about the likely effects of a large number of externalities are predicated on a preexisting security externality.

tively unconstrained states may still choose to intervene, but their actions will be driven by internal forces and not necessarily conducive to regional order. As security becomes more regionalized in the post–Cold War world, such disinterested states are likely to become quite common. While the Bush administration took the initiative in delivering food shipments to strife-torn areas in Somalia, for instance, this effort was predicated on estimates of extremely low casualties and material losses. When the attempt to capture the Somalian warlord Mohammed Farah Aideed proved frustrating and casualties began to escalate, the Clinton administration quickly reversed course and withdrew combat troops from the area. Today, even the largest state within the global system is unwilling to become involved in costly conflicts or carry through on costly commitments outside the regional security complexes in which it is embedded.[27]

As a corollary, it follows that the United Nations, as presently constituted, will also often fail to play an effective role in managing regional relations. As long as the organization remains dependent upon voluntary contributions to its annual budget and special missions, the United Nations will reflect the national interests of its member states—and especially the interests of the great powers on the Security Council. If the great powers do not possess a sufficient interest in a region to contribute directly to ameliorating or producing an externality, they are equally unlikely to possess an interest in contributing indirectly through an international organization. Indeed, given the larger number of states likely to be involved in multilateral decision making, collective-action problems or political differences that might be avoided by ad hoc coalitions of concerned powers may stymie more formal institutions. Edmond Keller's discussion (this volume) of the limited role of the United Nations in contemporary Africa appears to confirm this prediction.

While regional conflicts might be ameliorated by an infusion of external resources, the lesser interests of the great powers today suggest that such contributions will generally be limited. Although some states under some circumstances may choose to participate, the great powers cannot be relied upon to manage regional conflict or promote regional cooperation. States within a regional security complex must and will be the primary actors in

27. The Persian Gulf War is the obvious exception that so far proves the rule: in addition to securing the other regional powers, a politically fragmented Middle East produces the positive *global* externality of cheaper oil—the low price of which is clearly in the interest of the United States and the other large oil importers. For a positive argument that regional powers ought to police their own areas, see Maynes 1993–94.

building the regional order. And although multilateral operations may be attempted and, indeed, successful in some circumstances, regional actors would be unwise to rely upon them as universal panaceas.

This poses one of the central paradoxes of the post–Cold War world. International political problems are typically difficult to resolve because of the anarchic nature of the international system and the inability of states to make credible commitments to mutually beneficial agreements. One of the most important roles great powers can play in today's world is as guarantors of regional peace arrangements—whether monitoring and enforcing the Bosnian agreement, a peace settlement between Israel and the Palestinians, or a nuclear-free zone in Northeast Asia. Yet, in the absence of sufficient security externalities, the willingness of the great powers to absorb the costs of these actions is quite limited. Although bipolarity globalized security externalities and escalated interests for the superpowers in peripheral contests, today—at a time when reduced tensions enable the great powers to cooperate more effectively than ever before—their incentives to contribute to regional security management are greatly reduced.

Conclusion

At present, we lack well-developed theories of regional security systems. The purpose of this volume, and of this essay in particular, is to develop theories of regional order. The hypotheses posed above are tentative. The chapters below explicate some propositions developed here and open up additional avenues of inquiry.

The view of regional systems advanced here, of which transborder but local security externalities are the foundation, reveals new dimensions of variation in regional security systems, expands the research agenda, and, I hope, improves our understanding of regional order. Externalities also provide a handle for opening up the relationship between regional and global systems, a key issue for theoretical progress in this area. The concept suggests when and how regional politics will be globalized and why great-power solutions to regional conflicts are likely to prove elusive for the foreseeable future.

Studying regions can also help us refine our prevailing systems theories of global relations. The task of developing a theory of regional security systems forces us to consider the nature of the interactions that create and sustain all systems. Just as local externalities create regional systems, global externalities can be considered the foundation of the global system. And just as the number, magnitude, and distribution of externalities are likely to matter in regional relations, so too are they likely to influence global relations.[28] For instance, understanding how global externalities are created and managed, and how they change over time, may help reveal how our current international system differs from other anarchic and (increasingly) multipolar international systems. The seemingly more numerous and larger externalities found today have created a denser international system that may support greater international cooperation than found in earlier periods of global multipolarity.

28. For a related argument, see Ruggie 1986 and Buzan, Jones, and Little 1993. Whether global externalities are properly an attribute of the system or of the structure of the system is, to my mind, largely a semantic question. Externalities stand above the individual units; indeed, they epitomize the kinds of unintended consequences central to all systems theories. They also correspond closely, but not exactly, with Durkheim's notion of dynamic density, used by John Ruggie (1986) to open up Waltz's second dimension of structure. But, externalities do not, strictly speaking, define how the units "stand in relation to one another" (Waltz 1979, 80); thus, they do not fall within Waltz's conception of structure. Externalities do not fit easily into a structuralist conception of systems. They may nonetheless be an important source of interstate behavior and systems change. For a discussion of systems as networks of strategic choice and how they differ from the structural theories, see Powell 1994.

4

Economic Liberalization, Political Coalitions, and Emerging Regional Orders

Etel Solingen

This chapter examines the domestic determinants of regional conflict and cooperation at the end of the century. I address specifically the potential impact of economic liberalization, arguing that the nature of ruling coalitions may be a powerful predictor of how states manage regional cooperation or conflict. I explore the extent to which (1) coalitions more strongly committed to economic liberalization are also more likely (than their political nemeses) to undertake regional cooperative postures, *particularly when facing similarly committed regional partners,* and, conversely, (2) coalitions aggregating statist and nationalist interests—in many cases allied with con-

I would like to acknowledge the support of the John D. and Catherine T. MacArthur Foundation Program on Peace and International Cooperation, and the helpful comments of Jack Snyder, Joel Migdal, Steve Weber, Phillip Roeder, Richard Eichenberg, and Vinod Aggarwal. Permission to reprint has been granted by the *Journal of Theoretical Politics,* in which an earlier version of this essay originally appeared (vol. 8 [January 1996]: 70–114).

fessional movements—endorse less cooperative positions vis-à-vis regional partners.[1]

To some extent, it is safe to argue that domestic politics have not only always mattered, but could comfortably explain regional orders in the last forty years (Solingen 1994a). Undoubtedly, the Cold War era can be considered a "hard case" for domestic-politics interpretations, since few can dispute how forcefully the superpower rivalry framed the scope of action of regional actors. The post–Cold War era, however, makes it easier to argue the preeminence of the domestic over the structural in global power considerations. The new global order has largely reduced the global security externalities of regional processes, or, at the very least, has changed the nature of such externalities. What are, then, the general conditions—intellectual and empirical—that make domestic politics essential to a reconceptualization of regional relations at the end of the century?

First, the relationship between military endowments and genuine security is complex and indeterminate. The widespread recognition of this complexity has reinforced the natural tendency of domestic groups to frame their attitudes toward security on the basis of their respective political and institutional interests, rather than on vague assessments of national security. Second, the end of the Cold War and the growing regionalization of conflicts have sharpened domestic debates over the meaning of security within countries in different regions because it is no longer feasible to peg regional relations to the old, inexorable logic of superpower competition. Domestic processes have thus been gaining greater relevance in the formulation of regional policy. The politicization of regional policy, in turn, makes the relevant themes and actors more transparent, thus offering a unique opportunity for the analyst to study the domestic conditions that shape regional postures. Third, the new global order marks the end of aid to regional players that, by virtue of their strategic value, could rely on superpower military and economic support. The waning of such external rents has weakened certain domestic groups and institutions—such as the military—and strengthened others. The contraction of resources has narrowed the political space for

1. The confessional category includes ethnic or religious groups; where these embrace radical platforms, they are commonly labeled "fundamentalist." I use the terms "radical-confessional" and "fundamentalist" interchangeably, wherever it applies empirically, that is, nearly worldwide. Although not every confessional party or movement is radical, in this chapter I refer to radical forms of confessionalism for the most part. For a more nuanced perspective, see Solingen 1996b.

military expenditures and forced a redefinition of priorities. Understanding the new domestic distribution of costs and benefits from alternative security postures is thus essential in forecasting likely regional outcomes.

Fourth, the democratic-peace research program has turned the rarity of war among democracies into virtually an article of faith, even if methodological and theoretical debates continue to rage. A preliminary overview of the applicability of the democratic peace to understanding both conflict and cooperation in the industrializing world (Solingen 1996a, 1996b) suggests that (1) the democratic nature of states has not been *necessary* for regional cooperation to come about; (2) given the relative infancy of many democracies, the jury is still out on whether democracy will be *sufficient* to preclude regional wars; (3) the nature of democratic transitions introduces a high degree of complexity into the democracy-peace relationship, with some arguing that democratization may well heighten the probability of violent conflict (Mansfield and Snyder 1995). The emergence of regional cooperation in the absence of democratic dyads is entirely compatible with democratic-peace theorizing. It is nonetheless noteworthy that one of the most dramatic recent reversals from conflict to cooperation occurred in a region most lagging in democratic interlocutors, the Middle East. Paradoxically, there has been more cooperation in that traumatized region than, for instance, in South Asia, where the sharpening, enduring rivalry between two democracies—India and Pakistan—has turned them into the most likely site for the outbreak of a nuclear conflict.[2] Similarly, the absence of armed conflict among the ASEAN countries in recent decades can be traced to anything but a meeting of democratic minds. A coalitional argument building on the impact of economic liberalization goes a long way toward explaining these and other trends toward regional cooperation and conflict.

I discuss next the theoretical foundations of the hypothesis that the nature of domestic ruling coalitions and of their political-economic strategies provides important insights into the kind of regional postures their states embrace. Subsequently, I consider some qualifying conditions, hybrid cases, and unintended effects. Next I examine the relationship between presumed effects and observed outcomes throughout a range of situations where liberalizing and statist-nationalist coalitions face each other and their adversaries. I end with some conceptual and methodological advantages and limitations of this approach for the study of emerging regional orders.

2. See the statement by former U.S. director of the Central Intelligence Agency James Woolsey (*New York Times,* 22 February 1994, A15).

Domestic Coalitions, Economic Reform, and Regional Orders

An efficient way of capturing the impact of economic liberalization on regional orders is by focusing on the political coalitions that promote and those that oppose liberalization. The general question explored in this section is whether ruling coalitions pursuing economic liberalization are more likely to embrace regional cooperation than their political adversaries (often a collection of inward-looking, statist-nationalist, and confessional groups). This hypothesis is not strictly based on traditional arguments about the effects of interdependence among (regional) partners on their bilateral cooperative behavior. Rather, it builds on certain assumptions about the way in which political coalitions—in safeguarding their domestic interests and viability—define their association with the regional and international political economy as a whole.[3] The core assumption is that the kinds of ties binding different actors (institutions, economic sectors, groups, bureaucracies, political parties) to global economic and other international processes do affect their conceptions of interests, and that these conceptions are expressed domestically as well as regionally.[4] Actors (state and private) join forces in coalitions when some of their interests converge in order to safeguard their common interests against challenges from alternative coalitions. Political entrepreneurs constantly scan the coalitional landscape to logroll coalitions and effect exchanges that may otherwise not easily come about. Different coalitions develop competing grand strategies, which define not only a state's relation to global power and economic structures but also the regional strategic context and the domestic extraction and allocation of resources among groups and institutions.[5]

In dissecting the possible association between coalition type and regional orders a good starting point is the distributional consequences of

3. On regime survival as the main priority of ruling coalitions in the Third World, see Rothstein 1977. On domestic coalitions and international cooperation, see Snyder 1989. On nationalists and internationalists in U.S. foreign economic policy, see Frieden 1988.

4. Gourevitch 1978. As Cowhey (1990) argues, "[I]nterested actors anticipate the constraints imposed by the international system in their working out of domestic policies."

5. The grand strategy of political coalitions transcends the traditional disciplinary divide between "industrialization" strategies (often studied in comparative political economy) and security strategies (a core subject in international relations). On grand strategy as an economic, political, and military means-ends chain designed to achieve security, see Posen 1984, Kennedy 1991, and Rosecrance and Stein 1993.

economic liberalization, which create two basic ideal types of coalition: one favoring it, the other opposing it.

LIBERALIZING COALITIONS

The grand political-economic strategies of different coalitions transcend the domestic-international divide. Quite often, the interests of political coalitions favoring broader economic liberalization (market-oriented, privatizing, state-shrinking reforms) require openness to global markets, capital, investments, and technology. Hence the characterization of these coalitions as "internationalist."[6] Central to their agenda is the primacy accorded to macroeconomic stability and to the discipline induced by international competition. Liberalizing coalitions often include state agencies in charge of economic reform, and politicians and parties representing the beneficiaries of reform.[7] Beneficiaries include liquid-asset holders and export-oriented firms, such as large banking and industrial complexes capable of surviving without state protection, more receptive to structural adjustment policies, and opposed to external confrontations with the international financial and investing community.[8] The ability of big business (local and foreign-owned) to influence domestic investment patterns and to move capital abroad endows them with an important voice in shaping domestic and external adjustment policies. Smaller firms engaged in exports or supplying internationalized enterprises are normally part of these coalitions, as is the highly skilled labor force employed by these firms. A variety of professional groups that might be

6. Stallings 1992. Different coalitions emphasize different aspects of economic liberalization, depending on their interest in expanding exports, deregulating financial flows, opening the domestic market to foreign goods and investment, reducing state entrepreneurial activities, or some mix thereof. Liberalizing tendencies do not mean "laissez-faire" policies across the board; a "dirigiste" developmental state (Johnson 1982) can plan the direction, rate, and extent of liberalization, which does not exclude selective protection and continued regulation. Given a selective and gradual agenda, the adjective "liberalizing" is more appropriate than "liberal" in characterizing these coalitions.

7. On how global interdependence has strengthened key state financial institutions, big business, and transnational firms, see Cox 1986 and Strange 1992.

8. Structural adjustment is "a set of measures designed to make the economy competitive" (Przeworski 1991,144). Such measures often include, in different sequences and combinations, currency devaluation, deficit reduction, de-indexing of wages, reduction in consumer subsidies, price deregulation, and tariff reductions (Kaufman 1989). On why firms with strong international ties oppose protection, see Milner 1988. On the bankers' alliance and their populist nemesis, see Maxfield 1990.

aggregated under the category of "symbolic analysts" are similarly oriented toward an open global economic and knowledge (technological) system.[9]

From the perspective of liberalizing coalitions, cooperative regional orders may be most efficient for both their *domestic* political and *global* implications. Such orders, in general terms, are expected to have three consequences:

1. *Freeing up resources to carry out reform at home.* Conflictive postures must be backed up by an internal mobilization of resources for potential military conflict. Such mobilization often contributes to many of the ailments afflicting these countries' domestic political economies (from the standpoint of these coalitions): the expansion of state power, the maintenance of unproductive and inflation-inducing military investments, and the perpetuation of rent-seeking patterns.[10] In principle, therefore, liberalizing coalitions arguably resist such choices, by attempting to avoid inflated military budgets that increase governmental and payments deficits, raise the cost of capital, curtail savings and productive investment, deplete foreign exchange coffers, and distort the human power base.[11] In light of the high opportunity costs of military expenditures, these coalitions may be less predisposed to extract and mobilize societal resources for external conflict, because such extraction would threaten important macroeconomic objectives they endorse. The relationship between military expenditures, a bloated state, and economic decline seems clearer today, given the experience of the former Soviet bloc and the industrializing world.[12]
2. *Weakening groups and institutions opposed to reform.* The resolution of regional conflicts can have a detrimental impact on (*a*) the size and strength

9. "Symbolic analysts" include public and private managerial, technical, scientific, educational, information, and service-oriented elites who benefit from an integrated global economy (Reich 1991).

10. Ball 1988. On how predatory taxation—very often adopted for defense purposes—reduces profit margins and discourages private investment, see Feigenbaum and Henig 1994. On rent seeking, see Buchanan, Tollison, and Tullock 1980, 4.

11. This is not to say that liberalizing coalitions do not invest in weapons acquisitions at all, but that when they do so, it is likely that (1) their levels of defense expenditures will not endanger their liberalizing strategy, and (2) military investments will be considered an insurance policy, particularly against statist-nationalist adversaries or against generalized uncertainty (of the kind unleashed by the end of the Cold War). On East and Southeast Asian weapons acquisition as insurance, see Shirk (this volume).

12. On why the congruence of economic growth and war production in the United States in World War II was exceptional, see Kaysen 1990.

of the military as an institution, (*b*) the network of public and private enterprises thriving on the production and distribution of military and ancillary goods, (*c*) proponents of nationalist and/or radical confessional causes that prosper with regional conflict and competition with neighboring states (see below).[13] These groups often oppose economic reform because it threatens their material or ideal interests. Statist-nationalist and radical confessional movements often connect liberalization with global (Western) institutions, which they consider anathema to their own political agenda. Their challenge of these global economic actors makes them natural adversaries of liberalizing coalitions.

3. *Securing access to foreign markets, capital, investments, and technology.* Cooperative regional arrangements have positive global externalities for liberalizing coalitions because they erode risk considerations and enable (not guarantee) foreign investment, avoid potential sanctions and penalties from international private and public actors, and reinforce the coalition's ties to economic institutions (IMF, World Bank) with which these coalitions endear themselves by virtue of their reform programs. Intransigent regional postures, instead, raise the propensity for conflict and the risks for foreign investors and may trigger denial of bilateral or multilateral aid (as with the U.S. refusal to provide loan guarantees to Israel's Likud-led coalition), denial of technology, and other sanctions. Liberalizers aim to lower the probability of any of these punitive measures and avoid the uncertainty that each of them creates; they are averse to these risks even when they are fully aware of coordination problems that exist more with respect to sanctions than to foreign investments.[14]

The preceding points suggest that cooperative regional arrangements are not just the product of concessions to outside pressures. Liberalizing coalitions do not merely trade the right to pursue the national interest regionally (whatever that means) for the right to maximize their own wealth, as their opponents often argue (in the Middle East, for example). In fact, liberalizing coalitions aim at shrinking the size of the state but, if successful, end up strengthening the leaner state's institutional capacity for societal extraction and, by extension, for mobilizing resources for war. Liberalizing coalitions

13. On the affinity between economic nationalism and "national security" as the pivot of state behavior, see Gilpin 1987.

14. Mares (this volume) points to problems of coordination in imposing sanctions. However, he does not consider the distinction between punitive outcomes and the prospect thereof, or between sanctions and investment.

unite domestic groups and institutions that favor regional cooperation because such cooperation is instrumental in (1) advancing the agenda of liberalizing the economy, (2) reining in adversarial political forces at home, (3) securing certain international economic, financial, and political benefits—such as debt relief, export markets, technology transfer, food imports, aid, and investments—that can be used to maintain or broaden domestic political support and to strengthen the institutional framework underpinning economic liberalization at home and abroad. Where most of the positive externalities from regional cooperation are captured by a few groups with intense internationalist preferences and equally intense political access, these privileged groups, or *k*-groups (Lake, this volume), are particularly active in advancing the liberalizing agenda.

STATIST-NATIONALIST AND CONFESSIONAL COALITIONS

Statist-nationalist and confessional coalitions encompass eclectic groups that often collude in challenging different aspects of liberalizing agendas. Not all elements are present everywhere, and their relative strength varies across states and regions. Generally, these coalitions have an affinity with import-substituting models of industrialization and classical populist programs, involving a strong, active government controlling prices, protecting workers, wages, and state enterprises, allocating credit at low interest rates, and dispensing rents to private industry.[15] In their extreme form, outright economic autarky and self-sufficiency have been the cornerstone of inward-looking coalitions, as in the "hermit kingdom" of North Korea.

Opponents of economic liberalization worldwide often include threatened state bureaucracies and enterprises, politicians resisting the dismantling of such enterprises and the consequent erosion of their basis of political patronage, some popular sectors (unskilled, blue-collar workers, white-collar and other state employees, small businesses), import-competing firms with close ties to the state, and the underemployed intelligentsia as well as "symbolic analysts" associated with all these groups.[16] Arms-importing and arms-

15. Populism is distributive but not necessarily redistributive; the politically powerful benefit, not the very poor. It is generally biased toward an increase in middle-class (not poor) urban income at the expense of rural producers, exporters, and foreign capital (Cardoso and Helwege 1991, 46).

16. Kaufman 1989; Kallab and Feinberg 1989. Certain economic groups may support privatization in principle but profit at lower risks from expanded state economic activities and resources.

producing military establishments are often adversely affected by adjustment programs, as is the military as an institution. These coalitions thus reject orthodox stabilization plans, particularly as imposed by the IMF and other financial institutions, and favor a more expansionist course.[17] Civic nationalist and majority ethnonationalist and confessional movements are not merely natural partners in the logrolling of these coalitions, but the key to mass political mobilization. Such movements (as in the Middle East and South Asia) thrive on popular resentment over what they regard as externally imposed adjustment policies, over reliance on foreign investment, and over the "Western" principles and norms embodied in most international regimes. At times the coalition's material basis of opposition to internationalization and liberalization is stronger (as where state enterprises and import-substituting interests are powerful). At others, the confessional component becomes a driving force. Very frequently the two converge and tend to reinforce each other. The paradox of weakened former nationalist parties (such as Egypt's Socialist Labor Party) allying themselves with the Muslim Brotherhood quickly unravels when bearing in mind their calculus of potential gains from jointly challenging liberalizing coalitions.

The partners aggregated in statist-nationalist and confessional coalitions perceive regional cooperation as weakening them politically and economically, for many of the same reasons that liberalizing coalitions expect such outcomes to benefit them. From the vantage point of statist-nationalist and confessional coalitions, the prospect of peaceful settlements involves the following:

1. *The danger of legitimizing downsized allocations to the military and weapons-producing enterprises.* A more cooperative regional order weakens the justification for the extraction of societal resources, while leaving intact these institutions' mission of confronting regional threats.[18] Without such threats, the viability of military-industrial complexes is endangered, particularly since export markets have withered away in the

17. Stabilization involves restoring macroeconomic balance through short-term measures to slow down inflation and reduce balance-of-payments and government deficits (Przeworski 1991, 144). On the impact of economic liberalization on military-industrial complexes in various regions, see Solingen 1997. On the historical connection between the rise of nationalism, massive increases in armed forces and taxation, and the growth and centralization of nation-states, see Tilly 1994.

18. At the same time, nationalist coalitions are often more reluctant to mobilize resources abroad, and even if they are not, the new global realities—political and economic—preclude that option anyway.

aftermath of the Cold War. Militarization is not subsidiary to larger political-economic objectives, but built into the grand strategy of statist-nationalist and confessional coalitions, for which military prowess constitutes a core basis of legitimacy, as in Iraq and North Korea.

2. *Depriving statist-nationalist and radical confessional coalitions of a major source of political capital: mythmaking.* Mythmaking (Snyder 1991) entails the ability to mobilize militant religious, ethnic, or cultural groups against an actual or imagined regional adversary. Self-reliance is a central myth of inward-looking coalitions, either in their secular (North Korea's *juche*) or in their confessional form. Overall, these coalitions are far more prone to rely on legitimating principles—such as sovereignty, geographical and territorial integrity, self-reliance, and confessional purity—than are their liberalizing counterparts, which rely (often blindly) on markets and a leaner, effective state to broaden the constituency benefiting from liberalization, internationalization, and regional cooperation.[19]
3. *Cooperative regional orders, and their potential for helping myths wither away, weaken the ability of these coalitions to justify societal extraction and the allocation of fiscal resources to an array of economic and religious interests.* Consider, for instance, how Iranian state enterprises, including Islamic "welfare" patronages, have exploited such myths. The use of myths to expand state activities, revenues, and rents recalls Tilly's (1989) notion of external threats as a racket.

Where most of the negative domestic externalities from liberalization and regional cooperation are suffered by politically strong statist-nationalist and confessional groups with intense preferences, these groups resist the liberalizing agenda most forcefully and, sometimes, quite effectively. Given their constituent basis of domestic political support, inward-looking coalitions, unlike their liberalizing counterparts, are also more resilient to coercive international intervention, and excel in converting such external interventions into domestic political profit. Statist-nationalist and confessional coalitions have thus defied political and economic sanctions from great powers and international institutions, as in Iraq, Iran, Serbia, Libya, and North Korea. In all these cases (1) powerful import-substituting economic interests prospered from international closure; (2) despite potential bottlenecks in the sup-

19. On nationalists' affinity with the acquisition of neighboring land through military means, see Rosecrance and Schott (this volume). On trading states' emphasis on global resources, capital, technology, and markets, rather than territories and population, see Rosecrance 1986.

ply of inputs, the military and its productive complex were often "Teflоned" from the effects of sanctions; and (3) sanctions strengthened state agencies in charge of productive and distributive functions. These effects, however, are relatively short lasting and, over the long haul, can severely threaten the longevity of these coalitions.

To sum up the argument so far: Regional cooperative postures hold different payoffs for different coalitions. They are expected to have positive political effects (domestically and globally) for liberalizing coalitions, and negative ones for statist-nationalist and confessional ones. On the one hand, regional cooperation enables the pursuit of economic reform; it spells transparency, predictability, a good reputation, and the blessing of the international community (which connects liberalizing coalitions with the promise of rationalization and cooperation). On the other hand, the prospects for cooperation undermine the viability of state agencies and enterprises associated with military functions and production, threaten with extinction the state's ability to disburse unlimited resources among rent-seeking groups (erstwhile justified in "state-building" and national security terms), and deprive populist leaders of a rich fountain of myths. Nationalist coalitions, in other words, appear oriented either toward what Barnett (1992) labels an "accommodationist" strategy of mobilizing societal resources for security objectives (that is, a strategy that maintains the basic compact between a robust "state" and societal interests) or toward a centralizing restructuring strategy (increasing state control over the economy and society). Liberalizing coalitions, instead, restructure state-society relations by diluting state control, arguably expanding the country's material wealth. Liberalizing coalitions embrace regional and domestic policies that may be politically risky in the short term but potentially rewarding over the long haul (Israel's Labor-Meretz, 1992–96). Statist-nationalist and confessional coalitions rely on regional and domestic strategies that bear short-term political payoffs but are fundamentally counterproductive in the long run (Iran's Islamic republic).[20]

These are the general political contours shaping the grand strategies and regional postures of liberalizing and statist-nationalist coalitions respectively. This overview provides no more than a stylized account of contending coa-

20. Their behavior may be explained as a result of (1) a failure to act strategically, (2) acting strategically but miscalculating the future political benefits from "standing up to the world," (3) impermeability to "learning," or (4) absence of choice, given their political makeup, compelling an all-out (even if suicidal) strategy. On cartelized systems, immobile interests (assets), and short time horizons, see Snyder 1991, 49.

litions, abstracting a pivotal axis or political cleavage from a very complex reality, where no coalition classifies as a pure case. What it may risk in failing to capture every empirical variation, it gains in facilitating large-scale comparisons across regions through relatively parsimonious means. I turn next to more nuanced versions of the independent variable (coalition type).

Ideal Types, Hybrids, Unintended Effects, and Regional Outcomes

The following considerations are worth bearing in mind regarding ideal types, their imputed effects, and regional outcomes:

1. *Ruling liberalizing coalitions enjoy varying degrees of political stability and half-life.* The more unstable, narrow, and weak their political basis, (*a*) the greater the pressures to dilute their reform program, (*b*) the more compelled they may be to gravitate toward the themes and interests of political challengers to avoid their own collapse, (*c*) the less able they may find themselves (because of *b*) to downplay regional security threats, and (*d*) the lower their capacity to forgo the support of elements from the military-industrial complex. Thus, although scapegoating (the external enemy) is generally the tool of statist-nationalist coalitions, insecure liberalizing coalitions may use that instrument as well, particularly when facing statist-nationalist adversaries. Some contemporary evidence for weak liberalizing coalitions, with narrow and unstable political bases, appealing to their opponents' constituencies is found in India and Pakistan and, historically, in Jordan, Egypt, Israel, and Argentina. Whether liberalizing coalitions may be prone to political weakness—and, if so, why—leads to the next point.
2. *The weakness of liberalizing coalitions may be traced to their failure to distribute the spoils of reform more equitably, or to their tendency to pursue their shortsighted, instead of their enlightened, self-interest.* Although the phenomenon is quite widespread, Egypt provides the classic case, mostly because of the longevity of the process of reform in that country (since the mid-1970s), its tentative nature, and its meager successes. The reform process in Russia and Eastern Europe similarly reveals income

concentration and widespread impoverishment reminiscent of the experience of some developing countries. International conditionality requirements reinforce these coalitions' proclivity toward the unfettered pursuit of wealth and inattention to the risky political consequences of concentrated benefits. Stabilization programs often lead to recessions and reduced public subsidies and investments in infrastructure, while trade liberalization exacerbates unemployment. Food riots in Egypt, Sudan, Algeria, and Morocco followed the reduction of staple subsidies, as did the conservative Russian coup. A popular shift to nationalism and fundamentalism often follows, either through electoral (Algeria) or other available means. Shock-style "therapy" without safety nets ends up weakening, not strengthening, the power of agencies in charge of economic reform and their societal allies.[21] Domestic forces and institutions offering an alternative, if unreal, solution to the predicaments of economic transition reap the political benefits.

The net result of the political dynamics of nondistributive liberalizing coalitions can be summed up in a paradox: such coalitions—prodded by international economic institutions—may plant the seeds of their own destruction. Regional cooperation might (and has) become a collateral casualty, as liberalizing coalitions fight for survival by moving toward more symbolic, nationalist, or confessional instruments to attract political support. In other words, IMF-style conditionality arrangements that are unresponsive to the domestic distribution of the burden of reform may have negative security externalities throughout a region. Such dangers may loom on the horizon in the Middle East, India and Pakistan, and Africa. Where integration into the world economy evolved in tandem with a more egalitarian income distribution, as in South Korea and Taiwan, liberalization could gradually muster enough political support to sustain itself and to deepen. Significantly, there was relatively less regional adventurism, nationalist mythmaking, and saber rattling in these cases. In the postliberalization period, South Korea's cautious response to the vagaries of the North (including its nuclear threats) is symptomatic of a relatively strong liberalizing coalition's approach to regional security.

3. *Coalitions can embrace economic liberalization without abandoning their political reliance on a confessional mantle of legitimacy, as in Paki-*

21. On negative political effects of neoliberal economic reform, and on the flimsy knowledge on which international agencies rely, see Przeworski 1992.

stan and Saudi Arabia. However, in these cases—in contrast to the self-proclaimed "true" Islamic republics, Iran and Sudan—Islamic content is pursued insofar as it does not impinge on liberalizing political-economic strategies. The Saudi regime (i.e., the extensive royal family) is known more for its commitment to the accumulation and consumption of wealth than for its devotion to ascetic Islamic lifestyles. At the same time, the regime's distributive efforts may have foiled the decades-long prediction—thus far falsified—of its imminent demise. This reinforces the contention that where the benefits are relatively more widely distributed there is less need to rely on external scapegoating. Despite their shortsighted financing of a variety of infamous radical groups in the past, Saudi and GCC (Gulf Cooperation Council) policy in the region has been generally more restrained than that of other Islamic and secular statist-nationalist regimes in the region. In Pakistan, liberalizing coalitions have retained the selective application of the *sharia* where Islamic law could not cancel the benefits of economic reform and international exchange. Nawaz Sharif, a representative of Pakistani industrial interests backed by pragmatic Islamic groups, lamented the political energy invested in domestic debates over Islamization "while the world is marching fast to meet the challenges [of] the twenty-first century" (Mayer 1993, 131). Thus, the Saudi and Pakistani variants differ from radical-confessionalism in that they have subordinated the pursuit of Islamic values to their primary (internationalist) political-economic strategy. Their regional postures—in spite of heavy-weapons acquisitions—are reactive and arguably have more of an insurance than an offensive essence. Even as Pakistan, facing a nuclear-capable India, is suspected of harboring a nuclear deterrent, its feeble liberalizing coalition has advocated a nuclear-weapons-free zone in South Asia. In the Saudi case, the military often finds ample justification for its arms purchases in the need to counter statist-nationalist and radical confessional neighbors like Iraq and Iran.

This last point prompts an important consideration: the need to internalize the regional context in evaluating a coalition's behavior. The nature of ruling coalitions in neighboring countries acts as an important intervening variable in defining the extent to which liberalizing or statist-nationalist coalitions can implement their grand strategies, both domestically and regionally.

Coalitions, Interactive Effects, and Regional Outcomes

The nature of a ruling coalition creates regional externalities or spillovers. In supporting one coalition or another, domestic actors may behave strategically, in some cases more consciously or directly than in others. Israeli high-tech entrepreneurs, for instance, threw their political lot with the Labor-Meretz coalition in 1992, with an eye on the domestic, regional, and global windfalls from prospective regional cooperation. In this section I examine how the degree of coalitional homogeneity/heterogeneity at the regional level influences the foreign behavior of coalitions and the obtaining regional order. Most generally, higher levels of cooperation can be expected where liberalizing coalitions prevail throughout a given region than where statist-nationalist, or competing liberalizing and statist-nationalist neighbors, face one another.

Figure 4.1 depicts the simplified case of two regional actors, A and B, and all the possible coalitional combinations that may shape their relationship. The darker the shaded areas, the more cooperative the bilateral relationship is expected to be. Cooperation implies active attempts to adjust policies to meet the demands of others under conditions of discord or potential discord. Such attempts involve the willingness to forsake, in repeated instances, the unilateral pursuit of one's own interests and to undertake commitments on a basis of diffuse reciprocity. These commitments can run the gamut of substantive issue areas; very often, security and economic cooperation go together, not merely because of economies of scope (Lake, this volume), but because of the complementary role they play in the grand strategy (domestic, regional, global) of different coalitions.[22] The broader the scope of issues, the more extensive the cooperative framework. The deeper the level of commitments, the more intensive the cooperation. A pluralistic security community or security via integration amount to the most intense cooperative categories of all. How extensive and intensive regional cooperation becomes is a function of two interactive ingredients: (*a*) the type of coalitions facing one another in a given region; (*b*) the coalitions' respective strengths relative to their domestic challengers (hence the differentiation in Figure 4.1 between weak and strong coalitions). The wider and more stable

22. On definitional issues regarding cooperation, see Keohane 1986. For a more comprehensive analysis of the regional behavior—cooperation and conflict—of different coalitional types, see Solingen 1997.

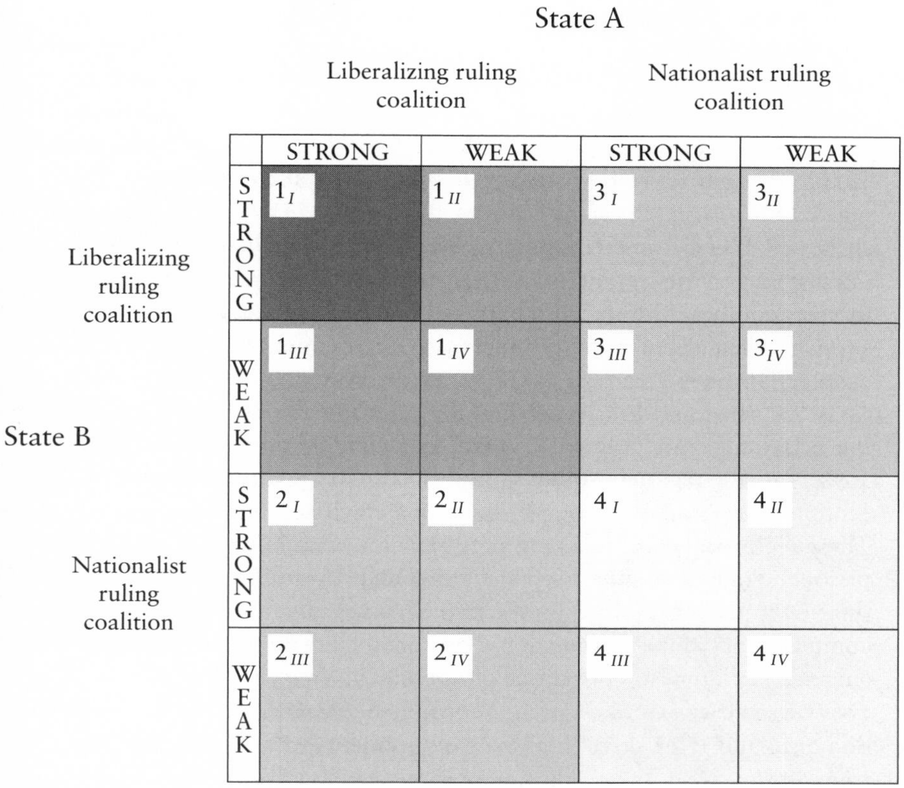

Fig. 4.1. Coalitional combinations and regional orders

the coalition's basis of political support, the more able the coalition is to pursue its preferred grand strategy. In the ensuing discussion I identify *dominant* patterns of interaction at different times in different regions, by way of illustration.

CELL 1: LIBERALIZING ORDERS: FROM CONVERGING GRAND STRATEGIES TO THE REGIONAL MANAGEMENT OF COOPERATION

Cell 1 captures a situation where both A and B are ruled by liberalizing coalitions. Despite variations among the four quadrangles in cell 1, this is generally the most extensive and intensive cooperative relationship of all those depicted in Figure 4.1. The synergies between economic and security cooperation become evident when the domestic implications of regional postures are taken into account.

In the realm of security, this interaction is characterized by the following features: *First,* as argued, domestic considerations of political survival drive economic rationalization—and military downsizing—as much as external factors. Therefore, there is an almost built-in guarantee that fellow liberalizing coalitions will be, *ceteris paribus,* reluctant to defect through militarized strategies. Liberalizing dyads and clusters tame their existing disputes, granting primacy to the stability required by their grand strategies and eschewing military conflict. Although not blind to potential regional threats to their own survival, their defense expenditures are often compatible with the world's average (about 4.5 percent of GDP), while those of statist-nationalist coalitions are three and four times higher. Extensive military buildups threaten the economic and political fundamentals of liberalizing strategies: fiscal conservatism, regional stability, and access to capital and markets. Such economic programs function essentially as tacit self-binding commitments. These reciprocal conditions not only alleviate what might otherwise become prisoner's-dilemma situations, they also help liberalizing coalitions defend their own platform (of economic reform, a contained or shrinking military complex, and cooperative regional postures) from attacks by domestic challengers. The domestic programs of liberalizing coalitions, in essence, create positive security externalities in the region. *Second,* the mutually reinforcing domestic and interactive (regional) inducements to allay conflict lower the transactions costs of an agreement between liberalizing coalitions. Thus, such coalitions beget the conditions for self-sustained, rather than externally imposed, regional cooperation, as in ASEAN and Mercosur (Mercado Común del Sur, or Southern Cone Common Market). Even where international actors do play a facilitating role in conflict management and/or conflict resolution, as in the Middle East, the engine of regional cooperation is progressively internal.

In the realm of economic cooperation, where liberalizing coalitions take firm hold throughout a region (as in the paradigmatic case of the European Union, or in the still evolving cases of ASEAN and Mercosur), their domestic political-economic strategies are often transferred to the regional institutional arena.[23] New regional cooperative regimes emerge that serve both to

23. On how ASEAN and the GCC operate with an eye on domestic challenges to their regimes, see Acharya 1992b. Malaysia's foreign minister argued: "The concept of free enterprise . . . is the philosophical basis of ASEAN" (quoted in Acharya 1992b, 152).

strengthen the liberalizing model at home and to lubricate external ties to the global political economy. Establishing markets requires harmonization of legal and administrative infrastructures, which, in turn, deepen the institutional links among liberalizing coalitions, as well as their mutual interdependence. Very often, liberalizing coalitions embrace trade-creating schemes with positive regional and global externalities. Although an absolute increase in regional trade and investment often results from the interaction among ruling liberalizing partners, regional economic integration is not always required for cooperative relations to be maintained. For instance, where competitive—rather than complementary—economies are involved, the drive for integration may be weaker. In effect, extensive intraregional economic exchanges are not a necessary condition for a cooperative regional order. The Egyptian-Israeli peace exemplifies why, even in the absence of substantial economic benefits from bilateral economic interactions, liberalizing coalitions find it in their interest to maintain cooperation.

The Argentine-Brazilian relationship exposes many elements of the generic ideal type identified in cell 1. In the early 1990s the administrations of Carlos S. Menem in Argentina and Fernando Collor de Mello in Brazil laid out a blueprint of cooperation. The political coalitions backing Menem and Collor (and, later, Fernando H. Cardoso, albeit to a more limited extent) endorsed effective economic liberalization, privatization, military contraction, and structural adjustment, with unprecedented commitment. A genuine integrative process (Mercosur) was set in place by 1995, after decades of integrative efforts during failed import-substituting and hybrid (including weakly liberalizing) phases. A mutual commitment to renounce nuclear weapons and fully to abide by the Treaty of Tlatelolco have replaced three decades of nuclear ambiguity and competition.

The most extensive and intensive levels of cooperation within cell 1 can be expected when both A and B are ruled by strong liberalizing coalitions (quadrant 1_I). Levels of cooperation decrease somewhat where a weak liberalizing coalition faces a strong liberalizing neighbor (quadrants 1_{II} and 1_{III}). A weak liberalizing coalition in Brazil (under pressure from statist-nationalist challengers) was more tentative about the cooperative process launched in 1991 than its counterpart in Argentina. President Itamar Franco wooed a nationalist, populist, and military constituency while denouncing international institutions and their domestic "allies," brandishing Brazil's sovereignty in nuclear matters, and taming the drive toward a new regional order. Argentina's stronger liberalizing coalition stayed the course, downsizing military expenditures, balancing budgets, and acceding unilaterally to the

NPT (Non-Proliferation Treaty), a step it had resisted for decades. Under such conditions, the strong coalition faces a dilemma: by maintaining its liberalizing program, it helps its weak liberalizing neighbor uphold cooperative postures; at the same time, however, it risks domestic censure for yielding to an unstable partner.

Cooperation is even more tentative and unstable, within the largely cooperative cell 1, where two weak liberalizing coalitions face each other (quadrant 1_{IV}). A weak liberalizing coalition (in A, for instance) finds it easier to survive politically (while pursuing compromising regional policies) in situations where B is steered by a strong (rather than a weak) liberalizing coalition. B's pursuit of state-shrinking policies, lower military budgets, and easier access to international markets, capital, and technology makes it easier for A's weak liberalizing coalition to justify its cooperative posture vis-à-vis B. On the other hand, where A's weak liberalizing coalition faces a similarly weak one in B, it is likely to find greater domestic resistance to accepting the risks of downsizing military endowments and engaging in diffuse reciprocity. The arguments of statist-nationalist challengers resonate far more effectively when they can point out the frailty of reform and the strength of their statist-nationalist and confessional counterparts in the neighboring state. This effect is particularly evident in the difficulties that the incipiently liberalizing Indo-Pakistani leadership has encountered since 1991, making it harder for each to transcend old patterns of domestic and regional policy. In a sense, the respective weakness of such dyads raises issues of involuntary defection. Under such conditions, the benefits of an alleviated security dilemma are more likely to dissipate than is the case for strong liberalizing partners. However, even where they face tough challenges at home, weak liberalizing coalitions are on far stronger ground to cooperate when they face a liberalizing interlocutor. Largely cooperative Arab dyads historically fall under this category: Egypt and Sudan (1970s–80s), Egypt and Jordan (1970s onward), Egypt and Algeria (1970s onward), and Egypt and Saudi Arabia (1970s onward). These relations, however, cannot be taken out of a broader regional context with highly diverse coalitions, which affects the ability of the liberalizing camp to transcend militarization and compels it to balance adversaries in the region.

To a significant extent, the Middle East peace process in the first half of the 1990s is the product of cell 1 conditions, where coalitions advocating openness to international markets and institutions have implemented breakthroughs in bilateral and multilateral regional cooperation. Variants of liberalizing coalitions of different strengths have emerged throughout that region, from the Gulf and the Arabian Peninsula, to Egypt and Jordan, with their financial, tourist-based, commercial-agriculture, and *munfatihun* ("openers") economies. Egypt has pioneered a regional rapprochement since the mid-1970s, when Sadat replaced Nasser's statism with a policy of liberalization (*infitah*), accumulation, and growth. Liberalizing agendas had overtaken important factions of the Palestine Liberation Organization by the early 1990s, once the convulsive energy of the *intifada* had spent itself. In Israel, the vast pool of technical, scientific, service, managerial, and entrepreneurial sectors supportive of liberalization gave Labor and Meretz a mandate in 1992: to launch the coalition's strategy of economic and social renewal within the "green line" (pre-1967 Israel) and to negotiate a territorial compromise beyond that line. The electoral campaign of 1992 pivoted on regional stability as a precondition for a revolutionary economic takeoff. All Middle East partners in the peace process became haunted by the specter of radical confessional and nationalist myths advanced by their oppositions, which opposed different aspects of globalization and the peace process.

As of 1996, this liberalizing cluster has made possible Israel's withdrawal from all populated areas of the West Bank and Gaza (except Hebron), after twenty-nine years of occupation. The new Palestinian-Israeli relationship highlights the tendency of liberalizing coalitions to maximize global and regional economic opportunities over land. Neither Greater Israel (Likud's myth) nor Islamic Palestine (Hamas's myth) has much affinity with a liberalizing grand strategy. At the multilateral level, unprecedented—if uneven—progress in economic, environmental, water, refugee, and arms-control negotiations has superseded decades of balancing power. The emergence of incipient collective security mechanisms has created a new balance of power, this time between the peacemaking parties and the statist-nationalist and confessional camp (mainly Iran, Iraq, Sudan, and Syria). That cooperative frameworks can have negative security externalities for third parties is nothing new. However, the electoral defeat of Labor-Meretz in 1996—aided by Islamist terror—has shattered the region's earlier coalitional balance, at least for now.

CELL 4: STATIST-NATIONALIST RIVALS: BALANCING POWER AND MYTHS: THE PRODUCTION OF HIGH-CONFLICT REGIONS

Statist-nationalist and confessional coalitions facing each other in a region (cell 4) produce regional orders distinctively different from the ones just depicted. In principle, where they face a virtual clone, ruled by nearly identical political, economic, and confessional interests, one might expect cooperation—even attempts at political and economic integration—to be more likely. Alas, the history of inter-Arab relations in the last four decades provides strong evidence to the contrary. The half-life of cooperative schemes has been quite brief, whether or not the ruling statist-nationalist coalitions were weak or strong. This is not entirely counterintuitive if we bear in mind the "inside-out" and "outside-in" effects of their grand strategy. On the one hand, given the political pillars of statist-nationalist coalitions, their domestic programs themselves (extensive state entrepreneurship, economic closure, and overall militarization) often have negative security externalities throughout the region. On the other hand, cooperative schemes in economics and security have the potential of forcing statist-nationalist, military, and radical confessional constituencies literally out of business.[24] Clearly the expected negative domestic externalities from regional cooperation lubricate the logrolling of sometimes unlikely coalitional partners. The ground is ready for unearthing myths and symbols—territorial "integrity," "economic independence," and confessional "purity" are particularly powerful mobilizers—which end up foiling attempts at panregional cooperation among otherwise "natural" allies. Weaker statist-nationalist coalitions may feel more tempted than stronger ones to rely on integrative efforts (particularly with a strong partner sharing its political platform) in order to bolster their own position at home. Yet, such efforts involve the risk of being swallowed by a stronger neighboring partner and, consequently, of impairing a weak coalition's position at home even further.

Thus, in the realm of security, statist-nationalist coalitions advance their parochial interests by creating a climate of risk, instability, conflict, and competition. Even if they are not invariably interested in resorting to war, the logic of their political-economic strategy and of their risky postures often leads—or makes them stumble—into armed conflict. The regional balance of power is more often than not the dominant mechanism by which these coalitions manage their mutual relations, as with Syria, Iran, and Iraq. The idea of multilateral conflict management (or of forsaking the unilateral pursuit of their own interests) is oxymoronic for regimes thriving on myths of self-reliance, military prowess, sovereignty, and national or confessional pu-

24. At best, the presence of liberalizing coalitions in the region might justify the maintenance of a common military effort, but such effort implies a division of labor (with would-be statist-nationalist allies) that could undercut the individual military-industrial constituencies of each statist-nationalist coalition. These constituencies are often very large, consuming between 15 and 25 percent of the GDP, or over three times the world's average.

rity. As if all these conditions were not enough to preclude cooperation, the fact that these coalitions quite often are held together by a strong leader adds a personalistic adversarial touch—and an important source of myths—to this interaction.[25] The scope of regional devastation and of the dense global externalities resulting from encounters between statist-nationalist coalitions often compels intervention from outside powers or institutions. In their extreme form, these coalitions spearheaded the nuclearization of regions, placing nuclear programs at the heart of "redeeming" solutions to regional threats (which in some cases were more real than in others).[26]

Historical examples of statist-nationalist coalitions include those of Pakistan's Zulfi Bhutto, Egypt's Gamal Abdul Nasser, Libya's Muammar Qadhafi, North Korea's Kim Il-Sung, Iraq's Saddam Hussein, and Argentina's Perón, and the leaders of Iran's Islamic republic. With few exceptions, these coalitions helped place their states among the most conflict-prone in the industrializing world. Particularly bloody were encounters between strong statist-nationalist rivals (quadrant 4_{I}) such as South and North Korea (1950s), Kampuchea and Vietnam (1978–79), India and China (1960s), India and Pakistan (1948, 1960s), and Iran and Iraq (1980s). The Serbian-Croatian-Bosnian debacle falls largely under this category as well. Territorial issues—highly malleable material in the construction of myths—were almost invariably central to these disputes. Weak pairs (quadrant 4_{IV}) and mixes of weak and strong ones (quadrants 4_{II} and 4_{III}) are similarly prone to slide into bloody confrontations, such as those between Indonesia and Malaysia (1960s), Somalia and Ethiopia (1977–78), and South and North Yemen (1994). In all three cases (quadrants 4_{II}, 4_{III}, and 4_{IV}) the weak coalition is particularly constrained domestically and can hardly afford to "appease" its neighbors. The transborder—including global—spillover effects of conflicts in quadrant 4 have been remarkably high. Even in the relatively benign Latin American system, whatever conflict and wars there have been in the last five decades often involved statist-nationalist rivals, with territorial issues looming large in their regional postures.

Regarding economic cooperation, statist-nationalist coalitions face conflicting incentives. On the one hand, satisfying the economic constituencies

25. The personalistic element is not unique to nationalist coalitions, but its incidence is higher, and its role more integral to a statist-nationalist strategy, than is the case for liberalizing coalitions.

26. This is different from arguing that nuclear programs everywhere in the Third World have similar origins, although an amazing proportion do. On the role of nuclear myths, see Solingen 1994b.

that sustain them may involve a measure of regional economic cooperation—for instance, where such cooperation broadens the market for import-substituting firms. This pattern largely characterized repeated but failed efforts at regional integration in South America (Mares, this volume). Quite often, economic cooperation between these coalitions results in trade-diverting schemes, with negative externalities for third actors in the region and beyond. On the other hand, private and state monopolies threatened with competition from regional counterparts resist lowering trade barriers. Where such monopolies play a critical role in sustaining ruling coalitions, they strive to maintain a regional system of competing, rather than complementary, economies. As a fundamental pillar of such coalitions, protected sectors, balking at cooperative undertakings likely to threaten their niches, generally prevail under these conditions, whereas, although present nearly everywhere, such sectors are never natural partners of liberalizing coalitions.

In the Middle East, statist-nationalist and confessional coalitions propose a political economy "genuinely" rooted in Islamic principles and reject many of the tenets of international economic regimes and their perceived associated scourges: inequalities, corruption, unemployment, and enslaving indebtedness. Not all Islamic movements see an inherent tension between international economic exchange and Islamic principles, but many do (Kuran 1995). In their proposed new social order there is no place for deviants, and violence is commonly used to sabotage the Middle East peace process itself and the "apostate" coalitions backing it in particular. Challengers of liberalizing coalitions are willing to drown the benefits from regional economic exchange in a politically more rewarding sea of nationalist or confessional radicalism. In Israel such political forces gravitate toward Likud and its radical religious and secular partners. Likud's free enterprise liberalism of the early years has shifted to accommodate populist groups disaffected with Labor. Historically a secular party, Likud has embraced fundamentalist themes and opponents of territorial compromise, many of whom are highly distrustful of international institutions and of "Western hypocrisy."[27] In recent decades, Likud has been unable to attract most liberalizing constituencies (notably big business), because of the estimated low probability that liberalizing objectives will dominate those of Likud's core constituents and coalitional allies. The performance of Benjamin Netanyahu's coalition in 1996 proved these estimates right.

In South Asia, India's fundamentalist Bharatiya Janata Party (BJP) ob-

27. On the anti-Western element among some religious fundamentalist groups in Israel, see Greenberg 1994.

tained a plurality of votes in the May 1996 elections. Its platform included—beyond Hindu supremacy and combative anti-Islamic and Pakistani postures—the banning of foreign loans, investments, and imports, with some of its prominent leaders advocating India's deployment of nuclear weapons. Pakistan's radical Jama'at-i-Islami party, whose principles resemble Hindu fundamentalism, challenges the Western-style modernization policies of Prime Ministers Nawaz Sharif and Benazir Bhutto and exploits confessional passions to advocate combative policies vis-à-vis India. The process of shifting from opposition to government is often expected to have a moderating effect, although two factors militate against such expectations in most of these cases: the political logic that sustains these coalitions, and the historical legacy and contemporary empirical record of statist-nationalist and confessional coalitions in power. Israel's 1996 Netanyahu coalition has, so far, defied incumbency's presumed pacifying effects. The Nixon-on-China analogy is far from an ironclad principle of international behavior.

CELLS 2 AND 3: MIXED DYADS: BALANCING GRAND STRATEGIES AND THE PARADOX OF RELATIVELY CONTROLLED REGIONAL CONFLICT

Cells 2 and 3 depict mixed dyads, where alternative coalitions face each other. Where liberalizing coalitions rule in neighboring states, the ability of statist-nationalist coalitions to embrace hypernationalist (or hyperconfessional) postures is heightened.[28] This is evident in the Middle East, where secular and radical-confessional challengers offer themselves as alternatives to an array of liberalizing coalitions (royalist with a pragmatic Islamic bent as well as secular). Statist-nationalist and confessional coalitions exploit the existence of liberalizing coalitions in the neighborhood to attract support for their agendas, rejecting religious or economic "apostasy," "moral decadence," and "cosmopolitan" values. They depict efforts to liberalize the domestic economy only through its negative fallouts, portray overtures to liberalize regional trade as hegemonic designs, and construe liberalizers' affinity with international regimes and institutions as complete surrender to foreign dictates. In essence, the presence of a liberalizer in the region offers yet another arena for carrying on the battle against the liberalizing opposition at home. The liberalizing neighbor, in response, becomes more constrained domestically in its ability to pursue a cooperative path. Moreover, the mili-

28. On hypernationalism, see Mearsheimer 1991 and Van Evera 1991.

tary contraction that might otherwise be preferred becomes more difficult. The basis for a stable cooperative framework is lacking, in varying degrees, throughout cells 2 and 3. Within a mixed region, alternative coalitions create negative externalities for, or impose costs on, their neighboring adversarial coalitions.

Where strong adversarial coalitions face each other in a mixed dyad (quadrants 2_I and 3_I), as in the Korean peninsula since the 1970s, cooperation is undermined by the fact that both sides feel compelled to reaffirm the political-economic strategy that sustains and legitimizes them, while keeping the adversary at bay. Yet, their respective strength allows such coalitions to achieve a certain *modus vivendi,* as the Koreas have done between the 1970s and early 1990s. To be sure, mixed dyads are not friendly—hardly the material that evolves easily into security communities. Although wars are a definite possibility, quadrants 2_I and 3_I do not elicit as many examples of extensive bloodshed as quadrants in cell 4. To some extent this might be a product of the overall scarcity of strong liberalizing coalitions in the industrializing world, particularly until very recently. An examination of the extant cases, however, is illustrative of the dynamics of strong adversarial coalitions.

South Korea and Taiwan pioneered in shedding statist-nationalist, inward-looking policies characteristic of the 1950s as their primary strategies of industrialization. They became paradigmatic cases of an integrative, export-driven model steered by the state, with growing support from powerful societal actors. Granting primacy to macroeconomic stability and to the discipline induced by international competition, these coalitions displaced private-sector initiative to a far lesser extent than did most import-substituting coalitions. Bureaucrats and *chaebols* in South-Korea, and Taiwan's Guomindang apparatus, nurtured a strategy that—despite some protected niches and considerable state entrepreneurship—leaned heavily on foreign markets, capital, technology, and investments.[29] Substantial threats to their physical existence compelled them both to develop sophisticated military-industrial sectors, but these were not allowed to harm the integrity of their grand strategies. South Korea's defense burden has absorbed on av-

29. Haggard and Kaufman 1992. On the Guomindang's overriding concern with economic stability, on Taiwan's shift from rabid militarism in the early years to "an ever-more absorbing interest in economic growth," and on the decline of the military institution in Taiwan's political economy, see Amsden 1989. On the minor and indirect role of Taiwan's defense burden on its GNP growth, export expansion, and improving income equality, and on Taiwan's reluctance to finance indigenous arms industries, see Chan 1988.

erage between 4 and 6 percent of the GDP once U.S. aid ended, not far from the average for the industrializing world (about 4.5 percent of GDP).

Low levels of regional conflict were an essential requirement in a grand strategy hinging on domestic political and macroeconomic stability. Since the 1970s, the ruling coalitions of South Korea and Taiwan have pursued the least confrontational postures possible under a highly adversarial regional context. Both renounced an expensive nuclear competition and joined the nonproliferation regime in fact (rather than, as Iraq or North Korea, merely in form). The phenomenon of extremely vulnerable states giving up the allegedly best option to secure their own survival is not easily explainable via U.S. security guarantees or coercive pressure alone. Such guarantees were not foolproof, and they can never be so within a neorealist framework of self-help, by definition. Nor have U.S. pressures invariably yielded their denuclearizing objective, as the cases of South Africa, Egypt, Pakistan, India, Israel, and the Southern Cone clearly show. The moderation of Taiwan and South Korea vis-à-vis intractable regional rivals might have been overdetermined by the domestic and international requirements of their grand strategies, including a deference to the United States, which was able to underpin internal political and economic stability and external protection. South Korean investments in the North and the promotion of a "soft-landing" endgame in the 1990s are a natural extension of a grand strategy premised on domestic and regional stability and peaceful change, which are key to the survival of a liberalizing project. The tame Taiwanese response to China's provocations falls in the same category. In neither case did the regional adversary represent a source of potential domestic threats, given the strength of liberalizing coalitions in both South Korea and Taiwan in the last two decades. Progressively, the reverse became the case, as the miracle "tigers" unleashed internal pressures in their opponent's home camps. The old *modus vivendi* was now obsolete, leading our discussion into a different quadrant.

A weak statist-nationalist coalition confronting a strong liberalizing counterpart (quadrants 2_{III} and 3_{II}) faces a strong dilemma. On the one hand, embracing a cooperative regional policy can weaken it further domestically, because such policy alienates its natural constituencies. On the other hand, following a combative regional policy (1) provides political ammunition to its liberalizing challengers at home, who accuse it of fabricating security threats where there are none, and (2) forces the adversary's ruling liberalizing coalition to deepen its military preparedness, thus causing the weak statist-nationalist coalition to miss cooperative opportunities and further weaken itself externally. The rationale for this latter argument is that a strong liberalizing coalition in the neighboring state offers cooperative opportunities because it has a built-in proclivity to downsize the state and the military industrial complex and to upsize its international status as a stable and reliable target of investments. These opportunities decline in the presence of an aggressive statist-nationalist neighbor. In essence, a weak statist-nationalist coalition is caught in a double whammy because it faces both a strong liberalizing coalition at home and a strong liberalizing neighbor at its borders, a situation that heightens the potential for a concerted political challenge by both. With the growing strength of liberalizing constituencies in the mid-1990s, Syria's ruling coalition may well be facing this dilemma.

A situation where a strong statist-nationalist coalition faces a weak liberalizing adversary (quadrants 2_{II} and 3_{III}) overturns the previous double-whammy scenario, allowing the former coalition to ride roughshod over the weak liberalizing opposition at home and a similarly weak neighboring opponent. These conditions whet the appetite of this nearly hegemonic statist-nationalist coalition for physical aggression. Cashing in on its own solid domestic political support and the neighboring coalition's absence thereof, the strong statist-nationalist coalition faces the optimal conditions for implementing its grand strategy, including the preferred *regional* policies of its core constituents. It is better able than in most other circumstances to extract vast resources from society and to convert them into a powerful military machine that, in turn, is able to extract vast resources from the neighborhood as well. The weak liberalizing coalition across the border, faced with a politically strong statist-nationalist challenger at home and in the region, is now afflicted with the double-whammy syndrome. It is highly constrained from implementing its domestic reform program, from translating economic efficiency and growth into an effective military deterrent, and from retaining internationalist postures that lubricate foreign trade and investment. It is thus compelled to turn to the themes of its own opposition to advance its short-term survival, and to embrace policies that run counter to its long-term interests, at home and abroad. The dynamics of quadrants 2_{II} and 3_{III} approximate relations between Syria and Lebanon in the 1970s, Libya and Morocco in the 1980s, and Algeria and Morocco in the 1960s.

Finally, quadrants 3_{IV} and 2_{IV} depict relations within a weak mixed dyad. The weak statist-nationalist coalition faces a more or less formidable opponent at home, ready to challenge any deepening of resource extraction and the continued expansion of state controls and activities, including those related to the military-industrial sector. The conditions to promote both the domestic and regional interests of this ruling coalition are largely curtailed. The weak liberalizing coalition, in turn, is fettered domestically by a relatively strong statist-nationalist front that resists liberalization and heightens the dangers of cooperating with the regional rival. This environment creates little incentive for reciprocal concessions and devalues the expected future benefits of cooperating in the present, a situation that appears to have characterized the interaction between a rather liberalizing coalition in Jordan and a similarly nationalist one in Israel during the 1991–92 interlude between the aftermath of the Gulf War and the electoral defeat of Likud in 1992.

Figure 4.1 depicts a simplified regional system composed of a single dyad. A single bilateral interaction is sometimes critical in determining regional conflict or cooperation. Other regions involve a more complex situation, where a larger number of states help define the regional order. Figure 4.1 retains its utility in accounting for such situations. One can think of A as "the regional environment" facing coalition B, or as an aggregate measure of the relative strength of liberalizing versus statist-nationalist coalitions. A liberalizing regional environment is one where a more or less homogeneous group of liberalizing coalitions holds power, and conversely, a statist-nationalist regional environment is one where statist-nationalist coalitions prevail. As in the dyadic mixed case, in regions where various coalitions compete to advance the legitimacy of their respective models, we might expect less cooperation, and a higher incidence of balance-of-power mechanisms, than where ruling liberalizing coalitions, particularly strong ones, share a common agenda. The more liberalizing the regional environment, the higher the region's reliance on concerts and multilateralism. A concert arrangement at the regional level enables the simultaneous implementation of the domestic components of their grand strategies. Liberalizing coalitions cooperate regionally among themselves to protect their own domestic viability against assaults from statist-nationalist rivals in the region. ASEAN countries initially excluded Vietnam, Cambodia, and Laos, while GCC (created in 1981) left out Iran and Iraq. After years of deriding ASEAN members as "puppets of Western imperialists," and while moving toward economic liberalization and military downsizing, Vietnam acceded to ASEAN's Treaty on Amity and Cooperation in 1992.

The competition between two ideal-type coalitions within a state sometimes fails to yield a clear victor, one that can hold on to power for any significant lapse of time. This situation is rather extreme among some African states, such as Somalia. In such cases, the absence of a central government backed by any type of coalition can precipitate regional conflict when neighboring regimes scramble to minimize the potential negative spillover effects of a power vacuum in the region. Thus, the absence of a winning coalition or the presence of intractable and fractious coalitional strife is among the worst scenarios in terms of generating preconditions for regional conflict. At the same time, such cases, as in Cambodia, offer an opportunity for the international community to develop a domestic coalition promoting broad-based reform and cooperative regional policies.

This general overview suggests that it is naive to ignore contextual variations across regional systems, even where liberalizing coalitions face each other. Initial (security) conditions do matter. Clearly, Israel and Egypt, let alone Taiwan and China, are not Brazil and Argentina. On the one hand, the constraints placed by genuine security considerations on the first two sets of partners are far heavier, but not insurmountable. The extent to which other important regional partners share a liberalizing agenda can soften the impact of such constraints. For many years, Syrian and Iraqi challenges to the legitimacy of the Egyptian regime loomed large in Egypt's inability to move beyond a "cold peace" with Israel. As liberalizing coalitions reached a critical mass in the region as a whole, a new collective path took hold, leading to the Declaration of Principles between Israel and the PLO (1993), the peace treaty between Jordan and Israel (1994), and multilateral cooperative breakthroughs. On the other hand, the absence of genuine security constraints is no guarantee of regional cooperation. Even benign security contexts (as in the Southern Cone) have produced conflict situations—and limited cooperation at best—particularly under statist-nationalist regimes, but also under *weak* liberalizing coalitions enjoying little popular support, like Argentina's and Chile's in the late 1970s. Only strong liberalizing coalitions in Argentina and Brazil embraced the opportunities of a benign security environment to introduce unprecedented economic cooperation and denuclearization.

Initial conditions can affect both the first- and second-order dimensions of cooperation. Thus, given a first-order form of cooperation that would fall within cell 1, there might be more or less intractable second-order forms of conflict, depending on past levels of regional security threats. Distributional struggles in the context of a cooperative Middle East peace process clearly reflect the shadow of a zero-sum past, whereas distributional struggles among Southern Cone partners bear the imprint of past variable gains from mutual interaction. That is, liberalizing coalitions differ in terms of their starting points for the construction of cooperative regional orders. And the distance traveled toward the Pareto frontier matters.

Implications for the Comparative Conceptualization of Regional Orders

What are the implications of this coalitional approach for international relations theory? First, symptoms of neorealism's poor health in accounting for important outcomes—including the end of the Cold War and the emergence of Arab-Israeli cooperation—cast doubt on its centrality to a theory of regional orders. Power distribution seems far less helpful in predicting either patterns of change or levels of conflict and cooperation than are coalitional grand strategies. The latter go a long way in explaining even the hardest case of regional security cooperation—nuclear regimes—for which neorealism claims theoretical supremacy (Solingen 1994b). At the same time, advancing the utility of coalitional struggles does not preclude a systematic concern with the shadow of past security trajectories in assessing the speed and, to some extent, the shape of cooperative processes and outcomes.

The relationship between coalitional grand strategies and regional cooperation hypothesized here departs—to some extent—from the classical, deterministic association between economic liberalism and peace postulated by general theories of interdependence:[30] (1) Far from assuming that expanded domestic welfare resulting from free trade fosters cooperative preferences, it suggests that where liberalizing coalitions prevail, their interests dictate compatible regional arrangements. Thus, the gains from trade could be highly concentrated and not contribute to widespread societal welfare in the short term. If maintained, nondistributive patterns impair both the coalition's survival and its regional policies. (2) Rather than assume a purely economistic aggregate calculus of costs and benefits from war and peace, the argument examines the domestic political foundations of a coalition's regional and global postures. It thus highlights the coalition's internal political opportunities, often ignored at the expense of its external "vulnerabilities."[31] (3) In

30. Classical formulations include Cooper 1968, Keohane and Nye 1977, and Rosecrance 1986. Despite the noted differences, the argument remains largely compatible with this tradition, and particularly with "devalued utility of war" (Kaysen, in Lynn-Jones 1991) interpretations that are sensitive to whose costs and benefits (among domestic actors) count in opting for peace or war. At the same time, far from implying an invariable relationship between capitalism and peace (Schumpeter 1955), this framework suggests a varying disposition for conflict and cooperation among different capitalist segments.

31. The argument has thus some affinity with the political-survival theme in Roeder (this volume), while taking account of realists' and materialists' concerns as well.

light of the first two points, a coalitional analysis provides a more proximate estimation of whose relative gains (those of specific coalitions) matter in the formulation of preferences. (4) The analysis is not contingent on the extent of economic interdependence between regional interlocutors. The grand strategies of liberalizing coalitions are particularly—but not solely—responsive to nation-to-system (Tetreault 1980) or globalizing interdependence. Regional stability, not regional economic interdependence, is the main conceptual link between the regional and global dimensions of a liberalizing grand strategy. (5) The framework does not require that states become "fully modern industrial nations" (Kaysen 1990) before they eliminate war, only that strong—particularly redistributive—liberalizing coalitions prevail over their challengers. (6) No linear progression toward economic liberalization or regional cooperation is implied. Statist-nationalist and confessional forces could be more resilient than "liberal optimists" (Snyder 1991) tend to believe. The possibility that economic liberalization (as democracy) may be part of cyclical "shifting involvements" (Hirschman 1982), and not an irrevocable process, is real.

This point suggests the need to explore further the ways in which international conditions influence domestic-coalitional struggles. Adversarial political coalitions do not aim at balancing, but at overtaking their rivals, domestically and regionally, and they can rely on international and regional institutions to prevail. Consequently, such institutions play an important role in determining the political longevity and strength of coalitions and, as a second-order effect, in shaping the conditions for regional cooperation. Without an open international financial, trading, and investment system, for example, the basic requirements for pursuing an internationalist grand strategy are undermined, and with it the domestic political platform of liberalizing coalitions. Protected markets in the industrialized world can have negative security externalities at the regional level. At the same time, international institutions imposing conditionality arrangements that deepen societal economic cleavages (which often overlap with confessional ones), may paradoxically contribute to the demise not only of liberalizing agendas but of cooperation as well.

The coalitional analysis explored here applies most forcefully to the end of the twentieth century, characterized by a highly integrated global economy, a rapidly integrating multilateral institutional foundation in world politics, tightly knit economic and security systems, a disintegrating revival of nationalist and confessional allegiances, and rising regionalism. Under this "world time," two issues related to the supply side (global management) are worth considering: one involves *willingness,* the other *capabilities.* On the one account, a new global order where Western hegemony is largely unchallenged (for the foreseeable future) could lead to yet another unintended and paradoxical outcome: diminished incentives to contribute to the maintenance of such order beyond the OECD (Organization for Economic Cooperation and Development) periphery. The extent to which regional conflicts will remain marginalized or create demands for intervention, together with the degree to which the conditions triggering such conflicts can be ignored, is now a subject of intense debate in academic and policy circles. On a second account, the international ability to influence the coalitional balances and regional outcomes—through a nested global economic and political institutional network—may be higher today than ever before. This network's weight can be applied to support liberalizing coalitions where they are bearers of regional cooperation, as in the Middle East. International efforts could also aid moderate statist-nationalist coalitions to "traverse the valley of reform" (Przeworski 1992) toward a new social pact, domestically and regionally. Some European powers apply this logic to renew economic exchanges with (not-so-moderate) Iran and Iraq, although it is hard to remove this European strategy from their ulterior considerations of domestic economic and political gain.

Any attempt to outline a broad framework explaining regional orders involves simplifications. While proposing a single transregional explanatory variable, the framework is flexible enough to allow for variations in the extent to which state officials or powerful societal forces play a more crucial role in steering a grand strategy. Since state autonomy is both a matter of degree and subject to empirical analysis, a focus on coalitions helps to avoid sterile debates between purely statist notions of an autonomous state and purely societal, reductionist conceptions of states as instruments of social (particularly economic) forces. At the same time, the approach transcends the idea of a unified state with monolithic interests. Certain state agencies are often allies of economic liberalization (central banks), while others frequently oppose it (planning, industrial policy, and import-licensing agencies). This point highlights the centrality of the domestic institutional foundation against which coalitions operate. Institutions allow certain coalitions of interests to prevail at some points and not others (Gourevitch 1986). Democratic institutions can strengthen diffuse interests at the expense of concentrated ones, in some cases benefiting liberalizing coalitions (1996 Palestinian elections), in others their opponents (1991 Algerian elections). Proportional representation may preclude the emergence of a "conquering" coalition of either brand, as seems the case in Israel. Weak political institutions may induce an unstable alternation of precarious coalitions and unstable shifts in regional policies. Institutions are central to the aggregation of preferences into coalitions, to logrolling patterns, and to the robustness and longevity of obtaining coalitions. Elsewhere (Solingen 1997) I outline institutional aspects of coalitional birth and strength, including the links between democratic institutions and coalitional type, on the one hand, and the interconnections between the democratic peace and a coalition-driven approach to conflict and cooperation, on the other.

The focus on coalitional competition allows a dynamic analysis, able to explain sudden regional departures from past trends as well as many civil wars arising from the irreconcilable demands of ethnic and confessional groups, often in alignment with economic ones. The framework thus accommodates internal as well as interstate competition, while transcending old level-of-analysis categories by linking the global and subnational (domestic) to explain regional outcomes. The international context is built into the argument, avoiding one of the common pitfalls in conceptualizing regional politics. The global externalities of a dense international system are directly incorporated into actors' conception of regional orders. Finally, the approach integrates "great-power" theories (Snyder 1991) with the rest of the international system. It thus eschews exceptionalist theories of Third World behavior while making allowance for the particular world-time under which these states define their choices for war and peace.

5

Geostructuralism and International Politics: The End of the Cold War and the Regionalization of International Security

Arthur A. Stein and Steven E. Lobell

The Cold War has ended and the debate about the postwar world rages. Some maintain that greater cooperation is emerging rapidly; others disagree and long for a return to the good old days—or what we may have mistakenly thought the bad old days.[1] This chapter assesses and criticizes both the optimistic and pessimistic schools of thought. We argue that assessment of the post–Cold War world depends critically on judgments about the nature of the Cold War and its end. We develop a regionally differentiated perspective on the post–Cold War world, one that recognizes the multidimensional character of its end.

Optimists who point to a more peaceful world emphasize the stabilizing influence of increased global trade and economic interdependence among

We would like to thank Amy Davis, Catherine Sweet, Kiron Skinner, the University of California, Los Angeles, and the University of Southern California graduate students in P.S. 221, and Alexandra Stein for their comments and corrections.

1. In a terminological shift, some now refer to the Cold War as "the long peace" (Gaddis 1986, 1987).

states and of political and economic liberalization, as well as the increased effectiveness of international institutions and regimes in managing conflict. From this optimistic outlook, the end of the Cold War has made it possible to link all areas of the globe in an economic web. It has also freed international institutions from the paralysis of U.S.-Soviet Cold War rivalry and brought the domestic liberalization of totalitarian regimes and the more pacific foreign policies that are presumed to accompany such liberalization.[2]

Pessimists point out, however, that the end of the Cold War has unleashed new violence and unrest in some regions and nations. To them, the end of the Cold War has simply led to the resurgence of long-suppressed hypernationalism, inter- and intrastate fighting among and within new states, and increased tensions within formerly united alliances. The emergence of multipolarity, they argue, means a more conflictual and unstable present and future.[3]

Optimists and pessimists agree that the Cold War's impact was transitory and that its end will have globally uniform consequences, but they disagree about the nature of those effects in both eras. First, all assume the Cold War to have had a short-lived effect on interstate relations. Optimists hold that because the Cold War divided the world into two distinct camps, its end will bring a return to the world economy that existed before World War I. Pessimists claim that because the Cold War suppressed ethnic hatred and restrained regional states, its end explains the recent return to ethnic cleansing and aggressive behavior. Second, both suggest that the end of the Cold War will have a single, uniform, and global impact on world politics. The optimistic view sees the end of the Cold War as contributing to greater global cooperation; the pessimistic one predicts greater global conflict. But in both cases, the ramifications are the same everywhere.

We offer an alternative interpretation on the Cold War era and the post–Cold War order. After describing the two standard perspectives on the role

2. The once moribund United Nations has successfully expelled Iraq from Kuwait and brokered agreements among disputants in the western Sahara, Cambodia, and Namibia. The Security Council had not approved an operation such as that against Iraq since its authorization of military force against North Korea in 1950, which was approved only because the Soviet delegation was absent from the Security Council meeting. For a recent discussion of UN operations, including those in Bosnia, Somalia, and Cambodia, see Diehl 1993.

3. Some of the pessimists are realists who see the end of the Cold War as a change in, but not of, the system. They expect that the international system will continue to be characterized by anarchy, which constrains the behavior of states and inhibits cooperation even among those with shared interests. They do, however, find multipolarity to be more unstable than the bipolarity of the Cold War.

of the Cold War and the permanence of its consequences, we offer our own view, that although the bipolar structure of the international system and the intense ideological competition between the United States and the Soviet Union globalized many regional, local, and even domestic disputes, the rate and extent of superpower penetration of regional politics varied greatly across space and over time. We then analyze four distinct but concatenated dimensions of the Cold War's end, and finally, we discuss the emerging post–Cold War order, especially the increasing regionalization of world politics and its impact on security (and trade). We argue that the end of the Cold War will have the greatest effect on regional relations in locales that were highly penetrated by the superpowers and will have little or no effect on regions and disputes that were unaffected by the Cold War or remained on its periphery.

As with the Cold War order, that of the post–Cold War era has been influenced by geographic pressures, especially the continued importance of regions and regionalism, as well as by structural forces of the international balance of power. We maintain that the interplay of these pressures constitutes a "geostructural" perspective of international politics. By ignoring either of these characteristics of world politics, it is difficult to understand the effect that the Cold War will have on regional relations in the post–Cold War world.[4]

Alternative Perspectives

There are two basic interpretations of how the Cold War and its end have affected regional relations. They disagree about whether superpower intervention in regional politics during the Cold War increased or decreased regional conflict and whether superpower disengagement from regional politics in the post–Cold War era will contribute to stability or conflict. The *conflict-suppression* school emphasizes the stabilizing consequences of superpower involvement even as it argues that the superpowers globalized local disputes. The *conflict-exacerbation* school emphasizes the superpowers' creation and expansion of small disputes as well as their militarization of political conflicts.

4. On the debate over the primacy of globalism or regionalism, see Gannon 1982 and Doran 1989.

GLOBALIZATION AND CONFLICT SUPPRESSION

One perspective, rooted entirely in a view of the Cold War as globalizing and suppressing regional conflicts, argues that age-old rivalries and animosities suppressed during the Cold War are again at the fore. This argument holds that the superpowers restrained their respective clients and suppressed regional conflicts by stationing troops, extending security commitments, rejecting or limiting the shipment of advanced offensive weaponry, applying political pressure, and using economic rewards and punishments to elicit certain behavior.[5]

Central to this argument is that the history of the Cold War is one of superpower involvements all over the globe. Military and economic support allowed regional conflicts to escalate well beyond the level that local clients could sustain financially. Sophisticated weaponry raised the intensity of wars by allowing local states to engage in large-scale modern warfare, while superpower arms resupplies helped belligerent states to prolong conflicts. The infusion of economic assistance allowed small powers to live beyond their means. The conflict between the Vietnamese, for example, both before and after the nation's partition, could not have been sustained for as long or as intensely without superpower support. U.S. aid was essential to the contras in their struggle against the Nicaraguan government. Many other local conflicts, although not begun by the superpowers, were clearly nurtured by their rivalry.

But the compelling element of this perspective is that the superpowers also restrained their clients, especially when events threatened to get out of control. Even when they encouraged their clients to pursue military solutions to regional conflicts, the superpowers restrained them as well—particularly when events threatened to suck them in. With Israel on the verge of crushing the encircled Egyptian Third Army Corps in 1973, the Soviets threatened unilateral intervention if Israel did not halt its operations. So to prevent the possibility of a direct great-power conflict, the United States warned Israel that it would not be allowed to destroy the Third Army (Quandt 1977).

This perspective reflects a seemingly contradictory vision of bipolarity, in which the bloc leaders contest every region and issue but manage their

5. Doran (1991) notes that one of the reasons that the war between Iran and Iraq (1980–88) lasted so long is that neither the United States nor the Soviet Union had ties to Tehran or Baghdad. In contrast, the Soviets refused to deliver the advanced weaponry that would have allowed Egypt to extend the Arab-Israeli War of Attrition (1969–70) to Israel's heartland (Breslauer 1979; Glassman 1975). In the case of the Indo-Pakistani conflict, the United States never supplied Pakistan with enough military supplies to wage an extended war (Barnds 1972).

clients and their conflict.[6] The common brief for the stabilizing effect of bipolarity is that competition between the superpowers comes to encompass all regions. There are no peripheries, since either power's gain will upset the delicate global balance of power. Accordingly, all local and even domestic conflicts are absorbed into the bipolar contest; in effect, all regions are globalized. This view implies that local conflicts were exacerbated during the Cold War, since they came to involve global stakes and the survival of the superpowers themselves. Yet this argument also emphasizes that the superpowers nonetheless suppressed regional disputes and restrained their clients for fear that a regional quarrel would ensnare them in a direct confrontation that might escalate into a nuclear exchange. In some instances, their shared interest in avoiding a war actually contributed to superpower coordination as they managed regional disputes.[7]

GLOBALIZATION AND CONFLICT EXACERBATION

A second, equally compelling argument about the current world, rooted entirely in a view of the Cold War as an era of superpower competition fostering regional conflict (Slater 1990–91; Hurewitz 1973; Weiss and Blight 1992), argues that without superpower kindling, regional disputes die down. Whether through the active mischief making of the superpowers or because of wily, manipulative clients, the Cold War generated conflicts in all parts of the globe.

From this perspective, superpower competition for global influence exacerbated and prolonged regional disputes in an intensive and extensive bipolar rivalry. Eventually encompassing the entire planet, this rivalry even reached regions in which the superpowers had only marginal interests. Vying to increase their influence and gain any advantage at the expense of the other, both sought new clients. Where they did not actively create local clients to oppose their opponent's clients, they nurtured and encouraged indigenous

6. During the bipolar Cold War, both superpowers sought to prevent a repeat of World War I, in which Austria pulled its great-power patron, Germany, into war with Russia. On the Middle East, see Miller 1990 and Freedman 1990. For a discussion of great powers exercising restraint on their clients even during a multipolar period, see Schroeder 1976.

7. In 1972, the United States and the Soviet Union signed the Basic Principles Agreement, which established a set of rules of conduct for the superpowers in the Middle East. In part, this agreement called for the superpowers to "exercise restraint in their mutual relations, and [to] be prepared to negotiate and settle differences by peaceful means" (Quandt 1977). In 1981, Premier Brezhnev called for a "code of good behavior" with the United States in regard to Africa, Asia, and Latin America (Allison and Williams 1990).

opposition. By setting brush fires and playing troublemaker, they tried to wear one another down.

The bipolar structure of the Cold War also allowed local disputants to maneuver the superpowers to advance those disputants' interests.[8] Those seeking support from Washington took on the mantle of anti-Communism; those looking for Soviet support sold themselves as opponents of Western imperialism. Local rivals could extort extensive political, economic, and military support from the superpowers by framing local issues in East-West terms and by threatening to abandon one superpower for the other. The end of the Cold War also implies, therefore, the end of such easily obtained and generous support.

Even when the superpowers did not actively encourage local conflict, their guarantees alone encouraged clients to pursue reckless foreign policies (Rubin 1988). Confident that a patron would come to their rescue, local states often took greater risks in relations with their neighbors. The patron's commitment could be presumed by even marginal regional clients whose defeat might damage the superpower's credibility in other regions or simply damage the reputation of its military hardware. Even implicit or presumed guarantees therefore tended to exacerbate local disputes.

From this view, the superpower competition for influence internationalized domestic disputes and globalized regional ones. The superpowers engaged one another in wars by proxy, and their military assistance increased the death and destruction wrought by poor players in local conflicts that persisted beyond their natural course. Hence, the end of the Cold War has meant the diminution of regional conflict.

These alternative perspectives are neither fully complementary nor fully contradictory. The first characterizes the Cold War as a superpower lid on regional hostility. The second sees the superpowers as stoking the flames of regional conflict. Both agree that the Cold War globalized international politics and expanded the scope and importance of regional disputes. Both agree that the impact of the Cold War will have been temporary and the post–Cold War world will witness a reversion to prior form—in one case to regional disputes uncontrolled by great powers, in the other to regional stability uninflamed by superpower involvement.

8. Although international relations theory focuses mainly on great powers, under some conditions the tail (i.e., the client) can wag the dog (i.e., the great power). There is a small literature, which emerged rapidly after the heightened activity of Third World states in the early 1970s and especially after the success of the 1973 Arab oil embargo (which transferred extreme wealth from the First World to the Third World), on the ability of small states to influence the behavior of great powers (Bergsten 1973; Keohane 1971; Handel 1982).

Superpower	Cold War: Ephemeral	Cold War: Lasting
Lid	Revert to Instability	Sustained Restraint
Stoker	Regional Solutions and Cooperation	Sustained Conflict

Fig. 5.1. The Cold War and its effect on regional relations

More generally, arguments about the post–Cold War world derive from assessments of the Cold War and its impact. The prospect for the emergence of regional security arrangements will depend upon whether the superpowers were involved in a region and, if so, whether they acted as lids on, or stokers of, regional conflict—whether they restrained their regional clients and suppressed conflict or encouraged competition and exacerbated regional disputes. It also matters how reversible the Cold War proves to be. The Cold War can be seen as lasting if it fundamentally transformed certain regions of the globe by the ideological cast given to domestic political struggles during the era, by the forms of political organization and control that remain as its residue, by the new levels of armaments that remain in its wake, and by the economic development it nurtured. Alternatively, the Cold War will prove to have had ephemeral consequences if the regions revert to their previous state.

Figure 5.1 highlights the possible impact that the Cold War era will have on regions in the post–Cold War order.[9] If the Cold War suppressed regional conflict but its effect is only ephemeral, the outlook is a reversion to regional instability. Similarly, if the Cold War fostered regional conflict and if this

9. Scholars with different views of the effect of the Cold War on regional relations can still arrive at similar conclusions concerning the nature of the new world order. Those who argue that superpower involvement in regional relations contributed to only temporary stability and those who hold that superpower competition has permanently exacerbated regional rivalry both anticipate that the new world order will be characterized by conflict. Similarly, scholars who believe that superpower competition only fueled regional hostilities temporarily and those who see that superpower involvement as having permanently dampened regional hostilities both expect a peaceful new world order.

rivalry left a lasting impression on the region, the outcome will be sustained conflict. In contrast, if the Cold War restrained local states and if this left a lasting imprint on regional relations, the product will be continued restraint in the behavior of the local actors. Likewise, if the Cold War provoked regional conflict but had no lasting effect on regional relations, cooperation among local actors will be possible.

In this chapter, we argue that different parts of the globe fall into these different cells and do so on different dimensions. We argue that the end of the Cold War is a multidimensional phenomenon with regionally differentiated implications. We begin our reanalysis by characterizing the regional variation that remained despite the globalizing consequences of the Cold War.

The Cold War and Regional Security

Two Cold War forces, the bipolar structure of the international system and the intense ideological competition between the United States and the Soviet Union, globalized many regional, local, and even domestic disputes. Eventually, the Cold War came to encompass the entire planet; local disputes in Asia, Africa, the Middle East, and Latin America came to be framed in East-West terms. The need of each superpower to demonstrate its willingness to defend or support local states that espoused its ideology militarized and linked isolated conflicts, involving the United States and the Soviet Union in regions where neither had substantial interests or historic ties.

Yet even at the height of the globalization of the Cold War, regional differentiation remained a salient feature of world politics. On the one hand, Europe, the Middle East, and Asia were highly penetrated by the superpowers and were drawn into the Cold War competition in its initial stages. Much of Africa and Latin America, on the other hand, remained on the fringe of the superpower rivalry for most of the Cold War.

This interaction of geography and power, this geostructural perspective, suggests that the end of the Cold War and the demise of the dual globalizing forces of bipolarity and ideology imply a growing regionalization of world politics and a localization of conflict management. The end of the Cold War, whether characterized as unipolarity or emergent multipolarity, will produce neither a global policeman nor a global concert but a localization of security relations.

FRAMING REGIONAL DISPUTES: BIPOLARITY AND IDEOLOGY

As World War II drew to a close, the United States and the Soviet Union emerged as the dominant states in the international system. Their confrontation originated at the intersection of their respective zones of occupation in Europe and other borders of the Soviet empire. A circumscribed (although multiregional) politico-economic conflict eventually became worldwide as many local disputes were framed in East-West terms. It also became military as well as political and economic. Two Cold War forces, the *bipolar structure* of the international system and the intense *ideological competition* between the United States and the Soviet Union, were primarily responsible for this state of affairs.

The bipolar structure of the Cold War absorbed regional conflicts into the U.S.-Soviet struggle. Local states sought superpower support in the form of arms and economic aid, and the United States and the USSR competed for local allies and influence. Eventually the United States and Soviet Union became involved in all regions of the globe, linking disparate regions and nations that had no historic ties. That the superpowers attempted to gain any advantage meant that each allowed the other to dictate its regional interests and that both were dragged into places in which neither had any prior interests and that made little contribution to their respective security.

The second globalizing force was ideology. Both the United States and the USSR claimed universal objectives in their competition. The United States exported market capitalism and opposed the spread of Communism everywhere; the Soviet Union wanted to export Communism. The United States felt that it could not allow Communism to triumph, especially by expansion, without responding; the Soviets could not allow a Communist regime to succumb without making some effort on its behalf. The United States, for example, which left the Korean peninsula shortly after World War II, returned when North Korean forces invaded the south. The Soviets felt they had little choice but to support a Communist outpost in Cuba, even though they lacked the power to deter or defend territory so far from their home.

During the Cold War, local conflicts were sometimes absorbed by the superpower rivalry. The conflict between Arabs and Jews in Palestine antedated the Cold War, but was sucked up by it (just as it had been by World Wars I and II) as the United States replaced Britain and France as the primary supporter of Israel and the moderate Arab states. The Soviet Union championed Arab governments and nongovernmental movements that opposed the West and Israel.[10]

Similarly, the final collapse of the European empires in the wake of World War II and the struggles to achieve independence from European colonial rule were also absorbed by an ever more encompassing Cold War.[11] Vietnam provides a poignant case. After 1945 the French returned to Vietnam in the hope of reestablishing their colonial rule. But the years of wartime occupation by Japan had strengthened Vietnamese nationalists, who already had ties to the Soviet Union. The French government wanted American support in Southeast Asia and framed the conflict in Vietnam as a struggle between Communism and the West. Initially, Washington perceived the struggle as nationalist and resisted French requests for support.[12] But the outbreak of the Korean War brought a dramatic change in American policy toward Vietnam as the United States came to see the Cold War in global terms and so accepted French arguments.[13] Eventually, the United States replaced the French militarily and waged an ill-fated battle against those Vietnamese supported by the Soviet Union.

GLOBALIZATION VERSUS REGIONALIZATION DURING THE COLD WAR

Even during the Cold War, scholars disagreed about the extent to which the United States should intervene in regional politics, though they all identified

10. On how the Jewish-Arab conflict was drawn into the great-power rivalry before World War II, see Brown 1984. Brown devises for the Eastern Question (the decline of the Ottoman Empire) a set of rules that outlines the behavior of regional and outside players since the nineteenth century. Two of his rules of the game are that "political initiatives generated within the area [the Middle East] are undertaken—more than in other parts of the world—with an eye to the reaction of the outside" and "outsiders are brought in until all are involved." Middle East actors "internationalize" any regional conflict, pulling outside states into the region. For Brown, these characteristics of the Middle East explain why no single great power has been able to dominate the region.

11. See Kent 1993 and Louis 1977 on how the Cold War helped Britain retain its Asian empire. See Masoa 1977 on how the Cold War internationalized the Korean conflict.

12. Opposition to France was tempered, however, by the U.S. need for French support in Europe and by American worries about the plight of the French people and the possibility that they would choose a Communist government themselves.

13. As the Cold War began to replace the notion of postwar U.S.-Soviet cooperation, the United States reversed its anticolonial stance (Rotter 1987; VanDeMark 1991; LaFeber 1975; Herring 1977). For studies of the early history of U.S. involvement in Vietnam, see Young 1991 and Hess 1987. Ironically, a domestic debate within the United States during the Vietnam War involved precisely this question whether the war in Vietnam was a nationalist struggle with local roots or part of the global war between the Communist world and the West.

key regions of the globe, particularly Europe and Japan, as crucial to U.S. security and to the global balance of power.[14] Soft-line realists like Walter Lippmann, George Kennan, and Hans Morgenthau argued that not all regions of the globe were of equal value to the United States.[15] Instead, they wanted to distinguish between vital and nonvital commitments and called for American restraint throughout most of the Third World, which they considered nonvital.[16] They opposed the universal commitment of the Truman Doctrine's call for the United States to defend any state threatened by Communism and objected to the general military buildup demanded by NSC-68.

Kennan held that only five centers of industrial and military power in the world (the United States, Great Britain, Germany and central Europe, the Soviet Union, and Japan) were important to the United States (Kennan 1951, 1967a; Gaddis 1982, 25–88). Since only one of these was in hostile hands, Kennan saw containment as intended to ensure that none of the others fell into Soviet control. For only by conquering some or all of these vital power centers could the Soviet Union, or any other challenger to the United States, shift the balance of power in its own favor.

The Cold War had a critical *economic dimension,* for successful regional and national economic development would signify the success of a superpower's economic system, strengthen its clients as a bulwark, and tie its allies and clients more tightly to it. The United States initially focused on the economic recovery of Europe in order to contain Communism and subsequently emphasized economic development as the key to containing Soviet expansion elsewhere.[17] In varying degrees, the United States promoted the establishment of institutions and policies intended to promote the economic growth of its allies and clients. Taking the lead in re-creating a multilateral trading system, the United States oversaw the creation of the Bretton Woods agreement (1944), International Monetary Fund (IMF), International Bank for Reconstruction (World Bank), and the General Agreement on Tariffs and Trade. Several collective management systems, such as the Group of Ten

14. Although realists disagreed about whether the United States should pursue a policy of limited containment or total containment of the Soviet Union.

15. Here we adopt Combs's (1983) distinction between soft-line and hard-line realists. David (1989) identifies Combs's soft-line realists as hyperrealists.

16. In many ways, the Nixon Doctrine embodied soft-line realism. It called for the United States to retreat from the Third World while reaffirming the primacy of Western Europe and Japan.

17. Beginning in the mid-1950s, the literature on modernization theory made a similar assumption. Scholars such as Lipset (1960), Lerner (1958), and Rostow (1960) argued that there was a direct link between a state's level of economic development and the likelihood of its becoming a democracy.

(1961) and the Organization for Economic Cooperation and Development, emerged to coordinate economic policy among the industrialized powers. Finally, the United States sponsored several regional economic development programs. The Marshall Plan, for example, was a key ingredient in the reconstruction of Europe, especially Germany.

Rejecting the West's trading system (including participation in the World Bank, IMF, and Marshall Plan) for itself and its allies, the Soviet Union established its own trading bloc, the Council for Mutual Economic Assistance.[18] Historically most Eastern European trade had been with the West. But by the 1950s, the Eastern European nations traded primarily within the Soviet bloc (Spulbar 1968; Kaser 1967). Outside its sphere of influence, the Soviet Union sometimes coerced and sometimes encouraged others to adopt its economic system and centralized economic policies.

Although initially waged in political and economic terms, the Cold War soon took on a military cast as well.[19] The United States and USSR stationed troops around the world, and both sailed fleets on all the planet's oceans. Yet they never confronted one another directly in a hot war and rarely contributed their own forces to the exclusion of regional powers. Rather, they created highly militarized clients as both sold weapons that local states could not themselves produce and subsidized weapons purchases their clients could not otherwise afford.[20] These transfers of sophisticated weaponry allowed local states to engage in large-scale modern warfare.[21] One legacy of the Cold War is that a large number of advanced weapons, such as supersonic fighter planes and surface-to-air missiles, remain in the periphery.[22]

18. By the end of the Cold War, this dual economic system had created relatively more prosperous U.S. allies and relatively more backward, stultified, and stagnant Soviet ones. More important, those linked politically and militarily to the United States were more part of a larger global economy than were Soviet clients.

19. In later years, a dispute emerged about the character of containment. George Kennan, widely credited as the doctrine's intellectual parent, protested that his prescription had been inappropriately given a military character (Kennan 1967b). Although the struggle was initially political, the military component was central to foreign- and defense-policy planning (Leffler 1992).

20. The great powers also helped many small powers develop indigenous arms industries (Neuman 1984).

21. The number of tanks engaged in the Sinai and Golan during the 1973 Arab-Israeli war was second only to the World War II battle of the Kursk between Germany and Russia. In a single battle, Egypt deployed nearly 1,000 tanks and Israel 700 (Safran 1981, 305, 331). In all, Egypt and Syria lost more than 2,000 tanks and Israel more than 800; the Arab states lost some 500 aircraft and Israel lost 114.

22. Regional states have learned to use sophisticated weaponry most effectively. The Mujahideen in Afghanistan used U.S.-supplied Stinger missiles against Soviet fighter planes and helicopters. During the Gulf War, Iraq launched Soviet Scud missiles against both Israel and Saudi

Neither superpower had direct security or economic interests in many of the regions in which it became involved, but *reputation* provided the key externality that linked regions and superpower involvement in them.[23] A superpower committed either to encouraging or to preventing Communist expansion around the world could not afford to be seen as reneging on that promise. The wars in Korea and Vietnam were fought as much for Europe and the Middle East as for any intrinsic interest in either.[24] More than concrete interests, credibility was on the line.

The importance of reputation and credibility underlay the position of hard-line realists who advocated a policy of global anti-Communist containment.[25] They called for an activist U.S. policy worldwide, warning of the dangers of falling dominoes and the damage to American credibility in core regions should the United States fail to defend its commitments in peripheral locales. Not surprisingly, Kennan strongly objected to the notion that the United States had to resist Communism everywhere. He saw no need to contain the Soviets in the Third World, since even substantial Soviet conquests there would not alter the global balance of power.[26]

Moreover, the centrality of reputation derived not from considerations of power as much as ideology. Although a great power's commitments are linked, it can typically distinguish vital from secondary interests and so decouple its commitments and guarantees. But the ideological overlay of the Cold War, by linking reputation through a universal issue other than that of credibility alone, made it extremely difficult to do so. A great power com-

---

Arabia. There is, of course, a danger that sophisticated weapons will be used against the supplier or its allies. In 1982, Argentina sunk two British ships with French Exocet missiles, and in 1987, Iraq heavily damaged the U.S. frigate *Stark* with an Exocet missile.

23. On externalities and spillovers, see Lake, this volume.

24. This point is made by LaFeber (1993). See also Jervis 1980. For a review of a number of works that examine U.S. intervention in the Korean War as a signal to American allies, see McMahon 1988.

25. More recently, the Reagan Doctrine went beyond a strategy of total containment. It called for "rollback," or pushing back, the Soviet position in the Third World (Copson and Cronin 1987).

26. The debate about what parts of the world matter and which should take primacy predates the Cold War. During the interwar period and immediately after World War II, Europe Firsters and Asia Firsters disputed the proper priorities of U.S. foreign policy. Today's debate questions whether the Third World matters. Walt (1989) and Van Evera (1989) contend that American vital interests have not substantially changed since Kennan identified five strategic regions, although they add access to Persian Gulf oil as a strategic concern. According to Walt's calculation, Western Europe is the largest "prize," producing roughly 22 percent of the gross world product. In contrast, he notes, the entire Third World produces less than 20 percent of gross world product from more than one hundred countries. Africa has an aggregate GNP lower than Britain's.

mitted to the defense of freedom and the containment of Communism could not easily renege on one of its commitments without affecting all of them.[27]

Although the Cold War globalized many regional and local conflicts, regional differentiation remained a salient feature of world politics (Lobell n.d.). Although U.S.-Soviet competition eventually came to encompass the world, the timing and extent of superpower penetration, and the intensity of the rivalry, varied across space and over time. Europe generally; the Northern Tier States of Greece (Kuniholm 1980; Fawcett 1992; Hess 1974; Stavrianos 1952; Knight 1975), Turkey, and Iran; and the Far East were drawn into the superpower competition early in the Cold War; Africa, the Persian Gulf, and Latin America were drawn in much later or remained on the periphery. Several factors, such as the loss-of-strength gradient (Boulding 1963), the strategic value of a region, and the presence of local states with an ideological affinity for one of the superpowers, contributed to the variation of superpower penetration of regional politics.

According to the standard interpretation, the withdrawal of American and Soviet forces from the Korean peninsula delayed the Cold War's coming to Asia until the Korean War began there in 1950. Our alternative formulation holds instead that the Cold War came to East Asia as early as it did to Europe. The United States and USSR occupied countries they had liberated in both regions in order to create states in their own images. The primary difference between the European and Asian experiences was that ideological and military competition between the superpowers occurred simultaneously in Europe. In Asia, only the ideological competition was manifest during the initial stages of the Cold War; military competition began later (Gallicchio 1988; Iriye 1974).

Africa, the Persian Gulf, and South America remained on the sidelines for most of the Cold War, drawn into the fray much later or not all. Until the Angolan crisis in the mid-1970s, Africa remained largely marginalized, with the United States devolving much of its putative "global" responsibilities there to the former European colonial powers of the region.[28] The super-

27. The USSR created a hierarchy of socialist states as the basis for signaling their relative importance and differentiating its commitments to them (Wallander 1992; Luttwak 1983; Bialer 1986).

28. Noer (1981) titles his chapter on Africa "'Non-Benign Neglect': The United States and Black Africa in the Twentieth Century," and notes that the United States has historically neglected Africa, pointing out that as late as 1958 the United States had more diplomats in West Germany than in all of Africa. See also Laidi 1990 and Jackson 1982. One bibliographic index on the origins of the Cold War has not a single citation on Africa (Black 1986). The United States replaced Britain and France as they retreated from the Middle East but did not do so in Africa.

powers remained aloof from the conflict over the Western Sahara, with the Americans extending only limited support to Morocco and the Soviets offering no support to the Polisario. In the Persian Gulf, where the United States built the shah's Iran into a regional hegemon, the Soviet Union had no opportunity to establish a toehold until the shah's fall in 1979. South (although not Central) America also remained largely uninvolved in the Cold War. Almost all Soviet arms deliveries to Latin America went to Cuba until after the rise of the Sandinistas in 1979, when Nicaragua also got Soviet munitions.[29]

During the Cold War, each superpower dominated a sphere of influence in which it established and enforced a set of rules of behavior and over which the other was not prepared to challenge its primacy. Beyond each sphere of influence, there were a number of highly penetrated regions. The primary difference between a sphere of influence and a highly penetrated region was that both superpowers refrained from direct intervention in the latter for fear that a local confrontation could escalate into a nuclear exchange. Instead, the United States and the USSR both extended substantial military and economic support to create surrogates, as they did in the Middle and Far East, that could police the regions for them.

The degree of superpower penetration of local politics varied as widely as the timing of their interventions in regional affairs. As measured by arms transfers from the superpowers to their clients, U.S. and Soviet military support (as well as economic assistance) for clients in Africa and Latin America never reached the proportions found in the Middle East.[30] Variation existed not only regionally but over time. American and especially Soviet arms transfers to Africa greatly increased in the mid-1970s, whereas U.S. arms sales to the Middle East peaked during the Reagan years. Finally, the types of weapons delivered to clients varied across regions (ACDA 1979, 159–64; 1985, 135–37; 1988, 137–39; 1994, 145–47). The superpowers delivered

29. From 1984 to 1988, the Soviets delivered more than $9.7 billion worth of weapons to Latin America. Of this, $7.4 billion went to Cuba, $2.1 billion went to Nicaragua, and $.2 billion went to Peru (ACDA 1990, 117).

30. Between 1964 and 1991, the value of U.S. arms transfers to the Middle East was nine times greater than to Latin America and fifteen times greater than to Africa. During the same period, Soviet arms transfers to the Middle East were four times greater than to Latin America and two times greater than to Africa. Oceania (Australia and New Zealand) remained completely outside the superpower rivalry, with the United States transferring a negligible amount ($6.3 billion in arms between 1964 and 1991) and the Soviet Union transferring no arms to the region (ACDA 1975, 67–71; 1985, 42–44; 1990, 32–34; 1994, 135–39). Other great powers remained active in the politics of regions to which they had colonial ties. China became increasingly active in East Asia, and France and Britain were active in the Middle East and Africa. Indeed, French arms transfers to Africa often exceeded American deliveries there.

a greater number of arms, and more sophisticated ones, to their clients in the Middle East than to those in Latin America and Africa combined (Neuman 1986).[31]

Although the Cold War internationalized many regional conflicts, this differentiated perspective highlights two characteristics of world politics. First, regions were incorporated into the Cold War rivalry at different rates, some early and some late. Second, the degree of superpower penetration varied across regions, with some at the center of the Cold War rivalry, while others remained on its periphery.

The End of the Cold War: Multiple Dimensions

The end of the Cold War simultaneously represents four analytically distinct phenomena. It signals the relative collapse of a great power. It closes an era of global bipolarity. It concludes an ideological struggle of some seven decades. And it ends the existence of the last great multinational empire. Each of these has distinct implications for future world and regional politics.

The USSR has experienced an economic and military collapse of immense proportions. Its core successor, Russia, remains a great power but a substantially weaker one. In itself, such a relative decline would lead to power vacuums, especially within that power's sphere of influence, as well as to international realignments among major and minor powers. The relative decline and retrenchment of British and French power after World War II, for example, led the United States to enlarge its global commitments and brought regional realignments.

The relative collapse of the Soviet Union means not only the loss of a great power but of one pole in a bipolar world. This has led some to assert a new era of unipolarity (oh so shortly after an overwhelming emphasis on relative American decline), whereas others who perceive an emergent multipolarity assume the current international structure will be short-lived.

31. Between 1973 and 1991, the United States transferred roughly 270 subsonic fighter planes and 1,180 supersonic fighter planes to the Middle East, 300 subsonic fighters and 100 supersonic fighters to Latin America, and only 6 subsonic fighters and 70 supersonic fighters to Africa (during this same period, Britain and France transferred 135 subsonic fighters and 175 supersonic fighters to Africa). The USSR transferred roughly 400 subsonic and 2,395 supersonic fighters to the Middle East, only 300 subsonic and 100 supersonic fighters to Latin America, and 165 subsonic and 1,515 supersonic fighters to Africa.

The end of bipolarity has had marked effects, including contradictory ones, on the foreign policies of American and Russian client states. In some instances, it has encouraged greater caution and conservatism. For Russian protégés, the collapse of Soviet power, coupled with the USSR's subsequent retreat from its global commitments, has meant that they can no longer rely on the support of a patron superpower to rescue them. The collapse of the Soviet pole has also served to lessen the strategic worth of U.S. clients, and the United States has been less likely to rescue a reckless or besieged ally.[32] Once strategically important U.S. clients can no longer count on unconditional economic and military assistance in wartime and fear that they will be abandoned without warning. Having to bear the full risk of their actions, some regional powers have adopted more cautious foreign policies and have sought to resolve local conflicts short of war.[33] This tendency is reflected, for example, in the recent Israeli-Palestinian Basic Principles Agreement, which was primarily the product of indigenous actors (Pervin, this volume).

Yet the end of the Cold War and the collapse of bipolarity have also created opportunities for aggressive behavior by local states (Ayoob 1991). The decline of the patron's restraining influence and the reduced likelihood of superpower intervention on the part of a besieged client has encouraged some to act more recklessly and behave more aggressively toward their neighbors.[34] One consequence is that their neighbors feel less secure than in the past, contributing to a regional security dilemma and encouraging the proliferation of conventional and nonconventional weapons.

The collapse of the Cold War also brings the end of an ideological struggle. Realists, who emphasize relative military power, treat the history of the twentieth century solely in terms of the rise and decline of powers and changes in the distribution of power. They see ideological differences as either fully irrelevant or merely as by-products of differences in power. For others, however, the Cold War was an ideological struggle between opposing

32. Some have argued that the decline of the Soviet threat to the Middle East means that the United States no longer needs Israel as a strategic ally (Barnett 1991; Telhami 1992; Keddie 1992). The end of the Cold War has also reduced Turkey's strategic value as a listening post on the Soviet Union (Cowell 1993, A3). In the Caribbean, the United States recently closed its embassy in Grenada (Holmes 1994, A1).

33. In the insurance industry, this is called moral hazard. The presence or absence of an insurance policy will alter an individual's behavior. An individual with no insurance is likely to behave more cautiously. An individual with insurance, however, is more likely to behave recklessly, since damage will be covered by the insurance company. Deductibles, which force some burden sharing, are a way to decrease the insured's risk taking.

34. At the same time, the presence of massive Soviet or American weapon stockpiles grants further independence from the great powers.

conceptions of political order and legitimacy. Hence, they count the end of the struggle between Communism and capitalism as a defining element of the Cold War's end.[35] The triumph of capitalism, they argue, has left the international and domestic landscape fundamentally changed, a reorientation that entails changes not only in external alignments but in domestic political systems as well.

During the Cold War, both superpowers wanted to install political leaderships linked to them. Political realignments during the Cold War almost always entailed wholesale shifts in the political leadership of client states. The collapse of Soviet ideology has again brought changes in the holders of political power and even in the nature of the political system within most former Soviet clients. The political conflicts that have erupted in parts of the world and within nation-states are not just a product of the collapse of a great power, therefore, but of the collapse of an ideology, resulting in intensified domestic rivalries, internal political transformations, and the search for new mechanisms for political mobilization.[36]

A second consequence of the ideological component of the Soviet Union's demise has been economic. Those parts of the world that find themselves cut off from Soviet financial assistance and economically adrift are now forced to choose between the continued immiserization of self-sufficiency or the internally difficult and wrenching requirements of economic transformation. In contrast, states most closely linked to the United States during the Cold War remain tied to a growing global economy even as the maintenance of continued military ties comes into question.

The collapse of Soviet power has meant not only the collapse of a great power and systemic pole, and not only the loss of an ideological competitor—it has ended the last great multinational empire and resulted in the creation of separate states where there had been just one.[37] In itself, such a splintering of one into many powers would likely generate regional conflicts in the

35. During the period of Soviet decline, some American conservatives debated the Cold War's meaning. Some hailed the dissolution of the Communist Party as constituting the end of the Cold War. Others countered that the struggle had never been ideological and that since as many nuclear weapons were aimed at the United States as before, the Cold War had not yet ended. They awaited more tangible manifestations of a change in the military balance before being willing to close the book on the era.

36. In this sense, the relative decline of Soviet power is much more consequential than the decline of British and French power in an earlier era. For a discussion of the import of these factors, see Stein n.d.

37. Realists have a difficult time explaining the Russian core's peaceful acquiescence in the dismantling of the empire it had dominated.

area previously controlled by the once-unified multinational empire.[38] Combined with the delegitimation of Communism, the result is a local political vacuum likely to generate regional conflicts among new states and outside powers.[39]

The end of the Cold War is simultaneously a collapse of a great power, the end of a bipolarity, the end of an ideological struggle, and the collapse of a multinational empire. These are analytically distinct changes that have distinctive impacts on the security environment.[40] Making sense of the current international environment requires understanding all of them.

REGIONALIZATION OF SECURITY

Even during the Cold War, the most globally polarized period in world history, regional differentiation remained a salient feature of world politics. Although this suggests a preeminent emphasis on the structural, we have highlighted the continuing importance of the geographical and regional.[41] The end of bipolarity constitutes a changed structural condition for international politics, but also one in which the geographic and regional will become increasingly more important, influencing security relations in the post–Cold War era.

The end of the Cold War means the decline of the globalizing forces of bipolarity and ideology and the growing regionalization of world politics. Concomitant with this trend in world politics is the growing localization of conflict management.[42] Instead of a global concert composed of the great

38. The decline of the Ottoman Empire resulted in several crises between outside powers and among newly independent states in the region (especially in the Balkans) between 1832 and 1878 and two great wars, the Crimean War and the First World War (Anderson 1966).

39. The end of the Cold War has meant different things to those areas that were part of the Soviet empire and that, although dominated by it, were politically stable, with indigenous and viable political systems. For a discussion of political stability and the emergence of regional cooperation, see Shumaker 1993 and Weber 1992 and 1997.

40. One way to perceive the difference is to think counterfactually about the consequences of a dramatic decline in American power. Such a decline would have one set of consequences in and of itself. But a decline in American power would have different consequences should it occur in the context of a collapse of U.S. representative institutions.

41. On the impact of geography on politics, see Mackinder 1904, Kelly 1986, Saul Cohen 1991 and 1994, and Krugman 1991.

42. The end of the Cold War has an economic dimension as well. The Cold War era witnessed a growing commitment to trade among the Western powers and a reduction in protectionism. One explanation for the increasing globalization of trade during the Cold War is that there is a close relationship between economic and military power and a tendency for trade relations to co-vary with security arrangements. Commercial relations often "follow the flag" and reflect

powers, like that which formed after the Napoleonic Wars, security arrangements in the post–Cold War era will increasingly be local in breadth and scope (Morgan, this volume), and the form and composition of security regimes will vary across regions.[43]

The relative incorporation of a region into the Cold War superpower rivalry will affect regional relations in the post–Cold War world. In regions in which the superpowers were uninvolved, the end of the Cold War will have little effect on regional relations. Disputes like the India-Pakistan conflict, divorced from the Cold War and sustained locally, will continue irrespective of the demise of the Cold War, whereas regions like Oceania (Australia and New Zealand) will remain peaceful. Similarly, regions of low penetration, like Africa, will also remain largely unaffected by the end of the Cold War. The end of the U.S.-Soviet competition for clients will mean that such regions will become ever more marginalized, although France and Britain are likely to continue to participate in African affairs. The primary legacy of the Cold War in such locales is the continued presence of large stockpiles of sophisticated military weapons that will contribute to deadlier and more destructive conflict.

Although the end of bipolarity will somewhat affect areas penetrated by the United States, Cold War inertia means that, for the moment, the United States will remain involved in the politics of areas in which it has historic ties.[44] The call of some policy makers and scholars for the United States

---

patterns of alignment, resulting in an increase in intra-alliance trade and a decrease in cross-alliance trade (Pollins 1989a, 1989b; Gowa and Mansfield 1993; Mansfield 1993; Gowa 1994; Skålnes 1993). Rivals are unlikely to trade, for fear that economic gains will be converted into military power. During the Cold War, as alliances became globalized, cross-regional economic links developed among member states. With the end of the Cold War and the rising importance of regional security arrangements, it remains unclear whether international trade relations will become more global. The implication for states that become involved in regional security arrangements is that trade will increasingly become local as well. However, for states that continue to participate in extraregional security arrangements, trade is likely to remain global.

43. Here we differ with a number of scholars who anticipate that a new concert of great powers will form (Rosecrance 1992b; Kupchan and Kupchan 1991).

44. According to Newton's laws of motion (or the first law of physics) "every body continues in its state of rest or in uniform motion in a straight line unless it is compelled to change that state by forces impressed upon it." Similarly, only regions that were penetrated by the superpowers will be affected by the end of the Cold War. Regions that were not will remain in "uniform motion": those characterized by conflict during the Cold War will remain conflict-ridden, and those characterized by stability will stay peaceful. In contrast, regions that were penetrated by the superpowers might no longer remain in "motion," depending upon the reversibility of the Cold War. The impact of superpower penetration might cause previously unstable regions to become peaceful or previously peaceful regions to become unstable.

to reduce its extensive foreign commitments to fit its capabilities will more likely be answered with respect to penetrated regions no longer deemed of critical strategic value. The U.S. sphere, however, will remain largely unaffected by the end of the Cold War. The United States will continue to be the dominant player in the Western Hemisphere, the regional balancer unilaterally intervening to settle local disputes, as it has done most recently in Haiti.

In contrast, the end of the Cold War will have its greatest impact in regions that were highly penetrated by the Soviet Union. The disintegration of the Soviet Union, as well as its subsequent retreat from its global commitments, leaves a large concentration of former Russian clients in its wake—ones whose internal political and economic arrangements and foreign policies are in flux.[45] Whether cooperation (as reflected by the recent Israeli-Palestinian Basic Principles Agreement and the multilateral peace negotiations between Israel and its Arab neighbors) or conflict (as seen in Serbia's aggressive nationalism in the Balkans) emerges in such regions remains uncertain.[46] Regional cooperation is most likely to emerge (1) if the collapse of the Soviet Union has discredited Communism, encouraging Soviet clients to adopt political and economic liberalism and integrating them into the global economy, or (2) if the collapse of the Soviet Union sustains caution in the foreign policies of local states.[47] Regional conflict will reign, however, (1) if it encourages Soviet clients to seek autarky or (2) if the end of Soviet dominance brings the reemergence of conflicts that Moscow had suppressed rather than resolved.

Conclusion

The interaction of structural and geographic pressures shaped the pattern of superpower penetration of regional politics during the Cold War. The differentiated nature of superpower penetration in that era will continue to affect regional relations in the post–Cold War world. In regions that were di-

45. In the former Soviet sphere, the emergence of fifteen new states has also created new conflicts, such as border disputes and regional realignments. The process of state building has also been fraught with conflict and instability, which could spill over into neighboring states.

46. A number of scholars maintain that Asia is "ripe for rivalry" (Friedberg 1993–94). For a more optimistic view of the prospects for peace in the Far East, see Shirk, this volume.

47. Solingen's chapter in this volume argues that regional cooperation is most likely to occur among liberalizing states.

vorced from or on the periphery of the Cold War, little change is likely in regional relations, whether peaceful or conflictual. In contrast, regions that were highly penetrated by the superpowers will be most affected by the Cold War's end. There, the prospect for cooperation or conflict will depend on whether superpower intervention in regional politics increased or decreased regional conflict and whether this involvement left a lasting imprint on regional relations. The implication for the post–Cold War order is twofold: regions that were unstable during the Cold War are not necessarily destined to remain unstable, and those that were stable might not remain so.

Part III

Problems of Regional Security Management

6

Great Powers and Regional Orders: Possibilities and Prospects After the Cold War

Paul A. Papayoanou

The United States and the Soviet Union played an active and important role in most regions of the world during the Cold War, competing against and checking one another by direct intervention or by supplying regional allies with money, matériel, and political support. Today, the role and the impact of great powers—those states which have the capabilities to "play a major role in international politics with respect to security-related issues" (Levy 1981, 585–86)[1]—are much more varied across regions. Sometimes the approaches to managing regional security complexes in the post–Cold War world involve great powers, and sometimes they do not.[2] And when great powers are involved in a regional order, their approaches vary from compe-

For their comments, I thank Richard Eichenberg, David Lake, Patrick Morgan, David Pervin, and Christopher Twomey. My thanks also to Matt Ruben for research assistance. I accept full responsibility for all errors and shortcomings.

1. The United States, Russia, Germany, Britain, France, Japan, and China are the present-day great powers.

2. A regional security complex refers to a given region's set of security-related issues (or security externalities). For extended consideration of regional security complexes (and regional systems more generally), see Chapters 2 and 3, by Morgan and Lake respectively.

tition to collaboration to hegemonic management. This chapter develops an explanation for the approaches great powers take to regional security complexes. The logic of the explanation is illustrated with empirical examples. In what follows, I make three interrelated arguments, and then discuss the possibilities and prospects for different regional orders involving great powers. I first argue that the local security externality that defines a given regional security complex (Lake, this volume) must affect a great power if that state is to participate in the security management of that region.[3] However, the approach taken, if any, depends on the nature of the regional security complex and the capacity that great-power leaders have to mobilize economic resources and political support from their societies for taking action in the region.

I then argue that mobilization capacity, and in turn the approach that great powers take, depend most of all on the level of a great power's economic interests in a particular region, for those will give rise to the most extensive societal support. Ethnic or ideological ties, and human rights concerns, may generate sufficient societal support for playing some role in a region, but they are not as politically salient. I note, however, that while mobilization concerns are going to be important for most great powers, some have domestic political institutions that leave their leaders unconstrained by societal interests; those leaders' mobilization capacities will be quite significant regardless of the interests at stake.

Finally, I argue that the mobilization process is crucial to the game that great powers play in regions. Borrowing from signaling-game theory, I argue that mobilization capacity has a strong effect on great powers' preferences, the beliefs that other states have about those preferences, and the way signals are interpreted in regional politics. In turn, this process determines the strategies great powers pursue and the type of regional order we see.

Regional Security Complexes and Great Powers

During the Cold War, regional politics tended to be characterized by superpower competition, or by U.S. or Soviet domination over geographically proximate states. The two great powers saw the possibility of one another's

3. Consistent with Lake and Morgan, but not all contributors to the volume, I am using the traditional and narrow definition of "security," which refers to the survival of the physical and territorial integrity of the state from military harm.

expanded territorial influence as potentially threatening, and tended to compete against and check one another by direct intervention or domination in regions, or by supplying regional allies with money, matériel, and political support. Thus, bipolarity gave U.S. and Soviet leaders a strong incentive to balance vigorously against one another all over the globe. To a significant extent, systemic imperatives shaped the behavior of great powers in regional politics and determined what regional security complexes looked like.[4]

In the post–Cold War world, the constraints of the great-power system are more limited. As a result, regional politics themselves are an important motivation behind what great powers do in regions. That is, regional security complexes are more often determinants of great-power behavior in regions than they were during the Cold War, when regional security complexes were often defined by the bipolar competition of the great-power system.

Thus, whereas most regions were battlegrounds of the Cold War up to 1989, they have since been characterized by varied modes of conflict management. Sometimes these include great powers and sometimes not. Sometimes we see competition and conflict, and other times collaboration, hegemonic management, or quietude. These results at the regional level are due in part to the change in the international system.

It is important to recognize, however, that whether security motivations for great-power behavior in regions are systemic or regional in origin, they are often not sufficient to account for behavior. During the Cold War era, the exigency and clarity of the threat from the Soviet Union may have facilitated the cultivation of domestic support in the United States necessary to oppose the Soviets, but this was not enough. Societal interests, particularly internationalist concerns, complemented the security motivations of U.S. leaders, giving them a great capacity to pursue containment policies. Without such domestic support, leaders of the United States and other great powers in earlier eras have often been constrained from pursuing effective security policies (Papayoanou 1996, 1997, n.d.). Such a mobilization process is just as important in the post–Cold War world for most great powers. We must therefore examine whether the security concerns that leaders of great powers have about a regional security complex are complemented by domestic concerns, and how that affects the mobilization process and, in turn, behavior.

In short, regional security complexes are necessary but not sufficient conditions to explain the approaches great powers take in regions. The nature of the regional security complex—the type and degree of conflict to be managed—gives rise to the motivation that leaders have for taking action

4. The classic theoretical statement explaining this trend is Waltz 1979.

and determines the approach they deem appropriate. Whether a leader can pursue a particular approach, however, depends on his or her mobilization capacity and what approach a given regional security complex requires. The more extensive the approach required by the regional security complex, the more mobilization capacity leaders must have. For example, some regional security complexes may simply require diplomatic mediation by, and money from, great powers, as in the Arab-Israeli conflict. The mobilization capacity necessary to pursue such approaches is minimal. In other cases, such as in the Persian Gulf in 1990–91, military force is required, and mobilization capacity must be much greater.

Determinants of Mobilization Capacity

A great deal of scholarship demonstrates that state leaders typically have to extract economic resources from society and mobilize domestic political support for security policies (Barnett 1990, 1992; Barnett and Levy 1991; Haskel 1980; Lamborn 1983, 1985, 1991; Mastanduno, Lake, and Ikenberry 1989; Organski and Kugler 1980). State leaders of most great powers charged with national security concerns are typically not autonomous from their societies, but rather are often constrained by domestic political and economic concerns. That is, they do not work in a political vacuum or have unlimited resources at their disposal.

What determines a leader's mobilization capacity to pursue security policies in a particular region? Most important, I would argue, is the level of economic interests a great power has in that region. The more trade and financial links a great power has in a given region, the greater the number and size of powerful domestic vested interests with a stake in that region, and the greater the adjustment costs for that great power's economy should the economic ties become the victim of armed conflict. Thus, as economic dependence in a particular region increases, the stake in that region for both narrow and broad economic concerns increases. Vested interests in the great power will, therefore, have a strong interest in supporting security policies that protect trade, financial links, and investments. And to the extent economic interests are significant in a region, the society at large will also be supportive of security measures aimed at reducing any shock to the economy that would come from the disappearance of markets (i.e., the adjustment costs). Economic ties to a particular region therefore have high political salience and will affect mobilization capacity, for security policies in that region will have implications for both narrow and broad economic interests. Hence, state leaders' capacity to mobilize economic resources and political support for playing a role in a region increases with the level of economic ties, since leaders will be able to garner support from societal interests for security policies that can protect their economic interests abroad.[5]

Ethnic or ideological ties that great powers have to states in particular regions, and human rights concerns, may have some political salience as well. However, noneconomic interests are typically less concentrated and powerful. Interests that represent ethnic groups or those with particular ideological or human rights concerns are likely to be diffuse and lacking in political strength. Broad and deep support is therefore likely to be lacking, and so mobilization capacity will be limited. Thus, while some state leaders of great powers shed their initial reluctance to intervene in Rwanda and Somalia for humanitarian reasons because public sentiment favored action, these were quite limited operations. All in all, then, it is possible that noneconomic concerns will lead to societal support that will enable great-power leaders to play a role in a region, but mobilization capacity will tend to be quite limited.

In some cases, such mobilization concerns are not going to be an issue. When a great power's domestic political institutions have leaders unconstrained by societal interests, those leaders' mobilization capacities will be quite significant regardless. While most of today's great powers are democracies with significant, though varying, degrees of access for societal interests to impact policy, and leaders of those states need to be sensitive to societal concerns, there are some nondemocratic regimes in which leaders are not so constrained. For instance, in many authoritarian regimes the leadership is not held in check by interest groups and median voters. China's closed political system, for example, limits society's impact significantly, though it does appear that the Chinese leadership's supporting coalition includes internationalist economic interests. And in praetorian polities, the institutional framework may ineffectively assimilate struggles between competing groups, and so narrow interest groups with a disproportionate influence can capture

5. This argument follows on the work of Hirschman ([1945] 1980) and of Keohane and Nye (1977, 1989). See also Arad and Hirsch (1981) and Arad, Hirsch, and Tovias (1983), who discuss how states may try to create vested economic interests to establish political support for peacemaking. The argument is also fleshed out in Papayoanou 1996, 1997, and n.d. Note also the rough parallel here between the argument I am making about the effects of economic interests on great powers promoting the search for better management of regional relations and Etel Solingen's argument in Chapter 4 on the economic interests of region members in promoting cooperative regional management.

national policy. Russia's political system, being in a transition period, has some such characteristics. All in all, then, to the extent that domestic political structures fail to provide narrow and broad societal interests with political influence, the mobilization capacity that leaders have to play a role in regions will not be impacted.[6]

Great Power Interaction in Regions: The Signaling-Game Process

Because the mobilization capacity that great power leaders have to play a role in regions will vary across regions and over time, great powers will have varied preferences over possible outcomes in their interactions. A great power with strong economic or other interests in a region, for instance, will tend to have strong preferences for a cooperative regional order and be willing to contribute to regional stability, while a great power without such ties may have only weak preferences for these same outcomes and be willing to make only minor contributions. Great powers are thus different "types," in game-theoretical language, and in an uncertain world the behaviors they pursue may be signals of their types.[7]

How signals are interpreted and affect states' strategies depends significantly on the beliefs that states have about the preferences of the signaling state. While foreign leaders will be uncertain what a given great power's preferences are, they will have beliefs—a probabilistic assessment—about the intentions of the great power in question. Since the mobilization process is inherently political and somewhat transparent, the expectations foreign leaders have about the likelihood that prospective partners will come through on commitments or be adversaries will be influenced by the nature of that process. Hence, assessments of others' intentions are influenced by the domestic politics of mobilization processes.[8]

6. The arguments I am making about domestic political structures and societal interests draw from, and are consistent with the premises of, theoretical work on political institutions and foreign policy, such as Doyle 1986, Lake 1992, Gordon 1974, and Snyder 1990 and 1991.

7. I am drawing on the logic of signaling-game theory here. For a review of the literature, see Banks 1991.

8. The logic underlying this discussion draws on Jervis's [1970] 1989 discussion of signals and indexes in international politics as determinants of states' behavior.

In short, then, the mobilization process gives rise to a great power's preferences. Other states' beliefs about those preferences are then influenced by what they see in the domestic politics of the mobilization process; this will provide strong indications about the political implications leaders of great powers face, or are likely to face, in attempting to play a role in regional politics. There is still likely to be some uncertainty, however. While leaders of great powers may be constrained in the mobilization process, what decisions they are willing to risk domestically will be a source of uncertainty.

Nonetheless, because a great power's behavior depends to a significant degree on the capacity that its leaders have to act abroad, its response to a regional security complex will be a signal to other powers that tends to reinforce beliefs. That is, the nature of a great power's behavior will tend to be consistent with assessments that states have about a great power's intentions and resolve, and so others will update (or revise) their beliefs accordingly. However, when the signaling great power has political institutions that make its leaders highly unconstrained, its preferences will be unclear, and signals will carry little weight.

Mobilization capacity is thus an important influence on great powers' preferences, beliefs, the interpretation of signals, and in turn the strategies states pursue in regional politics. Mobilization capacity thus determines whether great powers play a role in a region, how extensive that role will be, and whether the role played is cooperative or not. Because the domestic politics of mobilization affect a state's beliefs, the credibility of commitments is influenced. As such, regional states and other great powers will make assessments about the staying power and the sincerity of cooperative gestures made by a given great power. Thus, the credibility of commitments will be influenced by the information provided by the mobilization process, and this has important implications for what strategies will be pursued and the type of regional order that obtains.

Given the discussion above on the determinants of mobilization capacity, it follows that strong economic interests in a particular region are most likely to make a great power's security commitments in that region relatively extensive and credible. In such cases, vested interests with a significant stake and concerns with the broader economic consequences of developments in a regional security complex will give leaders the capacity to make credible commitments. Ethnic or ideological ties, or human rights concerns, may have a positive impact on the capacity state leaders have to make credible commitments, but will do so at a generally lower level, since domestic interests will be more diffuse. If state leaders are highly unconstrained by their societies due to their domestic political structures, however, they will have a great capacity for acting as they see fit. But since they can make and break commitments with relative ease, it will be more difficult for these state leaders to make credible commitments. Thus, a country like China is likely to have problems making credible commitments because of its authoritarian political structure. Russia too will have difficulty convincing others of prospective faithfulness given the flux that its institutions are in presently and their uncertain shape in the future. Nonetheless, even if there is a bit more room for leaders to choose, for "reasons of state" leaders are still likely to pursue and follow through on commitments that protect significant economic interests, in particular, but perhaps also ideological or ethnic ties in a region.

Great Powers and Regional Orders

State leaders' capacities for playing a role in a region and the possibility of making credible commitments are important determinants of states' strategies in regional systems. In turn, the type of regional order is influenced. When great powers play a role in a region, one of five possible orders seems likely: hegemony, balance of power, concert, collective security, or a pluralistic security community.[9] I turn now to a discussion of these various possibilities, and show how the logic of the argument is illustrated by the various patterns of great-power behavior in or toward particular regions in the post–Cold War era, and what the likely trends for the future are.

HEGEMONY

A hegemonic regional order is one in which a single great power plays a leading role managing regional security relations. Where a great power acts as a hegemon, it may adopt one of three approaches to managing relations with smaller states.

The great power may adopt a "balancer approach." In the role of bal-

9. This typology is similar to, and draws on, that outlined by Patrick Morgan in Chapter 2. However, for my analytic purposes, I find it useful to distinguish between "hegemony" and "balance of power," which he lumps together under the category of "power-restraining-power" regional orders. I also ignore "integration" as a possible regional order for lack of real-world referents.

ancer, a characterization often associated with Britain's period of "splendid isolation" in the nineteenth century, a great power is not permanently identified with the policies of particular nations or groups of states and only seeks to maintain the stability, or "balance," of the system by alternating its support between different sides in a regional conflict. Without concrete ties, the balancer gets involved only when it sees fit and perhaps by playing an "honest-broker" role (Morgenthau 1960, 194).

A great power may, alternatively, attempt to create what could be called a Bismarckian alliance system. In this approach, named after that taken by German chancellor Otto von Bismarck in central Europe from 1871 to 1890, a great power attempts to provide for regional security through a network of alliances with smaller powers in the region. The hegemon will use these alliances as tools for the control and management of conflict in a region (Schroeder 1976).

Finally, a hegemon may employ its disproportionate power over lesser states in a region to establish order in ways elucidated by what is commonly referred to as "hegemonic stability theory." This school of thought suggests hegemons may seek to dominate and exploit smaller states as a way of establishing order, or that a hegemon bears the costs of providing public goods—in this case, security—for a region.[10]

The theory implies that a hegemonic regional order depends on a single great power being part of a regional security complex and having significant economic, ideological, or ethnic ties to, or human rights concerns with, states in that region. The leaders of such a great power will then have the motivation to deal with security externalities and the capacity to mobilize resources and support for pursuing a hegemonic role. This mobilization capacity, and in turn the great power's approach to hegemonic management of a region and the credibility of its commitments, will be a function of its economic links particularly, but ethnic or ideological ties, or human rights concerns, may lead to some political support as well. There are several examples of the varied forms of hegemonic management.

With rivalry and competition between the United States and Soviet Union no longer the norm in the Middle East, the Arabs and Israelis are seeking to cooperate on issues such as water, the environment, economic ties, refugees, arms control, and regional security. However, there remain reasons to be concerned that spillovers may adversely affect the security interests of

10. On the various strands of this theory and a review of the literature, see Snidal 1985 and Lake 1993.

great powers outside the region. This has been a motivation for the United States to keep its hand in the Middle East peace process, particularly in regard to negotiations between Israel and the PLO, and between Israel and Syria. In addition, there is domestic support for pursuing such a role, since the American Jewish lobby has historically been quite influential in the U.S. government, particularly with the Democratic Party. Nonetheless, this is a relatively narrow interest group, so its impact is unlikely to be very great when it comes to garnering the support necessary for an extensive U.S. role in the region. Such an approach has not been necessary, however. The United States has been able to pursue something of a balancer approach, being an "honest broker" to some extent and offering side payments to the different sides to facilitate agreements. For instance, in the historic accord signed in Washington, D.C., in September 1993, President Bill Clinton promised to help raise some $4 billion to alleviate the West Bank–Gaza economic crises (LaFeber 1994, 777). Hence, the United States has pursued a balancer approach commensurate with limited domestic support for American intercession in this area.

We also see a hegemonic pattern in the former Soviet Union, with Russia taking an approach toward the successor regimes of the former Soviet republics that is somewhere between a Bismarckian system, with its Commonwealth of Independent States (CIS) collective security agreement, and outright domination, as it attempts to strong-arm some successor regimes. For Russia, there are clear security externalities that provide a motivation for managing security in the region. Strong domestic political reasons exist for pursuing something of a hegemonic role. In particular, there are substantial economic interests given the level of integration achieved under the former Soviet Union. There are, as well, concerns with potentially disruptive ethnic conflict spillovers, which can affect the Russian leadership's prospects for survival.

In Central America, there has often been hegemonic management as well, but by the United States. This hegemonic pattern has a long history—the Monroe Doctrine, the Roosevelt Corollary, the Good Neighbor Policy, and the United States' active behavior in the region during the Cold War—and is likely to continue. Besides the obvious strategic importance of regional stability to the United States given its geographical proximity, the United States and Latin America have large, mutual, and complementary economic interests. There are also ideological ties between the United States and the newly emerging and established democracies in the region (Pastor 1992,

108–10). Hence, U.S. leaders have a capacity to mobilize societal support for activist policies in Central America; we should continue to see the United States playing a hegemonic role in the region to impose some semblance of order.

We have also seen somewhat transitory hegemonic approaches, perhaps most notably by the United States in Somalia and France in Rwanda, where the great powers have attempted to impose some order. Human rights concerns have prompted these interventions, and such efforts have, as the theory leads us to expect, been limited and short-lived because of the difficulty of sustaining public support for humanitarian missions.

BALANCE OF POWER

A regional balance-of-power system involving great powers is a competitive system in which great powers balance against one another internally (i.e., by their own means) and/or by alliance. This is possible where at least two great powers are part of a regional security complex and have significant but divergent economic, ethnic, or ideological ties in a region. Their leaders will have the capacity to mobilize to play a role in such a region, but for dissimilar purposes, so competition between them is likely.

Whether such a competitive system leads to conflict depends on the ability of the great powers to make credible balancing commitments. Hence, the greater their economic, ethnic, or ideological ties and thus the greater the apparent societal support, the more likely commitments are to be credible and conflict to be avoided. If state leaders are quite unconstrained by their societies due to political structure, however, their intentions will be less clear, and this will diminish their ability to make credible commitments. Hence, to the extent that leaders in a balance-of-power system work under unconstraining domestic political institutions, competition is more likely to lead to conflict.

My theory suggests that a competitive and potentially conflictual balance-of-power system among great powers is likely in the Asia-Pacific, where China, Japan, Russia, and the United States are the great powers that are part of the regional security complex (see Shirk, this volume). All four see that regional conflict is a possibility to be avoided, as Susan Shirk points out in Chapter 11. However, contrary to Shirk's argument that a concert of powers is emerging, my conception predicts conflictual balance-of-power politics, for the great powers have significant but divergent economic, ideological, and ethnic concerns, and two of the four have political institutions that are quite closed (China) or are undergoing an uncertain transition (Russia).

While U.S.-Japanese commercial and financial ties are substantial, if sometimes conflictual, their economic links with China and Russia are not terribly significant. There are also few Sino-Russian economic ties. Yet the regional economic stakes for the United States, Japan, and China are quite significant, so each has strong but often divergent economic incentives for playing a role in the region. Moreover, there are sharp ideological differences between the four as well, particularly between the United States and China, who clash over different conceptions of human rights. Ethnic ties, meanwhile, are also nonexistent among the four powers. Finally, China's and Russia's domestic political institutions lack the accountability to societal forces that would help make their intentions clear. Together these factors make the potential for credible commitments low and conflict a distinct possibility. For these very same reasons, the possibility of an Asia- Pacific great-power concert that has any teeth seems remote, for the bases of meaningful cooperation are absent.

CONCERT

In a great-power concert, two or more great powers agree to collaborate on maintaining order and security in a region (Jervis 1983 and Morgan, this volume). This is most likely when the leaders of great powers that are part of a regional security complex have the capacity to make credible commitments to one another. A concert is thus most apt to form when great powers have significant and complementary economic interests in a region. While it is possible that common ideological, ethnic, or human rights concerns may also serve as the glue for a concert, these factors typically have less domestic political salience, so such a concert will be weaker in strength and duration, since state leaders will have less capacity for making credible commitments. Thus, while the major European powers established the Concert of Europe following the Napoleonic Wars, based largely on ideological grounds, it had significance only from 1815 to 1823, and then continued only as a very limited and weak arrangement up to the Crimean War in 1853 (Jervis 1983).

The region that appears most likely to see a great-power concert is Western Europe. In Western Europe, the great powers in the regional security complex—Britain, France, Germany, and the United States—have the capacity to make credible commitments to one another given their extensive economic and ideological ties and their democratic political institutions. Indeed, NATO has made substantial progress toward transforming into a concert since the end of the Cold War. However, NATO appears to be moving toward something that is not simply a great-power concert, but rather a mix of a concert and a collective security system that includes small states, as I now discuss.

COLLECTIVE SECURITY

A multilateral collective security approach pursued by states in a regional security complex includes both great and small powers. Although like a concert, in that collaborative management of regional politics for a common good of order and security is the goal, management is not the prerogative of the major states alone. As with a concert, such a regional order is more likely to the extent there are common economic, ideological, or ethnic ties in a region, for these give leaders the capacity to make credible commitments for collaboration.[11]

Western Europe is the region most likely to see a collective security order, or a hybrid of a concert and collective security arrangement. Both great and small powers are working through security institutions created in the postwar era, such as NATO, the CSCE (Conference on Security and Cooperation in Europe), and WEU (Western European Union). Hence, in the post–Cold War era, the OSCE has gone beyond its CSCE predecessor by taking on concrete security functions such as peacekeeping and election monitoring. Moreover, the Partnership for Peace has been pursued to expand NATO membership. Although there has, to date, been a fair amount of confusion in the process, and coherent collective security arrangements have not been realized, the United States and its European allies are attempting to transform the security orders of the Cold War for a new era.

Western leaders are motivated to do so because they see that nationalist or ethnic conflicts and associated instabilities of bordering states to the east

11. Such arrangements may go one step beyond this, to a type of regional order Morgan identifies as "integration." Integration rests on supranational institutions, so member states, unlike those in a collective security system, must cede some sovereignty. This, however, seems to be a utopian chimera, since states appear unwilling to relinquish that much sovereignty on security matters. Even the European Union, which has achieved a great deal of integration on economic affairs, has been unable to do so on foreign-policy matters.

pose potentially serious security externalities. They also have a good deal of capacity to deal credibly with such problems on a multilateral basis because of their extensive economic and ideological ties. Collective security in Western Europe is thus a possibility. Unlike the experience of the League of Nations, which by 1924 was insignificant without the membership of the United States (Rosecrance 1992b), today there are many more complementary economic interests. The United States and the European Union have extensive economic ties, and despite some arenas of conflict (e.g., agriculture), domestic support for the postwar liberal economic order remains strong. Thus, security institutions in Europe may be transformed into a collective security system or a hybrid of a concert and collective security arrangement that is viable and durable, although there will undoubtedly still be something of a large-*n* problem.[12]

PLURALISTIC SECURITY COMMUNITY

The last type of regional order that may involve great powers is a pluralistic security community (PSC). A PSC has no formal security arrangements and none are necessary, since states in the region give no thought to the use of violence (Morgan, this volume). A PSC thus reflects the absence of a regional security complex.

The question then becomes, why is there no regional security complex? First, the existence of a single great power with overwhelming capabilities in a region may vitiate any thoughts that successful aggression is possible. The great power sees no need, as a result, to take a particularly active approach to managing security relations. Or, if there is substantial economic integration, the stakes may be so high that states eschew any thought of resorting to force for gain.

North America most closely approximates a PSC. No significant regional security arrangement exists or is likely there. The United States, Canada, and Mexico share strong economic ties, and America's vast preponderance over its neighbors makes contemplation of the use of military force unlikely. Hence, there is little need for a security arrangement.[13]

12. On large-*n* problems in collective security arrangements, see Brian Job's contribution in Chapter 8 of this volume.

13. In Chapter 14, Yuen Foong Khong sees ASEAN as a nascent pluralistic security community, but because it does not involve great powers I leave it out of the present discussion.

Conclusion

The role of great powers in regional politics during the Cold War was typically characterized by a pattern of competitive balance-of-power politics as the United States and Soviet Union opposed one another in the various regions of the world. The pattern of great-power behavior in regions since the demise of the Cold War is more varied, and this essay has advanced a theory to account for these outcomes and provide insight into future developments.

Theoretically and empirically, I have shown that the approach great powers take to a regional security complex since the end of the Cold War is a function of state leaders' capacities to make credible commitments. This mobilization capacity, I argue, is affected mostly by a great power's economic interests in a region, for these entail high domestic political salience, but ideological or ethnic ties to a particular region, or human rights concerns, may also carry some weight. Thus, the post–Cold War era is, and will continue to be, qualitatively other than it was for more than forty years, for the ability to muster the necessary domestic support for regional security policies now varies to a greater extent from region to region. This means, in general, less competition and greater opportunity for collaboration than during the Cold War, yet the specific outcome depends on the region in question. There is unlikely, therefore, to be anything like a "new world order." On the other hand, there is not apt to be a "new world disorder," for some regions are finding—with or without great-power involvement—effective modes of regional security management.

7

Concerts and Regional Intervention

Richard Rosecrance and Peter Schott

The Cold War is over and the pattern of bipolarity has broken down. Ideological and power differences no longer divide the erstwhile superstates. This evolution has made for two new features of the international system: (1) the partial autonomy of regions of the world, which are now somewhat freer from great-power intervention than before; (2) the gradual construction of a concert of great powers. A "concert" is a club or group of powers that agree collectively to lower security costs for a given geographic (regional or world-wide) area. Since U.S. and erstwhile Soviet intervention has declined or disappeared, regional conflicts will continue unless and until concert intervention takes place. The costs of local conflicts are usually low, at least at the beginning; the prospect of concert intervention greatly raises those costs. Thus, this chapter seeks to achieve two goals: the first is to outline the general conditions that must be met for a concert—an oligopoly of great powers—to function effectively; the second is to indicate how this concert might apply (or has historically applied) to the solution of regional conflict. We also hope to provide a conceptual guide to present and future concert intervention.

The Theory of International Concerts

The basic problem confronting any international concert mechanism is solving the collective-action problem. Why should any of the great powers join in a cooperative endeavor to reduce conflict in the international system? This is a particularly pertinent question when we recall that balance-of-power mechanisms confront the same problem and do not typically solve them (Rosecrance and Lo 1996). Indeed, "shirking" or "free riding," rather than cooperation, should be the typical outcome (Jervis 1988; Waltz 1979). One possible solution to this difficulty is through "hegemonic leadership," but some systems do not contain a hegemonic power, and those that do characteristically experience hegemonic decline (Krasner 1976). Yet it is too simple to conclude that cooperation cannot exist among more or less equal great powers. Both everyday experience and the literature tell us that it does. Eichengreen's recent works (1989, 1992), for example, inform us that even cooperation typically dubbed as "hegemonic" was actually far more "multilateral" in character. In addition, Snidal (1985), Schelling (1978), Margolis (1982), and North (1981) give useful examples of solutions to the collective-action problem in multiple-actor systems. Thus, our problem is not to debate whether such cooperation can take place. It is to explain the cooperation that actually exists (Rosecrance 1992a).

CONCERTS AS OLIGOPOLIES

Oligopolies, or cartels, succeed when there is considerable inelasticity of supply due to barriers to entry or some other factor, as, for example, the lack of viable substitutes (Fellner 1965; Samuelson 1976; Tirole 1988). Consequently, an oil cartel like OPEC may succeed when none of the member producers is tempted radically to violate its quota by increasing production. High prices can be maintained because the lack or relative expense of alternatives, such as oil substitutes or other forms of energy, keeps demand from falling. In analogous terms, security oligopolies (or concerts) succeed when the international system needs provision of underlying security and when there is no other group to provide it. Nonmembers of the concert (or the oligopoly) benefit because they can free ride on the security (price) provided by the member states (firms). For instance, Britain, Mexico, and Norway benefited from the higher oil price derived from the operations of OPEC, without having in any way to decrease their own production. In regional contexts where there is no local self-sufficiency in security (or military balance), smaller countries also gain from general concert involvement to create that balance or diminish conflict, possibly forming a regional concert linked to its international counterpart. In economics, oligopolies form where large firms can influence the price and where, through agreement (collusion), it is possible to raise the oligopoly price above the competitive price. In international relations, great powers are the greatest consumers of and beneficiaries from the creation of security as a public good. In the absence of minimal security more resources have to be devoted to military expenditure and less to domestic welfare or state returns. In the absence of oligopolistic cooperation, a balance-of-power system obtains, costing each of the great powers more money and involving a less favorable guns-butter trade-off. In the contemporary post–Cold War world, a concert system is in de facto operation, including the most important members of the European Union, Russia, China, Japan, and the United States. These states do not earn monopoly rents from other members of the system. Rather, they diminish security costs *for themselves* by cooperating. Security oligopolies maintain coherence when their members are not tempted to "free ride"—that is, when there is the danger that they might get considerably less security if they undermine concert cooperation. It is important to remember here that the breakdown of the concert instates a balance-of-power system in which security and balancing requirements are set at a much higher level than under a concert. Under the balance-of-power system, great powers have to "balance" against each other, not simply against small powers in regional contexts.

Oligopoly competitors can collude when they face "games of ruin" as the possible alternative. *Perfect* collusion takes place when firms reach agreements that are tantamount to merger. This cannot occur in international relations short of world government. *Negligible* collusion occurs when there is no cooperation among firms. This can have two consequences: (1) either profitable (harmonious) peace (Keohane 1984) or (2) games of ruin. In the former case profits might be higher than those achieved under perfect competition (but lower than monopoly prices) due to the existence of "quasi-agreements" on price (Fellner 1965). Under such agreements, unilateral lowering of price is avoided because it might initiate a price war. The second possible result is "games of ruin," in which oligopoly competitors seek to force one another out of the market. In international relations, the first consequence would suggest that major war would no longer occur (Kaysen 1990; Fukuyama 1989). The second result would indicate the opposite: major war could be risked (Van Evera 1984; Snyder and Diesing 1977).

Imperfect (or intermediate) collusion exists when cartels are formed to increase oligopoly profits and (incidentally) to benefit free riders (Olson and Zeckhauser 1966). In international relations the analogue is the formation of an international concert of great powers. This takes place when cooperation among a few major states reduces security problems both for the world and for the states themselves. In formal terms, they form a *k*-group (Schelling 1978; Snidal 1985; Rosecrance and Taw 1990). For an international cartel to meet the *robust* requirements of continuing to exist (as a *k*-group), the defection of one member must cause the whole group to receive a negative outcome. This, however, infrequently occurs. *Less strenuous* requirements would allow collusion (cooperation) to continue even though one or more members "cheated" or partially "defected." In this situation, such "cheating" would not automatically produce negative returns for the group as a whole. Technically speaking, an oligopoly that did not engage in "games of ruin" would still not approximate a "cartel" in which states/firms agree on production quotas of the security-good in question.

In the less strenuous situation, members would continue to cooperate even though they might obtain a higher return by free riding (moving to the NC, or noncooperation, line; see Fig. 7.1). Why? Douglass North (1981) contends that some form of shared "ideology" solves the collective-action problem, causing, for example, an individual to pay for an orange rather than steal it. In this instance, though some form of opportunity cost is incurred through restraint, ideology and group solidarity would make that payment worthwhile. The cost of cooperating in an existing order can be thought of as inversely related to the perceived legitimacy of its goals. As legitimacy rises, the advantage of free riding declines (North 1981). It is also important to remember that underlying agreement on goals (ideology) does not mean the absence of conflict among concert or cartel members. In the 1980s Iran and Iraq were able to cooperate to regulate production in OPEC even though they were simultaneously fighting each other in the Gulf.

In more precise terms, agreed ideological beliefs facilitate common expectations about behavior under conditions of uncertainty. Going one step further, cartels establish standards of price or quantity of production. Then they seek to enforce policies of transparency so that member violations can be speedily detected. Greater information also reduces the temptation to vio-

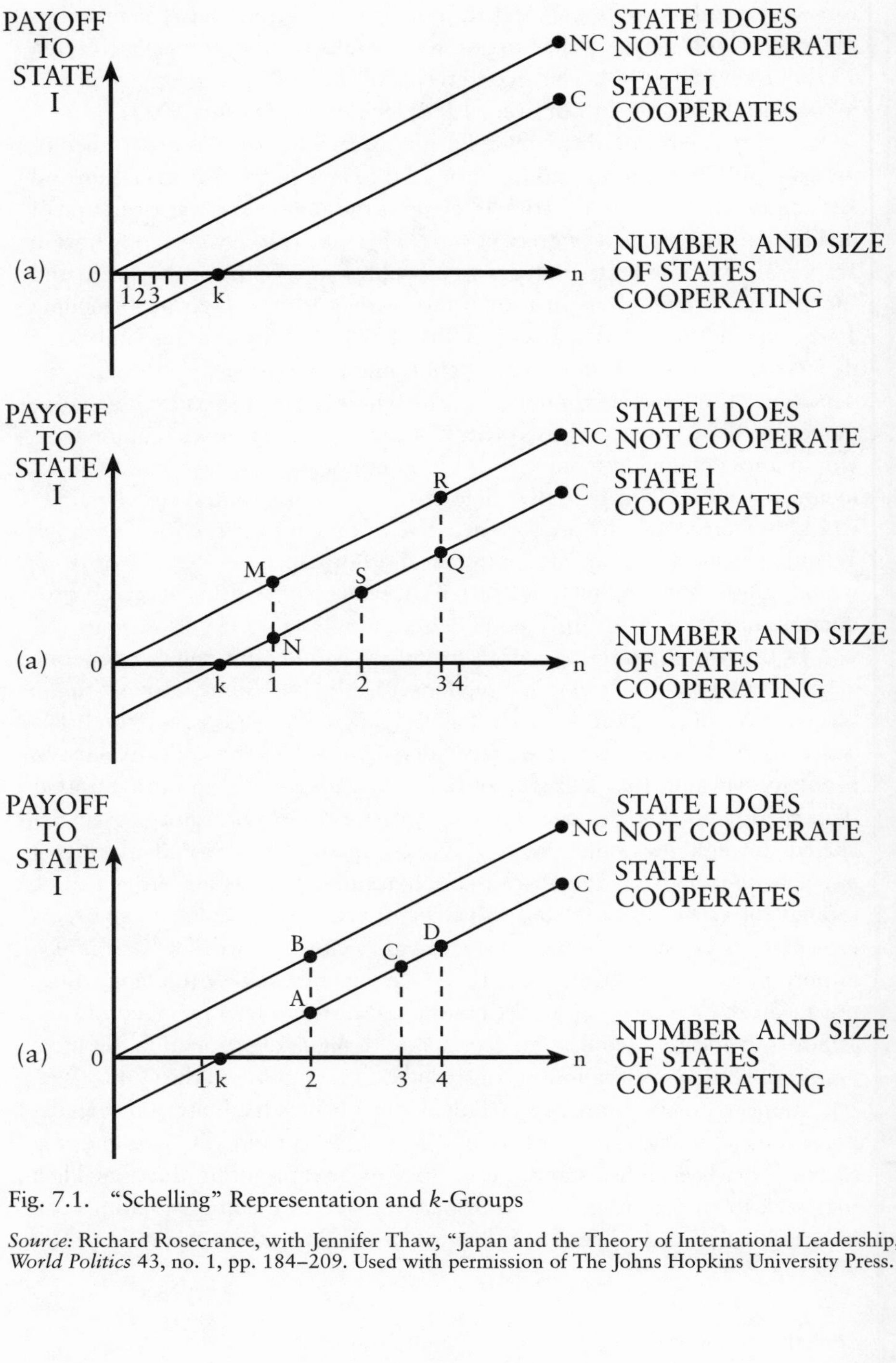

Fig. 7.1. "Schelling" Representation and *k*-Groups

Source: Richard Rosecrance, with Jennifer Thaw, "Japan and the Theory of International Leadership," *World Politics* 43, no. 1, pp. 184–209. Used with permission of The Johns Hopkins University Press.

late agreed standards of behavior and facilitates retaliation if violation occurs (Scherer 1980). In static analysis, oligopolistic firms often confront a "kinked demand curve" in that any increase in price reduces revenue, but any decrease in price also reduces revenue. The kinked demand curve, however, does not tell us how colluding firms arrive at their particular focal point. Dynamic analysis, however, also does not resolve this problem, because of the "Folk Theorem," which tells us that in iterated prisoner's-dilemma games with little discounting of future returns there is no ESS (evolutionary stable solution) (Friedman 1971, 1977; Fudenberg and Maskin 1986; Tsebelis 1990). An infinite number of points may each constitute an equilibrium. Ideology helps to center oligopolists or states upon particular salient equilibria and thereby makes collusion successful. Ideally, ideological accord also facilitates strategies of concert or cartel maintenance, such as punishing cheating through TFT or TTTFT methods (Lomborg 1996).

SHARED IDEOLOGY

Generally speaking, concerts do not meet the robust requirements of cooperation. A regional concert of Western powers continued to function after 1945–47, even though Russia and China had defected from the overall international arrangement.[1] In this instance there is little doubt that common ideology offered a cement to international cooperation. Furthermore, in the nineteenth century the Concert of Europe continued to operate on ideological agreement (albeit at a reduced level of effectiveness) even after England lessened her involvement in concert decisions and actions.

The Concert of Europe functioned most efficiently when its members were agreed on ideological goals as well as on the need to prevent war among their number. In such circumstances, while members might get more by "shirking" (thereby avoiding opportunity costs), ideological solidarity provided the necessary ingredient to induce cooperation (Margolis 1982). When both the fear of war and ideological agreement declined, however, the concert no longer operated powerfully, ratifying rather than controlling international outcomes. The fear of war declined when it was proved in the 1850s and 1860s that a major military clash between great powers no longer had disastrous social or political effects. Indeed, successful war could actually ce-

1. Strictly speaking, a Western concert preceded bipolar alliances in that it offered the Soviet Union membership (in the Marshall Plan) in 1947. When the Soviet Union refused, the regional concert became an alliance (NATO).

ment a shaky regime's hold on power. These changes undercut the agreement on international purposes that had sustained the concert mechanism since 1815 (Rosecrance 1992b).

FINANCIAL AGREEMENT

A variety of cements bind concert members together. Ideological agreement is the primary one, and when that collapses, the concert emerges in weakened or truncated form, if it continues to function at all. Nonetheless, in the nineteenth century, the concert could still meet (and occasionally resolve particular questions) after ideological divisions had surfaced. It solved the Russian-Turkish problem in 1878 and made some inroads in apportioning colonial real estate in Africa in 1884. One of the threads still knitting concert members together in those days was the continuance of financial ties among them. Of course, in an age of laissez-faire, this would not have great political significance for foreign-policy direction. Nonetheless, financial agreements were used to buttress political links between Russia and France after 1894, and as late as 1907 the British and German central banks continued to work closely together.

Financial relationships became much more important after economic issues had become central to government policy making in the twentieth century. In the contemporary world financial links are necessary to underpin political relationships. When the international financial system ruptured after World War I, allied solidarity vanished, the preexisting concert collapsed, and Germany was allowed to go her own way. As Beth Simmons (1993) shows, the Bank of International Settlements could not put Humpty Dumpty together again. When financial agreement falters, the last vestige of cooperation is lost, and the (international) political system cannot cohere. A broadly supported conclusion would thus be that financial ties were not *sufficient* to underpin the concert in the (laissez-faire) nineteenth century. Today, they may also not be *sufficient,* but they appear to be *necessary.* This is because financial ties among states buttress ideology in a way they did not do in the nineteenth century. In the nineteenth century, financial ties frequently cross-cut ideologies; today they reinforce and sustain liberal, capitalist, and democratic notions.[2]

2. Some will question the importance of financial links. Today, we mean, particularly, foreign direct investment in each other's economies by great powers. This means that local production depends upon close ties with other economic units. It also means that countries cannot easily withdraw from production interdependence. They can much more easily withdraw from trade interdependence.

CONCERTS AND THE BALANCE OF POWER

Some will now be saying that since the requirements for maintaining a concert system are so demanding, why not let the system relapse into the traditional balance of power? Many believe that the "balance of power" is the only critical international constituent structure—that balances of power have an intrinsic tendency to form (Waltz 1979). Hedley Bull (1977) thought that "balance" was an essential element in creating and maintaining "international order." Kenneth Waltz (1979) believed that international theory ultimately revolved around the balance of power. Many historians of international relations devote most, if not all, of their attention to shifts in the international balance of power (Dehio 1962; Hinsley 1963).

There are two reasons for seeking to avoid the excesses of a balance-of-power system. First, because of public-goods problems, balances of power frequently fail to form or take place too late to avoid war. The nineteenth century is largely a period of missed balancing opportunities—whether directed against Napoleon or Bismarck (Schroeder 1995). Before World War I, a balance of power did begin to form, but it solidified too late to prevent conflict. The British did not declare themselves until 29 July, when it was already too late to stop the Austro-German steamroller. In 1939 the same pattern transpired: Hitler thought that England would stay out of the conflict, since the British could not prevent the German invasion and occupation of Poland. In these cases the balance of power was the proximate occasion of war, not its preventative. Only after World War II did the balance of power begin to have greater effectiveness, but this was partly because of the high degree of ideological conflict between antagonists, in addition to the constraining effect of nuclear weapons on both sides.

A second disadvantage of the balance of power, as noted above, is its high opportunity costs. By definition, the balance of power is likely to operate against another great power; "balancing" then must involve formidable rearmament to contain that state. A great power is a state that cannot certainly be defeated even by a combination of others. In these circumstances, expensive rearmament and balancing operations are likely to come at the cost of economic growth.

Of course, it is also true that concerts depend upon a solution to the collective-action problem, and that is why a degree of ideological unity is prerequisite to concert action. A balance of power comes into being when that unity is lost. In a concert, therefore, it is even harder to solve collective-action problems unless, fortuitously, the threatened aggressor is on one side of the ideological divide and the balancers are on the other. In the Napoleonic case even this advantage was not sufficient to bring reliable balancing (Rosecrance and Lo 1996).

Central Concerts and Regional Concerts

The same incentive that produces central concerts (i.e., the desire to save on security costs) also gives rise to regional concerts. In the contemporary world there is an expanding European concert, centered on the European Union, its members and associates, that offers a degree of cooperative security to Western and central and in limited fashion also Eastern Europe.[3] It has not been able to defuse the conflicts in Bosnia. On the other hand, by holding out membership in EU only to democratic, stable, and economically open states, the European concert provides incentives for feuding ethnic nations to resolve their own disputes.

In the Far East, there is an informal regional concert composed of Russia, China, the United States, and Japan to solve conflicts in the East Asian region (Shirk, this volume). This concert has had to deal with disputes over North Korean nuclear capabilities. There is, however, no single ideological basis for concert agreement, save, among its Asian participants, some acknowledgment of common Buddhist and Confucian cultural standards. The more China and Russia are brought into the Western international trading system, however, the more likely they are to respond to world problems and trouble spots in ways similar to Japan and the United States.

It is premature to speak of regional agreements or concerts in the Middle East (Pervin, this volume). In Latin America small groupings within the Organization of American States have helped to defuse conflicts in Nicaragua and El Salvador. But low-level militarized disputes have continued among ostensibly democratic polities. Since the Chaco War between Latin America's two poorest states, Paraguay and Bolivia, however, none of these have been sustained wars of attrition, inflicting many casualties (Mares, this volume). The U.S. role in Latin America, increased by the likely further expansion of NAFTA, makes a relationship of more or less equal powers seem unlikely, but the relationship may continue as a hegemonic concert. In South Asia, for

3. We therefore disagree strongly with Patrick Morgan and Paul Papayoanou, who believe that today's European system is a full-fledged collective security system. It is not. The system is run by great powers: France, Britain, Germany, and one or two other key states.

similar reasons, Indian preponderance seems to make an egalitarian concert less possible, and a near-hegemonic system has emerged. In sub-Saharan Africa the OAU (Organization of African Unity) admits conflicts *within* states but has been remarkable in limiting the number of important conflicts *between* states (Keller, this volume).

There is an intimate relationship between regional and central concerts. Even with regional concerts in place, regions may not enjoy a self-sufficiency in security. The strictly European concert cannot handle conflicts in Bosnia without the participation of NATO and the United States. There is no self-sufficiency of security in the Middle East, which must call upon Russia and the United States from the central world concert to help to create it. It is difficult to imagine the Asian members of a Far Eastern concert (Japan, China, and Russia) containing military conflicts in Northeast or Southeast Asia without the presence and/or participation of the U.S. fleet and American ground troops.

In practice there could be some conflict between central and regional concerts. Local concerts might reach one agreement in their own area and then find that the central concert did not agree with their disposition of the dispute. As always in world politics, an international concert of great powers trumps a purely regional concert. A purely Arab concert (like the failed Arab League) in the Middle East could in the past agree to exclude Israel from Middle East peace efforts, but this only had the effect of stimulating the United States to bulwark the Israeli position, leading to an Arab-Israeli agreement that perhaps in time could include Syria and Lebanon as well as Egypt, Jordan, and Israel. In Latin America, the countries of the region could reach one conclusion only to have it nullified by the United States, but increasing closeness of economic relationships in the Western Hemisphere make this unlikely. Indian preeminence in South Asia might have to be counterbalanced by the influence of a central concert to achieve stability between India and a weaker Pakistan.

The central concert now reduces security costs and spreads them among concert members. Any effective regional concert's disposition of security tasks—reducing the need for central-concert intervention—*is* welcomed by the latter. Only if the regional resolution explicitly violated the principles underlying the cooperative agreement of the central concert itself would this not be true. Then a conflict between regional and central concerts could emerge. This, however, seems progressively unlikely given the gradual spread of liberalizing (if not democratic) tendencies (Solingen, this volume) conjoined with the world concert's desire to economize on both military effort and cost. The existence of an international concert today, formalized in the P-5 of the UN Security Council (with the addition of Germany and Japan), makes regional conflict both less likely and less dangerous than in the past.

The Practice of International Concerts

International concerts failed when (with the collapse of ideological agreement) "land" became or remained the most valued factor of production. "Land," an immobile factor, could easily be seized and, until the mobilization of underlying populations in the twentieth century, administered by an aggressor nation. In this sense it was not until the "rise of the trading state" in the late twentieth century that nations collectively became aware that mobile factors of production—capital, labor, and information—were more important (with certain exceptions) than land (Rosecrance 1986). After the 1970s, resource shortages no longer served to dominate international relations or domestic politics, and the ownership of "land" became less important. Raw material and commodity prices declined relative to industrial prices.[4] Countries now court multinational corporations because an increased rate of growth and employment will improve the lot of the domestic public (Strange 1992). The attraction of mobile factors of production into one's national economy has become more important than seizing new immobile factors. Because of the growing relaxation of capital controls, countries can plumb labor and capital markets in other nations (Wood 1994).

In the nineteenth century the international economy linking nations did not determine their international policies, because diplomacy and economics were conducted in different compartments. Because of growing laissez-faire, what individual investors and central banks did produced little or no impact upon political chancelleries. Indeed, the private sector often acted with little regard for political consequences. In the early 1900s, for example, British underwriters insured German ships against wartime losses, even if these were inflicted by the Royal Navy (Kennedy 1981). Thus, up until World War I, European bankers, insurers, acceptance houses, and investors formed a tightly knit fraternity. As a result, though the United Kingdom could benefit from German financial aid in 1907, this did not improve the political tenor

4. There has been a secular decline in real commodity prices since 1957 (Reinhart and Wickham 1994).

of Anglo-German relations. In the nineteenth century, therefore, there was no connection between economics and security.

After World War I the nineteenth-century separation between finance and political strategy vanished. The period of laissez-faire was over, and security and economics became intimately intertwined. Despite the large loans that America provided to Weimar Germany under the Dawes Plan, the reparations problem was never solved. Owing to French opposition, the total reparations bill was never scaled down to an amount liberal Germany could conceivably pay (Simmons 1993; Douglas 1977; Eichengreen 1992). France, because of its opposition to Berlin's foreign policies, refused to cooperate in economically refloating Germany.

Not until 1947–48 did a true international concert again emerge as a possibility. Security governance (the North Atlantic Treaty or the intention to form a security alliance) was associated with the success of the Marshall Plan. In 1947–48 a Western regional concert of nations formed, though it did not govern the Soviet sphere. The requisite political and economic constituents of cooperation were present only among Western nations. In that period, states and private investors desperately needed an overall climate of security to begin to take business risks (Gilpin 1970). The converse was also true. Unless concerts had the underpinning of financial and economic agreement, they were unlikely to last. In somewhat similar ways, Lane (1979) underscores the link between state protection for merchants and the growth of the world economy from medieval to modern times. Investors aim at long-run returns, but they remain paralyzed if there is an uncertain political and international climate.

A derivative but important question today is whether Russia can be refloated. In certain financial respects contemporary Russia equals Germany in the 1920s. Investment in Russia is now being held up as it was in Germany in 1927–31 or in France and Italy in 1946–47. Entrepreneurs do not see the long-term outcome, and retrograde Communists and the Mafia flourish.

Conclusions from Past Practice

Rivalry can and does emerge among previously united concert members. Some rivalry is to be expected, however, as occurs among oligopolists. Oligopolies collude with respect to one variable (quantity). Concerts collude with respect to one variable (military security). This may permit competition in respect to another variable (advertising in the one case or international trade in the other). Competition in these other realms could, of course, become more intense.

The resurgence of separate national interests may undermine shared ideology. The creation of major, exclusive alliances undermines concert viability. When the Triple Alliance was countered by the Triple Entente, the *multilateral* concert could not control outcomes. Today, if NATO continues to expand without offering a link to Moscow, there could be a long-term impediment to general concert cooperation.

Concerts also succeed when they pursue realistic goals. There is the problem of trying to do too much as well as the problem of trying to do too little. *Too little:* If there is no intervention, nations conclude that the concert is not controlling events. Outcomes may emerge that all (or most) concert members would deplore (e.g., revolution in the 1840s). Too little intervention emanates from too little cooperation and the inability of a *k*-group to form.

Too much: The OPEC cartel initially tried to control too drastically the production of its members—allowing no cheating. Saudi Arabia sought to deal with violators by suddenly and punitively increasing its own production, thereby decreasing the world oil price. But with the rise in industrial prices, this strategy turned out to be too ambitious; even the Saudis had to cheat occasionally to keep their balance of payments in line. In like manner, concerts cannot aim at unrealistically high levels of security. The concert cannot intervene in all local conflicts, and the Concert of Europe propitiously declined to intervene in the Greek revolt in the 1820s—though it did seek to keep Russia from intervening on behalf of the Greeks. Equally, the concert could not intervene to overturn the revolutions of 1848, though Russia put down the revolution in Hungary in 1849. Seeking to intervene in each case of domestic change, the concert risks failure. The present-day concert did not intervene in Liberia, Angola, Mozambique, Tajikistan, the southern Sudan, Portuguese Timor, Tibet, or other places. Perhaps it should not have been involved in Somalia.

It is important to remember here that while cooperation provides a *k*-group-style return, it does not produce the highest individual payoff (movement to the NC line). This is why ideological agreement is still necessary—to find other values in the situation: solidarity and participation (Orbell, Dawes, and van de Kragt 1990). Concerts do need to intervene in salient cases where the general tenor of international cooperation in the system as a whole will be affected if they do not do so—specifically, where unimpeded local conflicts are likely to escalate, with regionwide or global consequences. A regional concert might be able to handle these, at least in the first instance. Where escalation is not likely, or where it is contained by regional force, the central concert does not need to be involved. In addition, as we shall see later, the cost of intervention must be compared to the benefit derived. An extremely high cost can cancel even a substantial prospective benefit. The United Nations, for example, has intervened in so many situations ineffectually that some major powers, including the United States, have not paid their peacekeeping assessments. The concert, patterning future action after the success of the Gulf War, does not want to make a similar mistake. When the concert does intervene militarily, it wants to intervene crushingly. But concert intervention need not be military. Diplomatic pressure or economic sanctions may suffice.

An economy of interventionist actions smoothes the path of agreement among concert members and softens the impact upon their domestic populations. The concert can then maintain its ascendancy and also provide payoffs to concert leaders, which may be very important in domestic politics. But if the concert intervenes everywhere, it garners few additional benefits and incurs much higher costs. The result is analogous to insisting upon too onerous production cutbacks for OPEC members. The efficient operation of regional concerts may make a great difference here.

The balance between extremes is sketched in domestic affairs by Howard Margolis (1982). Individuals as well as nations may have group, as well as selfish, utility functions. Under the conditions of Margolis's model, individuals and nations may seek individual interests, but moderate their selfish goals to serve group interests on some occasions. Realists would accept few examples of this behavior. But it is interesting to note that Japan and Germany, once known as leading free riders in security matters, are now seeking to join the great-power political club: the permanent membership of the United Nations Security Council. To do so, they must help underwrite security operations by other concert members that they may not entirely support. They did so in the Gulf War, which actually led to a brief U.S. current-account surplus. Not to participate and pay the costs was to indicate that one was not qualified to be a full concert member.

To sum up, concerts succeed when

1. fundamental agreement continues;
2. there are no exclusive alliances;

3. they do not attempt too much;
4. financial links obtain between parties.

When the obverse is true, concerts fail.

The Present Practice of International Concerts

A number of guidelines for present practice may be advanced. As opposed to the balance of power, a concert mechanism offers a cost-effective solution to many conflicts. It does not follow, however, that the concert should intervene everywhere. As one notices with the record of United Nations peacekeeping, intervention alone is not enough. The UN has troops in many places but has found solutions only in a few.

COST-EFFECTIVENESS

The goal of concert intervention is to end conflict and integrate the previous combatants into the world economy. This is not a simple task. It certainly cannot be attempted in a vast range of cases. Thus the underlying factor of cost-effectiveness is useful in judging potential interventions. Achievement of this objective is assisted by the centripetal effect of the world economic mechanism. The fundamental difference between the nineteenth- and late-twentieth-century economies is that industrial self-sufficiency is no longer a possibility. In the nineteenth century, "latecomers" could expect to match or exceed the record of the "first industrial nation." They could buy the latest technology and industrial practice off the shelf, confident that they could gain economic equality or superiority even if they then cut themselves off from the world economy by imposing high tariffs. This degree of certainty no longer exists. Today early pioneers reinvest to cancel or overcome the gains of latecomers. Nations that "de-couple" themselves from the world economy after a few key industrial investments now risk obsolescence. Nations must be involved in all major markets and in all realms of technology if they expect to keep up.

The new argument for strategic trade and "increasing returns" augments this point. It is now possible to create "comparative advantages" where they did not naturally exist. By making key initial investments in new sectors of technology, countries can create and multiply their competitiveness. They need continually to reinvest and to sell abroad to keep those advantages (Krugman 1991). In this way, the world economy retains a strong centralizing effect: to be cut off is to wither and die.

This phenomenon was first understood by the major powers, even by Russia and China. It is now coming to be recognized by regional states like Israel and the Arab nations. The most basic fact animating peace between Israel and her neighbors, including the Palestinians, is opportunity costs. What have Middle Eastern nations given up in four major wars, 1967 to the present, compared with the gains of East Asia, Latin America, and northern Europe? Thus the cost-benefit criterion must place as much emphasis upon "benefit" as "cost." Great-power intervention to limit regional conflict can be less costly and more successful if the parties themselves recognize what their regional wars have sacrificed in terms of lost benefit.

In this sense, international relations is less anarchic than has sometimes been assumed. For some, the end of the Cold War was an apparent invitation to let the conflictual flowers bloom in region after region. Local conflict could regain its ascendancy and ultimately preponderate over the distortions of the past bipolar struggle. Yet, as regions have sought to gain the advantages of First World economic growth through trade with Western countries, they have begun to recognize that unremitting local conflicts hurt not only individual countries but regions as well (Solingen, this volume). The lesson is clearest in the Middle East, but it could take hold in Southeast Asia (Vietnam and Cambodia), Eastern Europe (Croatia and Slovenia), and perhaps even in India, Pakistan, and Sri Lanka. The net result of the spreading international economy is that concert involvement is easier than it might otherwise have been. Such factors also favor the development of regional concerts. Costs could lower as benefits increase. There will, however, always be areas, like Rwanda or the southern Sudan, where tribal and ethnic hatreds prevent nations from taking advantage of their economic possibilities.

REGIONAL SELF-SUFFICIENCY

Second, interventions can be tempered or avoided if a region is self-sufficient in terms of security. Some regions do not need the equilibrating effect of outside intervention. Self-sufficiency means that through regional concert, balance of power, or multilateral security arrangements, security questions can be handled locally. This seems to be true in parts of Asia, Africa, and Latin

America.[5] Security issues may arise, but they can either be coped with or ignored by local powers. The past struggle in Angola no longer spills over into the South African conflict; it does not constitute an issue for the great powers, and Africa ignores it. The Sudanese civil war lingers on, but it has not engaged the interest of major powers. Settlements will probably take place in Mozambique, and possibly in Angola, as they have already done in South Africa. The Liberian conflict simmers, but it is not clear that outside intervention could be more successful there than it was in Somalia. The Rwanda-Burundi conflict between Hutu and Tutsi could break out again. In this case intervention by the OAU would not have been sufficient to deal with the conflict. In this way, African conflicts could spill over and produce regional or global effects. Still, it is appropriate to hazard the judgment that despite widespread human misery in the subcontinent, Africa is relatively more self-sufficient in security (that is, able to contain the effects of one conflict leading to another) than most other continents.

There will, however, be a continuing need for great-power intervention in regions that do not attain self-sufficiency in security: the Middle East is a characteristic example. Since the Middle East disputants have depended upon an arms supply furnished by outside powers, that supply has to be collectively regulated or turned off. Equally, a supply of economic aid has to be collectively turned on to reach lasting agreement. Under outside pressures, Jordan has reached a settlement with Israel. Syria temporarily abstains, but if it delays too long, it risks losing potential economic and security gains. It is not clear what will happen to Iraq. Saddam Hussein has not been fundamentally weakened, but he remains ostracized by the international community.

EXISTENCE OF A REGIONAL PROTÉGÉ

Another factor of importance is whether great powers have a protégé in the region. If so, they cannot fully stand aside; Russian support of Serbia is one example of this phenomenon. In like and opposite fashion, the United States cannot dissociate itself from Israel, nor, probably, can Russia completely sever its ties with Iraq and Syria. Under traditional bipolarity, this meant that Middle East settlements were impossible. Today they are possible because of

5. Though humanitarian interventions in Africa may be more necessary in the future than they have been in the past.

the link between the United States and Russia. Russia may not actively promote a settlement but, unlike in the past, it does not resolutely oppose it.

TIMING OF INTERVENTION

The general rule is never to intervene in a defense-dominant situation (Posen 1993). This seems to indicate that intervention is timely *before* the parties have fully armed themselves and fashioned strong defense lines. In a narrow sense, offense dominance versus defense dominance refers to the respective advantages conferred by the weapons technology possessed on both sides. More broadly, it also includes the fortifications, terrain, and force imbalances that they have been able to accrue or to take advantage of before the conflict begins. If the offensive appeared dominant before 1914, it was because rapid mobilization facilitated by railway timetables allowed one power to amass a decisive superiority in the very first battles. The same is true in charting concert intervention in the contemporary age. Before Serbian troops poured into Bosnia and Croatia, rapid foreign intervention might have succeeded, because it did not confront a negative force imbalance. Of course, the difficult mountain terrain in Bosnia, strengthening the defense, would always have complicated intervention. Hence, to avoid defense dominance, early intervention is preferable.

It is also possible *after* several rounds of war, when the parties are tired of fighting and are ready to accept compromise. In this phase, even effective defense forces may be so worn down that they will be vulnerable to a sudden infusion of interventionist troops. It is most unpropitious in the *intermediate* phase, when the conflict and the cost of intervening are at their height (Fig. 7.2). Foreign intervention may then draw antagonists to oppose the interventionists rather than each other, as occurred in Somalia. The United States administration has held back from Bosnia because it missed phase I. It has now (with NATO) intervened in phase III.

This presentation assumes, of course, that countries can more or less tell when the "first" and "third" phases have arrived. They may not be able to do so. The result depends upon good intelligence, on gauging enemy morale, and on the enemy's likely supply of weapons. In Vietnam, the United States never found an appropriate time to intervene in the conflict between the South and the North, because its intelligence was lacking and because it could not interdict supply from Russia and China. Periodically it concluded, erroneously, that Vietcong morale was collapsing. It also relied, incorrectly,

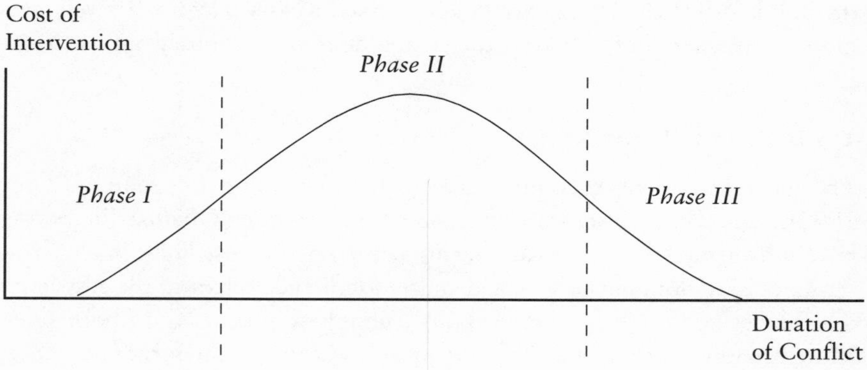

Fig. 7.2. Cost of intervention versus duration of conflict

on Soviet restraint in supplying Hanoi. The terrain in Vietnam always favored the defense, unless there was a very substantial advantage in intervening numbers, perhaps ten or more to one. In Afghanistan, on the other hand, the United States turned the tables in supplying arms to the Mujahideen, who had both the necessary morale and numbers to prevent the Soviets from gaining victory.

Unfortunately, this proper timing may be inverse to that proposed by domestic politics and the media. While public opinion may not be ready for early intervention, it may clamor for involvement at the most difficult (intermediate) time (Fig. 7.3). When the time ripens for intervention later, the public may have lost interest. Only strong foreign-policy leadership on the part of domestic elites can square the circle and educate the public on this complicated matter. This dilemma may encapsulate the difficulties the Clinton administration faced between 1993 and 1995.

THE PHASING OF INTERVENTION

Phase I: Offense-Dominant Phase

The combined problem is illustrated by Somalia. If the United States and the United Nations had insisted on disarming the Somali clan leaders in the early days of intervention, they might have succeeded. Equally, if the United Nations had sent large forces into Bosnia at the time of Slovenian independence, such vigorous action might have deterred the Serb offensive. This notion may also have applications in finance. If the great powers had been will-

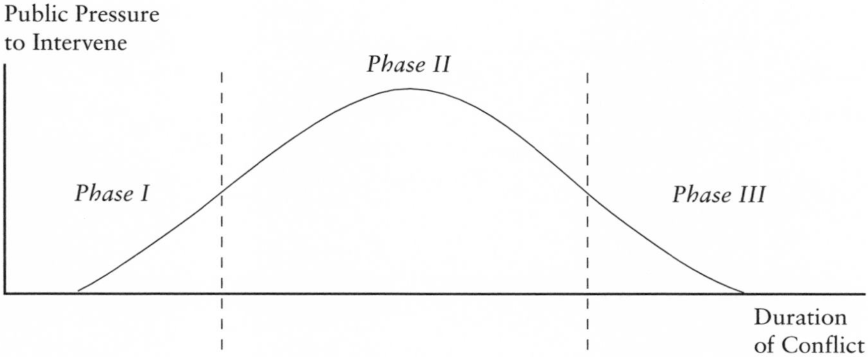

Fig. 7.3. Public pressure to intervene versus duration of conflict

ing to deal with the reparations issue in 1927–29, a solution might have been possible before financial collapse. But no such strategy was attempted. The problem in each of these cases, of course, was that such actions were considerably in advance of those mandated by public opinion.

Phase II: Defense-Dominant Phase

In the second, defense-dominant phase, United Nations peacekeepers are likely to be stationed in the area of conflict, impeding offensive action. Peacekeeping in this way may vitiate peacemaking. Peacemaking requires clearing off the bureaucratic and theater decks. It seems unlikely that the United States could have invaded Iraq if UN peacekeepers had been there in force on the ground. In this second phase the regional conflict is proceeding full tilt. It will not yield to anything but a massive intervention. This is the time, paradoxically, in which domestic publics call for action. The success of the Gulf War may have been fortuitous in this respect. As in Afghanistan, at this phase the concert may seek to provide covert aid to one of the parties to produce a military stalemate. Military equipment was covertly shipped to the Bosnian Muslims as governments held back from deeper involvement.

Phase III: Offense-Dominant Phase

The best phase for intervention (having missed early opportunities) is late in the game, when the parties are weary and when it is by no means certain who will win and where. The first flush of offensive gains has now worn off. If a stalemate has emerged or might emerge, the parties will be more compliant and less resistant to foreign military intervention. Further, while massive troop commitments might have been required at phase II, the threat of air strikes may be sufficient in phase III. As domestic publics begin to see this possibility, they (while initially resisting any new commitments) may be willing to accept limited intervention.

Global and Regional Interactions

The cost-benefit outcome of concert intervention in different regional contexts, as we have seen, depends upon the degree of security self-sufficiency each region possesses. The most self-sufficient regions will have no local conflicts or will operate regional concerts to defuse those that exist. The incentive to form concerts on the regional level does not exist at the global level. Regions may wish to be free of global intervention, and thus the public-goods problem could in theory be more easily solved at regional than at global levels. In Latin America the concert is partly hegemonic, with the United States at the helm as a major integrating force. In the former Soviet Union, Russia will be the regional concert leader as the Commonwealth of Independent States develops into a more cohesive grouping. The ASEAN concert has been important in defusing conflicts in Southeast Asia, but in East Asia as a whole the appropriate concert is that of four great powers: China, Japan, Russia, and the United States. In Europe the growing diplomatic and political unity of the European Union—as it grows to embrace former Eastern European as well as northern European countries—constitutes an effective European concert of powers. NATO adds America to this arrangement in the political-military field. Regional concerts are not yet possible in the Middle East, where the Arab League has broken down, or in South Asia. In Africa, they will remain at best inchoate unless or until the Organization for African Unity gains greater strength.

If regional concerts are not in place, a global concert faces the difficulty presented by regional bipolar or multipolar conflict and the operation of balance-of-power systems. In Southeast Asia, it took the great powers, China, Japan, Russia, and the United States, to moderate the conflict between

Vietnam and the Khmer Rouge. The same intervention may ultimately be required in South Asia, where the former Russian client India faces the former U.S. ally, Pakistan. Yet it is possible that India and Pakistan, for all of their differences in Kashmir and the Sind, may decide to reach a regional agreement in preference to outside concert intervention. Though it is very unlikely, the same sort of outcome is ultimately conceivable between North and South Korea, who may in time come to resent agreements among China, Japan, Russia, and the United States that may seem to be won at their expense. As long as the United States, South Korea, and Japan are offering important economic and technological benefits to Pyongyang, this phase may not occur. Very occasionally, however, local conflicts could be reduced because of the prospect of outside intervention.

Conclusions and Present Implications

SPECIFIC CONTEXTS

As we have seen, concerts need to focus on areas where there is no self-sufficiency of security. In a number of regional cases the parties will not necessarily vie to a stalemate. The creation of a stalemate depends upon outside powers and a degree of concert intervention. In the Middle East, this suggests regulation of further armaments, as well as the provision of economic incentives, leading toward a settlement. Such measures have been used to press the Bosnian contenders toward peace. Somewhat similar incentives will be used with North Korea to prevent it from developing its fledgling nuclear status. Pakistan will be treated differently from North Korea because it is not part of the IAEA (International Atomic Energy Agency) regime and faces intransigent opposition from a militarily more powerful and already nuclear India. If New Delhi does not give up nuclear weapons, it is difficult to argue that Pakistan should do so. In the North Korean case, however, South Korea has already renounced weapons and abandoned its nuclear program. American nuclear weapons have been removed. Japan will not go nuclear unless Pyongyang proves intransigent. The key here is denuclearizing North Korea by carrot rather than stick. It appears that China and Russia will cooperate in this task.

In the former Yugoslavia the best that can be hoped for is an uneasy federation between the Muslims and the Croats, with the Serbs retaining their extended position. In Kosovo province and Macedonia (still in phase I) the West has staked its prestige on halting Serbian designs and maintaining the autonomy of one area and the independence of the other.

THE GENERAL CONTEXT

The critical difference between concert practice in the nineteenth century and that today is the now far more important role of the international economy in political calculations. The countries that yield to concert pressures do so in part because they believe that agreement will open a cornucopia of economic possibilities. This is the rule that even Vietnam has followed. It will be very important in the Middle East and Northeast Asia. In time it could even have some relevance in Sarajevo, Zagreb, and Belgrade.

But the economic context is important not only for smaller states. The chief motivator keeping China and to some degree Russia on track as concert members is access to the Western, and now world, economy. This was never an issue in the nineteenth century, and for two reasons: (1) because all major European powers were already participants and (2) because economic levers were seldom or never used (in an age of laissez-faire) to achieve political objectives. In selling in the United States' market today, or borrowing money from the IMF, however, foreign countries enjoy a privilege, not a right. That access depends upon good behavior. The economic and security systems are today unified in ways that were never true in the nineteenth or early twentieth century. There were no economic costs to Britain's abstention from, or Germany's violation of, concert mandates. Today there are powerful economic restraints against similar policies, and that is what gives the concert an impetus it could not have in previous periods.

Finally, in market terms oligopolies (by narrowing the range of competition) effectively earn rents from consumers. It is less clear that diplomatic concerts of powers obtain a similar return. Of course, great powers are always the major beneficiaries of the systems they head, and would be the first affected by any major disruption of those systems. Their own trade, economic development, and placid pursuit of their livelihoods would be disturbed by huge political upheavals on the fringes of the system. Along with ideological agreement, this is the reason for the great powers' willingness to cooperate in solving the public-goods problems that confront them. On the other hand, unlike economic cartels, concerts make important contributions to the welfare of others, not only to themselves. They perform actions that most small powers would be incapable of or unwilling to undertake. They garner benefits from so doing, but they also provide benefits to free riders. So long as the concert continues, it prevents aggression by its own members and in addition disapproves actions by small aggressive states.

8

Matters of Multilateralism: Implications for Regional Conflict Management

Brian L. Job

This chapter addresses the role of multilateralism within the evolving post–Cold War international security order, focusing upon the potential for multilateralist forms of interstate behavior in the management of regional conflict. Whereas other chapters assess the prospects for specific forms of conflict management, for example, concert mechanisms or collective security mechanisms, or focus upon the recent conflict-related experiences of actors in particular geographic regions, this chapter proceeds with a more general and abstract mandate.

Earlier versions of these arguments were presented in a paper of the same title delivered to the 1994 annual meeting of the American Political Science Association, Chicago, and at Queen's University, Kingston, Canada, at the conference "Multilateralism and Regional Security," May 1995. This research was supported by grants to the Institute of International Relations at the University of British Columbia through its Military and Strategic Studies Program and the Co-operative Security Competition Program. The author acknowledges the able assistance of Brian Bow and Annwen Rowe-Evans. The opinions expressed in this chapter are the author's alone, as is responsibility for any errors or omissions.

The line of argument below advances in three stages. The first involves a consideration of the general definition of multilateralism and its defining features as a distinctive mode of state behavior, along with a subsequent examination of the varying nature and quality of multilateralism involved in Morgan's typology of the different forms, or prototypes, of orders (this volume). The second entails an analysis of the patterns of divergent security interests that might arise within any given regional security complex, and the conflicting incentives of various types of regional players to participate, or not participate, in multilateral and multilateralist mechanisms for conflict management. This establishes the groundwork for the third and final stage, which begins by drawing attention to the characteristics of contemporary regional conflict. It then assesses the capacities of existing regional security institutions to cope effectively with such conflicts—in the short term, through conflict-management strategies, and in the longer term, through community-building processes that mitigate the occurrence of conflict.

The examination below leads to quite mixed conclusions about the prospects for multilateralism in regional contexts. Regional dynamics in the post–Cold War order have proved to be especially complex and highly variable from one context to the next. The lifting of what Buzan (1992, 79) has termed the Cold War "overlay" of superpower influence upon regional security complexes has not led, in overall terms, to brightened prospects for the diminution of regional conflict or for effective multilateralist, collective security arrangements, at least in the short term. As discussed below, regional multilateralist institutions are proving largely incapable of addressing the conceptual and practical issues that must be confronted in contemporary, deadly, regional conflicts. The greatest majority of these are intrastate disputes among communal factions contesting for control of governance in what have come to be termed "weak" or "failing" states. The nature of the parties involved, the tactics employed, the issues at stake are all not amenable to the traditional post–World War II modes of dispute mediation and peacekeeping undertaken by the UN and regional organizations. However, while the immediate prognosis is not optimistic, the longer-term picture may be becoming brighter, with the evolution of multilateralism through the nurturing of common identities and norms of intraregional relations that, in turn, will enhance the development of regional pluralistic security communities. In Western Europe and the Americas such trends have been under way for some time; in other regional contexts such as Southeast Asia, they have gained momentum with political and economic transformations occurring since the late 1980s.

Multilateralism

GENERAL CONSIDERATIONS

There are two senses in which the terms "multilateral," "multilateralist," and "multilateralism" can be applied to state behavior. It is important to differentiate between them. The first is as a nominal, or quantitative, descriptor; that is, the term "multilater*al*" used as an adjective to refer to instances of coordinating national policies or behaviors by groups of three or more states. Multilater*al* activities would therefore be distinguished from unilateral or bilateral actions, essentially on the basis of the number of actors engaged.

The term "multilateral*ism*," on the other hand, has come to be used to distinguish the character or qualities of the behavior of coordination among states. In this qualitative sense, multilateralism is a form of state practice that accords with certain principles and that involves the development of norms, collective identities, and institutions (formal and informal) concerning cooperation and conflict management over extended periods of time.

This second notion derives from the work of scholars, such as John Ruggie (1993), who view multilateralism as a "generic institutional form of modern international life"—one that states demonstrate only when their attitudes and behaviors sustain three key principles: *nondiscrimination, indivisibility,* and *diffuse reciprocity*. The first, nondiscrimination, signifies that states perform their agreed-upon behaviors or satisfy their obligations without any contingencies or particularistic qualifications based on which states are involved. The most commonly cited example of nondiscrimination is the obligation of states to extend MFN (most-favored-nation) status to all other states in the GATT/WTO trading regime. In security relations, nondiscriminatory behavior entails that the members of a collective agree to treat each other in identical fashion by offering the same security guarantee to all members. Thus, in an alliance, all members would have to agree to commit to the defense of each and every other member that might be threatened or attacked by nonmembers. Indivisibility refers to the understanding among the cooperating states that critical conditions or premises that define the nature or purpose of the group or institution in question be treated in equivalent fashion by and for all members. Thus, in a security institution, the nature of the "peace" or the character of "aggression," for example, should be viewed (*a*) in similar terms by all members and (*b*) as applying equally to all members. In an alliance or collective security institution, the notion of peace should be inviolate, in that a breach affecting one member is seen as a violation of all others. (Thus, for instance, the failure of the League of Nations to act in response to aggression against a member contradicted the principle of indivisibility.) Continuity is the essential third characteristic. Single-shot, or even episodic, instances of interstate coalition behavior, while multilateral activities, do not necessarily demonstrate multilateralism. Instead, collective action has to range over an extended time period and, in doing so, come to be predicated upon, and become the basis for, anticipations about the longer-term functioning of the collective. In other words, participating states extend their shadow of the future beyond the immediate and short run. They provide benefits and undergo costs on behalf of other members at one time, feeling assured that equivalent benefits will be extended to them as necessary in the future. Such an environment exhibits what Keohane (1990) refers to as diffuse reciprocity.

Some scholars, including Ruggie (1993, 8), go a step further to ascribe generative or reproductive or expansionary qualities to multilateralism. Morgan (1993, 333) regards the distinguishing feature of multilateralism as "the fact that states involved seek to use [norms and their application] to push cooperation among themselves to an unusual level . . . cooperation into realms of interaction where it is usually absent." Caporaso (1993, 55) sees multilateralism as a self-promoting "ideology" designed to promote multilateral activity, combining normative principles with advocacy and existential beliefs. Kahler (1993, 299) regards multilateralism as involving "an impulse to universality"—that is, an impetus on the part of involved states to expand their collective to compass others within some relevant geographic or functional context.

When it comes to examining actual state practice, a wide variety of state behaviors and collective practices will be seen to exhibit greater or lesser qualities of multilateralism; multilateralism needs to be treated as ranging across a spectrum of behavioral and institutional forms—formal and informal in terms of their rules and organizational structures. To focus only upon those few examples that are fully developed according to all the criteria noted above would be to ignore instances of nascent multilateralism in transitory environments, typical of most current regional orders. Alternatively, the presence and operation of formal interstate organization(s) cannot be taken as either necessary or sufficient indicators of the existence of multilateralism. In fact, institutional mechanisms have been designed to facilitate distinctly non-multilateral principles of behavior, including imperialism, hegemonic dominance or bilateralism (as seen, for instance, in the "hub-and-spokes" architecture of the U.S.-centered, post–World War II Pacific security order). As

Martin (1993, 99) points out, there are circumstances in which the efficient operation of institutions that are multilateral in the nominal sense could inhibit the promotion of conditions and behaviors of multilateralism.

For analytical purposes, the multilateralist arrangements struck by states can be arrayed over two dimensions: the first referring to the nature of the commitment undertaken by and for members, and characterized here as varying from "deep" to "shallow"; the second referring to scope of membership, and described as varying from "narrow" to "broad."

Regarding the first dimension, commitment, the essential feature of multilateralism in a security-oriented context is "some expression or other of collective security or collective self-defense" (Ruggie 1993, 7). States deeply committed would promise to go to war on behalf of one of their membership threatened or attacked by another state. Shallower commitments would involve undertakings of lesser assistance, such as aid, arms, and so on, or contingent commitments, for example, not to assist aggressor states or to remain neutral. The matter of membership, the second dimension noted above, concerns the question of to whom commitments are extended. Thus, a narrowly conceived association would involve few states, relative to the overall number of states within the region or system with mutual security interests. One that was broadly conceived would be inclusive of its potential regional or systemic membership. In these terms, a concert composed of three of five major powers would be viewed as narrow, as might an alliance of half of the states in a region, while a regionally inclusive organization such as the Organization of African Unity or the United Nations, a global institution, would be seen as broad.

While not logically necessary, in practice one sees a tension in contemporary regional orders between these two dimensions of multilateralism. Thus, within the same regional security complex, there may be two contending dynamics among member states. Those whose primary interest is to guarantee their security through "deep" collective security commitments will work to establish and sustain institutions whose membership is exclusive, limited to those like-minded states whose reliability and capability are sound. On the other hand, other regional actors may be more interested in focusing upon the longer-term prospects for a more broadly based regional security community. Accordingly, they will seek to de-emphasize immediate security irritants and to engage non-like-minded states in dialogue and processes designed to promote the growth of common understandings, collective regional identity, and security community.

Experience, however, argues that the depth of effective multilateralist commitment is likely to be inversely related to the size of group membership. The tendency to invite in new members, or accede to the requests of outsiders to join, while expanding the aggregate number of states espousing the principles of the group, may prove counterproductive to the collective's fulfillment of its commitments. For a variety of reasons (many of which have been exposed by collective-choice theorists), larger multilateralist cohorts are capable of sustaining only intermittent, partial, or shallow commitments. On the other hand, smaller associations, which define their membership bases narrowly and with an eye to their common interests and capacities, will likely be more effective in sustaining deeper commitments. The trade-off, however, is that such groups will be exclusionary, and may be self-isolating and resistant to changes in their security environment.

MULTILATERALISM AND FORMS OF MULTILATERAL CONFLICT MANAGEMENT

With these points in mind, it is useful to recall and review the typology of alternative regional "security-management options" set out by Patrick Morgan (this volume), with an eye to (1) the requirements for their effective functioning as conflict-management mechanisms, and (2) the differing natures and qualities of collaborative behavior exhibited in each. Recall that Morgan set out five ideal types—power restraining power, great-power concert, collective security, pluralistic security community, and integration—as rungs on an imaginary ladder of increasing levels of cooperation among regional players. What I am interested in is the characteristics of qualitative multilateralism identified with each ideal type and the transformations in collective attitudes that underlie the transition from one institutional form to the next. For my purposes, Morgan's initial category, "power restraining power," is separated into two phases, or "rungs," on the regional security collaboration ladder.

BALANCE OF POWER

In the prototypical self-help conditions of Waltzian "anarchy," there is little opportunity or rationale for interstate collaboration. Short-term self-interest may lead actors to form coalitions to offset perceived threats to their security, as in a classic balance of power, but any such cooperative arrangements will be fleeting. In the extreme, this is a regional environment of "relentless security competition" (in Mearsheimer's words, 1994, 9), virtually devoid of qualitative multilateralism. In perceptual terms, states' interactions with each other are framed within the classic security dilemma.

Theoreticians, intrigued by the premises of interaction among unitary, rationalist actors, have given considerable attention to devising the minimal necessary conditions that will lead states to undertake collaboration, and have gone on to show that with specified "structures of interest" some more than minimal forms of coordination, assurance, and suasion can be expected (see, e.g., Martin 1993). In practice, systemic and regional structural circumstances and configurations of attitudes militate toward regularized patterns of balancing behavior among states. Some degree and form of interstate collaborative behavior is the norm, rather than the exception, in international relations. Often, within regional contexts, this collaboration is invoked by a hegemonic actor. In environments characterized by enmity within or between regional contexts, "stable" balancing of the major powers is achieved through maintenance of threat systems and deterrence relationships that prevent destabilizing (sub)systemic conflicts from taking place (see Papayoanou, this volume). In such contexts, limited aspects of qualitative multilateralism will be present.

COLLECTIVE DEFENSE

The most common form of security collaboration in such circumstances is a multilateral agreement among states motivated by their common perception of a security threat posed by another state or group of states. Collective defense arrangements, usually alliances, are formed and reformed in response to changing threat circumstances and attitudinal patterns, such as the ideologies of the Cold War camps. Collective defense arrangements, in essence, subdivide systems or subsystems into exclusionary membership subsets. Norms of diffuse reciprocity, indivisibility, and nondiscrimination may well apply *within* an alliance, but obviously do not hold toward outsiders.

Historical experience suggests that alliances are transitory phenomena, subject to changing endogenous and exogenous influences—"temporary marriages of convenience," in the eyes of realist scholars (again, Mearsheimer 1994). The general wisdom is that the depth of multilateralist commitment among alliance members is directly related to the magnitude of perceived external threat. However, even the perceived Communist (or Western) threat of the Cold War era proved insufficient to sustain or enliven most regional defense pacts, for example, CENTO, SEATO, and the PRC-USSR pact. NATO, therefore, represents the exception, rather than the rule, for collective defense, and deserves particular notice. Its members shared common attitudes that facilitated the creation and growth of a security community among them, as well as an integrated economic community. The internal multilateralist characteristics of the Euro-Atlantic alliance thus were very "deep." Membership, while broadly inclusive of Western European states, however, remained exclusionary vis-à-vis the Soviet Communist empire. Interestingly, one of the effects of the confrontation of the two alliances, NATO and the Warsaw Pact, within the context of the European continent was to make it more, rather than less, difficult to promote panregional multilateralism.

COLLECTIVE SECURITY

A collective security arrangement entails an "all-for-one" commitment by members to act, automatically and in concert with others, to assist a member state that has been threatened or attacked by another (Kupchan and Kupchan 1991, 120). Unlike collective defense mechanisms, collective security mechanisms are not motivated by the need to plan or act against a particular perceived external threat, that is, a state that is thereby excluded from the group. In a systemic or regional collective security context, the security dilemma among states is attenuated, in that no immediate, identifiable threat is perceived by any of the players. They, therefore, form an inclusive compact with each other to respond collectively against any player who threatens the peace. In an ideal (Wilsonian) collective security arrangement multilateralist norms of nondiscrimination, indivisibility, and diffuse reciprocity must be operative in order to create and sustain an inclusive "community" of member states that do not regard each other as immediately threatening and whose future behavior may be counted upon.

The historical record, however, shows that collective security mechanisms have been beset by difficulties. As Kupchan and Kupchan (1991, 118) point out, there is a duality of logic within any collective security arrangement. On the one hand, there is sufficient perceived commonality among states that none sees the immediate need to plan or act directly concerning its security vis-à-vis another state. On the other hand, future threats and challenges to security are foreseen, motivating the desire to establish a potential, aggregated deterrent capability sufficient to deter any aggressive intentions.

The trick, of course, is to orchestrate a distribution of capabilities among regional members that does not promote or provoke what it is trying to avoid, namely, engendering perceived security dilemmas among individual states, resulting in the collective dividing itself into competing coalitions or collective defense pacts. It is here that the cognitive or attitudinal component of collective security arrangements becomes fundamental for their survival. Some sense of "community" involving shared notions of identity, commonality of values, acceptance of the status quo vis-à-vis the security of other members, and agreement on norms and rules of interaction has to be sustained. States will continue to recognize that threats may arise from within the collective, *but* they have a common appreciation that they can reduce or remove these prospects through their joint, rather than individual or subset, behaviors.

In forming collective security arrangements, there has often been an impetus toward membership breadth, that is, an impetus to make the association as large as possible, in order to enhance a broad common denominator of attitudinal similarity and multilateral commitment. However, the result has almost always been institutions of large numbers but inadequate or failed performance because of states' unwillingness to honor their commitments to act for each member or for all other members. It is in collective security institutions that the tension, noted earlier, between depth of commitment and breadth of membership is most pronounced. (Witness the ongoing dilemmas regarding NATO enlargement.)

In practice, the success of collective security mechanisms has depended heavily upon the degree of involvement and commitment by the subset of "larger" or more powerful members. Absent the inclusion of all relevant major powers as members, and a consensus of attitudes among them, collective security institutions have failed at critical moments. Accordingly, resort to a concert mechanism has come to be viewed in both theory and practice as a, if not the, solution to the performance problems endemic to large collective security arrangements.

CONCERT

A concert involves major-power management of the global or regional system according to generalized principles of conduct acceptable and applicable to this subset of key players. The requirements are that the major powers (1) do not view each other individually or in coalition as imminently threatening, (2) accept for the foreseeable future the status quo vis-à-vis their own sovereignty and security interests, and (3) agree not to attack each other and to come to the assistance of one attacked. While they undertake to provide a collective security guarantee among themselves, they do not forswear the use of force in their international relations, nor do they extend any multilateral guarantee to minor players. While major-power war may be successfully averted, conflicts between major and minor powers as well as major-power intervention in the affairs of minor states may in fact be increased.[1]

A concert, therefore, embodies a peculiar combination of qualities of multilateralism and collective security—the commitment among members is relatively deep, although qualified in scope; membership is limited to those perceived to meet capability requirements; some "benefits" are distributed unevenly between major and minor players, although the system as a whole is viewed as better served by major-power management. Indeed, "minilateralism," that is, the operation of a concert within the context of a larger multilateralist framework, has come to be viewed by many analysts as the only effective path to international management of a large system (see Kahler 1991). Kupchan and Kupchan (1991, 137ff.), considering the post–Cold War environment, advocate a "concert-based collective security" arrangement as the answer to regional (European) and global peace maintenance (see also Rosecrance 1992b; Rosecrance and Schott, this volume).

PLURALISTIC SECURITY COMMUNITY

The next step on the ladder is the security community, a concept originating with Deutsch's investigations of the processes and institutions in the post–World War II European order. Members of a security community exhibit "a sense of community and of institutions and practices strong enough and widespread enough to assure, for a long time, dependable expectations of peaceful change" (Deutsch et al. 1957, 5). Qualitative multilateralism is enhanced among the members of a security community, but membership itself is restricted and, in practice, closely guarded by members. This is understandable given the high degree of like-mindedness, of mutually created common identity, required to realize and sustain the principles of behavior involved, especially a long horizon of diffuse reciprocity. The existence of a security community hinges upon the definition and realization of such a

1. Most contemporary discussions of concerts of powers are based on analogies to the nineteenth-century Concert of Europe. For an extended discussion of the institutions and experience of the Concert of Europe, see Holsti 1991, 142–43, 167–68.

"common identity"—a social construction of generative and self-reinforcing attitudes and behaviors (see Adler and Barnett 1994; Hurrell 1995).

The distinctive character of a security community, as contrasted to a collective security or concert arrangement, is the cognitive transition that has taken place whereby states, in principle, no longer regard or fear force as a mode of interaction *among themselves*. In other words, what Morgan has termed "the most profound form" of the security dilemma among them has been eliminated in that states within a security community do not envisage future circumstances for which they must strategize to protect and enhance their security *autonomy* vis-à-vis each other.[2]

INTEGRATED SECURITY COMMUNITY

The culmination of interstate security cooperation would be the formation of an integrated security community (in Deutsch's terms, an "amalgamated security community") in which the identities and policy-making capacities of individual states have been consolidated or unified. For our purposes, a fully integrated group of states is not especially interesting per se, because an amalgamated community would function as a single entity in the international order, with a common security outlook and common defense policy. In logical terms, the preconditions for interstate multilateralism will have been eliminated. What remains interesting, however, is the behavior of any such integrated collective, or integrating collective (as in the case of the European regional community) toward nonmembers. Is it (are the members) willing to extend multilateralist principles of nondiscrimination and diffuse reciprocity toward other actors in a regional subsystem, and is it (are they) willing to take on new members? With the regionalization of international economic and security relations in the post–Cold War era, much attention is now focused upon institutions like NATO and ASEAN, and APEC (Asia-Pacific Economic Cooperation forum) and NAFTA on the economic side, to see how effectively they deal with such challenges. And again, as with the transitions at earlier points on the multilateralist continuum, it is the tensions of deepening versus broadening multilateralism that persist in debates over extension of membership, the definition of a common security identity, and so on.

2. Quoting Morgan (1993, 340): "The most profound form of the security dilemma is that defining autonomy as they do puts states in the position of setting the security of being safe from attack at odds with the security of sustaining autonomy." It was overcoming this sense of the security dilemma that was at the heart of the transformation of the Cold War European security order.

WHAT DETERMINES THE FORM OF REGIONAL CONFLICT MANAGEMENT?

Structural, cognitive, and behavioral elements are involved in any form of regional security architecture. In the first instance, structural features of the regional environment will determine the viability of regional orders (Lake, this volume). The configuration of power among the major powers—its distribution, stability, and shifts—establishes constraints on the mode of security institutions or architecture of the system or subsystem in question. Thus, for example, an attempted collective security arrangement that does not include all relevant major powers is likely to fail. A collective defense agreement of small states oriented against a global or regional hegemon will have little utility.

However, structural factors play only a limited role in determining the extent and nature of both multilateral activity and multilateralism in a given regional security complex. It is the cognitive features of the environment—the attitudes of the players toward each other, the rules and norms governing international interaction, the scope and nature of the security dilemmas that the actors perpetuate among themselves—that effectively determine the particular form of regional order that results.[3] Within the same structural distribution of power, any of a variety of security orders might arise. Whether a transitory balance of power holds sway, or a concert among major powers is established, or a polarized system of antagonistic coalitions occurs depends upon the nature and division of the shared understandings among states, especially the relevant major powers (Hurrel 1995, 335). This certainly has been the case in multipolar contexts. Even in a region with a potentially dominant hegemonic power, collective defense, collective security, concert, or even security community could evolve—dependent, of course, on the attitude of this key state.

3. Consideration of the intersubjective dimension of states' relations is necessary to understand how states construct their mutual security dilemmas and the formation of collective identities in groups of states. "Global politics has a profoundly social character"—to borrow Adler and Barnett's phrase (1994, 3). "It is how political actors perceive and interpret the idea of a region that is critical: all regions are socially constructed and hence politically contested" (Hurrel 1995, 334). While the line of argument in this chapter stresses the importance of the cognitive component of regional severity, it does not adequately explore the theoretical foundations or implications of this perspective. The author believes that a fuller consideration of the processes of multilateralism, especially those involved in the formation of collective identities of states, such as found with security communities, would require moving toward a reflectivist or constructionist theoretical perspective (see Wendt 1994).

In circumstances of basic structural continuity, movement from one form of regional order to another, from one rung to another of Morgan's ladder, is brought about by "cognitive transitions" of key actors concerning their perceived security dilemmas. Across the continuum of conflict-management forms discussed above, there are three such important junctures of mutual perception and understanding. The first occurs in the formation of collective defense coalitions or alliances. It entails the realization of sufficient commonality of security interests, vis-à-vis some external actor(s), to sustain joint collaboration and longer-term cooperation among contracting members. The second occurs with the establishment of collective security mechanisms and involves a substantial transformation of the security dilemma for a larger number of actors. The states in question now orient their security concerns inwardly, rather than outwardly. Perceiving no other member as an imminent threat, they focus their efforts upon establishing a credible collective threat against an unknown actor within their midst *and* upon sustaining a common set of collective attitudes. A similar logic, but involving fewer members, operates as the basis for a concert. The third cognitive transition is effected through the achievement of a security community. This involves the disappearance of the traditional security dilemma among a select group of states to the point where contemplation of the resort to force toward each other has been eliminated.

In reality, of course, such transitions involve incremental processes rather than discontinuous processes or discrete steps. Developments within regional systems take time; multilateralism is engendered through slow, and sometimes halting, processes involving increased interaction and mutual confidence building. In this regard, it is useful to refer to the reflections of Deutsch and his colleagues (1957) on the subtle dynamics and timing of post–World War II European integration as a prelude to the body of contemporary analysis on the "new regionalism" of the post–Cold War era (see Hurrell 1995 for a review of this literature).

The Regional Context

In order to get a sense of the possibilities for multilateral and multilateralist security institutions within regional security complexes, it is useful to begin by analyzing, in the abstract, the patterns of divergent security interests that can arise among states. The following discussion looks first at how prototypical states within a regional security complex might respond to their external security dilemmas; then it considers how states might advance or avoid regional multilateralist institutions in light of their internal security dilemmas.

For purposes of this discussion, let us assume a typical regional security complex could involve some combination of up to four different types of states: (1) a global power or powers, that is, states that define their interests and may project their power in any or all regions; (2) major powers, that is, states that define their interests and project their power, to a limited extent, beyond their own geographic region; (3) regional powers, that is, states that define their interests and project their power across their own geographic region; and (4) small states, that is, states that cannot project power, that cannot provide for their own security, except vis-à-vis each other, and that cannot, even in coalition with one another, contest or defend against states of the other types.[4]

EXTERNAL SECURITY DILEMMAS

States have been traditionally concerned with establishing their independence and sustaining themselves against direct territorial threats and challenges to their sovereignty from other states. However, over the last several decades and particularly with the end of the Cold War, such external threats and their associated external security dilemmas have substantially diminished. Nonetheless, in specific regional complexes, such as South Asia, external security threats remain an overriding and preoccupying concern; in other regions, such as Southeast Asia, states are anxious to establish regional orders that will militate against their revival (see Ayoob 1995, chaps. 6 and 7).

The majority of the actors in a typical regional security complex will be small states. Providing for and protecting their external security interests can only be accomplished in conjunction with other, more powerful states. They cannot by themselves or in cohort with their fellow small states provide credible security guarantees. Therefore, small states will wish to form col-

4. Under these rubrics, in the current post–Cold War system, the United States would be a global power; Russia, France, the UK and China major powers; and India, Brazil, Nigeria, and Indonesia regional powers. One could object that not all of the remainder are appropriately regarded as small states. However, for the moment, designation of states as "middle powers," for example, Canada, Australia, Italy, introduces complications that cannot be covered in a necessarily short overview (see, e.g., Cooper, Higgott, and Nossall 1993).

lective defense pacts or bilateral agreements with major or global powers. However, unlike during the Cold War, in today's world the latter may find little to attract them to such entangling commitments.[5] As a result, small states will have substantial interests in enhancing multilateralist arrangements within their region and the system. They will be drawn to support broadly based collective security mechanisms at both the systemic (e.g., the UN) and the regional (e.g., the OAU) level, for two reasons: first, to promulgate norms of sovereignty and noninterference (in effect to bolster their rights as members in the international system), and second, to acquire assurances that aggression against them will provoke a response by other, more powerful states. However, they face the dilemma that their individual memberships and the commitments they can make are largely symbolic. In light of their perceived vulnerability to the more powerful states within their own region, small states will strive toward enhancement of norms of multilateralism and toward regionwide security communities—as has been seen in Europe with the CSCE (now OSCE) and in Asia with the ASEAN Regional Forum.

It is more difficult to characterize abstractly the security dilemmas and multilateralist interests of the other types of regional states. Per earlier discussion, if sufficient commonality of security interests and shared norms exist among the major powers in a region, the formation of a concert or collective security institution is possible. However, it is our contention that this is more likely to occur at the systemic, rather than regional, level. Perceived threats to global norms and/or to the substantial security interests of all or most of the major powers, for example, the Iraqi takeover of Kuwait and its oil resources, will engender a concert of major powers to act. But such occasions are rare. At the regional level, analogous circumstances will arise no more often and perhaps even less frequently. Within regional security complexes, major and regional powers are quite likely to find their security interests at odds and, even if they are relatively unengaged, insufficiently motivating to cause them to act collaboratively to engage in conflict management.

This is a relatively pessimistic vision of regional orders; despite the rhetoric of globalization, democratization, and the advance of free market principles in regional contexts, the evidence to date of the emergence of effective regional concerts in the post–Cold War era is scant. Witness the failure of

5. During the Cold War, small states were sought after by the superpowers for two reasons: to create encompassing regional coalitions to array against rival(s) and provide strategic resources or base locations. Neither of these provides a strong rationale in the present environment; witness, for example, the U.S. abandonment of their Philippine bases.

European powers to act early regarding Yugoslavia, or the autonomous behavior of China in the Asian regional security complex.[6]

Probably the most intriguing combinations of external sovereignty and security interests within regional security complexes today are those of the so-called regional powers (for a fuller discussion, see Ayoob 1995, 59–65; Vayrynen 1984; and Myers 1991b). These states, for example, India, Brazil, Indonesia, and Nigeria, possess complicated security interests, leading them to be somewhat ambivalent or even recalcitrant about regional multilateralism. Their primary concerns will be to orient regional actors and institutions around their interests and ambitions and to avoid the domination or restrictions that could be imposed on them by major powers in whatever mode—intervention, interference in their domestic affairs, constrained membership in collective defense arrangements, or management through major-power concerts. Multilateral mechanisms that foster any such results will be eschewed by regional powers. On the other hand, institutions that foster principles of regional identity, that is, to the exclusion of geographic outsiders, will be attractive to them. For instance, Nigeria's support for the OAU or Indonesia's support of ASEAN can be seen in this light (see Acharya 1993). Furthermore, such institutions may provide potential opportunities for regional leadership (as in both of the instances cited above), by providing regional powers with institutional frameworks in which they can block or advance collective initiatives according to their own interests. However, if the development of regional or subregional multilateralism is perceived to advance norms and/or institutions that may ultimately constrain the autonomy of regional powers, they are likely to avoid involvement or tend toward minimalist commitments.

INTERNAL SECURITY DILEMMAS

The subsection above focused upon states' reactions to their perceived external security dilemmas, that is, tensions arising from the intersection of their interests with those of other states. States also face internal security dilemmas, in that the regimes in power find themselves threatened by forces seek-

6. This argument is somewhat at variance with those of Rosecrance (1992b) and Rosecrance and Schott (this volume), who speak to the commonality of values of democratization and economic liberalization that provides the basis for a concert of powers in today's world. Also, Shirk (this volume) argues that there is an intermittently operative (an "inchoate") concert of powers in Asia, and offers the solution to the crisis over North Korea's nuclear weapons program as an example of concert behavior.

ing to remove them individually from office, to secede from their jurisdiction, or to alter radically the principles of governance (Job 1992a). Such security dilemmas are characteristic of what have been termed weak states (Buzan 1991, chap. 2) and/or failed or failing states (Holsti 1995)—descriptions that can be applied to many players in today's international system and, to one degree or another, to almost all of today's key regional players.[7]

What will be the perspective of such states toward systemic or regional multilateralism? The fundamental interest of those in power in these states is regime survival and maintenance of the status quo or restoration of the status quo ante. Thus, within their international context, their concern will be to shore up the principles of noninterference in domestic affairs, preservation of territorial integrity, and entrenchment of sovereignty. International institutions will be attractive to them to the extent that these institutions foster such norms and are capable and willing to mobilize on their behalf. In practice, this has led to support for two forms of multilateral arrangements: (1) inclusive institutions established on the traditional premises of state centricity and providing multilateral commitments to maintain and restore them, and (2) coalitions of states that undertake collective commitments to sustain their current leaders or existing common form of government.

There are a variety of historical precedents of this latter type, including the Concert of Europe and, in more recent times, the Gulf Cooperation Council (GCC) and ASEAN, that is, multilateral arrangements among states within a geographic subregion who felt the need in the 1960s and 1970s for collective action to stave off commonly perceived internal threats (see Acharya 1992a).

As for institutions of the first sort, they emerged as a result of the anticolonialism and independence waves after World War II. Newly created states flocked to the United Nations, a global institution committed to fostering and preserving their existence and providing them a voice in the international system. They moved to create regionwide institutions, such as the OAU, whose missions, in principle, were to promote noninterference in regional affairs by outsiders and to preserve the territorial integrity and sovereignty of member states (see Jackson 1990). However, in practice, in

7. Thus, for instance, Russia would certainly qualify as a substantially "weak state," as would the entities of the former Soviet Union. In South Asia, both Pakistan and India exhibit certain characteristics of the prototypical weak state. In Asia, while the central governments of certain key states sustain authoritarian control, as in China, North Korea, or Burma, these regimes are under stress due to leadership transitions, political generational change, dramatic domestic economic restructuring, and penetration by global communications.

both regional and global contexts, the participation of weak states has been largely confined to norm enhancement. Being generally also small states, they provide little weight, even collectively, toward enforcement of multilateral commitments. With their precarious internal situations, they have been extremely reluctant to sanction or participate in any actions that might establish precedents for "intervention" in domestic affairs or for alteration of the territorial status quo. Thus, organizations such as the OAS have historically sustained themselves through their inaction, rather than through multilateral activism (see Mares, this volume).

In sum, four conclusions may be drawn concerning the incentives toward multilateralism in regional security contexts. First, in regional complexes in which the ongoing security interests of the major powers are perceived to be incompatible, the prevalent mode of multilateralism will continue to be collective defense arrangements among subsets of state members.[8] Second, in regional complexes in which the security dilemma is dampened—that is, there are no immediate threats to the peace among major players—more inclusive forms of multilateralism oriented toward development of common attitudinal bases for security architectures may be found. However, this is by no means assured. Aspiring regional powers, for instance, even if they do not evidence ambitions that threaten other regional actors, may not be eager to place themselves within multilateral frameworks in which their autonomy is limited directly or indirectly. Thus, the likelihood of the emergence of regional concerts involving these players is questionable. Third, to the extent that clashes of ideology (political, economic, religious, or otherwise) are avoided within regional security complexes, there is the opportunity for furthering multilateralist regional attitudes and norms of interstate behavior. Through the enhancement, within regional "strategic cultures," of norms of transparency, defensive defense doctrines and deployments, principles of nonconflictual resolution of disputes, and mutual trust-building mechanisms, progress toward multilateralist institutions such as collective security mechanisms and security communities will be achieved. (For reference to Europe, see Morgan 1993; to Asia, see Ball 1993.) Fourth, for a variety of reasons, smaller regional players will be attracted to regional institutions that espouse collective security commitments to sustain their territorial integrity and preserve their internal sovereignty. The positive impact of these institutions will be seen through their promotion of common identities and further-

8. With the demise of the Cold War, there are at present no regional environments polarized to this extent. Perhaps the deepest divisions are within South Asia, between India and Pakistan. While each has attempted to garner the greater favor of key states in the system, especially the United States, one could not characterize this situation as one of confronting alliances.

ance of norms and community building. On the other hand, as discussed below, such institutions are unlikely to be able, in the short-term future, to engage in proactive conduct on behalf of the security interests of their individual members and collective membership.

Regional Conflict and Multilateralism

In this section, the prospects for the extension of multilateralism in the mitigation and management of regional conflict are addressed more directly. Starting with a look at the nature of the problem, that is, the extent and characteristics of conflicts in the contemporary system, I go on to assess the prospects for multilateral action and multilateralism to prevent, mitigate, or resolve these conflicts. There are two avenues to be explored: First, in the short term, what are the capabilities and the record of existing global and regional mechanisms? Second, in light of the relatively dim picture that emerges from this stocktaking, what are the longer-term prospects for conflict prevention and management within regional security complexes through the development of multilateralist institutions such as collective security arrangements and security communities?

Such discussions must proceed with an appreciation for the nature of regional conflicts. While the falling of the symbols and structures of the Cold War brought an initial wave of optimism about a more peaceful world and the blossoming of multilateralism, the experiences of the past decade have replaced these positive predictions with more hard-nosed appreciations of the intractability of conflicts and the limitations of international cooperation. Systematically gathered empirical evidence supports these concerns. Surveys of the post-1989 years (such as Wallensteen and Axell 1993; Holsti 1995) demonstrate that the frequency of deadly conflicts remains much the same as in the prior decade. The most striking features of the distribution of post–Cold War violence are

1. that virtually all conflicts qualify as "regional conflicts"—only the Persian Gulf War would have counted as a global conflict in the last half decade;[9]

9. Existing inventories of conflicts, such as Wallensteen and Axell 1993 and those found in the SIPRI (Stockholm International Peace Research Institute) yearbooks, do not categorize cases as "regional conflicts." However, if one quickly reviews these lists, applying Morgan's criteria of location and spillover (this volume), almost all cases quite obviously qualify for this designation.

2. that well over 90 percent of conflicts are *intra*state conflicts, with the majority of these being contentions over governance, a minority being secessionist conflicts;
3. that with regard to regional geographic distribution, there has been a sharp rise in the proportion of conflicts in Europe, brought about through the disintegration of the Soviet Union's Eastern European empire; and
4. that there has been a decline in regional conflicts arising through "outside" intervention ("wars of interest"), contrasted with the rise in intrastate violence spawned by ethnic, religious, or social tensions ("wars of conscience") that occur and spread across traditionally defined state borders.[10]

GLOBAL AND REGIONAL INSTITUTIONAL EFFORTS TO MANAGE REGIONAL CONFLICT

An imaginary two-by-two grid can be constructed in which to distribute this array of conflicts, the dimensions of the grid being conflict type (intra- and interstate) and multilateral conflict-management institution (regional and global). Thus, the four cells of the grid become global institution/interstate conflict, global institution/intrastate conflict, regional institution/interstate conflict, and regional institution/intrastate conflict.

GLOBAL MULTILATERAL EFFORTS

To answer the first question posed above, consider the response and capacities of global institutions in the management of regional conflicts, noting again that interstate conflict is a rare species in the post–Cold War environment. There has been the Persian Gulf War, and there remain a number of recurrent interstate hot spots: India and Pakistan, North and South Korea, the Taiwan Straits, and more recently the South China Sea.[11] Mobilization of

10. "Wars of interest" and "wars of conscience" are terms used by the *Economist,* 5 December 1992, 3–5. Note that for my purposes, "outside," as in "'outside' intervention," needs to be set off in quotes, because in one sense any state whose security interests intersect with others in a region is a member (hence inside) of the relevant regional security complex. Buzan (1992) treats the Cold War and accompanying superpower intervention in regional affairs as a special set of conditions that were overlaid on top of the underlying regional security dynamic.

11. While the ongoing conflicts within the territory of the former Yugoslavia could technically be termed interstate, given the recognition of the state status of Croatia and Serbia, most analysts regard this violence as "intrastate," given the questionable premises and capacities of these "states."

the UN in response to an interstate conflict or crisis can occur only when and if the concert of major powers in the Security Council (the P-5 states) wills it, that is, when they perceive sufficient common interests are at stake to facilitate, directly or indirectly (through peacekeeping missions), conflict management. During the Cold War, when substantial numbers of interstate regional conflicts proceeded under the auspices of the global powers and their clients, collective action by the UN was initiated only when these same powers saw that the situation threatened to escalate to the panregional or global level, for example, in the Middle East wars. In the current environment, the logic of action is no longer driven by ideology, but may in terms of its bottom line not be that much different. Thus, one assumes that the P-5 states would be mobilized to action in the South Asian or Korean peninsula situations to prevent escalation to nuclear thresholds and to prevent widespread spillover effects (see Papayoanou, this volume). It is not easy, however, to assess the prospects for any global multilateral action to intervene to settle an interstate conflict among small states. One has the impression that, absent exceptional factors involving substantial human suffering, effective delivery on the multilateralist commitments of UN organization members will continue to prove difficult.

In comparison with interstate conflict situations, intrastate conflicts pose serious dilemmas to international institutions and their members. The result is that global institutional response to *intrastate conflicts* has not been, and is not likely to become, either frequently attempted or particularly successful when tried. In general terms, the contemplation of such actions runs against what most members regard as core multilateralist principles of the United Nations, namely, noninterference in domestic affairs and maintenance of territorial integrity and sovereignty.[12] Only occasionally will it prove feasible, or in the interests of the major powers in the UN, to mobilize regarding intrastate disputes. This is likely to remain so, despite the increasing number of deadly intrastate conflicts and the resultant calls for more frequent, more effective, and more forceful multilateral action by the United Nations.

Two issues arising in the post–Cold War context warrant comment. The first concerns the United Nations record in resolving conflicts in Angola, Afghanistan, and Cambodia. In these cases, the UN has been given credit for achieving settlements and for attempting to engineer transitions to peaceful, civil societies. Indeed, UN efforts in these instances were substantial. How-

12. The secretary-general's *Agenda for Peace* document, while advocating an enhanced role for his organization in promoting peace and peaceful settlement, remains adamant on such points. See also Damrosch 1993.

ever, a couple of caveats are in order that preclude regarding these cases as relevant predictors of the future: The exceptional characteristic of these cases must be noted, namely, that they constituted Cold War holdovers, whose resolution became desired when intervening powers sought to withdraw their support for the local warring factions. Also, the success of the "solutions" in these cases is proving to be short-lived, demonstrating once again the intractability of intrastate conflicts in weak states to resolution through the methods (peacekeepers, observer missions, and so on) and remedies (multiparty elections, and so on) traditionally prescribed in the UN's "developed"-state peacekeeping agenda (see Ayoob 1995, 140–41).

The second issue concerns the increased calls for humanitarian intervention to protect and sustain civilian populations caught in the ravages of intrastate conflict. The arguments and mobilizations on behalf of peoples (as opposed to states) are important because they represent an expansion of the bases of multilateralism and multilateral commitment in the current international order (see Jackson 1993). An assessment of the UN's actions and multilateralist potential in this domain is beyond the scope of the present investigation. Suffice it to say that the record to date is very mixed. The UN has responded with missions, for example, in Bosnia-Herzegovina, Somalia, Haiti, and Rwanda. But these efforts have been construed by critical participant and nonparticipant states as belated, expensive, understaffed, underequipped, inefficient, and insufficient, leaving a somewhat uncertain future for further UN humanitarian intervention.

REGIONAL MULTILATERAL EFFORTS

Chapter VIII of the UN Charter gives precedence to regional institutional responses in situations involving threats or outbreaks of conflict. Analysts too have tended to advocate regional initiatives as more appropriate and likely to be more successful than those of their global counterparts. A variety of rationales have been invoked: The spillover effects of regional conflicts are locally concentrated; as a result, regional states will presumably have more at stake in their settlement (see Lake, this volume). By sharing at least some minimal regional identities and common attitudes, there may be a larger basis upon which to build the understandings and confidence necessary to achieve settlement (see MacFarlane and Weiss 1992, for a good review).

The historical record, however, belies these arguments. Indeed, the general opinion among those who have examined the record is, in fact, just the opposite. That is, regional institutions have largely proved incapable of effective collective response in either interstate or intrastate regional conflicts. To quote the conclusions of MacFarlane and Weiss (1992, 11): "In reality these organizations are far less capable than the United Nations to deal with regional security. . . . The institutional capacities of regional organizations are extremely feeble, so much so that they have not been able to carry out mandates in peace and security. Finally, the so-called comparative superiority of organizations in the actual region in conflict—familiarity with issues, insulation from outside powers, need to deal with acute crises—are more than offset by such practical disadvantages as partisanship, local rivalries, and lack of resources."

Whether these conclusions about regional institutions should be qualified on the basis of action/inaction in interstate or intrastate conflicts deserves brief consideration. As noted earlier, most *interstate* regional conflicts during the previous four decades were substantially structured within Cold War parameters. The superpowers effectively managed both the course of the conflicts themselves and any conflict-management strategies that were deemed necessary. Regional institutions were largely cut out of the picture: Initiatives by inclusive regional institutions such as the OAS were blocked by their superpower members. Regional collective defense pacts (such as NATO) were generally themselves party to ongoing crises.

However, with the end of the Cold War and the decline of the Soviet Union, regional politics has taken on a quite different cast (see Stein and Lobell, this volume). While it is too soon to draw any conclusions concerning the performance of regional institutions concerning interstate conflict, some tentative observations can be drawn. In today's world, it is aspiring regional powers that fellow regional states often view as the greatest cause for concern to their external security, especially where such states do not appear content with the territorial status quo, for example, China, and perhaps India. In response, two sorts of strategies within regions have been adopted. Small regional states, generally individually, have sought security guarantees from major-power "outsiders" (e.g., agreements such as those between the United States and Singapore and Malaysia); and/or they have undertaken broader efforts, combining economic, diplomatic, and security-related initiatives designed to draw regional powers into accepting the multilateralist attitudes and norms of a regional community (e.g., ASEAN's strategy concerning China). Note, however, that commitment to this latter approach involves a longer-range and incrementalist vision that, in fact, can lead its advocates to avoid calling for action on short-term problems with regional powers, in order to keep them onside in the longer term. Thus, for example, ASEAN states have proved reluctant to confront China over its behavior in the South China Sea (see Segal 1996).

Regional institutional response to *intrastate* conflicts has proved problematic not only for the reasons stressed by MacFarlane and Weiss, but also because of the overall disposition of regional members to support norms of noninterference. In the instances when action has been taken under the auspices of institutions such as the ECOWAS (Economic Community of West African States) or OAS, it has generally been engineered by a dominating regional member. Absent such "leadership," regional institutions composed solely of small states have proved largely unable to mobilize action to prevent or manage intrastate conflicts, either through their own collective efforts (which would likely prove inadequate) or through capturing the attention of outsiders, be they major powers or global institutions.

The record of ASEAN in the resolution of the Cambodian crisis is instructive in this regard. With a strong interest in achieving stability in Indochina, especially in muting the presence and influence of contending regional powers, ASEAN made extensive efforts of its own over the years to achieve a Cambodian settlement, but with little result. Nor could the association internationalize attention to the Cambodian case through its collective diplomatic efforts at the United Nations (Lizee and Peou 1993). It was only when the major powers, acting on their own initiative, in light of the end of the Cold War, came together in the Paris Peace Agreement of 1991 that the Cambodian conflict was "effectively detached . . . from its regional and global dimensions," and only then was the United Nations peacekeeping mission put into place. Thus, while ASEAN states might take "justifiable pride in [working toward] the localization of the Cambodian conflict" (Acharya 1993, 14), the route to international remedial action in this case demonstrates well the relative capacity of institutions of its sort, that is, collectives of small states, to engineer management of regional conflicts, especially if they are ongoing and involve interests or action of major powers.[13]

Several factors appear important in determining whether regional institutions are capable of initiating collective action, that is, delivering on a

13. Thus, while the Central American states remained very concerned and made various attempts to resolve both the Nicaraguan and the El Salvadoran conflicts, movement toward a solution was possible only (1) when the interests of the United States were revised, in light of the end of the Cold War and a change in administrations, and (2) through the actions of the United Nations, that is, a global institution (see MacFarlane and Weiss 1994; also Mares, this volume).

multilateral commitment regarding intrastate conflict within their regional context. For certain institutions, this purpose in fact was central to their formation; member states sought to cooperate to fend off threats from internal forces, tangible or intangible, that were perceived to threaten the existence of their regimes. The six founding members of ASEAN, for instance, expressed a common interest in thwarting "Communist" insurgency; the members of the Gulf Cooperation Council similarly were concerned to preserve the traditional character of their regimes (Acharya 1992a). The evidence on how effective such regional institutions have been in regime preservation is hard to evaluate. While there are indications of bilateral cooperation in the sharing of information, transferring of suspect persons, clamping down on partisan groups, and so on, there is little evidence that regional institutions have been at all willing to mobilize in a formal manner around regime restoration.[14]

It is more likely that intrastate regional conflicts will prove to be divisive within regional institutional contexts. Either directly through their governments, or indirectly through the active identification and participation of sectors of their populations, regional member states will already be playing roles in such conflicts. The capacity to mobilize collectively for conflict management in such circumstances will be problematic and will likely yield suboptimal participation and results. Witness, for example, the difficulties in mitigating the conflict in the former Yugoslavia, or Ethiopia, Rwanda, Angola, Cambodia, and so on. The exception to this rule may be those instances when regional states are in accord that their primary interest is in halting the conflict within one of their neighbors. Such sentiments could arise through desires to stop unwanted spillover effects of fighting, of population movements, of ethnonationalist appeals to their minority populations, and/or desires to put a halt to the outside intervention by a major power. Movement by the Contadora group toward resolution of the Nicaraguan civil war could be cited as an example, as could the support of these Central American states for resolution of the El Salvadoran troubles. The resources available to small regional states in such situations derive in large part from their familiarity with the participants and their ability to devise specific, locally acceptable compromises (as MacFarlane and Weiss acknowledge), but obviously do not extend to their capacity to impose or even to police a settlement within another state or states.

14. The case of Grenada might be brought up as a counterexample. However, absent the "leadership" of the United States, it is not likely that any action would have been taken by the Caribbean Community (CARICOM) states (see Thorndike 1989).

What has occurred to date in the post–Cold War era, therefore, presents a dilemma for individuals looking for multilateralism in regional orders. The rise in the frequency and intensity of intrastate regional conflicts has been accompanied by a substantial increase in multilateral efforts to halt and remedy such conflicts, especially through the United Nations. However, these have been initiated largely at the global level, have been confined to a rather arbitrarily determined subset of cases, and have experienced substantial difficulties in engineering effective collective participation. The call has gone out, therefore, for a larger role to be played by regional institutions (Boutros-Ghali 1992). But, as discussed above, there are severe practical as well as attitudinal limitations to the capacities of regionally based institutions to address the challenges of management of the most prevalent and deadly forms of violence, namely, intrastate conflicts.

THE ADVANCE OF MULTILATERALISM WITHIN REGIONAL CONTEXTS

Therefore, it is the avenue of the second logic of multilateralism that must be pursued in considering prospects for mitigation of regional conflict and the internal and external security dilemmas that foster it. This is both because of, and despite, the incrementalism and minimalism that characterize processes of cognitive transition and community building around commonly perceived values and norms. Within the current international order several meaningful developments in this regard must be noted.

First, the end of the Cold War itself was effected through a fundamental cognitive transition regarding perceptions of security and the security dilemma, largely on the part of key leaders of the Soviet Union (see Lebow and Stein 1994). This basically undercut the rationale of the traditional multilateralism of the collective defense arrangements of the Cold War and, in turn, their accompanying overlay and penetration of regional security relationships. However, this transformation per se did not establish new attitudinal bases for security cooperation, particularly at the regional level. Instead, in many instances, long-standing social cleavages were brought to the surface, fueling interstate and intrastate conflicts.

Second, there were, of course, other forms of multilateralism present in the international environment. These ranged from the relatively "shallow" multilateralism of large collections of states seeking to affirm basic principles of self-recognition and acceptance, to pockets of "deep" multilateralism grounded firmly in the identification by their members with commonly accepted values concerning appropriate forms of economic and security orders and modes of governance. What have been set in motion by the attitudinal shift of the end of the Cold War are processes whereby states within the cores of these (nascent) security communities seek to expand and deepen their multilateral scope (see Adler and Barnett 1994). Again in the terms used earlier, committed states are seeking to effectuate cognitive transitions within relevant others in order to draw them toward identification in security communities. Much contemporary discussion, therefore, centers upon the spread of processes of democratization and economic liberalization and their presumed positive impact upon cooperative security relations within and among states (see Solingen, this volume, and Mares, this volume, for contrasting views). There are indeed signs, at both the regional and global levels, of the positive, long-term impact of these multilateralist developments.

Third, in the shorter term and with specific attention to regional conflict, no general optimistic conclusions regarding multilateralism in security relations appear warranted. Ongoing intrastate regional conflicts are not proving susceptible to effective management by either regional or global collective security institutions. Indeed, for reasons discussed above, those states that seek the expansion of their nascent regional security communities are and will remain hesitant to "interfere" in the internal affairs of other members or states they wish to draw into their communities. Thus, the longer-term prognosis concerning regional security multilateralism will depend on the achievement of a delicate balance between forces promoting common identity among regional players and forces that capitalize upon identities of distinction, either between states or between groups that intersect currently recognized state boundaries.

Part IV

Building Regional Orders

9

Regional Conflict Management in Latin America: Power Complemented by Diplomacy

David R. Mares

When we discuss violence in Latin America, intrastate violence rightfully draws our attention. But it would be an error to ignore either the history of or potential for interstate violence in Latin America. Military force has consistently been used in the foreign policies of Latin American countries. The twentieth century has seen more than two hundred instances in which Latin American states either threatened or used military force or were the subject of such threats or force by non–Latin American countries.[1] Democracies have shot at each other (Ecuador and Peru numerous times since 1981, culminating in the war of 1995);[2] a country with no army was invaded twice

1. Data are from the updated Militarized Interstate Dispute (MID) data set discussed in Gochman and Maoz 1984.

2. "Democracy" is a contentious concept, especially when an analyst disagrees with the institutional rules governing politics or the policies of the government in office. I use the latest version of *Polity II* for scores up to 1993, with 6 on a 0–10 scale (e.g., Chile up to 1973 was a 6) qualifying a state to be considered a democracy (Gurr, Jaggers, and Moore, 1994). By U.S. government criteria, all countries in the Western Hemisphere except Cuba were democratic in

by its neighbor (Costa Rica by Nicaragua under Somoza in the 1950s); and eight to nine Latin American wars have occurred.[3] In the 1970s Peru and Chile engaged in an arms race; in 1978 war between Chile and Argentina was averted at literally the last minute; and democratic Venezuela ordered full mobilizations of its armed forces against democratic Colombia in 1987 and 1993. Clearly, Morgan is wrong: these states do not form a Deutschian security community, in which war among members is not considered.[4]

Latin America, however, has made important progress in controlling violent conflict. Wars in the nineteenth century were long, spread beyond two parties, and entailed great loss of life and exchange of territory. Twentieth-century wars have been more limited affairs. Nevertheless, the potential for serious militarized conflict arising out of territorial, ideological, power-projection, resource, and refugee disputes continues (Morris and Millan 1990, 2; see also Dominguez 1984; Keegan and Wheatcroft 1986).

This study of how the search for security has historically been organized in this region and how it is currently being revised has four sections. First, I define the Latin American security complex and identify the issues to be managed. A second section examines the security-management framework proposed by Morgan's chapter. I find the cooperative modes of management discussed by Morgan inadequate for understanding Latin America's security complex.

1995 (DOD 1995a, 1). But we do not have to accept Mexico as a democracy to recognize that Peru was democratic in 1995, as domestic and international observer groups attested in the electoral campaign for president and Congress (Scott Palmer 1995).

3. The standard 1,000 battlefield deaths cutoff produces eight: Second Central American War, 1906; Third Central American War, 1907; Dominican Republic–Haiti, 1937 (not listed in the MID data base, but Mecham [1962, 175], notes that between "several thousand" and 12,000 Haitians were killed by Dominican soldiers); Bolivia-Paraguay, 1931–35; Peru-Ecuador, 1939–41; El Salvador–Honduras, 1969; Argentina–Great Britain, 1982; and Peru-Ecuador, 1995. (This last is too recent for the MID data set. But in my interviews with U.S., Ecuadorian, and Peruvian military analysts, all agreed that the official figures grossly underestimate battlefield deaths, which they all calculated at over 1,000 [from "over 1,000" to 1,500]. A dissident military lodge in Peru also reportedly is circulating a figure of 1,200 Peruvian deaths.) The Peru-Colombia clash in 1932 produced "only" 852 deaths, after more than 3,000 soldiers and a number of ships were dispatched to the area of conflict. Peru also mobilized another 25,000 (Wood 1966, 169–254; Pike n.d., 266–67).

4. Morgan claims that North America (Canada, the United States, and Mexico) is a pluralistic security community and that South America may also be one (see Morgan, this volume). He is right for North America since the 1930s (but see my qualifications in note 14 below). The evidence, however, clearly demonstrates that the use of military force is conceivable among South American states. Reporting on the January 1995 war between Peru and Ecuador the *New York Times* noted the wave of patriotism sweeping both countries (31 January 1995, A5). For a similar judgment about South America, see Hurrell 1996.

The history of inter-American security management is analyzed in the third section. The system has essentially been dominated by balance-of-power mechanisms, with the United States and some Latin American states imposing their will on weaker members. In the final section I examine current efforts to reorganize inter-American security management to satisfy U.S. interests as well as increase the security of Latin American states.

The Latin American Security Complex

An analyst could describe in any number of ways the geographic zone in which the Latin American countries are located. The Western Hemisphere would include the United States, Canada, and the Anglophile Caribbean, as well as Belize, the Guayanas, and Latin America. But for purposes of thinking about the security issues confronting the last, this "region" is too encompassing. Argentina and Haiti are connected to what happens in Central America in a way that has historically not affected either Canada or the Bahamas, although the U.S. invasion of Grenada in 1983 and Venezuela's attempt to project its influence in the Antilles may be changing historical patterns.

The primary security concerns that tightly link this group of countries arise from both self-perceptions and political competition. These factors link the United States, Latin America, Belize, Guyana, and Surinam into a security complex.[5]

Self-perceptions link the former Spanish and Portuguese colonies with the one former British colony that defined itself in opposition to the mother country (the United States) but not the one that never severed those peculiar political links (Canada). After independence the idea of a "Western Hemisphere," culturally and politically distinct from Europe (therefore not including undisputed colonial possessions in the Caribbean islands), permeated the diplomatic rhetoric, if not actual foreign policy, of these states. There was even discussion of "American" international law. At various times Latin American countries have tried, unsuccessfully, to make the Monroe Doctrine (promulgated unilaterally by U.S. president James Monroe in 1823) a security policy of the Americas (Whitaker 1954; Mecham 1962).

5. Large sections of Belize and Guyana are claimed by Guatemala and Venezuela, respectively. Guyana and Brazil dispute Surinam's borders.

But self-perceptions are usually a deceptive guide to behavior and outcomes when they clash with material interests and power. Thus the United States has always opposed multilateralizing the Monroe Doctrine, and in the early nineteenth century the Great Liberator Simon Bolivar and Argentina quickly discovered that the United States would not jeopardize its relations with Europe to defend other American nations.[6] In the mid–nineteenth century Mexico found to its dismay that South American states were unwilling to play a role in limiting U.S. expansion. In the twentieth century further examples of the inadequacy of perceptions for defining security complexes abound. Among the most notable examples were Brazil's frustrated claim to membership in the great-power concert in the Council of the League of Nations, Argentine perceptions that it belonged to a British-centered security complex during World War II, and revolutionary Cuba's belief that it could leave the regional security complex (Mecham 1962, 40; di Tella and Watt 1990; Cervo and Bueno 1992).

The security externalities that combine with self-identification to make "Latin America" a security complex arise from three different arenas: international, regional, and domestic. At the international level, the United States is a great power that, irrespective of Latin American wishes, identifies Latin America as belonging to its unique sphere of influence. U.S. power and geography have meant there would be no great-power concert or balancing in Latin America (on concerts, see Rosecrance and Schott, this volume). The United States has never recognized the right of any other great power to a unique sphere of influence, but from the time of the Monroe Doctrine through the Hay-Poncefort Treaty, the Roosevelt Corollary to the Monroe Doctrine and the Inter-American Treaty of Reciprocal Assistance, the United States has insisted on its unilateral right to "defend itself" anywhere in the Western Hemisphere (and elsewhere; see Dulles [1965] 1971; Munro 1964). United States defense interests produce fundamental security externalities for each and every Latin American nation.

A second security externality dates from colonial days: the prevalence of disputed territorial borders means that the management and resolution of

6. See the U.S. response to the Colombian minister in Washington (Perkins 1965, 69–70). Britain intervened actively in the region: in the 1828 Argentine-Brazilian war, Britain forced the combatants to create Uruguay as a buffer state; in 1833 it seized the Malvinas Islands and in 1843 a Honduran island; in 1841 it occupied a Nicaraguan port. The French were also active, occupying a Mexican port and an Argentine island in 1838 and participating with the British in a blockade of the River Plate in 1845. Aid would come only when the United States itself perceived a threat, not when a Latin American country defined the threat (Connell-Smith 1974, 69; Mecham 1962, 37–38).

one border conflict have an impact on the others. Many border disputes have been diplomatically, and some militarily, settled. Even today the vast majority of Latin American states have territorial disputes with at least one neighbor. The intra–South American militarized disputes of the last two decades all revolved around border issues, although the Venezuela-Colombia tensions also reflect guerrilla activity, the drug trade, and illegal immigration. In Central America, the Guatemala-Belize and El Salvador–Honduras negotiations are stalled in the legislatures, and Nicaragua and Colombia dispute some islands.[7]

The third security externality develops out of the highly stratified social structure in Latin America and the developing nature of its economies. Because states in the region identify themselves as a community, when the social structure in one country is threatened by revolutionary upheaval, elites in the rest of Latin America begin to worry. These Latin American perceptions of threats to regional stability are reinforced by the United States. The United States attempts to organize regional opposition, and thus engages in rhetorical excesses, if not the actual fabrication of "evidence" of revolutionary internationalism. In addition, the very willingness of the United States to act militarily in these situations raises the specter of internationalizing domestic conflict (as many feel was done in Central America during the 1980s).

Transborder spillovers of revolutionary upheaval are not the mere concoctions of perceptual overreactions by Latin America and U.S. elites. Traditionally, those seeking to change the social structure within a country appeal for support from their Latin brothers and sisters facing the same problems and offer to assist them in return. Sandino's fight against the U.S. intervention in Nicaragua during the 1920s, Cuba's Revolution, Chile's Popular Unity administration, and the Nicaraguan Sandinistas in the 1970s and 1980s all had significant extranational participation.[8] In addition, neofascist agents from Brazil's Estado Novo traveled South America in the 1930s

7. In 1993 Colombia accused Nicaragua of attempting to buy missile boats from North Korea to contest Colombian sovereignty over the San Andres Islands. Nicaragua denied the charges, claimed that it was downsizing its military establishment, and cited the sale of helicopters to Ecuador as an example (*Diario,* 7 August 1993, 32). The impact of such purchases on Ecuadorian and Peruvian calculations in their 1995 border war merits study. Peruvian president Fujimori claims that he was aware of Ecuadorian preparations for war in 1992 and sought to delay action until Peru defeated the Shining Path rebellion and revitalized its armed forces (*Hoy,* 4 April 1995; see also DOD 1995a, 12–14; Morris and Millan 1990, 8–16).

8. U.S. government officials and security analysts often point to such participation as evidence of "external" security threats. But they conveniently forget that the U.S. War of Independence itself attracted idealists from outside its territorial boundaries, as well as money and troops from prerevolutionary France, hardly a liberal polity.

to build a regional front against "Communists"; Peron's Argentine labor movement and Peru's progressive APRA (Alianza Popular Revolucionaria Americana) party tried to reproduce themselves elsewhere on the continent; Caribbean democrats set up the notorious Caribbean League to overthrow dictators; and Che Guevara tried to reproduce the Cuban Revolution in the heart of South America (Hilton 1991; Mecham 1962; Dominguez 1989; Bailey 1967, 150–52; Alexander 1973).

Latin America does not suffer from another security externality that characterizes developing countries, especially in Africa (Ayoob 1995; Buzan 1991; Keller, this volume). The nation itself is not an issue. Political regimes often confront legitimacy problems, but since the end of the Indian wars at the turn of the century, the surviving indigenous people have clamored for their rights as citizens rather than for separate nationhood.

If Latin America can be thought of as a security complex, what are the sets of issues to be managed? From a Latin American perspective, extracontinental threats ceased to be major issues once the United States became powerful enough to defend the hemisphere. (Mexico did worry about a Japanese attack during World War II, but neither Brazil nor Argentina was concerned about German aggression; for example, when the United States provided Brazil with equipment and supplies to defend its "bulge" on the Atlantic, the Brazilians preferred to focus resources on their southwestern border with Argentina [Mares 1988].) Although Germany tried alternately to woo and threaten Mexico, Chile, Argentina, and Brazil, these American states understood that the costs of playing balance-of-power politics were enormous, the chances of the United States accepting such an alliance small, and the threat from Germany minor (Francis 1977; Hilton 1991). Even the Cold War had its major impact only when it could be used to reinforce national interests.[9]

Because of the forced isolation of the region from great-power politics, its security issues arise from the region's own internal characteristics. In a region characterized by disputed borders, unequal levels of economic development, and broad disparities in the distribution of power, the main security issues for Latin American states revolve around sudden attempts at military resolutions of long-standing border issues and diplomatic stalemates, as well as the spread of revolution. Included in this regional security agenda is the manner and timing of U.S. intervention in the hemisphere. United States uni-

9. When Cold War "demands" conflicted with national interests, they were largely ignored. Thus in the 1970s Latin American countries began opening up relations with Cuba despite U.S. opposition. Even the Argentine military government that fought the "Dirty War" domestically against "Communists" could sell grain to the USSR during the U.S. grain embargo imposed against that country for invading Afghanistan. For further discussion, see Mares 1995.

lateralism and its inconsistent application (meaning that one cannot count on U.S. aid if attacked)[10] produce security benefits and costs for Latin American states that are largely outside their control. The unpredictability of U.S. behavior thus becomes a security risk.

Managing Latin America's Security Complexes: The Failure to Marginalize Military Considerations

Morgan identifies five management schemes for achieving order and security in a regional security complex: great-power concert (which actually represents only one type of great-power management); integration; pluralistic security community; collective security; and power restraining power (a.k.a. balance of power). Within each scheme military, diplomatic, political, economic, and cultural elements are combined in a variety of ways; in all except "power restraining power," however, national considerations of military force are subordinate to the other elements.

This section discusses the uses but ultimate shortcomings of the first four management schemes. In Latin America, military power considerations have consistently been paramount, with the other elements limited to modifying, rather than replacing, distribution-of-power considerations.

GREAT-POWER MANAGEMENT

The British sought to create a great-power miniconcert (including only Britain and the emerging great power the United States) in Latin America from independence in the 1820s until the early twentieth century, but the United States rejected such a scheme.[11] The United States clearly saw itself as having

10. Ecuador was abandoned to the Peruvians in the 1939–41 war, and Chile felt isolated in 1977–78 as it confronted war scares first with Peru, then with Argentina. The landed oligarchy throughout Latin America believed that the U.S. push for land reform after the Cuban Revolution meant that they were being abandoned by the United States. Anti-Communist military regimes in the 1970s also perceived U.S. human rights policies in a similar light.

11. The British first floated the idea of a joint British-U.S. declaration warning Spain and the Holy Alliance to stay out of the newly independent Spanish American states, but the U.S. rejected it and unilaterally issued its own warning to all non-American powers. The Clayton-Bulwer Treaty of 1850 provided for joint U.S. and British control over any transisthmian canal to be built in Central America, but the United States later forced renegotiations ending such British "rights" (Hay-Pauncefote Treaties) (Bemis 1955; Dulles [1965] 1971; May 1975; Munro 1964).

a paramount role in Western Hemisphere security questions: the Monroe Doctrine does not proclaim that the United States will keep its hands off the former Spanish colonies. The United States attempted formally to institutionalize its influence over Latin America by creating an American customs union in 1889, the Pan American Union (PAU). But Latin America rejected giving the United States economic advantages over Europe. Mindful of the risks of multilateralizing its foreign policy, the United States sought to keep "political" issues off the agenda (Mecham 1962, 53). But some Latin Americans wanted the PAU to play an active role in defending Latin American sovereignty and brought these issues to the regional agenda. While the United States could not turn the PAU into an instrument of hegemonic control, it could effectively immobilize it by not acting (see discussion under "Collective Security" below).

Based on its efforts one might be tempted to consider the U.S. conception of its role in the Latin American security complex as that of unilateral great-power management. But while such a scheme remains an open question in the former Soviet Union (see Roeder, this volume), it does not accurately describe inter-American relations. Historical experience demonstrates that the United States has not been able to act effectively as a security manager in Latin America. South America actually experienced its least conflictual period before 1919, the generally recognized date for the inception of U.S. hegemony (Mares 1995; 1996b, chap. 3). In defense of its own domestic and international interests, the United States behaved in a capricious manner, producing perverse incentives for other nations. The United States not only failed to punish regional aggression, but also rewarded (e.g., Peru's war against Ecuador in 1941)[12] or provoked it (Nicaraguan violations of Salvadoran and Costa Rican sovereignty in 1916; Honduran and Costa Rican violations of Nicaraguan sovereignty in the 1980s).[13] The United States also stayed out of regional conflicts that threatened to erupt into war (e.g., the 1978 Beagle crisis between Chile and Argentina). The United States itself is a

12. The United States was the driving force behind the peace negotiations that recognized Peruvian conquests in the 1939–41 war against Ecuador. English (1984, 239) believes the United States attempted to curry favor with Peru because Chile had pro-fascist sympathies.

13. The Bryan-Chamorro Treaty of 1916 gave the United States sovereignty rights over any canal using Nicaraguan territory. Costa Rica and El Salvador complained to the Central American Court of Justice that their sovereign rights were affected but that they had no part in the negotiations. When the court found in the plaintiffs' favor, the United States encouraged Nicaragua to ignore the ruling (Connell-Smith 1974, 35, 141–42); in the 1980s the United States organized, funded, supplied, and provided logistical support to the anti-Sandinista contra forces, who had camps in Honduran and Costa Rican territory (Walker 1987).

source of interstate militarized conflict in the region (via covert and overt intervention). Finally, the United States could not keep Latin American governments from accessing the international arms markets or developing indigenous military industrial complexes, both of which significantly increased the destructive power of their conventional arsenals (Child 1980).

INTEGRATION

Integration has both political and economic components. Political integration was the dream of some of Latin America's great liberators and statesmen. Bolivar himself created Gran Colombia, consisting of present-day Venezuela, Ecuador, and Colombia. Peru and Bolivia were at one time a confederated state, until Chile attacked them in 1836–39 (English 1984, 367). Central American leaders fought until 1907 to re-create the United Provinces of Central America, which had been dismantled in the civil wars of 1838–42 (Woodward 1976). The U.S. perception of security (as well as destiny) was also governed by an integrationist logic: it had to incorporate all westward territory to the Pacific Ocean. But only the United States was able militarily to defeat the opponents of integration, though in doing so the country itself (not to mention Native Americans and Mexicans) paid a high price: a bloody civil war.

Economic integration has also been attempted, partly out of security considerations and partly for developmental considerations. I have already noted the original U.S. intention for the PAU. During the early-twentieth-century naval arms race between Argentina and Brazil (which included Brazil's purchases of the largest dreadnoughts of the time) increased economic ties were advocated as a way of guaranteeing future amiable relations (PRO 1907). The Central American Common Market, Latin American Free Trade Association, Andean Pact, and the recently created Mercosur have been the major economic pacts. But the Central American nations of El Salvador and Honduras went to war in 1969, and Andean Pact members have shot at each other (Peru and Ecuador, twice) and engaged in a mini–arms race (Colombia and Venezuela). Mercosur is too new for its experience to be suggestive.

PLURALISTIC SECURITY COMMUNITY

The search for a pluralistic security community also has a long and unsuccessful history in Latin America. Between 1826 and 1889 at least fifty conventions among Latin American states pledged to resolve disputes amicably (Mecham 1962, 46). Yet this was the period of the bloodiest Latin American wars. Only in the post-1930s U.S.-Mexican relationship is there a pluralistic security community.[14]

Latin American countries have resolved disputes without recourse to military threats. Binding arbitration was popular among many countries at the turn of the century (Gros Espiell 1986, 16). Its use declined over time, but El Salvador and Honduras, and Chile and Argentina, recently arbitrated their border disputes. Nevertheless, the Central American countries continue to dispute the 1992 World Court ruling (*New York Times,* 5 February 1995, E4).

Mediation by both regional and extraregional actors has a long history in the region (Gros Espiell 1986; Mecham, 1962). The pope mediated the Beagle dispute between Chile and Argentina. Four Latin American countries (Mexico, Venezuela, Colombia, and Panama) unsuccessfully mediated the 1980s crisis in Central America (the "Contadora Initiative"). They were later joined by a "support group" of four other South American countries. Although the final resolution of the Central American crisis did not follow their lead, the experience was promising enough that the collaboration was formalized as the Rio Group (Frohmann 1989). The actual negotiated settlements to the Central American conflict were the result of diplomatic negotiations among the parties themselves (the Esquipulas, or Arias, negotiations).

Pluralistic security communities are likely to place great faith in international law as a mechanism for conflict resolution. This diplomatic approach is held in particularly high regard in Latin American international relations. Latins have historically joined with the United States in seeing the Americas as a special place, far from the power politics of Europe. This uniqueness was expected to produce a special style of international politics, governed by "American Law," which would protect the sovereignty of all states. Even when it became clear that this perspective did not prevent the United States or even Latin American states from violating the sovereignty of American states, the idealism of an "American system" remained. In a rebuke

14. This state of affairs is due to vast power disparities between the two nations and the decision by Mexican political leaders (in a one-party system born of military revolts and surrounded by the militarized polities in the rest of Latin America) to keep their military small and backward. Nevertheless, the United States has increasingly militarizing its southern border in a largely futile attempt to control the inward flow of drugs and people. The United States may not believe war is thinkable with Mexico, but they are coming to legitimize using military force against Mexicans.

to European and U.S. practice, Latin American diplomats and jurists formulated the first attempts legally to limit the ability of nations to use force to protect the interests of their national citizens in foreign countries (Calvo and Drago Doctrines) (Connell-Smith 1974, 111–15).

Sporadic efforts to delegitimize the use of force in interstate disputes demonstrate that states in the region understand the benefits of this type of security-management scheme. Historical experience demonstrates that American nations are not ready to trust their national interests to it.

COLLECTIVE SECURITY

Collective security schemes overlap pluralistic security efforts in Latin America. Two attempts stand out: the Pan American Union and the Inter-American Treaty of Reciprocal Assistance (Rio Treaty). The first failed even to materialize on paper, while the second was moribund from the time it was negotiated. Since many U.S. analysts erroneously believe that the Rio Treaty is a functioning collective security agreement, we should examine it closely.

Morgan notes that in a collective security order, at a minimum, "management is not solely the prerogative of major states; their actions are to have collective endorsement" (Morgan, this volume, 35). The historical reality is that neither the United States nor some of the major Latin American states have accepted subordinating their freedom of action to the inter-American community.

The years of the Pan American Union (1889–1945) included the heyday of overt U.S. intervention in Latin America, 1890–1933 (Goldberg 1986; Dulles [1965] 1971; Munro 1964). The United States attempted to keep political matters, including security issues, off the PAU agenda until the 1930s. But some Latin American states consistently pushed two security topics into the discussions. Argentina proposed the Drago Doctrine on debt collection, while others pushed for the obligatory peaceful resolution of conflict among American states. The United States was opposed to both measures, and important Latin American nations also refused to constrain their freedom of action. Brazil, a creditor itself, opposed the Drago Doctrine (Burns 1966, 120–21). Binding arbitration of inter-American disputes met with the disapproval of Brazil and Chile (Mecham 1962, 59–60), both of whom were busily establishing effective control over border areas in dispute.

United States hemispheric policy appeared to change with the adoption of the Good Neighbor Policy and the return home of the last U.S. troops in

Latin America (from Nicaragua and Haiti in 1933). Hemispheric cooperation became the rhetorical order of the day after 1936 as the United States sought to create a common neutrality position vis-à-vis the prospect of another European war, into which the United States worried that Latin America's European ties could draw the hemisphere.[15] Nevertheless, the United States was rebuffed in its plan for a strict neutrality stance that would isolate the Americas from Europe, and had to settle for a vague agreement to consult in the event of a threat "if they so desire" (Haglund 1984, 36–41; Mecham 1962, 124–35). In 1938, after the Munich crisis, the United States sought an outright mutual defense pact, but Latin American opposition limited cooperation to consultation.

The outbreak of war in Europe stimulated closer inter-American cooperation. A hemispheric neutrality zone was implemented in September 1939. In response to the fall of the Low Countries and France to Germany in 1940, the United States and Latin America declared that an attack against one American state by a non-American state was an act of aggression against all. Mexico participated in the Pacific war, while Brazil sent troops to Italy.

Even in the face of the global threat of fascism, there were important limits to cooperation. The U.S. effort to isolate the Americas from Europe before 1941 via a hemispheric economic cartel failed. In addition, the United States wanted Latin America to consult with it before taking any action that could provoke Axis retaliation, yet it did not consult with Latin America regarding the aid it provided Britain before Pearl Harbor. There was also no consultation with Latin America concerning the U.S. decision to join the European war. The United States also faced difficulties in undertaking bilateral military negotiations, particularly with Argentina, which only abandoned its neutrality stance in 1944, despite years of U.S. sanctions (Francis 1977; Mecham 1962, 186–87).

The period 1945–47 marks a watershed in the development of inter-American relations. The PAU was reorganized into the Organization of American States (OAS), with explicit recognition of its role in hemispheric political and security matters. The Rio Treaty of 1947 specifically allowed the use of force if necessary to ensure peace and territorial integrity.

The OAS and the Rio Treaty give the appearance of a farsighted collective security community. In addition to advocating peaceful resolution of conflict and military cooperation against aggression, the OAS Charter called

15. A similar issue arose in World War I when Mexico and Argentina rejected belligerency in favor of neutrality (Mecham 1965, 77–86).

for the defense of democracy and human rights.[16] Under Article 51 of the United Nations Charter regional disputes were to be referred to the OAS before the UN Security Council would intervene (Mecham 1962, 282–315).

The OAS conflict-management system had few successes. Some Caribbean and Central American disputes were at least temporarily settled under OAS auspices, but war was not prevented between Honduras and El Salvador in 1969. Most important, once the United States became involved in a dispute (as would occur when the United States sought to overthrow leftist regimes), the system usually was marginalized. The U.S. veto in the UN Security Council and denial of World Court jurisdiction effectively meant that there was no appeal of a U.S. decision to act unilaterally.[17]

The United States found numerous opportunities to act unilaterally against both perceived Communists (e.g., Guatemala in 1954 and Cuba in 1961) and non-Communists (e.g., embargoes against military regimes in the late 1970s and the invasion of Panama in 1989). In recognition of the reality, rather than the rhetoric, of the inter-American security arrangement, Canada explicitly refused to join the military components of the inter-American system when it recently became a member of the OAS. Chided by a U.S. diplomat for not wanting to undertake full responsibilities, a Canadian diplomat noted that Canada would join when the United States ceased to act unilaterally in security matters.[18]

The problem with collective security via either a military alliance or adherence to the norm of nonintervention was that it served few interests. Unable to restrain the giant, Latin Americans refused to bind themselves to a common response even in their struggle against revolutionary movements that threatened to overthrow their stratified social structures. In the 1970s Panama, Costa Rica, Mexico, and Venezuela provided aid and comfort to the Sandinista revolutionaries against the Somoza dictatorship in Nicaragua,

16. Despite widespread violations of human rights and the prevalence of nondemocratic governments, until the 1990s only two countries were sanctioned for violating these inter-American norms: the Dominican Republic and Cuba, both in 1960. The United States overcame Latin American unwillingness to sanction Cuba by reluctantly acquiescing in the sanction of the Dominican dictatorship (Mecham 1962, 282–84, 316–17, 389–423, 460).

17. Guatemala (1954) and Cuba (1960) appealed to the UN, and Nicaragua appealed to the World Court in the 1980s (Connell-Smith 1974, 215–19, 228–36; Kim 1987, 265). The OAS blocked the Carter administration from using an inter-American force to save the pro-U.S. regime in Nicaragua in 1978, but it could not stop the Bush administration from invading Panama (Einaudi 1991).

18. Comments during the workshop "North American Security in the Time of NAFTA," National Defense University, Washington, D.C., September 1994.

while the bureaucratic-authoritarian regimes of the Southern Cone collaborated in tracking down suspected Communists.

None of the four conflict-management systems examined in this section gives us significant insight into the Latin American experience. Historical analysis of these systems highlights three factors that have effectively undermined these paths to regional security: the United States and Latin America consistently put national above community interests, are unwilling to depend upon others for the defense of those interests, and believe that the unilateral decision to use force to protect national interests is legitimate. The de facto security-management system in Latin America reflects this reality.

The Historic System, 1889–1980s: Reproducing the Westphalian System

The Westphalian system, created in Europe and imposed on the rest of the world through European colonialism, instituted a conflict-management scheme with "power," "state," and "sovereignty" as core concepts. There was a sense of "community" because political units were identified as members or not (Chan 1984, 619–29); there were norms concerning behavior, in particular that of nonintervention in the internal affairs of member states (Mansbach and Vasquez 1981, 4); and there were occasional great-power concerts. Notwithstanding these constraints on international behavior, the conflict dynamics of the Westphalian system are best understood in balance-of-power terms, or what Morgan labels "power restraining power."

In this system power parity in a defense-dominated world produces low levels of militarized conflict, while power disparities in an offense-dominated world is most likely to lead to a breakdown of "management" and the imposition of solutions by military force (Waltz 1979; Jervis 1978). It is this conflict-management system that gives us the best insight into the Latin American security complex.

ADDRESSING THE U.S. THREAT

Latin American states have considered playing the international balance-of-power game to diminish the threat from the United States. During World War II Argentine leaders erroneously believed that Britain, which was happy to receive strategic raw materials from Argentina, would contain U.S. sanctions against its neutrality. Revolutionary Cuba used its island geography, revolutionary fervor, and massive Soviet aid (of a magnitude that Germany was simply unable to provide to potential allies in Latin America during either World War I or World War II) to slip slowly away from 1959 to 1961. It took a near nuclear war in 1962 to guarantee its right to balance against the United States. But 22,500 U.S. Marines at the beginning of a Dominican civil war in 1965, covert action and economic embargoes against a democratic government in Chile, and a proxy war against the Sandinistas in Nicaragua during the 1980s effectively kept Cuba the hemispheric exception.

Thus, for these states, as for the successor states in the former Soviet Union (see Roeder, this volume), external balancing against the United States is a virtual nonstarter. Given international power disparities and stratified domestic social structures, internal balancing is also essentially nonviable: defense is not possible, and deterrence via a Vietnam strategy is more likely to produce a civil war than to deter direct or covert U.S. action. One can interpret the breakdown of the Sandinista-led National Front after 1980 as a result of the internal balancing strategy used to deal with the Reagan administration's threat to post-Somoza Nicaragua.

In short, under a balance-of-power system in which there is no possibility of effectively balancing against one power (i.e., in which there is a condition of regional hegemony), weaker states can be expected to have a fundamentally difficult time restraining the powerful. The power disparity between the United States and any Latin American country is so great that whether the United States initiates a violent conflict with one of those countries depends largely on factors beyond Latin American control, except if it simply accedes to every whim of the United States. The U.S. decision on whether to use force varies by the domestic response to its costs and can be grouped into three periods: extensive use, 1898–1933; reliance on nonviolent means, 1933–59; and renewed intervention, 1959 to the present (Connell-Smith 1974; Mecham 1962; Munro 1964; Wood 1961; Francis 1977; Cottam 1994). The dynamics of a power-restraining-power conflict-management system explains why this particular threat in Latin America's security complex was beyond control of the management system.

DEALING WITH THE INTRA–LATIN AMERICAN THREAT

The intra–Latin American version of the Westphalian system did serve the other two needs of the Latin American security complex fairly well until the late 1970s. The danger of intra–Latin American war and large-scale use of violence was minimized by intra–Latin American power balancing and deterrence politics in a largely defense-dominated world, while the covertness of violations of sovereignty made containment of revolutionary threats manageable.

A combination of geography, the shift of Argentina, Chile, and Brazil to positions defending the status quo after gaining large expanses of territory, and the relatively low level and lack of sophistication of armaments in the region produced a strategic situation in which the defense had the advantage for most of the twentieth century until the 1970s (Kemp 1973; Child 1980). Balance-of-power-oriented diplomacy in Latin America's security complex sought to keep the level of armaments low. At the turn of the century the British helped broker a naval arms agreement between Argentina and Chile (Burr 1965). The Tlatelolco Treaty (1967) banned nuclear arms from the region (Redick 1981, 103–34). State leaders also seemed to understand the logic of deterrence, with sudden crises leading to quick arms buildups and arms racing producing periodic crises (Mares 1996a).

Military deterrence can be pursued not only by building up one's own forces, but also by aggregating one's military capacity through alliances. Most alliances in Latin America have been informal ententes. Chile has historically been concerned about deterring a possible Peruvian-Bolivian-Argentine axis (Burr 1965). A Brazilian-Chilean alliance long haunted Argentine security analysts. Peru assumes that if it became involved in a war with either Ecuador or Chile, the other would take advantage of the situation (Velit 1993, 233). In one of the most interesting examples of informal military aid, during the Malvinas War democratic Peru (with a center-left-leaning military) resupplied right-wing authoritarian Argentina with fourteen Mirages and Exocet missiles (English 1984, 401).

The seven twentieth-century wars up to 1970 confirm this balance-of-power view. The two Central American wars (1906 and 1907), Leticia (1932), the Chaco War (1931–35), and the Soccer War (1969) demonstrated that the defense had the advantage and that parity existed; only the Bolivians persisted in pushing a war to its ultimate consequences, and over a hundred thousand died. In 1937 preponderance allowed Dominican forces to massacre twelve thousand Haitians without fear of reprisals, and preponderance with new weapons systems and strategies allowed the Peruvians to implement a blitzkrieg across disputed Amazonian territory and deep into Ecuador proper.

Military power was thus a currency in relations among Latin American states, but statesmen well understood its limitations, given the distribution of power in the region.

CONFRONTING THE DOMESTIC THREAT

The Latin American security-management system addressed the threats of revolutionary contagion in a peculiar fashion. A de facto division of labor appeared adequate for a time. Confronted by a revolutionary movement in one country, Latin American diplomats would argue that nonintervention was in everyone's interests. If the revolutionaries failed to moderate their rhetoric, if not behavior, the United States would isolate and, if necessary, covertly overthrow the alleged "Communists." But even this constraint on Latin American behavior was violated: Latin American countries themselves covertly used money, intelligence, training, and supplies to reproduce preferred political regimes.[19]

BREAKDOWN

The regional security-management system began to break down in the mid-1960s and could not prevent crisis escalation in the 1970s and 1980s. For the first time since the 1930s, interstate war threatened to engulf Latin America. The Argentines prepared to take on the Chileans and fought the British; Peruvians clashed with Ecuadorians twice; Central Americans became intimately involved in each others' civil wars; and even the long-standing democracies of Colombia and Venezuela mobilized their troops. The United States invaded Grenada and Panama, threatened Cuba, and

19. Nineteenth-century liberals in power throughout Central America and Mexico helped each other gain and retain political power. The leaders of the Mexican Revolution initially felt more secure with radicals in power in Central America and supplied Sandino in Nicaragua during the 1920s. In the 1940s and 1970s Argentine military governments supported coups in Bolivia. Right-wing authoritarian regimes in Chile and Bolivia were suspicious of the left-wing military government in Peru, and vice versa. Venezuelan democrats overthrown in 1948 informally organized a "Caribbean League" to promote democracy in the subregion via covert action. In the late 1940s and early 1950s Perón's government in Argentina financed the ATLAS (Agrupación de Trabajadores Latinoamericanos Sindicalistas) labor movement throughout Latin America. Brazilian intelligence services helped track down Communists in the 1930s. Argentina helped train the contras in Central America from 1979 to 1982 (Woodward 1976; Francis 1977; St. John 1992; Mecham 1962; Bailey 1967; Hilton 1991; Kaufmann [1988] 1994).

stoked the Central American conflicts with military maneuvers, material, and rhetoric.

Three factors account for the collapse of the conflict-management system, two of which were embedded in the balance-of-power approach. Weapons became more destructive and offense-oriented, and diplomacy became more ideological, thus undermining the idea that diversity in domestic politics was not a threat to peace. In addition, the foreign-debt crisis made disputed resources seem more important and produced domestic political pressures that could possibly be mitigated via diversionary external conflicts.

United States unilateral arms control via military assistance programs faltered. In the 1970s, as Latin Americans sought to replace their antiquated equipment, the international arms market was tapped to increase military capabilities in the region dramatically. Soviet T-54 tanks and Sukhoi fighter bombers; French Mirages, Super Etendards, and Exocet missiles of various configurations; Israeli Dagger and K-fir fighters; British Hunter fighters and Canberra bombers; and finally U.S. F-16s and 4As—all made their way into Latin American arsenals. In addition, Argentina, Brazil, and Chile began to develop an arms industry that could retrofit existing weapons systems; develop missiles, light aircraft, light armored vehicles; and even embark on nuclear submarine and bomb programs (English 1984).

Diplomatic efforts to modify the arms race failed. A ban on bombers was discussed in the 1970s, but Peru's opposition apparently killed it, although Ecuador disposed of its small bomber force (three). After achieving parity with Chile for the first time in one hundred years, Peru called for regional arms control in 1974 and disarmament in 1985, but nothing concrete was achieved (St. John 1992, 204, 210). The Tlatelolco Treaty was accepted by all Latin American countries except the four most likely to proliferate: Argentina, Brazil, Chile, and Cuba. The United States embargoed a number of militaries because of their authoritarian governments. Alternative sources of conventional weapons overcame these efforts. Cuban, Soviet, and U.S. weapons flows to Central America produced perceptions of imbalances. Nicaragua's neighbors worried about the massive increase in its army's personnel and equipment, while the Sandinistas focused on Honduras's air superiority and the flow of resources from the United States.

One cannot simply attribute increased arms expenditures to the assumption of power by the military. Not all military governments increase arms expenditures, and not all countries that upgrade their military capabilities are run by the military. The left-leaning Peruvian military took power in 1968, but only began a major arms push in 1973, after rightist coups in neighboring Bolivia and Chile.[20] Democratic regimes have also not been willing to be caught in a disadvantageous military position, even with respect to each other. Venezuela and Colombia, both democracies since 1958, responded to a disputed border incident in the petroleum-rich Gulf of Venezuela by dramatically increasing their military expenditures and reinforcing borders.[21]

Latin American leaders also do not feel secure with a unilaterally and significantly diminished military presence, even in the absence of immediate security threats. Contemporary Argentina, democratic for over a decade and with clear civilian control of a dramatically downsized and politically weakened military, has significantly increased its radar capabilities in the most recent fighter aircraft purchases.[22] Not only the leaders feel the need for a deterrent military force. A 1992 public opinion survey indicated that 17 percent of Argentines and 36.5 percent of Chileans believed that military threats from neighboring countries were either likely or highly likely (Fontana and Varas 1992, 33).

The result of the disjointed efforts at arms control, arms buildups and reductions, and arms embargoes was to create a situation in which suspected imbalances and offensive advantages meant that strategic surprise might resolve long-standing disputes. Neither democrats nor authoritarians, economic liberalizers nor statists, pro-Communists nor anti-Communists, were immune to the new strategic environment. The Argentine economic liberalizers sought to surprise both the Chileans and the British; Ecuadorian democrats believed they could present Peru with a *fait accompli* in the Amazon; Sandinista pro-Communist statists feared a replay of the Dominican intervention; and Colombian democrats worried that Venezuelan actions were a prelude to a definitive settlement of their border dispute.

A new ideological rigidity also contributed to the recent ineffectiveness of the balance-of-power management system. The United States returned to more overt intervention and insistence on the limits of coexistence in the

20. St. John 1992, 203–5; Masterson 1991, 265. The Soviet Union provided Peru with 115 military advisors in the army and air force and trained 200 commissioned and noncommissioned officers (citing Pentagon sources, CLADDE 1988, 348).

21. *Defensa* (Madrid) 11 (November 1988): 127, as cited in Serbin 1988, 288 n. 43; CLADDE-RIAL 1988, 300, 301, 371. Venezuela had previously reinforced border defenses after Colombian guerrillas crossed. But the 1987 appearance of a Colombian navy vessel in Venezuelan-claimed waters provoked mutual military mobilizations. Similar incidents in the early 1970s also fueled arms acquisitions (*Diario,* 20 December 1993, 30).

22. *Los Angeles Times,* 4 March 1994, A4. Though old, the Skyhawks had been responsible for destroying some of the British ships during the Malvinas War (English 1982, 27–29).

hemisphere. The magnitude of the 1965 Dominican invasion (22,500 Marines) and the blatant subservience of the OAS in sanctioning the invasion after the fact (Lowenthal 1972) made it impossible for Latin Americans to gloss over U.S. unilateralism. The Alliance for Progress land-reform programs threatened the right-wing status quo in much of rural Latin America. In the 1970s U.S. liberals extended the purview of foreign policy to cover the domestic policies of Latin American countries (human rights and democracy), much to the chagrin of traditional U.S. anti-Communist allies in the region. An anti-U.S. siege mentality on both the Left and the Right began to grip Latin America twenty years after the start of the Cold War.

The Reagan administration fueled the ideological polarization of Central America, extended it into the Anglo-Caribbean (Grenada), and sought to reisolate Cuba from Latin America. The impact on Central American interstate behavior was predictable: interstate tensions increased dramatically. But the impact of the Reaganite "holy-war" mentality was not limited to fighting Communists in the United States' "backyard." The Argentine military government, actively aiding the United States in Central America, came to believe that the United States would remain neutral if Argentina unilaterally sought to resolve the Malvinas question (Kaufmann [1988] 1994, 3).

In this environment of suspected offense domination and ideological rigidities, the diplomatic structure of the security system became marginalized. This structure teetered in the wake of the U.S. invasion of the Dominican Republic in 1965 and the opening of Latin American ties to Cuba in the 1970s, and broke down dramatically with the Falklands/Malvinas War and the end of the Cold War. Not only was the OAS unable peacefully to resolve the war in the South Atlantic; the United States actively supported an extra-hemispheric power in a military confrontation with an American nation.[23] With the end of the Cold War in 1989, the legitimacy of the Rio Treaty (set up primarily for hemispheric defense), was seriously undermined by the absence of an extracontinental threat.

The economic collapse of many Latin American economies in the early 1980s may also have contributed to increased interstate conflict in South America. Oil is exploited on the Colombian-Venezuelan and Ecuadorian-Peruvian borders, and explorations were under way in the South Atlantic. Some Venezuelan analysts worry that developing their portion of the Ama-

23. A future Chilean ambassador to the OAS noted: "The mechanisms for the peaceful resolution of conflicts within the inter-American system did not function appropriately to manage the South Atlantic war precisely because they had been discredited and paralyzed along with the overall system" (Munoz 1984, 171).

zon could make it an attractive asset to seize.[24] But adverse economic factors alone do not explain the heightened level of regional conflict. Both Ecuador and Peru experienced strong economic growth before their 1995 border skirmish.

Ironically, democratization may also be partially responsible for increased tension. Democratic politicians in Colombia, Venezuela, Ecuador, and Peru used external tensions to garner domestic support (*Latin American Regional Reports,* 3 February 1994, 1; *New York Times,* 9 February 1995, A3). Diversionary threats, however, are not limited to democratic polities. The Argentine military may have engaged in a diversionary war (Levy and Vakili 1992; but Gamba [1987, 74–77, 131–33] presents a strong case against this interpretation).

Reorganizing Security: Parallel and Mutually Reinforcing Structures

Given the recent failure of the traditional system to dampen interstate conflict and given the new regional context of democratization, economic liberalism, and the end of the Cold War, discussion of new management schemes for regional security is widespread within diplomatic, military, and academic circles.[25] "Cooperative security," "collective security," even "pluralistic security community" have become buzz words once again. My evaluation of the historical experience and contemporary crises, however, strongly suggests that the underlying dynamics of interstate-dispute behavior has not changed significantly.[26]

24. *Globo,* 28 June 1993, 18, cites Alberto Muller Rojas, a retired general, current senator, and respected security analyst.

25. For example, the OAS created a committee to examine the relationship between the social-political-economic components of the organization and their military counterpart. The North-South Center at the University of Miami, the Latin American Program of the Woodrow Wilson Center of the Smithsonian Institution, and the National Defense University have had workshops for policy makers, officers, and academics on the new inter-American security environment, highlighting civil-military relations.

26. Solingen (this volume) disagrees. Solingen's argument requires that the "international economic order" sanction those who misbehave. But the liberal international economic order is not a unified structure, and the logic of sanction is not clear. At different points it appears to be the profit orientation of private sources of capital, the security interests of the governments of the advanced industrial countries, or the financial concerns of the major international economic

Economic growth and democratization in the absence of a stable and credible balance of power are more likely to be recipes for increased conflict, rather than the first steps toward integration or a pluralist security community. Even in the new regional context, Ecuador and Peru went to war, and border tensions brought Colombia and Venezuela to the precipice (*El Nacional,* 17 March 1995, 1). Historically, the Cold War made little difference in either U.S. intervention or Latin American interstate conflicts (Mares 1995). In the aftermath of the Cold War, the United States invaded Panama, pushed for an invasion of Haiti, and continues the embargo against Cuba, demonstrating that it is still willing to use a big stick.

I therefore expect the old balance-of-power system, with some modifications discussed below, to reemerge in a more stable form. This analysis suggests that prudence and cautious optimism, rather than euphoric idealism, promise to deliver more security to Latin America. The challenge in the current formulation of Latin American security arrangements is to push the military threshold further back, rather than to search for its elimination. The most viable alternative conflict-management system for Latin America must also recognize that the United States will continue to define its security needs unilaterally. The system must not be built on the assumption that the United States will behave as Latin America wants or that its behavior is irrelevant.

A multitiered and integrated security structure could meet these demands. It would be multitiered to facilitate working out disagreements locally first, and, as necessary, subregionally, regionally, and globally. It would be integrated in that military, diplomatic, economic, political, and social aspects of interstate relations would be used to support the nonviolent resolution of conflict. Structured in this fashion, the regional security-management system might convince the United States both that its legitimate needs were being addressed and that an early decision on its part to use force would meet opprobrium not only at the regional level but at the global as well.

---

organizations. Even with the end of the Cold War, the interests of these three groups of actors are not the same, either across groups or within them. Governments compete against each other; multilateral organizations disagree on who should be sanctioned and when; and the private sector not only is divided against itself but also may disagree with governments and multilateral organizations. The end result is a case-by-case evaluation by the various international forces. Note the disagreements over how to treat China or Iraq. Nigeria's execution of dissidents has not stopped Shell from investing there. The United States and Latin American governments condemned President Fujimori's coup in Peru (partly because democracy is believed fundamental to regional peace by all the current governments), but private-capital flows into Peru increased dramatically as the guerrillas were corralled and inflation came down (Peru 1993–94, 248).

Such a conflict-management system could also diminish the security dilemma among Latin American countries themselves.

The basic underpinning of the management scheme proposed here is found in the military and diplomatic structures in which Latin American conflict dyads play out. The chief elements of these structures are the balance of power, arms control, and confidence-building measures (CBMs). The challenge is to minimize the level of armaments and keep them defense-oriented, not to eliminate them.

While defense budgets in general have declined in most countries, the push for a professionalized military (which requires force modernization) should produce smaller but more powerful militaries.[27] Unfortunately, the Ecuador-Peru conflict will probably send ambiguous messages about the best use of that power. Ecuador's antiair capabilities kept Peru's superiority in fighter bombers and helicopters from making a difference in the war. For some analysts the experience will emphasize the advantages of defensive orientations, but others will seek new jamming capabilities (Pala 1995). Increased transparency in the arms acquisition process[28] could stimulate both a more defensive orientation and perhaps even a greater sense of security at lower levels of armament. Negotiated force levels in Central America helped diffuse the level of tension. Bilateral and multilateral meetings among Latin American militaries for confidence-building purposes have been gaining momentum for the last decade (CLADDE-RIAL 1988), but clearly more is needed. The Andean Group presidents renounced weapons of mass destruction in December 1991 (Declaration of Cartagena).[29]

Building on a stable and minimal balance of power would be military, diplomatic, political, and economic groupings at the subregional (i.e., Latin American subgroups) and regional (the OAS,[30] possibly a hemispheric free

27. There is an inter-American consensus that military professionalization keeps the military out of politics. For the theoretical justification, see Huntington 1957.

28. Not all countries participate in the United Nations' arms registry, and the data produced by the Washington-based Arms Control and Disarmament Agency (ACDA) and the London-based International Institute for Strategic Studies (IISS) are not identical.

29. The Latin American Center for Defense and Disarmament (CLADDE) edits an annual study of progress in this area, *Estudio estrategico de America Latina* (Santiago). The OAS Working Group on Hemispheric Security prepared three reports on the security of small states, the relationship between the OAS and the Inter-American Defense Board, and arms proliferation (OAS 1992). The United Nations has a Regional Center for Peace, Disarmament, and Development in Latin America and the Caribbean in Peru.

30. OAS diplomats are attempting to revive the inter-American security system but to render it less necessary by addressing political, economic, and social factors they believe affect peace and security (OAS 1992, 1993).

trade regime along the lines of President Bush's Initiative for the Americas) levels. Their basic contribution to security in the region would be via developing and training for defensive missions, support of confidence-building measures, economic development that promotes economic interdependence, political development that reinforces democratic government, and mediation of disputes when these other measures fail.

Many of these subregional and regional groupings are currently functioning.[31] It would be important, however, that any regional or subregional organization that had the United States as a member not have a military capacity. United States resources would overwhelm everyone, and the group would fall under its influence, repeating the unhappy experience of the Rio Treaty. Hence, collective inter-American security schemes are inappropriate.[32]

The next level up in the security system would incorporate the diplomatic/military structure of the United Nations. Its role would consist of mediation, confidence-building measures, coordination of sanctions when necessary, provision of peacekeeping forces where appropriate, and training of peacekeepers in Latin America. Argentina has participated in numerous UN peacekeeping missions and has offered to turn a military base formerly used to guard its Brazilian border into a peacekeeping school. It is more appropriate that Latin Americans collaborate with UN-provided trainers than with the United States in this mission because U.S. forces are trained to seek military victories rather than to help keep a tenuous peace. (For example, the U.S. decision to go after one faction in the Somalia conflict not only increased the level of violence but also turned U.S. public opinion against the mission when U.S. casualties increased).

Finally, and, one hopes, far down the path to peace and security, comes the traditional U.S. presence. One cannot eliminate this bull in the regional china shop. But incorporating Latin American bilateral, subregional, regional, and global structures into a multitiered and reinforcing security system offers the best hope for keeping red flags from the bull's sight.

31. For example, Group of Eight, Group of Three, Andean Pact, Mercosur.

32. As soon as the United States began discussing the possibility of using force to overthrow the dictatorship in Haiti, Latin American as well as Canadian diplomats objected (*New York Times,* 19 May 1994).

10

From Hierarchy to Hegemony: The Post-Soviet Security Complex

Philip G. Roeder

Following the collapse of the conservative coup against Mikhail Gorbachev, leaders of the Soviet Union's fifteen constituent republics began to make good on their threats to escape from Moscow's rule. At the time, many Western analysts predicted that intense nationalism plus the intoxication of newly gained independence would make any reimposition of dominance by Moscow unlikely; analysts rushed to repeat the once clever description of the Commonwealth of Independent States (CIS) as "the world's largest fig leaf" to cover Russia's loss of empire (Goble 1992, 57). Yet, a mere three years later, Western analysts began worrying about exactly the scenario that was deemed improbable in late 1991: the regime in Moscow began to reestablish its predominance within the region. Specialists now warn that many successor states are "reverting to Russian control" (e.g., Sunley 1994; Bondarevsky and Ferdinand 1994; Fuller 1993; Morrison 1993). The CIS is described as one of several tools by which Moscow has created "a partial reincarnation of a Russian empire, or at least a well-defined sphere of Russian influence, throughout the territory of the former Soviet Union" (Porter and Saivetz 1994, 77).

Despite the centrifugal forces that tore the Soviet Union apart in 1991, most of the successor states are still closely bound together; the space previously within the Soviet Union now constitutes a distinct international region. Despite nationalistic animosities toward Moscow in many of these states, Russia has established a sphere of influence over them; that is, the post-Soviet region is characterized by Russian hegemony. This chapter asks: How might we explain this outcome? And what alternative regional orders are possible?

Explanations for the tight hegemonic structure among many Soviet successor states have focused on Russia's motivations and its strong-arm techniques. Thomas Goltz (1993, 116) summarizes his analysis of Russian hegemony over the Transcaucasian states with the Russian aphorism "there is no defense against a crowbar." Yet, it is simply untrue that there are no defenses against crowbars, and the prevailing explanations beg an answer to why some strategies designed to resist the Russian crowbar have failed. Moreover, an explanation that focuses on Moscow's ambitions alone tells less than half the story: The prevailing explanations also beg an answer to why so many of the successor states have willingly acquiesced in, and some even actively sought, Russia's hegemony.

In this chapter I seek to unravel this puzzle. First, I begin by describing the dependent variable, examining the nature of the regional security complex that currently prevails within this region. Second, I analyze alternative explanations for the present form of the regional security complex, asking why some states of the former Soviet Union have accepted Russian hegemony and others have resisted. Third, I consider alternative security complexes that might emerge if or as Russia changes its strategy—or other states change theirs.

In this chapter I argue that the pattern of security relations among the Soviet successor states is constrained in the first instance by the survival objectives of the successor governments. That is, the benefits and costs, including transactions costs, that constrain the structure of the regional security complex (see Lake's chapter, this volume) are measured not with a financial yardstick of profits or revenues, but by the political metric of survival in office and power. Governors assess alternative alliance partners according to the contribution each can make to their own political survival. This differs from the neorealist survival postulate employed by Kenneth N. Waltz (1979); it reorients our analysis from the motivations of (and interactions among) fictional entities such as the state to the motivations and interactions of politicians in posts—governments. It notes that these politicians who have reached the highest post to which they can aspire seek first of all to hold on to their posts. A number of analysts have begun their investigations with this survival postulate (Bueno de Mesquita and Siverson 1995). In studies of domestic politics this postulate has been a fruitful assumption for both Americanists (Mayhew 1974) and comparativists (Ames 1987; Geddes 1994). In the field of international politics Steven David (1991a, 1991b) introduces the concept of "omnibalancing" to capture the notion that in forming interstate alliances Third World leaders seek to counter *all* threats—both external and internal.[1] In short, in selecting a survival strategy political leaders must weigh domestic against foreign threats to their survival and weigh the value of incentives offered by foreign as well as domestic coalition partners.

In most circumstances the survival of the state itself is an essential precondition for the leader's own survival, and so in most circumstances the realist survival postulate employed here does not diverge from Waltz's neorealist postulate. In some circumstances, however, leaders who face overwhelming opposition at home may sacrifice some of the sovereignty of their states in order to hold on to power.[2] This chapter argues that the conditions prevailing in the post-Soviet region constitute exactly this less common circumstance: many governmental leaders concerned with their own political survival have delegated some of their states' decision-making prerogatives and submitted to Russian hegemony.

The Post-Soviet Security Complex

The central structural features of the post-Soviet regional security complex are its relative autonomy vis-à-vis outside powers and Russian hegemony within it. In this Russian sphere of influence bilateral relations between Moscow and each of the other successor governments are more important than direct relations among the others or between these and governments outside the region. Whether they like it or not, the dominant security problem for

1. Michael Barnett and Jack Levy (1991) include domestic survival among the motivations for formulating interstate alliances, but they do not privilege either state or government survival among the eclectic list of motivations they posit for government leaders.

2. The willingness of some fascist and Communist leaders in this century to accept annexation or foreign domination in order to ensure their control of their states is an obvious case in point.

each of the other successor states is its "Russia problem"—how to respond to its overwhelming and sometimes overbearing neighbor.

To demarcate its sphere, Russia has sought to win global recognition of an external border that separates the post-Soviet security complex from others. To reinforce the autonomy of the regional security complex and its own hegemony within the complex, Russia has stationed troops along much of this outer CIS border and on the territories of many of its constituent states and has worked to exclude the troops of outside powers from the region. At a joint meeting of foreign and defense ministers of the CIS members in 1994, Russia's foreign minister, Andrei Kozyrev, argued that "Russia has an historic duty to guard the border" because "it is a frontier of the CIS." He justified Russia's unique role in the region: "It is clear that except for us, no one can resolve these issues" (Interfax, 16 March 1994; ITAR-TASS, 16 March 1994). By agreement Russia controls all Belarusian borders (ITAR-TASS, 3 November 1994). To maintain the external border in the Caucasus against Turkey and Iran, Russia has signed agreements with Armenia and Georgia for joint border control (*Nezavisimaia gazeta,* 26 August 1992; ITAR-TASS, 3 February 1994). In Central Asia, Russia brokered agreements for maintaining the "external" border of all states with China, Afghanistan, and Iran (Radio Rossii, 8 November 1992; *Slovo Kyrgyzstana,* 16 February 1993; ITAR-TASS, 26 June 1993, 15 July 1993, 16 July 1993; Ostankino Television, 22 July 1993). In order to block the flow of troops from Afghanistan, Russia has rallied the Central Asian states behind a multilateral commitment to defend Tajikistan's borders: At Alma-Ata and again at Minsk leaders of Russia, Kazakhstan, Kyrgyzstan, and Uzbekistan endorsed collective security agreements that they would take "all necessary measures" to guarantee Tajikistan's border with Afghanistan (*Nezavisimaia gazeta,* 5 September 1992; ITAR-TASS, 26 June 1993, 15 July 1993, 19 January 1996; Ostankino Television, 22 July 1993). In November 1994 the commander of Russia's Border Troops estimated that as a consequence of agreements signed with almost all successor governments, "there remain only two windows in the common border of the CIS," Azerbaijan and Moldova (*Rossiiskaia gazeta,* 12 November 1994; Russian Television, 27 November 1994).

By basing Russian troops throughout the successor states, Russia establishes a physical presence in its sphere. In 1994 the chief of the Russian General Staff predicted that Russia would conclude bilateral agreements for thirty bases with all successor states except Ukraine and the Baltic states (Interfax, 28 February 1994, 8 June 1994; ITAR-TASS, 3 February 1994, 9 June 1994). Russia has stationed so-called peacekeeping forces in Tajikistan, Georgia, and Moldova (ITAR-TASS, 23 February 1994).[3] Russia and Kazakhstan have agreed to create joint forces and to permit Russia to station troops within the latter (ITAR-TASS, 20 January 1995). Turkmenistan has placed the new Turkmen national army under joint Russian-Turkmen command and permitted as many as fifteen thousand troops under direct Russian command to be stationed on its soil (*Kazakhstanskaia Pravda,* 9 March 1993, 3 June 1992; KyrgyzTAG-TASS, 1 June 1992; Radio Rossii, 8 November 1992; *Slovo Kyrgyzstana,* 16 February 1993).

Equally important to maintenance of Russia's hegemony and the autonomy of the post-Soviet security complex has been the exclusion of troops from outside the region. Russia has objected to any discussion of granting NATO membership to the other successor states—specifically, to the Baltic states (Lieven 1995; *Komosomolskaia Pravda,* 11 June 1996). It has successfully resisted the introduction of "external" peacekeeping forces, leading the Committee of Senior Officials of the OSCE to protest Russia's obstruction of its efforts. Russia has sought instead to win endorsement from the UN and OSCE for an exclusive peacekeeping role in the region, with no "external" oversight, no limits on unilateral actions, and no provisions for timely withdrawal (RFE/RL, 14 June 1994, 15 September 1994, 17 September 1994, 21 November 1994; Interfax, 6 October 1994). As Boris Yeltsin told an assembly of Civic Union (a centrist political grouping) on 28 February 1993, "The moment has arrived for authoritative international organizations, including the United Nations, to grant Russia special powers as the guarantor of peace and stability in this region" (ITAR-TASS, 1 March 1993).[4]

The primary multilateral institution within the regional security complex has been the Commonwealth of Independent States. At first CIS served mostly as a vehicle for managing the Soviet armed forces during the breakup of the Soviet Union. Yet, as Stephen Foye (1993, 46) notes, the CIS and Russian military commands "worked in tandem to maintain Moscow's position as the focal point of an integrated security system on the territory of the former Soviet Union." Despite initial resistance from the other successor states, Russia increasingly pressed to transform CIS into a vehicle for broader integration in military and economic affairs under Russian leadership: on

3. Not all of the "host" countries, such as Moldova, have welcomed these peacekeepers and instead label them an occupying army (ITAR-TASS, 16 February 1994).

4. See also Yeltsin's discussion of basing rights within the CIS (*Krasnaia zvezda,* 11 June 1993) and Presidential Decree No. 174 (5 April 1994), approving these. This produced a furor, since the list of hosts included at least one country (Latvia) that claimed it had no intention of permitting Russian bases to remain.

17 March 1993 Yeltsin appealed to the CIS heads of state to coordinate foreign policies, to create collective peacekeeping forces, and to establish a "united defense . . . against aggressive nationalism" (Lough 1993). In 1994 Russia began pressing to transform the Joint Armed Forces Command into a headquarters for coordination of military activities (ITAR-TASS, 24 February 1994). At their April and October meetings that year the CIS heads of state accepted Russia's plan to create the Common Security Council and endorsed a memorandum for CIS integration in the military sphere, envisioning joint peacekeeping operations, a joint CIS rapid-deployment force, and joint production of military hardware (ITAR-TASS, 14 April 1994; Interfax, 14 April 1994, 15 April 1994, 5 October 1994). Within two years, nine members concluded the CIS Collective Security Agreement, and the CIS chiefs of staff held their first meeting in Moscow (ITAR-TASS, 5 June 1996). To promote economic integration Russia has pressed for creation of supranational bodies to manage transnational systems left over from the Soviet economy, including power grids, pipelines, transportation, and communications; it has urged transformation of CIS into an "EU-like arrangement" (Interfax, 23 August 1994, 7 September 1994, 8 September 1994). At their October 1994 meeting the CIS heads of state created the Interstate Economic Committee, which will serve as the executive arm of the CIS Economic Union; the agreement stopped short of the Russian plan for a supranational body that could impose sanctions on member states, but Russian leaders see this as the next step, and Yeltsin has announced that "the question of delegating powers" to this body is next on the agenda (Interfax, 5 October 1994, 21 October 1994, 24 January 1995).

To date, CIS has served more as a vehicle to reinforce Russian hegemony than as a multilateral constraint on Russia. Leadership positions within CIS are held by the Russian president or his appointees; the CIS Joint Command has served as an agent of the Russian Ministry of Defense. Within CIS bodies Russia's voice is predominant. For example, in the Interstate Economic Committee Russia holds 50 percent of the votes (substantive decisions require supermajorities of 75 percent) (Interfax, 5 October 1994). With this apportionment of power inside CIS Russia can use the organization to constrain other successor states, if it can win support from a few of them, but Russia cannot itself be bound against its will.

Typical of a sphere of influence the hegemon is a major party to each of the international conflicts of the region. In all four "theaters," or subregions, of the former Soviet Union, Russia is the major antagonist, the primary ally of each side, or the principal mediator. In the western theater (which includes Ukraine, Moldova, and Belarus) Russia has been the major antagonist in the four international crises that have plagued this subregion after the breakup of the Soviet Union—the Russo-Ukrainian disputes over the Black Sea Fleet, nuclear weapons, and the Crimea, and the Russo-Moldovan dispute over Trans-Dniestria. In the Baltic theater (which includes Estonia, Latvia, and Lithuania) Russia has similarly been the major antagonist in the subregion's three international conflicts—the withdrawal of Russian troops, the treatment of Russian minorities, and the demarcation of borders. In the Transcaucasian theater (which includes Armenia, Azerbaijan, and Georgia) Russia is not a major antagonist, but at various times has been the primary ally of both sides, and the principal mediator in the search for a resolution, of the three wars that have scarred this region—the Armenian-Azerbaijan war over Nagornyi Karabakh and Georgia's wars with Abkhazia and South Ossetia. In the Central Asian theater all five governments (Kazakhstan, Kyrgyzstan, Tajikistan, Turkmenistan, and Uzbekistan) have accepted Russia's leading role in managing security—particularly in the Tajik civil war—permitting Russia to establish its most complete protectorate over any theater (Page 1994).

These developments within the region have produced diverse reactions from the successor states that range from outright rejection to enthusiastic support of Russian hegemony. A rough ranking of these responses might group the fourteen other successor states into six groups (Interfax, 10 September 1994, 5 October 1994; Basapress, 31 January 1994; Ukrainian Radio, 22 August 1994):

1. Estonia, Latvia, and Lithuania have been most successful in distancing themselves from the post-Soviet security complex and have remained entirely outside the CIS.
2. Moldova has joined the CIS, but cooperates only in its economic activities and refuses to participate in military programs, claiming to be a neutral state. Moldova's government would prefer to follow the Baltic states and exit the post-Soviet security complex, but it has been unable to find similar levels of support from outside the region.
3. Turkmenistan and Ukraine, while participating in both the military and economic negotiations within CIS, are intent on limiting the extent to which members delegate decision making to CIS institutions (see, e.g., Rumer 1994; Page 1994). Both governments have refused to sign the CIS Collective Security Agreement (ITAR-TASS, 5 June 1996) and have re-

sisted creation of supranational bodies. Ukraine has objected to the concept of a common "external" border for the CIS and the implication that all other borders are "internal" (Interfax, 6 January 1996).

4. Armenia, Azerbaijan, and Uzbekistan have supported Russia's proposals for regional integration, but have sought to limit Russian hegemony within the regional security complex. Uzbekistan has been the most vociferous of the three. It rejected proposals to make CIS resolutions binding on members and, like Azerbaijan, initially refused to sign the CIS treaty on external borders. Nonetheless, all three states have acceded to the CIS Collective Security Agreement. While supporting regional integration, these three governments have held out for greater power sharing and multilateralism within the regional security complex (*Pravda,* 22 February 1996; Uzbek Television, 25 April 1996; ITAR-TASS, 7 May 1996, 11 June 1996).
5. Georgia, Kazakhstan, Kyrgyzstan, and Tajikistan have actively pursued integration with Russia and seem more willing to accept its hegemonic role within the post-Soviet region. As a result of their civil wars, the Georgian and Tajik governments have become thoroughly dependent on Moscow's support against domestic opponents and have reciprocated by endorsing Russia's plans for tighter integration of the CIS. For Kazakhstan and Kyrgyzstan large and strategically significant Russian minorities that could wreck these regimes make close cooperation with the Russian empire a necessity. In 1996 Kazakhstan joined a customs union with Russia and Belarus (ITAR-TASS, 3 January 1996), and Kyrgyzstan joined with these three states to form an integration committee (ITAR-TASS, 20 April 1996).
6. Belarus has been an enthusiastic supporter of tighter integration under Russian hegemony. In signing a series of agreements that culminated in the Russo-Belarusian Community on 2 April 1996, Presidents Aleksandr Lukashenka and Boris Yeltsin announced that their "goal" is "unity" with common legislative and executive organs (ITAR-TASS, 28 February 1996, 2 April 1996, 29 April 1996).

Why Is Moscow Once Again Dominant?

The prevailing explanations for Russia's hegemony within this security complex tend to emphasize its foreign-policy objectives. Yet, these explanations for hegemony beg an answer to why so many of the other successor states have acquiesced. This acquiescence is typically explained by the power disparity in the region, but this then begs an answer to why successor states have not used traditional balancing or alliance strategies to counter the Russian threat to their sovereignty. Failure to balance is typically explained by the absence of alternative alliance partners willing or able to enter the region, but this in turn begs an answer to why some successor states have not simply acquiesced, but enthusiastically encouraged growth of the relationships that underpin Russia's hegemony. Indeed, contrary to a common neorealist assumption that states jealously guard their sovereignty, several Soviet successor governments seem to be rushing to limit their states' sovereignty. In this section I consider each of these issues—Russian objectives, the regional power disparity, and the failure of traditional balancing strategies. I conclude by addressing the issue of support for Russian hegemony and offer an amendment to the prevailing neorealist explanation.

MOSCOW'S FOREIGN-POLICY OBJECTIVES

Central to the emergence of the Russian sphere of influence is unquestionably Russia's own hegemonic aspirations—a necessary but not sufficient condition. For Russia's government under Boris Yeltsin the foreign-policy agenda concerning its "near abroad" has been dominated by the problem of maintaining or reestablishing Moscow's influence within the post-Soviet region: Kozyrev explained that "Russia's vital interests are concentrated in, and being threatened from, that space" (Ostankino Television, 18 January 1994; Interfax, 18 January 1994). The Russian president stresses the centrality of Russian interests in the near abroad, including concerns for the Russians living there, and Russia's role as "a great power" that must be "first among equals" in the region (Russian Television, 1 January 1994; *Rossiiskaia gazeta,* 12 January 1994). The Russian Foreign Ministry issued the first of two foreign-policy "guidelines" on 1 December 1992, according to which, "[t]he most important foreign-policy tasks, requiring the coordinated and constant efforts of all state structures, are curtailing and regulating armed conflicts around Russia, preventing their spread to our territory, and guaranteeing strict observation in the near abroad of human and minority rights, particularly of Russians and the Russian-speaking population." On 3 March 1993 the Russian Security Council approved a second series of "conceptual principles," which also emphasized Russia's security interest in maintaining peace within the borders of the former Soviet Union. It added special emphasis to defending the external border of the former Soviet Union, warning that "Russia will actively oppose any attempts to increase the military-political presence of third states in the countries contiguous with Russia" (*Nezavisimaia gazeta,* 4 March 1993, 29 April 1993). Governmental spokesmen define this sphere of vital interests to include all successor states and not simply CIS members (Interfax, 6 January 1994; Info-TAG, 23 November 1994). The Russian president and his spokesmen frequently proclaim that their ultimate objective is the integration of the near abroad with Russia in either a confederation or even a new union (*Rossiiskaia gazeta,* 29 April 1994; *Izvestiia,* 21 July 1994; Interfax, 16 June 1994, 28 July 1994, 1 November 1994).

Explanations for Russia's hegemonic aspirations tend to be overdetermined, including objective security interests, Russian culture, and domestic Russian politics as sources. For example, concerning the first, Alvin Rubinstein (1994, 576) argues that in Central Asia "Moscow's aims are a combination of security, traditional great-power influence over weaker neighbors, and strategic denial." The Russian government's own explanation of its foreign policy, of course, stresses its roots in objective national interests, specifically, protecting the territorial integrity of Russia and the rights of Russian citizens in the near abroad. For example, Yeltsin's deputy prime minister for nationalities and federal affairs observed that the civil war in Georgia "must be regarded as a direct challenge to the vital interests of Russian security" (Russian Television, 14 July 1993; *Rossiiskie vesti,* 15 July 1993). In the official view the most important structural change following the end of the Cold War has been the rising importance of regions: According to the Foreign Ministry's guidelines, "the changing structure of the world balance of influence" has meant "the disappearance of the bipolar structure in its global dimension and the development of regional power-center tendencies" (*Rossiiskie vesti,* 3 December 1992); this, they reason, necessitates Russian regional hegemony.

Few analysts have been content to say that Russia's foreign-policy objectives are normal for a great power within its own region. Thus, many explanations for Russia's hegemonic aspirations tend to cite its cultural bases as well. The Russians' imperial culture is purportedly a consequence of a psychological ambiguity in their own identity as a people, an ambiguity that is in turn rooted in a legacy of the premodern empires under tsars and Soviets: the Russians never developed an identity that could be contained within a modern nation-state and that could reconcile them to a loss of empire (Goble 1993, 81; Dunlop 1993–94). The loss of the union republics has been a bitter pill to swallow for Russians of many political stripes. In late 1991 and early 1992 the reform movement split over the loss of the non-Russian republics; particularly distressing for many reformers was the loss of Ukraine (Tolz 1993). Russian conservatives (i.e., Communists and nationalists) and a good part of the Center were incensed at the breakup of the Soviet Union. For example, Vice President Aleksandr Rutskoi, writing for the moderate Right, claimed that "the historical consciousness of the Russians will not allow anybody to equate mechanically the borders of Russia with those of the Russian Federation and to take away what constituted the glorious pages of Russian history" (*Pravda,* 30 January 1992).

A third theme in the explanation of Russia's hegemonic aspirations stresses the domestic politics that constrain the Yeltsin government (Adomeit 1995).[5] Until the president's coup of September-October 1993, Yeltsin purportedly labored under the mounting threat of removal by the Congress of People's Deputies and Supreme Soviet. After that coup the strong showing of conservative parties in the parliamentary elections and the demands of the national security apparatus (the Armed Forces and successor agencies of the KGB and MVD) are allegedly driving a liberal president to more conservative policies. Those unwilling to reconcile themselves to the loss of empire gained a strong voice in the State Duma. The first chairman of the Duma's Committee for CIS Affairs claimed to be "an admirer of empire if this means imperial peace." He prescribed a special relationship with the "near abroad," in which Russia will guarantee the rights of ethnic minorities in all republics —particularly in existing and new autonomous regions such as Abkhazia, South Ossetia, eastern Moldova (Trans-Dniestria), southern Moldova, eastern Ukraine, Crimea, and northern Kazakhstan (*Nezavisimaia gazeta,* 5 May 1994). Other analysts explain Yeltsin's policies by citing the politics within his executive branch: Alexei Pushkov (1993) traces the waning influence of radical democrats such as Andrei Kozyrev and the growing influence of statist democrats and statist bureaucrats. Still others cite Yeltsin's dependence on the security apparatus and his debts to them following their loyal support in the October shoot-out with the former parliament (Walker 1994, 3). Yeltsin's appointment in 1996 of Yevgenii Primakov as foreign minister certainly has strengthened the hand of the statists within the foreign-policy establishment.

Whatever the sources of Russia's hegemonic objectives, the existence of these objectives is not a sufficient explanation for the outcome of a Russian

5. For a variety of perspectives on Russian national interests that reflect different points along the post-Soviet political spectrum, see Johnson and Miller 1994 and Sestanovich 1994.

sphere of influence. That is, a "reductionist" explanation at the level of analysis of state-actor motivations cannot explain a systemic (regional) outcome. For the latter, the neorealist explanation typically focuses on the distribution of power among successor states.

POWER DISPARITY

An overarching international reality of this region is the disproportionate power of Russia; the post-Soviet region is unipolar. As Table 10.1 shows, the Russian Federation contains over half the population of the region, having between 3 and 92 times as many people as any other successor state and about 30 times the median among the other states. Similarly, the Russian economy, despite the depression that has swept all economies in the region, is significantly larger than that of any of its neighbors—between 4 and 120 times as large as any other and about 57 times the median for the other successor states.

An additional disparity in international relations has emerged because Russia inherited the Soviet Union's central foreign-policy and national security apparatus. Although the Russian government has faced significant problems in transforming these, it still enjoys a considerable advantage over its neighbors: most successor governments lack the institutions and expertise to conduct activist foreign policies on the world stage. To this day national armies are only on the drawing boards for most of the other fourteen successor states; many have had to rely on foreign troops or mercenaries (so-called contract soldiers) as a substitute for a national army. As a consequence, Russia's armed forces overwhelm those of the other successor states in size and preparedness: Russia's range from 3 to 600 times the size of the other armed forces, approximately 132 times the median among all fourteen of its neighbors. Even Ukraine, which is the one successor state that could offer armed resistance to Russian coercion, can at best stage a delaying action if Russia chose a military strike against part of its territory. Bowing to the harsh reality of limited capabilities, the General Staff of the Ukrainian Armed Forces recognizes that it would be futile to plan for complete (360-degree) defense of its country's borders and has committed itself to developing mobile forces that could move in quickly in the face of enemy thrusts; yet, even this is at present something of a pipe dream (*Narodna armiya,* 11 May 1993, 1 June 1993).

In the context of this power disparity, interdependence among societies becomes a source of unequal vulnerabilities that give Russia special leverage

Table 10.1. Relative size of Soviet successor states

	Population, July 1995 (millions)	G D P, 1994 est. (billions dollars)*	Armed Forces, 1995 (manpower)	Ratios (Russia is x times larger)		
				Population	GDP	Armed Forces
Armenia	3.6	8.1	60,000	42	89	25
Azerbaijan	7.8	13.8	86,700	19	52	18
Belarus	10.4	53.4	98,400	14	14	15
Estonia	1.6	10.4	3,500	92	69	434
Georgia	5.7	6.0	9,000	26	120	169
Kazakhstan	17.4	55.2	40,000	9	13	38
Kyrgyzstan	4.8	8.4	7,000	31	86	217
Latvia	2.8	12.3	6,950	54	59	219
Lithuania	3.9	13.5	8,900	39	53	171
Moldova	4.5	11.9	11,850	33	61	128
Russia	149.9	721.2	1,520,000	—	—	—
Tajikistan	6.2	8.5	2.500	22	85	608
Turkmenistan	4.1	13.1	11,200	37	55	136
Ukraine	51.9	189.2	452,000	3	4	3
Uzbekistan	23.1	54.5	25,000	6	13	61

*Purchasing power parities
Sources: U.S. Central Intelligence Agency 1995; International Institute for Strategic Studies 1995.

over the fourteen other successor governments. For example, Russia is the major trading partner of most successor states, and this trade is proportionately more significant in the economies of the fourteen other successor states than vice versa (that is, regional trade represents a smaller share of Russia's total trade and of its total GDP). Russia has run trade surpluses with most of its neighbors and has extended credits, which it now characterizes as foreign aid, to the CIS. In Russia's reckoning, by 1993 these credits constituted over two-fifths of the total GDP of at least four successor states and sizable portions of the others, and by early 1996 CIS debts to Russia amounted to $9 billion (*Izvestiia,* 16 September 1993; Russian Television, 26 March 1996). A major component of these trade surpluses and credits originate from the purchase of Russian oil and gas. Russia has aggressively exploited this imbalance in order to swap debt for economic and political concessions that increase Russian control over its neighbors. John Morrison (1993, 686) asserts that "dependence on Russian energy supplies has since emerged as the Achilles heel of the Ukrainian economy and is a weapon used by Russia in predictable fashion to press Ukraine into concessions on other issues." Martha Brill Olcott (1994, 561) adds that "while Karimov and the Uzbek elite dream of a day when their nation is free of Moscow's influence, for now Moscow is the source of energy and food."

In light of the regional power disparities cultural or demographic interdependence of societies has given Russia additional leverage over the other successor governments. Hypothetically, the large Russian communities outside Russia could either provide Russia leverage over the host countries or be held hostage by the hosts for reverse leverage. In fact, it is the former that has turned out to be most important, since Russia has used the status of Russians in the Baltic, western, and Central Asian theaters to press for concessions from the host governments. Presidential decrees issued in November 1994 extend Russian citizenship (and the right of dual citizenship) to Russians living in the near abroad (despite protests from the host governments) and grant the president power to send troops into these countries in order to evacuate Russians in emergencies (ITAR-TASS, 3 November 1994; *Trud,* 23 November 1994). Russia has pressed each successor government to recognize this dual citizenship.

The neorealist explanation that focuses on this power disparity, nonetheless, begs an answer to why Russia's neighbors have not turned to the balancing strategies that small powers traditionally use to protect themselves against threats of a more powerful neighbor. Small powers traditionally band together or turn to other great powers in order to protect themselves against the greatest threat to their survival. Thus, in the nineteenth and the first half of the twentieth century, southern and western neighbors of the Russian Empire and Soviet Union turned to the West for alliances. On this basis England built up Afghanistan and Persia as buffers, and France constructed the cordon sanitaire. Why has this not happened at the end of the twentieth century?

FAILURE OF TRADITIONAL BALANCING STRATEGIES

Most successor states have failed to form alliances to resist Russian hegemony. Only the Baltic states have successfully constrained Russia through their alliance strategies. Azerbaijan, Georgia, Moldova, and Ukraine, despite their efforts, have had only limited success. The other successor states have had virtually none.

In light of the enormous power disparity, alliances limited to states within the region are not likely to constrain Russia—unless all fourteen could band together. Aside from the enormous collective-action problems of such an alliance, too many animosities among successor governments prevent such a grand coalition against Russia. Smaller, informal groupings have emerged instead. Moldovan spokesmen have suggested that their country relies on a tacit alliance with Ukraine: "Ukraine's wish to defend its independence plays an exceptionally important role for the defense of our own country's interests. . . . Ukraine provides an umbrella against those forces which want to bring down our independence and bring us into a neo-Soviet brotherhood" (Basapress, 15 February 1994). Still, this and the routine cooperation among the Baltic states and periodic cooperation among Kazakhstan, Kyrgyzstan, and Uzbekistan constitute loose webs of interaction rather than tight alliances to constrain Russia (Reuters, 11 January 1994; Interfax, 16 January 1994, 8 July 1994; Olcott 1994; Rumer 1993).

Those external powers that have been most willing to ally with successor states have tended to be too weak to constrain Russia and have demanded too high a price from the successor governments.[6] Iran has actively sought closer ties in Central Asia and Azerbaijan, but many of these states have been cautious because the Iranian regime seems to champion partisans and policies within these states that threaten the existing governments (Hyman 1993). Romania has actively sought political union with Moldova, but this is a price that the current government of Moldova is unwilling to pay (ITAR-TASS, 16 February 1994; *Moldova Suverana*, 20 October 1994).

Great powers from outside the region have largely eschewed balancing within it. In those few instances where NATO governments have been willing to make firm commitments, Russian hegemony has been kept at bay. Most notably, the Baltic governments have used their ties with the United States and European states as a counterbalance to Russian pressure (Radio Lithuania, 11 February 1994; Reuters, 16 February 1994; BNS, 12 September 1994; Interfax, 13 April 1994). For example, in the summer of 1994, as Russia threatened to delay withdrawal of its troops, Estonia used Western pressure to induce Russia to reverse its policy. On 6 May 1994 Russia's defense minister, Pavel Grachev, had warned that "withdrawal is closely linked to guarantees of normal life for the Russian-speaking population [in Estonia]. If talks stall, Russia will keep its 2500 servicemen there. If the situation changes, it won't take long to send reinforcements" (AFP, 6 May 1994). Yeltsin announced in July that withdrawal would actually be delayed due to Es-

6. Studies of the relations of Iran, Pakistan, and Turkey with Central Asia point up that the domestic politics of Pakistan and Turkey have prevented them from playing the role of balancer, but the successor states themselves have kept their distance from Iran. See Belokrenitsky 1994 and the essays by Malik and Smolansky in Malik 1994. See also the study of India's role in Central Asia by Singh (1995).

tonia's restrictive citizenship laws. This brought a swift appeal from Estonia to the U.S. Senate, which then voted to block further aid to Russia if its troops failed to leave Estonia on schedule (Interfax, 5 July 1994, 10 July 1994; AP, 13 July 1994). Yeltsin quickly reversed his position. As this one incident illustrates, alliances with external great powers can permit even the smallest successor states to resist Russian hegemony.

The efforts by Azerbaijan and Moldova to elicit similar levels of Western support have met with far less success. The Gaidar Aliev government in Azerbaijan has found Turkey standoffish, particularly when it comes to providing arms to limit Azerbaijan dependence on the Russian army (Hurriyet, 10 February 1994). Azerbaijan's requests that OSCE play a larger role in the Karabakh negotiations and contribute a share of the peacekeeping forces have not brought strong support from OSCE in the face of Russian resistance (Interfax, 7 July 1994, 8 July 1994; AP, 29 September 1994). Moldova's president has sought to enlist the Council of Europe, OSCE, European Union, EFTA (European Free Trade Association), and NATO to press Russia for withdrawal of its troops from Trans-Dniestria (Basapress, 12 January 1994, 16 March 1994, 7 June 1994; Interfax, 5 October 1994). Indeed, Moldova attempted to convince the Political Commission of the Council of Europe that it should make Russia's membership in the council conditional on withdrawal of these troops (ITAR-TASS, 13 September 1994). Still, the agencies have been unwilling to take strong action on Moldova's behalf.[7]

Despite pleas from the governments of Georgia and Ukraine, Western powers have so far made only minor commitments. Eduard Shevardnadze asked President Clinton to support UN peacekeeping forces for the Abkhaz conflict, but received little support. Shevardnadze framed his choice in stark balancing terms: he announced on Georgian Television that if the UN would not provide peacekeeping forces, the only alternative was to rely on Russia (ITAR-TASS, 14 March 1994, 5 May 1994; AP, 21 March 1994; Georgian Television, 23 March 1994). Ukraine's first president talked of a new cordon sanitaire in central and Eastern Europe to contain Russia, but was frustrated by the unwillingness of great powers to offer his country security guarantees. During his last year in office he became increasingly bitter over this indifference: "I think Ukraine is interesting for them only because it has nuclear

7. Although the explanation of Western foreign policies is exogenous to the analysis of this chapter, it is worth noting that for the powers of the North Atlantic community, commitments to the fourteen other successor states are partially constrained by expectations of Russia's reactions.

weapons on its territory" (quoted in Morrison 1993, 699; *Uryadovyi kuryer,* 2 March 1993; Solchanyk 1993; Burant 1993).

Yet, the failure of the other successor states to form counterbalancing alliances (as predicted by traditional balance-of-power theories) cannot be explained solely by the absence of external partners. Indeed, some successor states have rejected closer ties to parties outside the region that might have provided alternatives to Russian hegemony, and they have actively sought tighter integration with the post-Soviet security complex. For example, at the Turkic summit in October 1992, the presidents of Kazakhstan and Uzbekistan refused to agree to binding commitments to a pan-Turkic community that would jeopardize their commitments to the CIS (Robins 1993, 599–600). In June 1994 Kazakhstan's president, Nursultan Nazarbaev, with the endorsement of Kyrgyzstan's Askar Akaev and Georgia's Shevardnadze, proposed tighter integration of the post-Soviet region in a Euro-Asian Union with a common border, common currency, coordinated economic policy, and joint parliament (*Nezavisimaia gazeta,* 8 June 1994; Ostankino Television, 17 September 1994). Belarus's president, Lukashenka, has urged integration of his country with Russia and Ukraine in a Slavic state (ITAR-TASS, 18 May 1994; Belarus Television, 28 August 1994). Tajikistan's president, Imomali Rakhmonov, has urged speedy economic integration of his country with Russia (Radio Dushanbe, 8 May 1994). Paradoxically, while Russia today poses the greatest foreign national security threat to many successor states, the governments of these states are increasingly turning to Russia as the guarantor of their survival.

REFORMULATING THE REALIST EXPLANATION

The apparent failure of some successor governments jealously to guard the sovereignty of their states, as well as their willingness to accept Russian hegemony, raises questions about the assumptions of the neorealist explanation and its utility in analyzing the pattern of relations in this region. Two closely related amendments to this explanation would help us better understand the patterns among the Soviet successor states. (I would argue that these amendments simply make the original core assumptions of realism more precise, but that is a thesis for another essay.) The first amendment concerns the nature of the principal actors and their motivations. Specifically, the structure of the region is defined by interactions among governments, not states or societies. The modal, proximate objective of these post-Soviet governors is to maintain power—that is, to ensure their own political survival within their new states. The state's survival often is a necessary precondition for this, but where governors can ensure their own survival only by sacrificing the sovereignty of the state, they may seek annexation, embrace foreign protectors, or accept external limits on independence (cf. Waltz 1979, 91–92). The second amendment to the realist explanation concerns the international consequences of the selection process that determines whether these governors and their international ties survive. Those intergovernmental patterns of association that have made a positive contribution to the domestic survival of post-Soviet governors have been more likely to endure. Thus, the structure of coalitions among successor governments reflects their contribution to the domestic political survival of the governments.[8]

In the competition among powers for influence over the successor governments (and in the search by successor governments for allies) Russia has been more successful than powers external to the region for at least four reasons:

1. *Russia has been willing and able to make a more direct military contribution to the domestic political survival of the successor governments.*

Its significant military presence in many successor states has given Russia unusual leverage to determine whether successor governments survive or fall. In Central Asia, for example, Russia's willingness to contribute troops to the defense of the borders of all states, to create new national armed forces in several, and to protect the governors from their domestic opponents in at least one has made Russia far more valuable than Iran, Turkey, or the West as an ally to these governors. In the Transcaucasus and Moldova, Russia has played an equally direct and perhaps more manipulative role in making its contribution to the survival of these regimes indispensable. In these states Russia appears to be the mainstay of the chief opponents of the governors, but weak Transcaucasian governments without a solid popular base have had to turn to Russia to keep these opponents at bay and guarantee their own survival. In Georgia, when the Shevardnadze government was uncertain of its domestic popular base, it turned to Russia's central government as the sole guarantor of its survival; Shevardnadze agreed on 25 July 1993 to Russian terms for an Abkhaz cease-fire—Georgian military withdrawal from the Abkhaz capital and supervision by a tripartite Georgian-Abkhazian-Russian

8. This treats the system as a selection mechanism, much as Alchian (1950) proposes treating the market. As Alchian notes, not all actors will attend to their own survival prospects and in the competition are likely to be selected out.

commission—that are seen by many Georgians as severe violations of their state's sovereignty (*Nezavisimaia gazeta,* 3 February 1993; *Iberia ekspress,* 15 June 1993; *Izvestiia,* 21 April 1993; BGI, 2 February 1996). In Azerbaijan, Russia provided strong support to Gaidar Aliev following his June 1993 coup; as Elizabeth Fuller (1993, 33) observes: "Aliev, for his part, must have been acutely aware that his chances of political survival depended overwhelmingly on achieving some kind of settlement of the Karabakh conflict, which had precipitated the ouster of his three immediate predecessors; and, pragmatist that he is, he would have been prepared to pay whatever price the Russians chose to attach to their offer of assistance" (see also Goltz 1993; Sunley 1994).

2. *Russia can make a more direct contribution to the survival of individual constituents in the supporting coalitions that sustain these governors.*

The tightly centralized Soviet economy and national security apparatus left behind many enterprises and military formations that are critical to the successor states but that depend upon complementary units within Russia for fulfillment of their missions. Where these enterprises or military formations are major constituencies or power bases of the government, Russia can make direct contributions to the survival or failure of the constituents and through these to the survival of the governors. Belarus may represent an extreme case of nearly complete integration with Russia before the breakup of the former Soviet Union. After the breakup, a solid majority in the Belarusian parliament and cabinet favored integration with Russia; for the leaders of the military-industrial complex who have dominated both organs, there are few alternatives to closer ties with Russia (Radio Minsk, 7 April 1993, 9 April 1993; Belinform, 9 April 1993). Within the armed forces the Union of Officers of Belarus agitated against independence; military organizations such as the Union of Afghan Veterans, Slavianski Sobor, and Belaya Rus have since pressed for closer ties with Russia (Bela-TASS, 7 February 1992; *Narodnaya gazeta,* 11 March 1993; Radio Minsk, 23 February 1993; *Respublika,* 26 February 1993; *Vo Slavu Rodiny,* 27 February 1993). Russia is able to make a direct contribution to the survival of similarly situated interests within the supporting coalitions of many successor governments.

3. *Russia has been willing to make direct financial contributions to the political machines that sustain the ruling coalitions in power.*

A majority of the successor governments, whether democratically elected or not, maintain their support base through the distribution of material favors. Authoritarian and democratic regimes alike have maintained the loyalty of bureaucrats through high salaries and other financial incentives; this has been particularly important in states where the bureaucracy remains a powerful force in politics and the private sector offers few organized alternatives (civil society) that can hold the bureaucrats in check or few lucrative career opportunities for them outside the state apparatus. Russian infusion of rubles (through credits, debt forgiveness, and monetary subventions) have been essential to the governments of Central Asia seeking to cover their payrolls, to maintain pensions, and to meet other state obligations (*Kommersant,* 14 August 1993). For example, with Russia's support Turkmenistan was at least initially able to maintain subsidized prices and to raise bureaucrats' salaries (*Izvestiia,* 24 June 1993). Russians claim that in the first two-thirds of 1993 their central bank infused 87 percent more rubles into this small country of under five million inhabitants than it had infused into Russia itself (*Izvestiia,* 16 September 1993). Fiscal support in the form of central government subventions begun in the Soviet period have provided the basis for a post-Soviet pattern of financial supports that give Russia an advantage over other powers.

4. *Russia has been less concerned than extraregional powers with the ethics and ideological coloration of the successor governments.*

As a consequence of its Realpolitik in the region, Russia has been willing and able to make a stronger contribution to the survival of these governments: Unlike many outside powers, Russia has not been squeamish about its financial support going to political machines or authoritarian regimes, and Russia has been willing to ignore the ideological coloration of successor governments. Conversely, Turkey has been handicapped in dealing with the successor states of Central Asia and Azerbaijan by what Philip Robins (1993, 600–601) calls its "highly ideological view of itself." Turkey's Foreign Ministry has been uncomfortable dealing with the "old elites" who currently rule in these republics, and so more reticent with regimes that do not conform to Turkey's vision of secular democratic governments committed to liberal market-oriented economics. Similarly, Western governments and their international organizations, such as the IMF, have been reluctant to support such repressive regimes as exist in Uzbekistan or command economies as have existed in Belarus and Ukraine. Russia's behavior betrays no such compunction.[9] Typically, Western leaders demand economic reforms that are specifi-

9. One issue on which Russia may be vulnerable and at a disadvantage is Russia's demand that the successor governments recognize the rights of Russian-speaking minorities within their borders. Only a few other external powers—for example, Poland in its relations with Lithuania (Burant 1993)—are so constrained.

cally designed to shrink the patronage and end the corruption that sustains political machines. Where they have found the domestic orientation of a successor state acceptable (as in the Baltic states), Western powers, the European Community, and the IMF have given the governments means to escape Moscow's hegemonic security complex. Nonetheless, in the selection process of competition among powers that determines which ties dominate in the region, Realpolitik has won out over more ideological strategies. Russia offers incentives that are more appealing to unstable successor governments and directly contribute to their longevity, and so Russia has more alliance partners.

In the future these advantages enjoyed by Russia could erode. The foregoing analysis stresses three constraints on Russian hegemony. First, if the Russian government itself were to experience a severe domestic crisis of power, it might well loose its ability to support neighboring regimes against their own opponents. Second, the survival postulate implies that if the other successor governments consolidate power within their new states, by establishing popular bases of support or eliminating their opponents, they may become less dependent on Russian assistance for their survival and better able to pursue independent foreign policies. For example, despite Turkmenistan's manifest weakness in most power resources, President Saparmurad Niyazov's firm hold on the reins of power within that country has permitted him to pursue a more independent foreign policy. Third, if outside powers become more tolerant and supportive of the successor regimes, the latter may become less dependent on Russian assistance for their survival. Iran has reportedly become somewhat more pragmatic in its policies toward Central Asia (Halliday 1995); with Turkmenistan it has signed agreements on oil, gas, agriculture, and transportation (IRNA, 23 January 1996). Nevertheless, most Central Asian states remain cautious, and allegations that Iran continues to train guerrillas fighting the Tajik regime reinforce this caution (Reuters, 22 January 1996). Similarly, in order to encourage resistance to Russian hegemony, the United States by 1996 had become more open to relations with such successor governments as Ukraine, despite its slow pace of economic reform, and Uzbekistan, despite its abysmal human rights record. In March 1996, following a meeting with Ukrainian officials, Warren Christopher announced that the United States did not want to see Ukraine become a Russian satellite, and in June the Pentagon welcomed a visit from Uzbekistan's president.

Alternative Regional Orders

The future of the post-Soviet region, thus, depends on the three constraints mentioned above. Through the end of the century and beyond, the structure of the post-Soviet security complex is likely to remain fluid; choices by the Russian and other successor governments could lead to radically different orders within the region or even to the dissolution of the regional security complex altogether. Ranked from most tightly integrated to least integrated, five possible scenarios for alternative regional orders include the following:

1. *A unified state led from Moscow.* A more tightly integrated region than the present sphere of influence might reverse recent history and transform the international hegemonic region into a domestic (hierarchic) polity. Statements by some Russian leaders appear to envision exactly this outcome. For example, the chairman of the Russian Council of Federation and the CIS Interparliamentary Assembly argued in 1994 that the post-Soviet space needs supranational bodies to save what can be salvaged from the Soviet Union and to create "a sort of union" through CIS; he urged CIS to issue model legislation such as a civil code and law on local administration that would be adopted in each successor state to provide uniformity throughout the region (ITAR-TASS, 29 March 1994; Radio Rossii, 5–6 November 1994). The ever closer integration of the Russo-Belarusian Community, with the expressed objective of "unity," is celebrated by the Russian government as a model for its relations with other successor governments.
2. *Collective management of security.* If the other successor states could create regional institutions to wrest from Russia control over security issues, they might institute a form of multilateral management (see Morgan's discussion of multilateral collective management of security, in this volume). This would require that the other successor states develop stronger ties among themselves in order to balance the bilateral ties that each has with Russia; it would also require that they replace the existing CIS structure with one that gives them a larger voice. Indeed, some leaders of successor governments have championed plans for greater multilateral control within CIS as the best guarantee of their own independence. In early 1993, as Russia pressed to subordinate the CIS command to the Russian command, as had been the practice in the Warsaw Pact, Kazakhstan and Ukraine held out for a NATO-like joint command structure that would

give them greater voice in CIS military policies. In January 1994 the president of Ukraine endorsed a plan for a stronger CIS that would coordinate the dealings of the other successor states with Moscow and increase their leverage against the hegemon (Walker 1994, 5). Nonetheless, there is as yet little reason to believe that Russia will tolerate such limits on its prerogatives within the regional security complex or that the other successor states can coordinate to such an extent that they can limit Russia's dominance.

3. *A regional concert or balance of power.* At present no single successor state can engage Russia as an equal in terms of power, but if the other successor states could first band together in some way, they might create the basis for a purely regional concert or balancing complex (see the discussions of these by Papayoanou and by Rosecrance and Schott, in this volume). The minimum size of such blocs would probably be the four theaters: if each theater were to achieve a degree of integration that gave them the ability to take a common stand against Russia, the resulting five-power regional system might develop either a balance of power or concert of powers. Alone, the Baltic and Transcaucasian blocs would still be too weak to constrain Russia, but with assistance of either the Central Asian or western blocs, these could be counted as lesser powers within a region dominated by one great power and two major powers. Standing in the way of this fantastic scenario is, of course, the reality of subregional disunity. With the exception of the Baltic, none of the theaters has shown much ability to act in concert—certainly not when confronting Russia.

The first three scenarios assume that the regional security complex will retain its autonomy vis-à-vis other major powers, but if outside powers were to play a greater role within the regional security complex, at least two additional scenarios open up:

4. *Involvement of great powers from outside the region in collective security, a great-power concert, or balance of power within the region.* As the essays by Patrick Morgan, Paul Papayoanou, and Richard Rosecrance and Peter Schott (in this volume) point up, great powers from outside the region can play substantial roles in regional security complexes. If the United States, Japan, and Germany were to play larger roles in its various theaters, the post-Soviet regional security complex would differ from the regional security complexes in Africa (described by Edmond Keller) and

the Middle East (described by David Pervin), in that one of the great powers in the regional security complex would also be part of the geographic region itself. It would differ from the Asia-Pacific security complex (described by Susan Shirk), where Russia's presence within the geographic region is checked by that of the United States, Japan, and China. It likely would resemble the regional security complex in the Americas (see David Mares's description of Latin America), where the United States has used its physical presence and overwhelming local power to limit outside great powers (such as the Soviet Union until 1991) to minor roles.

5. *Dissolution of the post-Soviet security complex altogether and integration of the successor states with other regions.* The region that currently embraces the fifteen successor states might simply disappear as a meaningful frame of reference, and with it the post-Soviet security complex could dissolve as well. All successor states might simply be subsumed within other regional security complexes—the Central Asian theater within the South Asian security complex, the Transcaucasian theater within the Middle Eastern security complex, and the Baltic and western theaters within the European complex. The specific regional security complexes that exist in the last decade of the twentieth century have not been and are not likely to remain fixtures of global politics; the post-Soviet security complex, as the youngest of these, may have the least durability. Already the boundary of the region appears to be shifting as the Baltic states make good on their bid to be included in the European security complex. If more successor states were to follow, the boundary of the post-Soviet region would become more ambiguous and begin to dissolve.

Among the five alternatives listed here, this last scenario and the autonomous regional concert or balancing system (the third scenario listed above) seem least likely. Although the other three scenarios are more likely, it is probable that no single pattern of relations will characterize the whole Russian sphere of influence. That is, as the sphere matures, it may come to resemble the American sphere of influence in its complexity. With some states, such as Belarus, further integration may shift still more decision making to Moscow so that a new hierarchic state is established. Governments that preserve their formal independence but depend on Russia for their survival, such as Georgia, may remain subjects in a hegemonic relationship. With those states that establish strong domestic bases of support and receive security guarantees from outside powers, such as Ukraine and Uzbekistan, Moscow may rely on regional, multilateral institutions to manage security relations. With sufficient domestic and external support some states, such as the Baltic states, may exit the regional security complex altogether and rely on other regional bodies, such as the Council of Europe, to manage their security relations with Moscow. In sum, the current hegemonic post-Soviet security complex is likely to continue in its broad outlines, but it is also likely to shrink slightly (in the Baltic region), lose a little of its autonomy (in the western theater with regard to Ukraine), and grow more diverse in its internal structure as individual member states develop diverse relationships with Moscow.

Summary

The post-Soviet international region has been characterized in the first years of its existence by a transition from hierarchical domestic politics to hegemonic regional politics. The collapse of the Soviet Union formally brought to an end a highly centralized domestic political order, but it left behind ties among successor governments that give the government in Moscow strong influence over most of the former Soviet Union. The weakness of most successor governments and their dependence on Russia provide the Russian government leverage that it is exploiting in order to institutionalize a hegemonic regional order.

This chapter has examined the pattern of relations among these successor states, focusing on the role of Russia and the policies of other successor states toward it. It began with a question—why (despite nationalistic animosities toward Moscow in their societies and the intoxicating elixir of recently gained independence) have these successor governments once again submitted to Russian leadership and in some instances enthusiastically embraced it? I argued that these choices reflect first of all a domestic political, rather than international, economic, or ideological, logic—the governments have assessed alternative alliance partners according to the contribution each could make to their own political survival.

The agenda of this chapter has not been to develop a comprehensive explanation for the pattern of security complexes under different global or regional conditions, but instead to analyze a single security complex under very specific conditions. Nonetheless, the present analysis touches on a number of theoretical issues that imply an agenda for further theoretical development. Permit me to refer to just two of these before concluding this chapter.

First, although I have stressed the limits of neorealist analysis in explaining the structure of the post-Soviet security complex, the amendments based on the survival postulate are thoroughly within the older realist tradition of political science. The motivational postulate that politicians seek power sets political realism apart from political economy, which begins from a materialist postulate that often sees politicians as concerned with rents and revenues. In the realist tradition the costs and benefits that constrain such choices as alliance partners and institutions are measured in terms of gains and losses to power. In this sense my analysis diverges in key assumptions from that of Etel Solingen's examination of the economic constraints on regional conflict and cooperation (in this volume) even though we both focus on domestic constraints on international relations.

Second, this realist analysis treats regional security complexes as real, but not fixed. The existence of individual complexes (for example, whether the post-Soviet security complex survives) and the relative significance of these complexes within global politics depend on the contribution they can make to the political survival of governments. This approach treats security in an expanded sense that encompasses the many—both foreign and domestic—threats to the power of governments and sees governors operating simultaneously in global, regional, and domestic political arenas in order to find coalition partners.

11

Asia-Pacific Regional Security: Balance of Power or Concert of Powers?

Susan L. Shirk

The Asia-Pacific enjoys a peace and prosperity that is the envy of the rest of the world. Yet Asia-Pacific leaders worry that their good fortune is vulnerable to future security uncertainties. The contours of the post–Cold War relations among the regional powers—China, Japan, Russia, and the United States—are becoming more multipolar than during the previous four decades, and the new structure of multipolarity is in a state of flux. The relative strength of the four powers is shifting as China grows economically and militarily more powerful, Japan becomes economically and technologically stronger, Russia sinks into economic and political decay, and American economic capacity and political will appear to weaken.

Intentions are even more uncertain than capabilities. What international role does China want to play now that its national power has revived? Is Japan willing to continue to rely on the United States, or will it begin to assert an independent security role? Will the United States muster domestic support for sustaining its military presence in the region?

If the United States reduces its forces, will regional rivalries and arms races destroy the peaceful environment upon which Asian prosperity depends? East and Southeast Asian nations devote more money to buying military hardware than any region in the world except the Middle East. In recent years Asian governments have acquired weapons as insurance in case the United States closes its security umbrella (Ball 1993–94, 78–112). Their booming economies can easily afford new fighter planes and submarines. But the danger is that arms buildups typically produce security dilemmas: the defensive actions of one country are perceived as aggressive threats by its neighbors (Jervis 1978, 167–214). Existing territorial disputes can ignite such mutual suspicion into overt conflict.

Everyone agrees that the greatest threat to peace and stability in the Asia-Pacific is war between its regional powers. (Although Asians concentrate their attention on economic issues, their definition of security remains the traditional one of preventing military conflict from threatening the survival of their countries.) Before 1993, Asians focused their anxieties on Japan, which remains the object of deep suspicion in many parts of Asia. Recently, the focus has shifted to a concern with the threat of China's burgeoning economic and military power. The prospect of China and Japan in a contest for regional dominance triggers painful memories and fears for the future in the minds of many Asians. Americans are beginning to worry that their commitments to Asian allies could lead them into a war with China. From the perspective of all the countries in the region, conflict among the regional powers in the "strategic quadrangle" (Mandelbaum 1994) is the greatest threat to regional stability and national prosperity.

This essay argues that successful management of the relations between these powers will be difficult to achieve by power-balancing alone and that a regional concert of powers could emerge, although there are serious obstacles to the establishment of such a regional order. The first section identifies some of the relevant characteristics of the Asia-Pacific as a regional security complex, and the second discusses the historical experience of major power relations within the region. The third section discusses the reasons why balance-of-power methods are likely to fail in this regional security complex. The fourth section suggests that the North Korean nuclear threat is a catalytic event for an emerging cooperation among the Asia-Pacific powers that could evolve into a concert of powers.

Defining the Region and the Regional Security Complex

The definition of the Asia-Pacific is the subject of considerable debate. Because the focus of this essay is relations among the four major regional powers—China, Japan, Russia, and the United States—I define the region as the China-centered area of East Asia, and the regional security complex as East Asia plus the United States.

Defining the region as East Asia with China at its core and encompassing eastern Russia, the Korean peninsula, Japan, and Southeast Asia is justified both structurally and historically. Structurally, China is the dominant land power that links the subregions of Northeast Asia and Southeast Asia. The reunification of North and South Korea would affect Southeast Asia only indirectly, largely through China's response to such an event; likewise, military conflict in the South China Sea would affect Russia and Korea only through China's involvement. A conflict between China and Japan would have direct impacts on both Northeast Asia and Southeast Asia.

Historically, the China-centered area of East Asia was a distinct region. Over many centuries, geography produced frequent economic, cultural, diplomatic, and military interactions among the societies of East Asia surrounding China. This Chinese culture area, which came to be known by Europeans as "the Far East," formed the core of the Chinese empire. Japan, Korea, and Vietnam adopted Chinese Confucian ideas and institutions, including the writing system, examination system, and the imperial monarchy and bureaucracy (Fairbank 1968, 1). The Chinese culture area, separated by geography from West and South Asia, was the "most distinctive of all the great culture areas."

The China-centered world order was the external expression of China's Confucian value system. It was a hierarchical order in which peoples and states acknowledged the moral and political authority of the emperor as the link between Heaven and the world by accepting vassal status and offering up tribute to him. One of the most remarkable features of the Chinese empire was that it was sometimes headed by non-Chinese dynasties, the Mongols (1279–1368) and the Manchus (1644–1912), who preserved the tradition of Sinocentrism based on Confucianism.

Although the reach of the Chinese empire was broad, it was not truly imperialist in the modern sense of the word, according to Mark Mancall.

Chinese goods were in greater demand abroad than foreign goods were in China. Nor did the Chinese have a sense of mission to civilize the rest of the world. They welcomed people who wanted to adopt Chinese culture, but had no drive to uplift people by means of this culture (Mancall 1989, 10–11).

Centuries of Chinese hegemony in Asia left a strong imprint on the historical memories of Asian leaders and citizens. They remember a China that dominated them not primarily by military force, but by its size and its material, moral, and political superiority. Although the tribute system was resented by countries like Korea, Japan, and Vietnam for keeping them in a subordinate position, it also provided them with economic benefits and a measure of military protection, and did not intrude in their domestic affairs.[1] In exchange for acknowledging their vassal status, these countries received access to trade and a promise by China not to attack them or take them over.

Chinese hegemony was brought to an end by the coming of the European "barbarians," with their superior military and economic might and an entirely different conception of world order as a system of sovereign nation-states. The nineteenth and twentieth centuries were a period of economic decline and political disunity in China. Disabled by internal decay, Chinese leaders were unable to resist the challenge of the Europeans or to enforce the limited access to the country normally allowed under the tribute system. Chinese experienced these 150 years of internal and external weakness as a deep humiliation. Meanwhile the Japanese embraced European economic and military technologies and European notions of state sovereignty to strengthen themselves and challenge the hierarchical China-centered regional order.[2]

During the nineteenth and twentieth centuries European states and the United States came to play active economic, diplomatic, and military roles in the region. As Lake and Morgan point out in Chapter 1, we can distinguish a regional security complex, a set of states whose security depends on one another, from a region that is defined by geography. In this sense, the European states (particularly Great Britain) and the United States became part of the East Asian regional security complex, although they were geographically separate from the region. Paul Papayoanou notes in his chapter that an out-

1. "Chinese power intruded into the internal affairs of tributary states only when developments threatened the position or person of the segments' leader in his relations with the emperor" (Mancall 1989, 35).

2. One reason why the Japanese made more effective use of Western learning for self-strengthening than did the Chinese may be the motivation of Japan to balance against China's dominant power in the region.

side power's diplomatic and military presence in a region often is motivated by its economic interests there; this was the case with Great Britain's role in Asia during the nineteenth and early twentieth centuries. When Great Britain gradually reduced its role in the regional security complex during the interwar years, the United States increased its military presence (the U.S. Pacific Fleet was created in 1919). After World War II, the United States became one of the two dominant military powers in the regional security complex (along with the Soviet Union) because of its global responsibility to contain Communism.[3] With the China mainland hived off from the world economy by Communist policies of autarky, the United States became a dominant economic actor in the Asia-Pacific as the largest market for Asian manufactured products.

Now that the Cold War is over, the definition of the region is up for grabs. A debate is raging between those who define the region as the Asia-Pacific and those who define it as Asia or East Asia. This contestation over cognitive definitions reflects real-world changes in both economic and security externalities. Increases in intra-Asian foreign investment and the economic opening of China have increased trade among Asian nations and reduced their dependence on the U.S. market; and the disappearance of the Soviet threat has reduced the value of U.S. protection to them. The end of global competition with the Soviet Union means that Asia has become less important for U.S. security interests, but more important to its effort to revitalize the domestic economy through foreign trade.

For economic reasons, the countries outside of Asia, led first by Australia, then Canada and the United States, are pressing the Asia-Pacific definition of the region and the Asia-Pacific Economic Cooperation (APEC) as the best organization for promoting regional economic cooperation. The economic benefits to be gained in Asia and the importance of the sea lanes there for international trade make the United States all the more determined to continue its important role in the regional security complex even though it no longer has to deter the Soviet Union. President Clinton's notion of the "Pacific community" and his initiative to establish an annual summit meeting of APEC state leaders reflect his administration's desire to lead a process of economic and security cooperation in a region defined as the Asia-Pacific.

3. Barry Buzan argues that since the end of World War II Japan's security dependency on the United States has created a global "overlay" that prevents a full emergence of the regional security complex (Buzan 1992, 172, 182).

The Asia-Pacific definition of the region is contested by Prime Minister Datuk Seri Mahathir bin Mohamad of Malaysia, who advocates Asia-for-the-Asians and an East Asian economic bloc. He boycotted the first APEC summit meeting in Seattle and was dragged kicking and screaming to the second one in Indonesia. Mahathir's views are explicitly anti-Western, emphasizing the cultural differences between Asian collectivist values and the individualist notion of human rights that he sees the United States trying to impose on Asia.

Most East and Southeast Asian leaders favor an Asia-Pacific definition of the region over the Asia definition of Mahathir. United States markets, although relatively less important than before, remain the destination for 25 percent of Asian exports.[4] And in the uncertain post–Cold War security situation, the American military presence still has perceived value as a counterweight to revived Chinese power and a restraint on Japanese remilitarization. For these reasons, Asian leaders have forced Mahathir to downgrade his notion of a regional economic bloc to an East Asian economic caucus (EAEC) within APEC. If the expansion of intra-Asian trade further reduces reliance on the U.S. market or the U.S. cuts its military forces in Asia, the Asia-alone option will increase its appeal.[5]

The Asia-Pacific regional security complex is unique because it contains four states—United States, Russia, Japan, and China—that are global as well as regional powers. The United States is the most global of the powers, playing a major role in the security complexes in the Western Hemisphere, Europe, the Asia-Pacific, and the Middle East. The United States also is the outside power geographically. Unlike the other three, it could cross the ocean and go home; its military involvement in regional conflicts is optional, not automatic (note, for example, that the United States did not intervene to defend China from Japan until Japan attacked Pearl Harbor). Russia is both a European and a Pacific power. China and Japan are regional powers whose size (in the case of China) and wealth (in the case of Japan) have made them global powers. China, like Russia and the United States, is a permanent member of the United Nations Security Council, while Japan joins the United States and Western Europe in the G-7 and hopes to become a permanent

4. Based on 1993 statistics; the comparable 1989 figure is 30 percent (International Monetary Fund 1994).

5. Some Japanese have said they would support EAEC if it included Australia and New Zealand and therefore could not be labeled "anti-Caucasian." Another Japanese idea is to expand Latin American participation in APEC so that the non-EAEC members in APEC would not be exclusively Caucasian.

member of the Security Council. Three of the four are nuclear powers, and Japan has a virtual nuclear deterrent because it could convert its civilian space technology and nuclear technology and material to military purposes almost overnight.

The Past: Security Management in a Multipolar Asia-Pacific Before World War II

BALANCE OF POWER

Before World War I, security relations among the Asia-Pacific powers were characterized by an uneasy multipolarity that operated according to balance-of-power principles. Russia, China, and Japan seized territory from and fought wars with one another. China's internal weakness left it helpless to resist the incursions of Russia, Japan, the European powers, and the United States; Russia and Japan, the ascendant powers, competed for territory in China and neighboring areas. The United States, just becoming a regional and global power, tried to check Russian expansionism by tilting toward Japan. Washington cheered Japanese victories in the Sino-Japanese and Russo-Japanese wars.[6] United States support for Japan reflected balance-of-power principles, although Americans also identified with Japan's modernization efforts.

Japan's astounding victory in its war with Russia allowed it to strengthen its hold over Manchuria and to annex Korea in 1910. The island nation threatened to replace Russian influence in the Asian heartland. By playing balance-of-power politics in Asia, the United States got not a stable equilibrium, but the threat of Japanese hegemony over the Asian mainland.

American policy makers perceived a potential danger of military conflict between Washington and Tokyo even before the end of World War I. The United States and Japan were growing stronger economically and militarily. Americans developed naval armaments to counter the growing might of Japan. Although the two countries benefited from extensive bilateral trade, they warily eyed each other because of Japanese expansion in China and Russia, and Japanese emigration to the United States. Perhaps reflecting a temporary balance between them, the United States and Japan gingerly avoided

6. See Theodore Roosevelt's letter to his son in Tompkins 1949, 21–22.

provoking one another. Washington did not encourage Korean nationalists when they looked for help against Japanese aggression, and were silent when Japan annexed Korea; Tokyo refused to aid Aguinaldo in his struggle against American rule in the Philippines (Iriye 1994, 32). Washington continued to promote the notion of an Open Door in China (originally propounded by John Hay in 1899) to prevent the powers from expanding their spheres of influence and to preserve American economic opportunities in China, but with little success. United States and Japanese approaches to China became increasingly divergent as the United States broadened its China policies to encompass China's modernization and its territorial integrity as well as commercial opportunity; Japan remained determined to maintain and increase its supply of raw materials from China.

MULTILATERALISM

Following World War I, President Woodrow Wilson sought to prevent another destructive free-for-all by building multilateral institutions. American ambivalence about international multilateralism—on the one hand, we believe in engineering cooperation,[7] but on the other hand, we jealously guard our autonomy and have a tendency toward isolationism—was reflected by the Senate's refusal to allow the United States to join the League of Nations, created by its own president.

In the Asia-Pacific, the United States also sought to replace balance-of-power politics with multilateralism. The U.S. government organized the Washington Conference of 1921–22, which produced a treaty that limited the navies of the United States, Japan, Britain, France, and Italy. This experiment in regional arms control failed to create a new regional order in the Asia-Pacific and was unable to deter Japanese colonial expansion, which ultimately resulted in World War II.[8] The United States hoped to defend its commercial and political interests in Asia without any risk of direct military engagement, and in the interest of fiscal restraint, it welcomed a ten-year naval-building holiday that allowed it to postpone fleet modernization without losing ground to Japan and the other powers (Ziemke 1992, 88). Japan also had an interest in reducing the costs of armaments while maintaining its strategic position, but Japan's military and many of its civilian politicians believed that the treaty ratios were unfair to Japan and that the agreement would threaten its hold on the mainland of Asia (Ziemke 1992, 98). Japanese

7. "Americans always want to create new world orders. Japan's fate is to try to get by in whatever world order it finds" (McDougall 1993, 521).

8. For a more positive assessment of naval arms control between the wars as a "limited success," see Goldman 1994.

decision makers were pressured internationally and domestically into the Washington Conference so as not to appear "contrary to the spirit of peace and humanity" (McDougall 1993, 516). In other words, the arms-control treaty was intended to stabilize a status quo that many Japanese leaders did not accept.

The Washington naval treaty had other flaws as well. The agreement lacked mechanisms for verification or enforcement of compliance. The two interwar pariah states, Germany and the Soviet Union, were excluded despite their long-term strategic importance, a decision that later fueled the hostility of both countries to the United States and its multilateral engineering. China remained a passive player under interwar multilateral arrangements. Although the United States sought to promote the development of China and its territorial integrity within the context of international cooperation—China now appeared well on its way toward modernization, with a pro-Western nationalist leader at the helm—Beijing resented the fact that the multilateral agreements left intact Japan's colonial empire and institutions of extraterritorial authority in China.

The pre–World War II historical experience of multipolarity in the Asia-Pacific region offers lessons about the methods of balance of power and multilateral cooperation to the U.S. policy makers of today. First, it is very difficult for the United States to play the role of balancer from across the Pacific.[9] Second, expectations about regional collective security arrangements should be modest. Multilateral cooperation may provide reassurance and ease security dilemmas, but even formal arms-control agreements cannot deter aggression by a state that wants to change the status quo.

Cold War Bipolarity in the Asia-Pacific

During the Cold War, international relations in the Asia-Pacific were globalized and lacked a regional character. The United States, a geographically distant power, dominated the area militarily and economically. Japan, depen-

9. John K. Fairbank (1972, 299) describes efforts to protect China from Japanese aggression during the interwar years as "a second-best and ineffective alternative at a time of isolationism, when it seemed impossible to mobilize unilateral American economic or military activity." Caroline Ziemke (1992, 99) also criticizes U.S. policies toward Asia: "The interwar political leadership in the United States wanted it both ways: they sought the fiscal and political advantages of arms control without having to give up the moralistic tough talk that had dominated U.S. policy in the Pacific since at least 1900."

dent on the United States for its security, lacked the autonomy to be a regional player. China isolated itself economically and diplomatically from its non-Communist regional neighbors. The non-Communist Asian countries, shut off by the Cold War from their traditional regional markets and raw-materials sources in China and Russia, diversified their trading relations and became highly dependent on U.S. markets. The level of regional trade integration within Asia was far lower than in Western Europe.

Yet the Cold War experience in the Asia-Pacific had distinctive regional characteristics. The divide between the Communist and free worlds did not dominate regional relations in the Asia-Pacific as completely as in Europe. And regional relations were characterized by bilateralism instead of the regional multilateralism that emerged in Europe.

There were several structural reasons for the Asia-Pacific patterns. For one thing, the Soviet Union appeared less menacing to Asians than to Europeans; in Asia, the Communist threat was more often internal (Kahler 1994, 119). Divisions between Asian Communist nations also created a crosscutting cleavage. The alliance between Russia and China, the two Communist continental powers, lasted only a decade before the logic of regional rivalry sundered it in 1960. The Sino-Soviet split was caused not by a Leninist ideological dispute, but by the unwillingness of Soviet leaders to give their neighbor a nuclear capability. The Communist governments in Korea and Vietnam maintained their autonomy by manipulating the Sino-Soviet rivalry. United States leaders, locked into a pattern of mobilizing electoral support by means of anti-Communist ideological appeals, were appallingly slow to exploit the Sino-Soviet split for U.S. advantage. Only when American public opinion revolted against a fruitless war in Vietnam did President Nixon discover that the leverage within the Sino-Soviet-U.S. triangle could help extricate the United States from the war.

In Europe, multilateralism enabled the United States to enhance capabilities against the Soviet Union by drawing on the might of Britain and France. In Asia, however, there were marked asymmetries of power between the United States and the available Asian allies. From the U.S. perspective, therefore, multilateralism in Asia would only increase its commitments, with little enhancement of joint capabilities (Kahler 1994, 20).

Because of these complicating factors, neither the Communist nor the free-world nations in the Asia-Pacific solidified into closely organized camps. In contrast particularly to Europe, but even to South America or Africa, the Asia-Pacific lacks a framework for regional cooperation on security issues. There are no regional arms-control agreements; nor has the region developed agreement on rules like sanctity of borders or the nonuse of force (Morgan 1994; Scalapino 1988, 1).

The dominant mode of post–World War II international relations in the region was bilateral. The United States contained Communist aggression and maintained regional stability by situating itself at the hub of a set of bilateral alliances with Japan, South Korea, and the Philippines. Until the Clinton administration, U.S. leaders clung to this "wheel-and-spokes" model and discouraged proposals for multilateral security cooperation in the region. The absence of a legacy of regular collective consultations on security matters raises the risk of security dilemmas developing now that the Asia-Pacific has returned to multipolarity.

The Future: Security Management in a Multipolar Asia-Pacific After the Cold War

BALANCE OF POWER

The prospect for managing multipolar relations among the four major powers in the Asia-Pacific region by balance-of-power methods is not good. As Chinese scholar Ji Guoxing (1994) has observed, "In the Asia-Pacific a new stable relationship among the big countries has not yet emerged and there is a disequilibrium in international relations. Relations among the United States, Japan, Russia, and China have decisive effects on the stability of the whole Asia-Pacific. These relations are under overall adjustment and a stable relationship among the four will not likely emerge soon."

Now that multipolarity has returned to the Asia-Pacific, academic theory and the region's historical experience suggest that balance-of-power methods are likely to fail. Most academic analysis favors bipolarity over multipolarity (Mearsheimer 1990; Waltz 1979). Multipolar balances are problematic for several reasons: greater complexity breeds a greater risk of miscalculation because of mistaken estimates of relative power and different interpretations of history; miscalculations can also be caused by confusion about the commitment of coalition partners to deter an aggressive state; countervailing coalitions are likely to form too slowly to deter an aggressive state; and shifting alliances inhibit cooperation among coalition partners.

CONFUSION ABOUT RELATIVE POWER AND HISTORICAL PRECEDENTS

Estimates of relative national power in the Asia-Pacific arena are particularly ambiguous because the regional powers have different sources of strength and are undergoing rapid economic, political, and military transformation. The difficulty of assessing present relative strength is particularly obvious in regard to China and Japan, the two rising powers; projecting future relative strength is even more problematic. China is a huge continental power. Its population, ground forces, quantity of weapons, and domestic market all are very large. Its economic growth rates are unprecedented. Japan is a maritime power with naval and air power, economic wealth, technological superiority, and control of a regionwide production system (Betts 1993–94, 60). Translating Japanese wealth and technological superiority into a metric of military strength is particularly problematic because the Japanese public is strongly opposed to rearmament (May 1993–94, 182–87). Richard Betts (1993–94, 61) argues that Japan's technological and economic advantages allow it quickly to balance and dominate China; he also predicts that a wealthy China would become the clear hegemonic power in the region.

Russia's situation also makes it difficult to determine its strength relative to that of its neighbors. Although acute economic problems have caused its military might and readiness to deteriorate (Moltz 1996, 181–96), Russia remains a nuclear power.

As for the United States, despite its nuclear superiority and its victory in the Cold War, Asians view it as a declining power in the region because of its domestic economic problems and its public mood of isolationism. Evaluating U.S. influence relative to the Asian powers is very difficult because it depends on estimates of the credibility of U.S. commitments as the geographically most distant power in the regional security complex.

Historically, China, Japan, and then the United States were each dominant within the region; there is no natural hierarchy among them. Which is the greatest threat to peace and stability today? How one answers the question depends on the cognitive principle one uses to interpret the lessons of history: The rule of the Chinese empire was the earliest, longest, and most durable; the rule of the Japanese Greater Asian Co-Prosperity Sphere was brief, recent, and brutal; the United States, racially and culturally alien and a distant power, was the most recent dominant military presence in the region.

COMMITMENTS OF COALITION PARTNERS MAY NOT BE CREDIBLE

Credible commitments of allies are more crucial in a multipolar system than in a bipolar one. Yet the complexity and shifting alliance patterns (see below) in a multipolar system also make it difficult to establish credible commitments.

The greatest source of instability in an Asia-Pacific multipolar system is the uncertain credibility of the commitment of the United States to the region because, as a distant power, it faces no direct threat from regional conflict. The U.S. policy of protecting its Asian friends from aggression was never entirely credible. The United States has since the turn of the century sought to limit its economic and military commitments to Asia despite its broadly defined interests in the region. Even at the height of the Cold War, U.S. extended deterrence proved ineffective (for example, the forward deployment of U.S. forces did not deter Chinese support for North Vietnamese aggression in Vietnam). President Nixon's effort to withdraw American forces from Vietnam without reducing the deterrent value of U.S. commitments in Asia and elsewhere ("peace with honor") did not succeed (Tow 1991, 49).

When the Cold War ended, U.S. policies, driven by domestic economic and political constraints, signaled a reduced military presence in Asia. The congressionally mandated review of U.S. Pacific military strategy resulted in the 1990 East Asia strategy initiative (EASI) (DOD 1990), which projected a 10 to 12 percent reduction of U.S. forward deployed forces in the Asia-Pacific region by 1993 (from 135,000 to 102,000).

Despite the drawdown, U.S. leaders have tried to persuade Asians that Washington remains committed to providing security in the region. Presidents Bush and Clinton, on their travels in Asia, attempted to reassure our allies by repeating the refrain that "the U.S. is a Pacific power." Admiral Charles R. Larson, the former commander in chief of the U.S. Pacific Command, in his May 1993 posture statement, emphasized that the forward deployed military presence of the United States, even at its reduced levels, made credible the U.S. commitment to protect its friends and deter potential bullies. The Department of Defense's 1993 bottom-up review recommended against any further near-term cuts in U.S. Pacific forces, a position reflected in its 1995 East Asia strategy report (DOD 1995b), which promised to maintain the 100,000 level so long as the threat of conflict on the Korean peninsula remained.

None of these expressions of commitment, however, are viewed by Asians as something they can count on in the long term. Since the end of the Cold War, the American public and Congress are perceived abroad as unwilling to spill blood or spend treasure to protect their friends and allies against aggression, even in Europe. In Japan and South Korea, although the U.S. commitment is backed up by formal alliances, policy elites admit to anxieties about the future. In an era dominated by economic concerns, a system of power balances that depends on the United States' acting as a policeman against aggressors is no longer seen as reliable.

BALANCING COALITIONS FORM TOO SLOWLY

Maintaining a balance of power in a multipolar system is impeded by the inability of leaders to form rapidly a coalition to deter an aggressor state. Particularly in democracies, legislatures, the mass media, and public opinion constrain the foreign-policy-making process and limit the speed with which executives can respond to external threats; delays can be expected especially when this response involves a partnership with another country. The classic example of belated balancing was the slow response of France, Britain, and the United States to Japan's initial aggression in East Asia or Germany's in central Europe during the 1930s. Current examples are abundant because domestic consensus over foreign policy in democratic countries broke down with the disappearance of the Communist threat. The controversy in Japan regarding its possible cooperation with the United States and South Korea in enforcing economic sanctions against North Korea in 1994 helped end the Hosokawa coalition government.

This tendency is especially relevant to the role of U.S. forward deployed forces in balancing relations between China and Japan. The model of Britain as external balancer in continental Europe during the nineteenth century is often suggested for the U.S. role in Asia.[10] Yet domestic constraints on the foreign policies of American presidents, imposed by legislators, the media, and public opinion, are much greater than were the constraints on the policies of British prime ministers. Look at the protracted process required for the United States to restore diplomatic relations with Vietnam, a country important for balancing rising Chinese power in Southeast Asia (Betts 1993–94, 62–63). The role of balancer suggests an impartiality that would be im-

10. For a revisionist view, see Rosecrance 1992b, 64–82.

possible to achieve so long as the United States has a security treaty with Japan. As Richard Betts (1993–94, 63) observes, "It is hard . . . to imagine Washington playing the game of agile external balancer, tilting one way then another, rather than faithful ally. Such unvarnished realism seems out of liberal character."

SHIFTING ALLIANCES IMPEDE COOPERATION

Although alliances are much more important in a multipolar system than in a bipolar system, they also tend to shift with perceptions of relative power; a country that stands with you today may go over to the other side tomorrow. Hence, leaders need to hedge against defections from their coalition and tend to be cautious in cooperating with coalition partners.

Such expectations of shifting allegiance help explain why the United States was reluctant to become more fully allied with China during the 1970s and 1980s when it was using that country as a counterweight to the Soviet Union. Transfers of U.S. military technology to China could have later backfired against Washington if the strategic environment changed.

The fluidity of alliances in a multipolar system also illuminates the increasing unwillingness of the United States to tolerate Japanese trade barriers. It once made sense for the United States to build up Japan's economic strength, because it was an important ally against the Soviet Union. The disappearance of the Soviet threat makes the U.S.-Japanese alliance less crucial to both countries and will cause Japan to behave as a more "normal" state with an independent foreign policy (Johnson 1992; Gowa 1994).[11] Anticipating such a situation, the United States is determined to get its fair share from the economic relationship with Japan (see Denoon 1993). States operating in a fluid multipolar context are more cautious about cooperating economically; economic rivalries in turn may make political-military conflict more likely.[12]

In view of the problems noted above, relying on power balances managed by the United States does not seem a safe bet for a multipolar Asia-Pacific.

11. Gowa (1994) explains the effect of enduring alliances on the propensity for economic cooperation.

12. The Clinton administration, by identifying national foreign-policy interests with domestic economic interests, reflects this transformation to multipolarity.

An Asia-Pacific Concert of Powers?

Lacking confidence that balance-of-power politics can prevent security dilemmas and preserve the peace, and with a heightened sense of regional identity based on increased economic integration, Asia-Pacific leaders are exploring various collective security arrangements.[13] The Southeast Asian countries established the ASEAN Regional Forum (ARF), which will eventually enable all the nations in the region to discuss security issues. It is hard to imagine that a regionwide security organization with twenty-one members (and growing) will provide a level of reassurance sufficient to prevent national defense buildups and security dilemmas. Collective action in large groups is prone to free riding and underprovision of the collective good (in this case, security) (Olson 1965); large-sized collective security organizations are also likely to be divided by disagreements over what constitutes aggression and when to take action (Kupchan and Kupchan 1991, 138). In the terminology proposed by Brian Job's chapter on multilateralism, the ARF is likely to remain "broad" (in membership) but "shallow" (in commitment by and for its members).

A regional concert of powers consisting of China, Japan, Russia, and the United States would be more workable than a larger body, and would provide the leadership consensus required to make the larger body effective. As Brian Job (this volume) notes, "The operation of a concert within the context of a larger multilateralist framework has come to be viewed by many analysts as the only effective path to international management of a large system." Several scholars recently have suggested that the current post–Cold War situation is well-suited to a new European concert (United States, Russia, Britain, France, and Germany) (Kupchan and Kupchan 1991, 114–61) or a global concert (United States, Russia, European Community, Japan, and China) (Rosecrance 1992b, 64–82). Might a concert of powers be in the future of the Asia-Pacific region too?

Regular cooperation among the Asia-Pacific powers would be a significant change from the status quo. Except for the United States and Japan, which closely coordinate their regional policies, the four states lack regular interaction even at the bilateral level.

13. As Rosecrance and Schott note in their chapter in this volume, the international economy has now assumed a more important role in the political calculations of national leaders than it had in the nineteenth century, and economic interdependence makes security cooperation more likely.

Yet each of the regional powers has evidenced a new interest in a more cooperative regional order. The most dramatic change of attitude has occurred in Washington under the Clinton administration. What lies behind the new American enthusiasm for regional security cooperation is the belief that it is a more feasible, and therefore more credible, way for the United States to sustain its security role in the Asia-Pacific. The creation of a new Pacific security order is viewed as a good investment for the United States because it will reassure East Asians about the permanence of U.S. commitment to the region, discourage the kinds of regional conflicts in which the United States might feel compelled to intervene, and keep the fast-growing economies of Asia open to U.S. exports. It also might ease U.S. relations with China, which are becoming increasingly strained by differences over global and regional issues.

Like Washington, Beijing has recently discovered the utility of regional collective security, although it is moving toward it much more warily.[14] Chinese leaders recognize that their country's extraordinarily rapid economic growth combined with its military modernization program has raised international anxieties about a "China threat." Most China watchers (e.g., Cheung [1996]) believe that the military modernization program is a catch-up policy after years of low defense budgets and antiquated technology, and not a drive to dominate the region. Because Chinese force capabilities and intentions are so opaque, however, many of China's neighbors remain suspicious. Chinese leaders are coming to appreciate the value of multilateral settings for reassuring their neighbors about their peaceful intentions. Beijing is also growing increasingly uncomfortable with the anti-China focus that, under balance-of-power politics, will inevitably replace the anti-Soviet focus of the U.S.-Japanese security treaty.[15] It hopes, therefore, that a new order among the major powers in the region might eventually replace the United States' bilateral alliances that surround and seem to contain it.

Japan looks to a regional order of collective security for help in resolving the internal contradictions in its international role. Japan is a world power by virtue of its wealth and technological capability, but its international behavior has been constrained by the apprehensions of its own citizens and

14. In the past, China enjoyed its role at the United Nations, but was unenthusiastic about regional multilateral initiatives that would subject its military programs and behavior to criticism and pressure from neighboring states (Johnston 1990, 173–204).

15. Chinese policy makers were very unhappy about the 1996 U.S.-Japanese summit declaration that the alliance would extend the scope of military cooperation throughout the region.

those of its neighbors about Japanese militarism.[16] Many Japanese elites believe that the best way for Japan to assume its legitimate role as a regional and world leader is to act within multilateral frameworks. Some Japanese officials also believe that although they can rely on the U.S.-Japanese security treaty now, in the long run the bilateral security ties must be transformed into a political partnership for leading a multilateral regional security framework (*Asahi Shimbun* 1995; Igarashi 1995).

Russia has always promoted the idea of Asia-Pacific security cooperation, and now that it is in a weakened position, without the resources to act independently, it welcomes it all the more (Miasnikov 1992, 95–113).

AD HOC MULTILATERALISM AMONG THE ASIA-PACIFIC POWERS

A concert of powers could emerge in the Asia-Pacific region not by purposeful design, but as a result of what Robert Scalapino (1991–92) has called "ad hoc multilateralism" to resolve knotty situations such as Cambodia and North Korea. In both cases, although international multilateral institutions played significant roles, the arena for working the problems was not the Security Council, but consultations among the regional powers (United States, China, Russia, and Japan, along with ASEAN, in the case of Cambodia, and South Korea, in the case of North Korea).[17]

The effort to prevent North Korea from withdrawing from the Non-Proliferation Treaty and becoming a nuclear threat created a new concertlike pattern of consensus building among the four Asia-Pacific powers along with South Korea. This consensus-building process began in 1991, when U.S. secretary of state Baker persuaded Japan to pledge not to establish diplomatic relations with North Korea unless it scrapped its nuclear program; and South Korean president Roh Tae Woo, meeting in Seoul with Chinese foreign minister Qian Qichen, obtained a Chinese statement that North Korean nuclear development "would endanger stability not only on the Korean Peninsula,

16. As Yoichi Funabashi (1991–92, 63) has written, "Whenever Japan tried to assert itself and assume a regional leadership role, Asian leaders recalled its culpability in the Second World War and repeatedly warned of its 'new ambition' and aspiration toward becoming a 'military giant' once again."

17. The Cambodian negotiations involved a formal international conference in Paris, but the North Korean negotiations have been informal. The Northeast Asia Cooperation Dialogue, organized by the University of California Institute on Global Conflict and Cooperation in May 1993, provides an informal forum for government officials (acting in a private capacity) and academics from North Korea, South Korea, Russia, China, Japan, and the United States to discuss issues related to the security of the Korean peninsula and Northeast Asia.

but also in Northeast Asia and the whole world" (*New York Times,* 14 November 1991, A6). During 1993 and 1994 the foreign ministers, premiers, and presidents of the five countries shuttled to each other's capitals to negotiate bilaterally a joint approach to North Korea. In particular, Japanese and South Korean officials traveled several times to Beijing to discuss the North Korean nuclear issue. A chronology of these discussions shows strikingly that the United States no longer serves as the hub among this group of five countries. Negotiations are conducted directly between all the pairs, not just with the United States. (Washington's consultations on this issue with Japan and South Korea, however, have been very close and constant.)

The prospect of imposing international economic sanctions required a consensus among the four powers. China, Russia, and the United States, as permanent members of the Security Council, had formal vetoes over a sanctions decision. China and Japan also had effective vetoes because the implementation of the sanctions would have depended primarily upon them. If China had agreed to withhold its supplies of oil to North Korea, or at least to implement its policy of requiring hard-currency payment for the oil, the sanctions would have had real bite. If China had continued to provide oil to North Korea, the sanctions would have been ineffectual. China, in other words, was the linchpin of any successful international effort to impose economic sanctions on North Korea. Japan's role was only slightly less crucial. The 250,000 members of the Chosen Soren, the main organization of Koreans living in Japan, provide large amounts of remittances (estimated at $600 million to $1.8 billion each year) to their relatives and friends in North Korea (*New York Times,* 14 June 1994, A12). For Japan to have enforced a cutoff of these remittances would have been complicated but feasible, though highly controversial politically because of the close ties between the Korean population and Socialist Party politicians in Japan.[18]

Achieving consensus among the four powers and South Korea on an approach to the North Korean nuclear problem was extremely difficult. The dynamics of the process revealed a tendency for the Asian governments to diverge from the U.S. position no matter what it was at the time.[19] Whenever the United States went out in front with a tough position on North Korean nuclear inspections, as it did in the spring of 1993, when it considered mov-

18. Russia did its part to induce North Korea to cooperate on the nuclear issue by canceling the delivery of three nuclear plants in 1994 (Hoon 1994–95, 14).

19. Moscow also complains that Washington does not consult adequately with it about the sanctions issue, and takes positions on sanctions that differ from those of the United States (see, e.g., *New York Times,* 17 June 1994, 9).

ing toward sanctions after Pyongyang threatened to withdraw from the Non-Proliferation Treaty, the other countries, South Korea and Japan in particular, espoused more flexibility (*New York Times,* 6 May 1993, A3). When the United States acted more flexibly, Japan and South Korea advocated toughness. For example, in the summer of 1994, when Washington offered a comprehensive approach to Pyongyang that concentrated on freezing its nuclear program and deferred special inspections that would provide information about past nuclear production, Seoul and Tokyo pressed for special inspections and called the U.S. position a "half-baked compromise."[20] The tendency of the Asian governments to check the U.S. actions toward Pyongyang reflects a desire on the part of politicians in South Korea, Japan, China, and Russia to demonstrate to their citizens that they have independent foreign policies.

The process of working out a consensus on the North Korean nuclear situation enhanced Chinese influence in the region. One might view the visits of South Korean and Japanese foreign ministers to Beijing as "supplications" to get the Chinese to join in international pressure against North Korea. The new state of affairs is difficult for the U.S. State Department to get used to. What it reflects is the existence of a genuinely multipolar regional structure and the beginning of a more cooperative regional order.

Since the signing of a framework agreement between the United States and the Democratic People's Republic of Korea, freezing the North Korean nuclear program and supplying North Korea with highly subsidized energy resources in the form of heavy oil imports and the building of light-water nuclear reactors, cooperation among the major powers has continued but has left out key actors.

The Korean Energy Development Organization (KEDO), the organization responsible for funding the oil supplies and reactor construction, is led by the United States, Japan, and South Korea, the countries that will provide most of the funds. China and Russia were not invited to become leading members of KEDO, because they were not providing funds. When they were later asked to become ordinary members, they declined. The United States and its two allies are in charge, and China and Russia sit by the sidelines, although Li Peng, during his December 1993 visit to Seoul, said that China was willing to support the framework agreement in any way it could. The

20. *New York Times,* 8 October 1994, 3. The United States responded by changing its position to insist that special inspections to clarify the history of past production be part of any Washington-Pyongyang agreement (*Los Angeles Times,* 15 September 1994, A6).

Russians have expressed their disappointment at being excluded, and continue to advocate a "two-plus-four" international peace conference to devise a replacement for the 1953 armistice agreement (Hoon 1994–95).

The 1996 U.S.–South Korean proposal for four-party talks on a peace agreement to replace the armistice is motivated by the desire to bring the North back into negotiations with the South. The proposal, which has not yet been accepted by North Korea, includes China, but leaves out Russia and Japan. The Russians have complained openly, and the Japanese foreign minister admitted "it would be false to deny the existence of sentiments desiring the addition of other countries to the four involved in the proposal" (*Korea Herald,* Yonhap, 2 July 1996, 1).

Might this kind of ad hoc multilateralism among the Asia-Pacific powers evolve into a regional concert of powers? To assess the prospects, we must define a concert and see whether the region offers a suitable context for a concert.

WHAT IS A CONCERT OF POWERS?

A concert of powers is a type of collective security arrangement modeled on the Concert of Europe established by Great Britain, Prussia, Russia, and Austria at the close of the Napoleonic Wars in 1815 (France joined the concert in 1818). The Concert of Europe preserved peace in Europe for more than forty years (Jervis 1986, 58).[21] Based on this single historical example, a concert of powers has come to be defined as a type of collective security system in which a small group of major powers agrees to work together to resist aggression, to meet on a regular basis to monitor events, and, if necessary, to orchestrate collective initiatives (Kupchan and Kupchan 1991, 120). Although the Concert of Europe was in effect a global management system, theories of concertlike behavior can be applied to regional contexts.

The primary objective of a concert is to regulate relations between the major powers. By sharing information about capabilities and intentions, the powers reduce the risk of security dilemmas among themselves. By creating norms of cooperation, the powers raise the cost of defection and aggressive behavior.

A concert also seeks to prevent conflicts among other regional states from provoking wars among the powers. In the nineteenth century, the great

21. The Concert of Europe existed from 1815 to 1854, but was most effective from 1815 to 1822 (Jervis 1986, 58).

powers could dictate to smaller, less powerful nations. Under the more egalitarian ethos of the twentieth century, such a notion would be resisted. It is unimaginable that in this age countries as formidable as Indonesia or South Korea would allow the major powers to order them around. Therefore a twentieth-century concert, unlike its earlier antecedent, would not be able to provide security for all nations, big or small.[22] Instead, it would establish a norm that the powers would not intervene militarily in conflicts among the less powerful states. The concert might also engage in collective mediation efforts to resolve such conflicts and undertake limited peacekeeping activities in states experiencing breakdown of internal order. In most situations, the concert would constrain the involvement of the powers in intra- or interstate conflicts that did not directly affect them.

A concert of powers is distinguished from other mechanisms of multilateral cooperation by its small size and its informality. In contrast to a formal arms-control agreement like the Washington Naval Treaty of 1922, a concert entails no binding or codified commitments. Decisions are taken through informal negotiations and the building of a consensus (Kupchan and Kupchan 1991, 120). Kupchan and Kupchan argue that the informality of a concert of powers enhances its flexibility and effectiveness. Cooperation can coexist with competition among the states in a concert. Balancing goes on among the concert members, but because of the cooperative framework, balancing is less likely to lead to overt conflict (Kupchan and Kupchan 1991, 120). Although a concert lacks the enforcement mechanisms necessary to deter an aggressor state, cooperation within the concert may facilitate the formation of a coalition to check the aggressor. The informal consensus-building character of a concert also serves to restrain action as well as promote initiatives. Whenever some of the states prefer not to respond to a threat of aggression, the concert will not act; in this way a concert becomes an instrument of constraint and prevents great-power intervention and conflict in many areas (Kupchan and Kupchan 1991, 140–41).

Although a concert is something of a compromise in that it does not entirely eliminate balancing or the risk of security dilemmas among the powers, it does promote cooperative behavior. States in a concert do not play the game as hard as they can; they do not take advantage of the vulnerabilities

22. Rosecrance and Schott, in this volume, conceptualize a concert as an oligopoly that provides the public good of security to all states. Morgan, in his chapter, also defines a concert as an arrangement by which the powers not only mute and manage their own conflicts, but also cooperate to "contain, repress, or manage" conflicts within or between other states.

of the other members of the concert (Jervis 1986, 59). Bilateral economic and political relations between concert members may still be fraught by disagreements, but the existence of the concert motivates them to mute these disagreements and prevents them from spilling over into military conflict.

A concert achieves this cooperation in several ways. It establishes a set of norms about cooperative state behavior; it encourages cooperative behavior by changing a state's expectations about how other states will behave; it gathers information on military forces to reassure members that no aggression is planned (transparency);[23] it creates disincentives against states' defecting from cooperation and behaving aggressively; putting many issues on the table, it facilitates agreement by means of issue linkage; and its regular interaction among members builds a sense of community and value consensus (Kupchan and Kupchan 1991, 130–33).

IS AN ASIA-PACIFIC CONCERT OF POWERS FEASIBLE?

The Asia-Pacific powers have strong interests in a cooperative regional order. All of them (except perhaps China) would prefer a process led by the major powers to the ASEAN Regional Forum, which is led by the smaller nations. The informality of a concert of powers would suit Asian norms better than a formal arrangement and would take advantage of the long experience of Asians in sustaining informal forms of cooperation. Yet there remain two possible obstacles to the formation of an Asia-Pacific concert of powers: a lack of ideological consensus and uncertain acceptance of the status quo.

Scholars have pointed to common ideological beliefs as essential for maintaining cooperation within a concert. In the earlier European concert of powers, the leaders of all of the states were united by a fear of domestic radical movements and by a belief that war could provoke revolution. The identification of a common internal threat gave the powers, in Robert Jervis's words (1986, 65), "more of a common basis of understanding than is usual in international politics." Ideological agreement was the glue that held the powers together despite their rivalries.

This kind of ideological consensus does not exist among the four Asia-

23. By increasing communication and transparency, states not only reduce the risk of misunderstandings that could provoke conflict, but also signal to one another that they are willing to forgo the advantage of surprise. This signal changes the expectations of each power about the behavior of the other powers, and thereby widens "the chances of cooperation by increasing the decision makers' estimates of the likelihood that others will cooperate" (Jervis 1986, 76).

Pacific powers. To the contrary, a major ideological cleavage divides China, an authoritarian country, from the United States and Japan, which are democratic countries, and even from Russia, which is trying to be a democratic country. Building trust and cooperation between countries espousing fundamentally different political values is extremely difficult. The Chinese may embrace market reform, but their analyses of foreign relations still reflect a profound suspicion of U.S. motives and behavior. And many people in the United States still believe that as long as China is Communist, it must be contained instead of engaged in cooperation.

The problem of ideological disagreement is exacerbated by the United States' criticism of human rights violations in China. Such criticism is fiercely resented by Chinese Communist leaders as interference in domestic affairs. Other Asian leaders, particularly in Southeast Asia, also find this U.S. attitude objectionable. They support China's position by asserting the superiority of Asian cultural values, which creates yet another ideological divide between the United States and the Asian members of a potential concert.

As a global power, the United States believes it has a responsibility to encourage democracy and freedom; the United States also wants to draw China out into a cooperative relationship. The contradiction in the global and regional objectives of the United States, by making ideological differences politically salient, undermines the possibility of a regional concert that includes China.

Kupchan and Kupchan (1991, 144) state that a prerequisite for a concert is that its members all be status quo powers, that is, satisfied with the existing territorial boundaries and power positions; they do not seek to conquer any new territory or to eliminate any rival. Is China a status quo power, or does it seek to reassert hegemony over the region? China's closed Communist political system and its past dominance in the region—not to mention its recent military intimidation of Taiwan—breed distrust of its intentions. No one believes that China aspires to be a larger version of Japan, economically powerful but militarily and diplomatically self-effacing. But what kind of power does China aspire to be? Instead of a status quo power, China might be a revisionist power, aiming to revive its empire after two hundred years of weakness and humiliation. In the manner it manages its disputed territorial claims in the South China Sea, its reincorporation of Hong Kong, and its relations with Taiwan, China has opportunities to reassure its neighbors that it is indeed a status quo power.

Conclusion: Policy Implications for the United States

The modern history of the Asia-Pacific region offers little hope that peace can be maintained by the United States, as a geographically distant power, operating by balance-of-power methods. Each of the four major powers in the regional complex engaged in military conflict with the others in the past century. Even during the period of Cold War bipolarity, U.S. commitments to deter aggression lacked credibility. American GI's were engaged in combat with Asian soldiers during half of the years between 1942 and 1972 (Mandelbaum 1994). In a multipolar regional arena, the challenge for the balancer is especially great when rapid transformations confound estimates of relative power and the balancer itself is viewed as declining in strength and hamstrung by democratic checks and balances.

The natural American response to a rising China is to maintain balance by reaffirming its bilateral alliances and military presence in the region. This strategy is likely to force China into a belligerent stance by creating a security dilemma. The United States could one day also find itself with commitments to deter aggression that it cannot fulfill. The American public and Congress are unlikely to subsidize U.S. basing of forces in South Korea and Japan at current levels forever. And if the two Koreas are reunified, American may be moved off the peninsula. This would leave the United States with only its Japanese bases and its carrier groups, which would be very vulnerable to a modernized Chinese air force in waters offshore China, including the South China Sea and the Taiwan Straits.

Instead of relying entirely on Cold War architecture, it makes sense for the United States to prepare for the future by diversifying its approaches to maintaining the peace and stability of the multipolar Asia-Pacific region (Pollack 1995). As Buzan and Segal (1994, 19) conclude, "The lessons of the 1920s and 1930s suggest that the only way in which a retreating United States can maintain its influence at a reduced cost is by establishing an effective multilateral security structure." There can be no such effective regional order without a close working relationship among the four regional powers.

Achieving a full-fledged Asia-Pacific concert of powers will be difficult so long as China remains a Communist country criticized for its lack of human rights by the United States. Despite their common objective of avoiding war and fostering economic ties, balance-of-power politics will pit China against the United States unless the United States plays down the human rights issue or China moves toward democracy. And if in fact China is determined to settle territorial issues by force and reclaim hegemony, no multilateral arrangement will be able to stop it, as the failed arms-control agreements of the 1920s showed. Yet an effort to forge a concert should be undertaken even if it is unable to reach the ambitious standard of the nineteenth-century Concert of Europe and achieves only ad hoc multilateralism or regular consultations among the powers.[24] Any improvements of trust will be welcome for attenuating the security dilemma between China and the United States and Japan. Without such an effort, balance-of-power politics played by a distant United States are almost certain to fail.

24. A concert of powers that consults regularly would undermine domestic hard-liners and help sustain political support for cooperation in all four countries (John Odell, personal communication, 1995).

12

Building Order in Arab-Israeli Relations: From Balance to Concert?

David J. Pervin

> I like to reflect that if anyone had predicted in 1871 that within a hundred years France and Germany would be living as part of a European community linked politically and economically, such a person would have been called mad. But even more mad would have been he who predicted that such an outcome would take place only after the awful bloodletting of a World War I and a World War II.
>
> —Dana Adams Schmidt, *Armageddon in the Middle East*

Arab-Israeli relations have historically been marked by hostility, antagonism, and hatred. The long conflict has taken a variety of forms: communal, between Palestinians and Zionists and then Israelis; interstate, between Israel and its neighbors; economic, via the Arab boycott on Israel; political, on the international stage in attempts to convince governments and peoples of the rightness of the respective causes; over resources, for example, the limited supply of water; and military, in the form of six wars and a multitude of skirmishes. Although conflict has dominated, there were also various attempts to achieve conciliation and, failing that, to arrange methods of conflict management that would ameliorate, if not eliminate, the confrontation. By and large these efforts have been unsuccessful.[1]

Beginning with the Madrid Conference in 1991, Arab-Israeli relations appear to have taken a turn toward comprehensive peace. To be sure, the

1. On early efforts to make peace, see Rabinovich 1991 and Pappe 1994. In the case of Syria, see Alan 1953.

process has been prolonged, has suffered setbacks, and at times has even seemed to have sputtered to a stop. Notwithstanding these difficulties, significant achievements have been made, ones that previously would have seemed inconceivable: the September 1993 Washington Declaration between the Palestine Liberation Organization and Israel, followed by the Cairo Agreement of February 1994 and the limited autonomy of the Palestinians in Gaza and Jericho, and the Jordan-Israel peace treaty of October 1994. There has also been progress in negotiations between Israel and Syria. These bilateral negotiations and agreements have been paralleled by multilateral talks on five regional topics—arms control, economic cooperation, refugees, water, and the environment—in which other regional and extraregional states have participated, although Syria and Lebanon have refused to take part until the achievement of bilateral agreements (see Peters 1994; Spiegel and Pervin 1995a, 1995b). In short, there have been a number of breakthroughs that are not only symbolic and psychological, but also pragmatic and concrete.

The transformations generated by the end of the Cold War and the demise of the Soviet Union as a superpower create an opportunity to reevaluate the interrelation between regional subsystems and the global system, and to distinguish the autonomous dynamics of the region from the impact of external influences. The presence of changes in the regional actors' behavior—in Arab-Israeli relations the slow transition from conflict to peace—provides an ideal laboratory in which to examine the impact of global, regional, and domestic influences. To the extent that explanations of the actors' behavior can be found at all three levels, comparing the differences between the periods before and since 1990 may shed light on the relative importance of each via comparative statics.[2] The progress toward peace provides an unusual opportunity to examine the reasons for and influences on attempts to build regional order.

This chapter examines how a specific international system, namely, the bipolar Cold War, created environmental incentives and disincentives that conditioned the dynamic of regional and domestic politics in the Middle East, and then how a change in the international environment, marked by the demise of the Soviet Union, affected the strategies of the regional states—given the extant domestic political and economic structures. It is assumed

2. As Powell (1994, 316) notes, "Fixing [systemic] constraints and varying units' attributes comprise the essential conceptual experiment underlying reductive explanations. . . . Fixing the units' attributes and varying the constraints facing the units comprise the fundamental conceptual experiment underlying systemic explanations."

that state leaders are rational actors who seek to maintain power. To meet this goal they seek resources—both material and symbolic—while they face both international and domestic constraints and opportunities. A change in either the international or the domestic environment affects the ability of leaders to obtain these resources and thus requires adjustment.

The Arab-Israeli System

At its broadest, the Middle East geographically extends from Morocco to Iran, including Turkey, and might even include Pakistan and Central Asia. The rationale for this scope is that the majority of countries included are either Arab, with the exceptions of Israel, Turkey, and Iran; Muslim, with the exception of Israel and Lebanon; and Sunni, with the exception of Iran. The difficulties in using such a scope, due to both the distinctiveness of "sub-regions" and the extensive spillover among them, are made apparent using Lake's (this volume) typology of externalities: in terms of *security,* while there are distinct dynamics that separate northern Africa (the Maghreb), the Levant (the Mashreq), and the Gulf (the Khalij), in an age of aircraft and missiles there is clearly overlap, as Israeli attacks on Tunis and Osirak, Iraqi attacks on Tel Aviv, and transstate support for terrorist or political organizations illustrate. Intraregional *trade* is low, with the primary trade partners for all states being the industrialized countries, although there have been extensive intraregional movements in labor and lesser in capital. The *environment* reinforces these distinctions, given the traditional separation caused by the desert and the islands of settlement along rivers or in mountains, although the scarcity of water creates local effects for Syria, Israel, and Jordan, on the one hand, and Turkey, Syria, and Iraq, on the other. *Information* spreads quickly among the Arab states, within the limits imposed by political expediency and frequently in the form of propaganda, at times for subversive purposes.

As to using the criterion of *values,* a basis of the psychological approach (Boals 1973), the difficulties raised are profound, precisely because it raises the question of identity. The conflict in the Middle East, most especially that involving Israel, is deeply rooted in contrasting values and conflicting identities, and is beset by cultural differences (R. Cohen 1990, 1994). The very choice of what name to use for the "region" is itself contested because it implies an identity, as is clear in the objection by many Arabs to Shimon Peres's vision of, as the title of his book puts it, "the new Middle East" (Peres 1993). Some argue, on the basis of perceived links among the Arab states due to a common language and history, that there is a distinct Arab region (Korany and Dessouki 1991; Noble 1991). From this perspective, while Israel is not *of* the region, it is *in* the system, because "interconnections are present with the result that changes in some parts of the system produce changes in other parts [and] relations between two actors depend in part on the relations between each of those actors and other actors in the system" (Jervis 1979, 212–13). Given war, military skirmishes, and the spiral of terrorist attacks and reprisals, clearly Israel and the Arabs have been interconnected. A focus on interconnections does not, however, help to explain the dynamics of the system.

Explaining the system's dynamics might be helped by defining a system as "a group of actors standing in characteristic relationships to each other (structure), interacting on the basis of recognizable patterns (processes), and subject to various contextual limitations" (Young 1968, 6). Yet attempts to characterize the structural distribution of power in the region are beset by conceptual and empirical problems. Indicative is Noble's ambivalence: "[T]he Arab system in the 1950s and 1960s stood between an unbalanced multipower system and a one-power system, although it more closely resembled the latter." Egypt's influence was based less on its material resources and more on the power of its example as the main state confronting Israel and imperialism. The extent of its appeal was thus dependent upon its ability to provide "emotionally satisfying answers to the central issues confronting Arab societies." However, Egypt's ability coercively to use its material and political superiority "was checked by physical and political constraints on the use of its military strength" (Noble 1991, 63–65). The sources of these constraints were the great powers and Israel, which "served as a stabilizing influence in inter-Arab affairs by preventing important structural shifts" (Binder 1958, 428).

This raises the question of Israel's role in the region. Was the system bipolar, with Egypt and Israel the poles drawing the other regional states into their orbits? This is problematic. For the Arab states, alignment with Israel was not an acceptable policy, although tacit cooperation was possible. Was Israel the holder of the balance, similar to that of Britain during the nineteenth century (Oren 1984; Sheehan 1989)? Was it either an aspiring hegemon (Irwin 1991) or one in effect as during the 1980s it "intervene[d] at will, unchallenged, from Baghdad to Beirut" (Hudson 1984, 156; see also Peri

1984)? Finally, taking into account Israel's geographic position, was it a central power (Niou, Ordershook, and Rose 1989, 330) that like Germany relied on a military strategy of preemption (Harkavy 1977)? If this perspective is adopted, then, as was the case with Germany, Israel's policies have considerable implications for the stability of the system. But even if Israel is seen as a central and hegemonic power, its ability to influence events is constrained both by its not "belonging" to the system and by the interests of external powers. Whatever the standing of theories linking structure to stability at the level of the great powers, their applicability to the Middle East is at best dubious, as Lake and Morgan (this volume) note.

Perhaps drawing on general international relations theory can help explain the region's dynamics. In the general absence of democracies and given limited trade among the regional states, clearly liberalism is on foreign ground. The predominant explanation of regional dynamics is that of the balance of power or the balance of threat (Walt 1987). Rustow (1989, 790–91) argues that two regularities of the Middle Eastern system have been a checkerboard pattern in which neighbors are likely to be opposed while countries once removed are likely to be allied (see also Binder 1958, 417) and a tendency to balance by supporting the weaker side in any conflict (see also Brown 1984; Evron 1994; Maddy-Weitzman 1993; Sayigh 1993). The balance of power has also served as a metaphor in descriptions of inter-Arab politics (Taylor 1982). The appeal of realism is not surprising, because the basic assumptions—that the system is anarchic and the actors seek to survive (Waltz 1979, 121)—apply.

Yet Middle East international relations may be a balance-of-power system only superficially. Given the historical appeal of suprastate ideologies, in particular pan-Arabism, and the considerable differences in the resources available to regional states, had the region been autonomous it is questionable whether all the states would have survived. But in contrast to the independent European system, where states disappeared and were absorbed into others, none of the regional states have disappeared. This is because regional relations have been heavily penetrated by external great powers. By providing assistance to regional states and at times intervening to protect their allies (see, e.g., Kaplan 1975), the great powers significantly affected, and limited, the options available to regional states. The Middle East is a subordinate system because regional states "have to play within certain parameters" (Azar, Jureidini, and McLaurin 1978, 45) and the "[g]reat powers can often structure the choices and preferences of minor powers and thus shape regional outcomes" (Stein 1990, 48). If, as Waltz (1979, 184–85) argued, small states can be irresponsible, *"since their security is mainly provided by the efforts that others make"* (emphasis added), then the utility of realism, which assumes that "no external guarantee of survival exists" (Waltz 1967, 215), in explaining Middle East dynamics may be vitiated.[3]

This is not to say, however, that there were no regional dynamics. Political competition among the regional states and the movement of people and capital clearly had and have great importance; so, too, attempts at subversion. And a security dilemma (Jervis 1978) between states existed while the dangers of entrapment and abandonment (G. Snyder 1984) were experienced in relations both among regional states and, of particular importance, between regional states and their great-power patrons.

What it *is* to say, however, is that caution is needed in drawing on general theories. The dynamics of Arab-Israeli relations are best explained by examining the impact of the global and domestic environments in which state leaders act and react. We must "come to terms with the fact that international and domestic politics are interactive. . . . [G]overnments act at home to meet international challenges and abroad to solve domestic problems, often simultaneously" (Mastanduno, Lake, and Ikenberry 1989, 458).

The Cold War and Arab-Israeli Relations: Conflict and Order

As Azar, Jureidini, and McLaurin (1978) suggest, during the Cold War the system tended toward an equilibrium of contention, rejection, and antagonism; any movement away from this condition stimulated various forms of negative feedback, including intervention from external powers, in the case of war, and domestic opposition, including violence, in the case of movement toward peace (cf. Meibar 1982). This mechanistic formulation may obscure as much as it reveals, because it ignores efforts to create ground rules and conceals important changes that developed over time.

Efforts to create or impose rules of the game took both diplomatic and military forms. Examples of diplomatic attempts, whether through direct contacts or via intermediaries, include the coordination between Israel

3. This confirms the difference between open and closed systems noted by Lake and Morgan in Chapter 1.

and Transjordan in the 1948 war to limit the fighting and divide territory (Shlaim 1990); Egyptian-Israeli efforts in the early 1950s (Oren 1992); the American-mediated agreement governing Syria's intervention in Lebanon in 1976 (Rabinovich 1984; Evron 1987; Seale 1988); and the negotiations between Egypt and Israel starting in 1974, leading to President Sadat's trip to Jerusalem in 1977 and culminating in the peace treaty of 1979 (Quandt 1986).

Such diplomatic efforts were overshadowed by conflict: verbal threats, limited attacks, mobilizations, and war. Military attempts to influence and limit the actions of other actors dominated and frequently led to escalation. Examples include Israel's attacks against Arab states in retaliation for armed incursions, in an attempt to impose high costs on those states and thus persuade them to prevent future incursions (Blechman 1972; Khouri 1966; Morris 1993; Shimshoni 1988). Such attacks contributed to the wars in 1956 and 1967, and the weakness and inability of the central state in Lebanon to constrain the PLO led Israel to invade in 1978 and 1982 (Yaniv 1987b). Egypt's mobilization in 1960 may have deterred Israel from escalating its attacks on the northern region (Syria) of the United Arab Republic (Shepherd 1960; Schmidt 1960), but a similar effort in May 1967 led to war in June (Brown 1991; Dawn 1968; Mor 1991; Parker 1993). After Israel's conquests in 1967, Egypt launched the War of Attrition in an effort to convince Israel that the occupation would be costly and the superpowers that instability would reign unless they stepped in, while Israel launched air raids deep into Egypt in order to convince it that if the war continued, the regime would be threatened (Bar-Siman-Tov 1980). Similarly, the 1973 war was a joint Egyptian-Syrian effort to demonstrate to Israel and especially to the superpowers the dangers of the status quo. A different type of battle was the Palestinian *intifada* in the occupied territories, which began in 1987.

By affecting the costs and benefits of certain courses of action, both Israel and the Arabs sought to convince the other side that certain rules should be followed. These efforts were not always successful, whether because the parties did not have the power to impose their version, because they did not have the authority to convince the other side that their version was legitimate, or because, in the case of Lebanon, the state was not able to enforce its sovereignty. Nevertheless, tacit arrangements were made. For example, Syria's intervention in Lebanon in 1976 to maintain stability, or at least prevent a dangerous escalation, was at the invitation of the Lebanese government, was coordinated with the United States and Israel, and received the subsequent approval of the Arab states (Dawisha 1980; Haley and Snider 1979).

Nor were superpowers impartial referees enforcing agreed-upon abstract rules. This is not to say that a situation of no war/no peace was desired by either the United States (Slater 1990–91) or the Soviet Union (Freedman 1975) as each sought advantage over the other; such an environment entailed dangers for both superpowers, not least that they would be drawn into direct confrontation. With that danger in the background, some tacit rules governing the superpowers' respective behavior in the region evolved (George 1983). Cooperation to ensure that the regional conflict did not escalate out of control took place between the superpowers (Golan 1991; Saunders 1988). Neither would allow an ally of its opponent to overthrow or threaten the stability of the regime of one of its own allies. The American intervention in Lebanon in 1958 (paralleled by a British intervention in Jordan) and response to the Syrian intervention in Jordan in 1970 are examples. So too is the deployment, with American acquiescence (see Kissinger 1979), of Soviet advisors and pilots to Egypt in 1970 in response to Israel's deep-penetration air raids that sought to destabilize President Nasser (Shlaim and Tanter 1978). The principle of sovereignty was consistently reinforced by the superpowers and was included in the formula provided by United Nations Security Council Resolution 242, the basis of all subsequent peace processes.

As the superpowers ensured external sovereignty, so too did they enhance domestic sovereignty. Patronage has played an important role in maintenance of regimes, including those of Syria (Sadowski 1987) and Jordan (Yorke 1988), and the availability of external assistance has "lubricated neo-patrimonial power structures and supported consumer subsidy programmes intended to ameliorate potential popular discontent" (Brynen 1991, 609). Over time, centralized state institutions took on a life of their own and affected the identities, choices, and options of the various actors (Krasner 1988). While the appeal of substate, or ethnic and sectarian, and suprastate, whether pan-Arab or pan-Islamic, identities remain, there has been an "almost involuntary inculcation in the people of a sense of identity with their own state gained through habit, vested interests, local peculiarities and sensitivities, and common experiences" (Harik 1990, 26); that is, a "territorial nationalism" (*wataniyya*) that emphasizes the unique historic identity of each country has developed (Baram 1990).[4] As a result, the states are less

4. On the Arab state more generally, see Anderson 1987; on authoritarianism in the Arab world, see Crystal 1994.

permeable and more able to weather the winds created by domestic shocks elsewhere in the region.[5] As was the case in Europe (Smith 1985), the state is making the nation.

Thus, as a result of this limited conflict, the fragile and weak states that became independent in the wake of World War II had the need, due to conflict, the time, due to externally imposed limits, and the opportunity, due to external assistance, to solidify their internal authority, if not necessarily legitimacy. This result can be contrasted with the fate of African states, which in the absence of interstate conflict have remained weak (Herbst 1990). In the hothouse environment of the Cold War and the Arab-Israeli conflict, regional states took root; they also increased their capacities (Gause 1992).

The consolidation of the regional states, or what Ben-Dor (1983) called the creation of "stateness," has corresponded with a growing pragmatism in Arab foreign policy (Hagan 1984), apparent in inter-Arab relations following the decline in the appeal of pan-Arab nationalism (*qawmiyya*) and the ascendance of *raison d'etat* (Ajami 1978–79; Korany 1988; Shamir 1981). This pragmatism was also evident in official policy toward Israel, marked by the change from the rejection of the Khartoum Summit of 1968, with its three noes (no negotiations, no recognition, no peace), to the limited recognition in the PLO's two-state policy adopted in 1974 (Cobban 1984), to Sadat's 1977 visit to Jerusalem and the Egyptian-Israeli peace treaty of 1979, to the resolutions of the 1982 Fez Summit that implicitly recognized Israel (Dishon and Maddy-Weitzman 1984). This change was prompted both by the recognition that continued confrontation with Israel was too expensive (Miller 1988) and by the increasing domestic strength and stability of the Arab states, which enabled them to pursue independent policies.

The End of the Cold War: Adapting to a New Environment

The end of the Cold War, brought about by the weakening and then demise of the Soviet Union, necessitated a reexamination of opportunities and constraints. This was particularly the case for the Arab states that were allied

5. On this point, contrast Nahas 1985 to Gause 1991 and Brynen 1991. A partial exception to this trend may have been Jordan's partial alignment with Iraq in 1990 (Brand 1991).

with the USSR. As early as 1987, at a Syrian-Soviet summit meeting in Moscow, Gorbachev explicitly stated that "military force has been completely discredited as a means of settling the conflict," and praised Syria for its "firm course at achieving a political settlement" (*Pravda,* 25 April 1987, 2). The declining Soviet support for Arab military efforts dealt a severe blow to Syria's efforts to obtain "strategic parity" with Israel (Eisenstadt 1992; Hannah 1989; Karsh 1988, 1991; Khalidi and Agha 1991).

Within the Arab world there was debate whether the world was becoming unipolar, dominated by the United States, or multipolar, as well as about the implications for the Arabs and how to react (Karawan 1994). Two perspectives were apparent at the February 1990 summit meeting of the Arab Cooperation Council of Iraq, Jordan, Egypt, and Yemen. President Saddam Hussein (1990) of Iraq warned that the end of the Cold War meant that the relative power of both the United States and Israel had increased dramatically, which might lead them to harm the Arabs. In response, Saddam suggested that the Arabs consider withdrawing their investments from the United States and called for "pan-Arab cooperation . . . in the economic, political, and educational fields, as well as other fields." He concluded that "all of us are strong as long as we are united, and all of us are weak as long as we are divided." In short, Saddam Hussein called for greater unity to enhance Arab strength as a counter to the United States and Israel. Jordan's King Hussein (1990), on the other hand, emphasized that in the wake of the Cold War, "among the distinguished features is the world's move to a stage in which the importance of the economic and political blocs is stressed." Either the Arabs would adjust, and "achieve . . . existence, stability, [and] development," or they would fall by the wayside. In other words, King Hussein advocated increasing emphasis on economic development and ties to the West.

Iraq's 1990 invasion and occupation of Kuwait, a heavy-handed attempt to create that unity and counterbalance, followed by the American victory, reinforced the importance of external actors and independent action by Arab states, and exacerbated domestic problems facing Arab states. One result of the war was that many Arab workers lost their jobs, and their home countries no longer benefited from remittances. The expulsion of Palestinians who had long worked in Kuwait and the Gulf had at least short-term negative effects on Jordan, which absorbed a huge increase in population at a time when its economy was already damaged by Gulf Arab and American withdrawal of assistance as reprisal for Jordanian neutrality in the war; on Israel, which saw an important safety valve for the occupied territories closed; and especially on the PLO, which saw financial and political assistance from the Gulf countries disappear as punishment for its support of Iraq. The dangers of discontent's spilling into instability were seen as significant.

With the demise of the Soviet Union in 1991, any remaining questions about American dominance were answered. The analysis of the Al-Ahram Centre (1994, 42) was indicative: "The United States occupies a unique position as the world's only superpower and is monopolizing power solely and absolutely, both in the international arena and in the Middle East. [While] the United States has not yet succeeded in enforcing an alternative 'new order' in the Middle East . . . [it] has traced the parametres of the regional players' powers and, especially, in the field of defence and security." Because of this change, the Centre argued, the Arab countries lost "the choice of initiating tactical ploys . . . in playing one of the superpowers against the other." Notwithstanding conjecture that with the end of the Cold War Israel would lose its importance to the United States (e.g., Barnett 1991), the Centre instead saw "closer strategic cooperation." As a result, "[t]he relative standing of the Arab countries in regional interactions has deteriorated. This means that Arab countries are more susceptible to blackmail and to being forced to work from a position of weakness with Israel, Turkey, and Iran" (Al-Ahram Centre 1994, 46–48).

The changes in the international environment affected not only the regional balance of power, in Israel's favor, but also the availability of external resources so crucial for regime survival. However, the extent to which the policies of the regional states changed in response to this new environment was not uniform and varied according to how pressing the perceived need was. In part the differences can be explained by the differing abilities of regional states to gain resources either from within the region or from the domestic economy. Other factors were inertial and included the magnitude of sunk costs, in terms of the normative value placed on the conflict; the internal political and economic distributional effects of any changes; and the perception of the likely duration of the current international system and what would likely replace it.[6] In all cases the problems faced by the Palestinians (PLO) and Jordan were far greater than those facing Syria, which helps explain the relative willingness of each to make peace with Israel, a precondition for improving relations with the United States. Israel too had to adapt, but its problems, both environmental and domestic, were far less severe.

For the PLO, the possibility that Israel would unilaterally determine the fate of the occupied territories—and their inhabitants—appeared to in-

6. These factors are culled from Hannan and Freeman 1977, esp. 931.

crease, while funding for the organization and its myriad institutions dried up, further diminishing its ability to support Palestinians in the territories. The PLO had long given up any hope of attaining the ultimate normative goal of regaining all of historic Palestine, as was indicated in its implicit acceptance of a two-state solution as early as 1974 and explicit recognition of Israel and renunciation of terrorism in 1988. Domestically, here meaning the West Bank and Gaza Strip, the PLO faced challenges not only from leaders in the *intifada* but also from Hamas. This radical Islamicist organization had a fundamentally different view of the "identity and the future direction of the Palestinian people" (Abu-Amr 1993, 6), obtained financial support from fraternal Islamicist movements in the Arab world, and engaged in military activities, thus showing an activist policy the PLO had previously espoused but then renounced. In its failure to demonstrate a capability to solve, or at least ameliorate, the Palestinians' plight, the PLO risked irrelevance. Thus the Oslo process and the Washington Agreement of 1993.

The situation for Jordan was not much better. For Jordan the conflict with Israel did not have an existential dimension, in part due to its weakness and need for pragmatism and in part due to the overlapping interests regarding the fate of the Palestinians and wariness over the PLO. Indeed, historically Jordan's primary competition was with the PLO (Bailey 1984). While King Hussein had accepted, at least symbolically, the decision of the 1974 Rabat Conference to make the PLO the "sole legitimate representative of the Palestinian people," it was not until the threat of spillover from the *intifada* that Jordan severed its ties to the West Bank, although this certainly did not mean that Jordan no longer had an interest in the political fate of the occupied territories (Susser 1990). Yet Jordan's ability to influence events was diminished by a weak economy—which resulted in riots in 1989 that were particularly troubling because they took place among Transjordanians—combined with a political transition marked by limited democratization via elections, which were troubling because of the strong showing of Islamic candidates (Brand 1991; Brynen 1992; Satloff 1992). Already unsteady, Jordan was buffeted by the winds of the Gulf War: the return of Palestinians, increased unemployment, a reduction in remittances, the cutoff of its exports to and transit earnings from Iraq, and the elimination of Arab and American economic assistance. The link between the deteriorating state of Jordan's economy and the need for peace was made explicit by King Hussein in two speeches, the first on 9 July 1994 to members of the Jordanian House of Representatives, the second on 14 July 1994 to the Fourth Mechanized Division of the Jordanian Armed Forces (see Hussein 1994a, 1994b). In both he explained that Jordan had become isolated internationally, in the wake of the Cold War, and regionally, due to its support for Iraq in the Persian Gulf War. This isolation, combined with Jordan's extensive debts, posed a threat to Jordan's economy and was detrimental to the strength of the army. There was no choice but to make peace, since the United States "linked" any consideration of the debt problem, as well as arms sales, to Jordan's stand on the peace process.

For Syria, too, the changed international environment "made it clear that [it] would have to come to terms with the West to gain a favorable deal in a negotiated solution" (Perthes 1993, 24). Nevertheless, although Syria had lost its superpower patron and its economy had suffered a downturn in the late 1980s, the considerable payments for its role in the Gulf War and an increase in oil exports, combined with a low level of debt, made its position relatively resilient. "The transformation in the state's 'environment' has internal consequences. . . . The regime is altering its master strategies: away from statism and toward economic liberalization, away from the struggle with Israel and toward diplomacy and compromise" (Hinnebusch 1993a, 2)—yet the pressures were less severe. To the extent that Syria has undertaken steps to liberalize the economy, they have been sponsored by and in the interest of the regime; as a result they have been measured, limited, and dictated more by political considerations—such as gaining the support of segments of the population and in turn tying their interests to the regime—than by convictions about efficiency, much less the fundamental value of private enterprise (Heydemann 1992, 1993; Hinnebusch 1993a, 1993b). Should the limited liberalization threaten the sectarian, institutional, or popular bases of the regime, due to its distributional effects, it will likely be reversed.[7] The economic liberalization is thus contingent; it does not include political liberalization. In this respect, too, Syria is in a stronger position than either the PLO or Jordan: there are no significant domestic challengers to the regime.

Because of these differences, the time pressure on Syria is less; its strength allows it to wait out the current international transition if such is perceived as necessary. The Syrian regime also has extensive normative sunk costs.[8] For Syria the *sine qua non* of any agreement is the full return of the Golan Heights, for security reasons but mainly because it is intricately linked

7. As the Economist Intelligence Unit (EIU 1995, 5) observed: "The requirements of the reform programme have always been held subordinate to the requirements of political and social stability and the regime will continue to judge the value of reforms in these terms. It will not take dramatic steps toward liberalization for fear of runaway inflation and unemployment."

8. As Hinnebusch (1995, 74–75) puts it: "If a settlement could be plausibly presented as vindicating the enormous investment Syria has put into the conflict . . . it would bring a substantial windfall of political capital that the regime could even 'invest' in political liberalization." Whether the result of peace would be political liberalization is open to doubt.

with the Syrian leadership's perception of Syria's regional role (Diab 1994a, 1994b; Muslih 1993): Syria is, as Foreign Minister al-Shar' (1994, 3) put it, the "Arab beating heart." President Asad (1994, 46–47), in a speech to the Syrian People's Assembly, emphasized that Syria is a strong state that can and should act as leader and protector of the other Arabs, and had they coordinated with Syria rather than entered separate negotiations from a position of weakness that forced them to make concessions, they would have "benefit[ed] from Syria's position, negotiating power and various capabilities in the arena of conflict." Syria's strength and pride ensure that it will "not do anything if it does not serve the interests of our country," and enable it to take the "strategic option" of making peace without "relinquishing any part of the homeland," because this "means relinquishing the homeland and the free will, and submission at the expense of rights, destiny and future." While the regime has used speeches by the leadership and the press to prepare the public for a settlement, this preparation coexists with a continued vilification of Israel (Zisser 1994).[9]

The changed international environment had mixed effects on Israel. While Israel's security was enhanced by the elimination of Soviet support for an Arab war option, it was diminished by the violence of the *intifada* and the potential threat posed by missiles; in terms of Israeli strategic discourse, there was no "basic" threat to Israel's existence, but a simmering "current" threat to the security of Israelis (Yaniv 1987a). Before becoming prime minister, Yitzhak Rabin (1993, 9, 12) argued that Israel has "more territories than we require or know how to deal with" and observed that the missile threat from Syria was far greater than had been the case from Iraq; as Diab (1995) argues, a situation of mutual deterrence has been created. Perhaps ironically, the massive immigration of Soviet Jews reaffirmed Zionist goals but called into question ambitions of controlling all of the historic land of Israel, especially since the United States had linked $10 billion in loan guarantees for immigrant integration to a change in Israel's policy toward settlements in the occupied territories.[10] This linkage had domestic ramifications in Israel,

9. An example of this vilification is an 8 January 1995 editorial in al-Ba'th entitled "Israel's Generals and the Dangerous Calculation," arguing that Israel seeks to block peace and "persist with the same arrogance that made the entire world oppose Hitlerism. . . . the impasse in the region continues, and it is no wonder that Israel turns this impasse into a disaster as its generals have developed Nazi-like feelings" (FBIS-NES-95-008, 12 January 1995, 39).

10. This connection was made explicit by Yitzhak Rabin before the 1992 elections: "If I win the June elections . . . I will change national priorities and put an end to the settlements, which are a response to political pressures and not security criteria. . . . It would also allow us to win

where concern about relations with the United States, and the preference for absorbing immigrants to strengthening Israel's hold over the territories by increasing settlements, worked against the incumbent Likud and in favor of Labor in the 1992 elections (Arian and Shamir 1995; Shachar and Shamir 1995), especially among the immigrants themselves, who voted overwhelmingly and with close to decisive impact for Labor (Fein 1995; Reich, Wurmser, and Dropkin 1995), which was able to cobble together a slight majority government. And while Israel's economy was comparatively strong, the continuation of conflict was perceived as creating barriers to exports, obtaining investments, and taking advantage of opportunities created by its high-tech industrial infrastructure.

The Evolution of an International Society: Cooperation and Competition

If the Cold War environment facilitated conflict, it also—by ensuring the survival of states and regimes and through the heavy inflow of weapons that made war more costly, a point emphasized by Rabin (1993)—created stability. The end of the Cold War and the repercussions of regional events—the *intifada* and the Gulf War especially—brought about a reconsideration of the costs of the status quo of constrained conflict. As Buzan (1993, 343) has noted, "Units that have no choice but to interact with each other on a regular, long-term basis, and that begin to accept each other as essentially similar types of sociopolitical organization, will be hard put to avoid creating some mechanisms for dealing with each other peacefully." The bases for an international society, recognition of the rights and obligations of sovereignty and the sanctity of contracts (Bull 1977), had been set.

That the actors involved so see it is clear: the PLO-Israel agreement was preceded by the exchange of mutual recognition—by Israel, of the PLO's being the representative of the Palestinians, and by the PLO, of "the right of Israel to exist in peace and security"—while in the preamble of the agreement each "recognize[d] their mutual legitimate and political rights."[11] The pre-

guarantees of American loans to integrate the new immigrants" (*Le Figaro,* 21 February 1992, as cited in *Near East Report* 36 (26): 1 (29 June 1992).

11. Exchange of letters in the *New York Times,* 10 September 1993, A8; text of the agreement in the *New York Times,* 14 September 1993, A6.

amble of the Israel-Jordan peace treaty speaks of "recognizing their right and obligation to live in peace with each other . . . within secure and recognized borders."[12] The parties involved have thus framed their agreements in terms of internationally recognized norms and values. As such, if the "defining boundary between international system and [international] society is when units not only recognize each other as the same type of entity but also are prepared to accord each other equal legal status on that basis . . . [creating] a shared identity in which states accept each other as being the same type of entity" (Buzan 1993, 345), then Arab-Israeli relations are in the process of making that transition.

The shift is far from complete, as is apparent in the nature of the agreements between Israel and the PLO. While the mutual recognition of "legitimate and political rights" involved each side's acceptance of the other as the "same type of entity," namely, a national movement, it did not and could not involve recognition of equality as sovereign states. While the agreements postponed any definite decisions concerning the future of the occupied West Bank and Gaza, to the extent that they provided for the progressive devolution of authority over functional and territorial domains they implicitly constituted a framework wherein the Palestinians could build institutions that would enable an evolution to sovereignty; central place was given to such important pillars of sovereignty as internal order, education, land, legislation, and elections.[13] The transition period to negotiations over the final status of the occupied territories was thus designed as an Israeli test not only of Palestinian intentions, but also capabilities to "act" like a state.

The acceptance of sovereignty and the sanctity of contracts both reinforces and ameliorates anarchy. In and of itself, anarchy implies little about the levels of competition and cooperation; what is critical is the strategic environment (Powell 1994). But the process of creating an international society means that "the process of reproduction becomes conscious and intentional" (Buzan 1993, 348): to the extent that actors have accepted the existence and legitimacy of the others, they have at least an implicit investment in the others' continuity as presently constituted, which enhances cooperation. So too does the acceptance of interdependence, the acceptance that "outcomes [are]

12. *New York Times,* 27 October 1994, A13; full text in *Journal of Palestine Studies* 24 (2): 126–43 (winter 1995).

13. In addition to the 13 September 1993 agreement, see also the "Agreement on the Gaza Strip and the Jericho Area," signed in Cairo on 4 May 1994. For the text, see *Security Dialogue* 25 (3): 359–64 (1994).

positively interdependent in the sense that potential gains exist which cannot be realized by unilateral action" (Wendt 1992, 416), which requires sensitivity to how one's own actions affect the interests of others. Examples of this investment and sensitivity include Israel's efforts to ensure that American aid to Jordan and the PLO would be maintained (Sciolino with Friedman 1994; Greenhouse 1995), objections to proposals to move the American embassy to Jerusalem (Seelye 1995), and rescinding expropriation of Palestinian land in Jerusalem in the face of Arab objections (Haberman 1995b); efforts, which were criticized on human rights grounds, by the PLO to clamp down on terrorism (e.g., Sciolino 1995); and Jordan's willingness to allow Israelis to lease lands that had been returned as part of the peace settlement (Greenberg 1995). Such efforts to avoid unilateral actions that can weaken the position of other actors constitute a change from the previous situation, in which such actions often had precisely the opposite intent. There is thus an increased recognition that efforts, whether unilateral or coordinated, to enhance the position of partners are in each actor's self-interest. This was also apparent in Egyptian efforts in the summer of 1994 to convince Syria that if it were more forthcoming in the peace process, the Israeli government would be strengthened domestically and thus better able to deal with the contentious issue of settlers on the Golan (Avidan 1994).

Cooperation nevertheless coexists with competition. That disagreements are likely to continue in the wake of peace agreements is indicated by the long-standing "cold peace" between Israel and Egypt (Ya'ari 1987) and the acrimony generated by disputes between the two countries. One example is Egypt's criticism of Israel's presumed nuclear capabilities, at the bilateral level, in the multilateral talks, and most prominently in the lead-up to the extension conference of the Non-Proliferation Treaty in 1995. This opposition was in part based on traditional balance-of-power concerns: Field Marshall Mohamed Hussein Tantawi, Egypt's defense minister, explained that Israel's nuclear capability was a threat to Egyptian, and Arab, national security because a situation of imbalance "often leads to the adoption of policies that are not well calculated" (Tantawi 1995b) and because in such a situation the superior state "will be tempted, in the absence of a power balance, to perpetuate aggression and try to realize its objectives and ambitions at the expense of its neighbors" (Tantawi 1995a, 25). But the opposition was also, even primarily, due to Egypt's objections to the implicitly unequal treatment of the two countries. The expectation that Egypt should sign the NPT extension while Israel had nuclear weapons was "not fair" explained Egyptian foreign minister Amr Musa to an Israeli newspaper (Granot 1994, 19); as Musa told *Al-Hayah*, the suggestion that Egypt sign while Israel is excluded "harms our national dignity."[14]

A second point of tension centers on the direction of economic cooperation in the region, largely because "[i]t seems that Egypt is concerned over Israel's potential economic domination of the region through the much talked about Middle East market" (Nassar 1995). Attempts to prematurely push proposals for economic cooperation, for example, at the highly touted Casablanca economic summit of October 1994 (Council on Foreign Relations 1995), may have been counterproductive, since they can be seen as an Israeli attempt to complement its military dominance with economic hegemony. Indeed, Uri Sagi, head of Israel's military intelligence, reportedly told a forum of senior reserve officers that "the Casablanca conference was a negative turning point in the [peace] process . . . [because] the oversized Israeli delegation as well as the manner of the conduct of its members was perceived by the Arabs as an Israeli tour de force, demonstrating its willingness to take over the Middle East economy" (Jerusalem Channel 2 Television, 1995).

Underlying these disagreements are the difficulties that change entails, since change can be "inhibited by actors' interests in maintaining relatively stable role identities. Such interests are rooted . . . in the desire to minimize uncertainty and anxiety, manifested in efforts to confirm existing beliefs about the social world" (Wendt 1992, 411). In this respect, Egypt perceives a threat to its claims to leadership in the region. As President Mubarak forcefully puts it: "Those who imagine that they can marginalize Egypt's role or end its leadership are living in a big fantasy. They think it could be marginalized because of its stability, wise and logical policy, commitment to principles and values, and its refraining from interfering in others' affairs or stirring up trouble. This is odd. Do we have to stir up trouble in the region and act as though we were solving problems to stop them from saying that nonsense? . . . Egypt's leadership status is firm and no one can take it away from us" (Mubarak 1995, 25, 27). To the extent that the peace means the continuation of competition through other forms (Sid-Ahmed 1976), Egypt's policies demonstrate a concern that Israel will come to dominate the region.

At a more general symbolic level the dispute is over identity. In the wake of reports of the presumably jocular request that Israel join the Arab League

14. Both themes were apparent in Foreign Minister Musa's speech at the NPT conference on 20 April 1995 (see FBIS-NES-95-077, 21 April 1995, 12–17). On the tensions, and especially the NPT dispute, see also Elon 1995 and Gerges 1995. For a critique of Egyptian policy, see Pervin 1994–95, 1995.

made at the Casablanca economic summit by Israeli foreign minister Shimon Peres to Esmat Abdel-Meguid, the league's secretary general, Mohamed Sid-Ahmed, a leading columnist for the semiofficial *Al-Ahram,* warned that "[Israel] is calling for a Middle East market in a bid to undermine pan-Arabism as a distinct identity and replace it with a notion of a Middle Eastern community"; he pointedly asked whether the "common medium of expression" would be Arabic—"Or should we all start learning Hebrew?" (Sid-Ahmed 1995). With progress in the peace process, the question of the region's identity and Israel's place, if it is not only *in* the system but also *of* it, has become more central: the question is "whether [Israel] will be merely a Jewish quarter in an Arab city or will become like the British India Company, which ruled the Indo-Pakistani subcontinent" (Nafi' 1995).[15] The potential dangers of accepting Israel as part of the system were dramatically drawn by Abd-al Halim Khaddam (1995, 35–36), Syria's foreign minister: "There are dangers that threaten our identity and fate. . . . When fate falls, the homeland is lost, and the nation falls into oblivion. There is a poisoned and planned campaign which seeks to undermine the Arab identity. . . . This campaign seeks to establish new relations which they call Middle Eastern relations. In this plan Israel would have the leader's position . . . a cultural invasion has begun to threaten our young generations, to drive them to a state of loss, to a loss of identity, and to separate them and . . . our values, principles, civilization, culture and heritage. . . . The ultimate objective of those hostile campaigns is to strip the Arabs of their values."[16]

15. This issue was also raised at the Islamic level in January 1995, when the mufti of Saudi Arabia, Sheikh Abdel-Aziz Ibn Baz, issued a *fatwa,* or religious ruling, interpreted as meaning that peace with Israel was permissible. Actually, he said that an "open-ended or a provisional truce is permissible if the man in charge [the ruler] finds this to be in [the national] interest" (Abdel-Latif 1995, 3; brackets in orignal). This met with vehement rejection by many Muslim scholars (see Abdel-Latif 1995 and Ibrahim 1995). Sheikh Ibn Baz's ruling was premised on two bases of *sharia,* or Islamic law, namely, *maslaha,* or interests, and *qiyas,* or analogy, in this case with the truces the Prophet Muhammed made with Jewish tribes near Medina. As Sheikh Ahmad al-Mahallawi pointed out, "God and his prophet did not allow peace with the Jews," and the truce was not with Jews who occupied Muslim territory (Al-Nur, 12 April 1995, in FBIS-NES-95-075, 19 April 1995, 3). Given the subsequent fate of the Jewish tribes at the hands of Muhammed, it is unlikely that even the limited concession of Sheikh Ibn Baz was reassuring to Israelis.

16. As Vice President Muhammad Zuhayr Mashariqah, representing President Asad, told the Syrian Teacher Union on 13 March 1995, while for Syria peace is "a strategic option," peace has yet to be achieved, because of "Israel's intransigence, noncompliance with the resolutions of international legitimacy, and its endeavors to bypass the peace process. It is also due to Israel's desire to subject the region to its hegemony and control its political, economic, military, and cultural resources by talking about a new Middle East order, which it can lead and run" (Damascus Syrian Arab Republic Radio, translated in FBIS-NES-95-049, 14 March 1995, 56).

As central as these issues may be on the symbolic level, their importance in terms of actual policies and impact on Arab-Israeli relations should not be exaggerated. To say that "far more threatening to the Middle East policy than the increase in bloody attacks by Islamic militants against Israelis are the recent strains in Egyptian-Israeli relations" (Gerges 1995, 69) is overblown. Notwithstanding the vitriol of the rhetoric employed, continued steps on the ground to maintain and even enhance relations should not be obfuscated. In the case of Egyptian-Israeli relations, President Weizman visited Cairo in December 1994; in March 1995 a delegation from the Knesset visited the Egyptian Assembly (El-Din 1995); and after a break of more than ten years, Israel had a booth at the Cairo Business Fair (Fiqi 1995).[17] In the multilateral talks progress was made on establishing a joint cleanup program in the Gulf of Aqaba (*Al-Ahram Weekly* 1995); in February 1995 there was a summit of the leaders of Israel, Egypt, Jordan, and the Palestinian Authority (PA) (Hedges 1995), and a meeting of the economy and trade ministers of Israel, Jordan, Egypt, the PA, and the United States;[18] and in March 1995 a high-level meeting among Egyptian, Jordanian, Israeli, and Palestinian officials took place in Amman to address the future of the displaced persons (Haberman 1995a).[19]

Will a Regional Concert Evolve?

This combination of increased cooperation, continuing competition, and profound ambivalence—even fears—about the future highlights the transitional nature of Arab-Israeli relations. Given the ambiguities, it would be rash to predict confidently that the new equilibrium will take the form of peace and cooperation. Nevertheless, one might ask whether a regional concert is forming, in part against the threat posed by Iraq and Iran. To see whether regional developments tend in that direction, it may be useful to examine the Concert of Europe of the first part of the nineteenth century (Elrod 1976; Schroeder

17. Israel's presence met with protests by opposition parties. The deputy chairman of the Labour Party, which has a heavy Islamist orientation, called Israel's participation a "rude challenge to the feelings of Egyptians," while the spokesman for the Wafd Party, historically liberal, had "expected the Egyptian people, with all their ranks, to boycott the fair. This is the least they should have done to preserve Egypt's dignity." And the secretary-general of the leftist Tagummu Party said that by participating "Israel has managed to infiltrate the Egyptian people" (Nahhas 1995).

18. See reports in FBIS-NES-95-027, 9 February 1995, 1–3.

19. See also the details in FBIS-NES-95-045, 8 March 1995, 1–8.

1986). Since there has been only one such phenomenon, it is hardly surprising that there are considerable differences concerning its causes, effects, and duration (Lipson 1994); as a result, any attempts to draw parallels are tentative.[20]

Among the bases for a concert are a recognition of the potential high costs of war; a dispersal of power in which no state has overwhelming superiority, so that all are "vulnerable to collective sanctions";[21] compatible views on the bases of international order and acceptance of the status quo; and a high level of transparency (Kupchan and Kupchan 1991, 124, 144). A critical element is elites' fear of the reciprocal relationship between domestic instability or revolution and war, in either direction. This leads to a situation in which "decision makers in each country . . . develop sufficient ties with their opposite numbers so that each wants the others to stay in power—a goal to which cooperating with the other states is likely to contribute" (Jervis 1985, 67).

If such conditions are conducive to a concert, there may be cause for optimism. As previously noted, there has been a general recognition that war has little utility and high costs. Israel may be the strongest actor, but it is not "overwhelming" in the sense of being able to impose diktats and is constrained not only by the ability of the Arab states to retaliate but also by the United States, whose interests would not be served by increased conflict and which is able to impose sanctions. While there has been general agreement on the basis of international order, namely, that of sovereignty, the status quo has not been accepted, whether by agreement, as in the case of Israel and the PLO, or because of disagreements, as in the case of Israel and Syria. Efforts to enhance transparency are a central part of the multilateral talks, especially those on arms control and regional security (Toukan 1995). In the Middle East "peace is a central part of a calculated policy to prevent . . . upheaval and chaos. It is a strategy of change to preserve the leaders' rule and to reinforce it as a barrier to extremism and internecine warfare" (Stephen Cohen 1994).[22] The desire to strengthen, or at least not weaken, the current regimes

20. For extended discussion of concerts, and an argument that more empirical examples exist, see Rosecrance and Schott (this volume).

21. As to the structural conditions, Schroeder (1992) has argued that the Vienna settlement and the peace that followed it were based on the benign hegemonies of Britain and Russia over the system as a whole, while other actors were dominant more locally; it was only when these broke down—when the interests of the various states began to overlap and conflict—that the concert collapsed. For criticisms of this argument, see Kraehe 1992, Jervis 1992, and Gruner 1992.

22. From the perspective of Martin Indyk (1993, 7), then National Security Council senior director for Near East and South Asian affairs, Islamic fundamentalism constitutes a "common threat to all the parties involved in the peace process."

has already been discussed. Just as the Concert of Europe coexisted with continued competition and conflict, albeit contained within limits, so do Arab-Israeli relations.

Optimism must be tempered with caution, however, because such changes have largely been at the elite level. Whether there is extensive popular support for peace is unclear, and what evidence exists is not encouraging. Israelis are reluctant to give up the occupied territories, especially the Golan (Arian 1994). In a poll taken among Lebanese Shiites and Sunnis, Palestinians in Beirut and Amman, and Syrians in Beirut and Damascus before the 13 September 1993 agreement, support for peace was limited; of those who supported peace, 28 percent did so because there was no alternative, 25 percent because it would block Israeli aggression, 32 percent because "it gives us a chance to reorganize ourselves," and fully 92 percent would not continue to support peace "if future geostrategy works against Israel" (Khashan 1994). Notwithstanding the peace agreement of 1979, even among Egyptians there is considerable hesitancy toward Israel: a poll conducted for Cairo's *Al-Ahram Weekly* found that more than 70 percent would not buy Israeli goods and would oppose Israeli factories in Egypt, while 53 percent opposed Israelis' visiting Egypt and 63 percent opposed visiting Israel (Shukrallah 1994–95). It is useful to recall that domestic factors, as much as changes in the international balance, helped undermine the Concert of Europe.

Conclusions

While actors cannot completely control their environment, under certain conditions there is greater leeway; anarchy may not always be what states make of it, but sometimes it is (Wendt 1992). The end of the Cold War was one of those times when there was greater leeway, more opportunities for the actors in the region to try to change their environment. The extent of these changes confounds the expectations of those who stress that the Middle East "has not changed fundamentally in terms of its basic structure and external linkages . . . [it] is probably going to experience regional instability in the years ahead mainly because of serious domestic socioeconomic, ideological, and political tensions" (Hudson 1992, 315; see also Norton and Wright 1994–95; Salame 1994). It is precisely this continuity at the *domestic* level, combined with fundamental changes at the *international* level, those "external linkages," that changed the calculus of the various actors. As Buzan (1993, 347) notes, "[R]uling elites may favor the arrangements of international society simply because they facilitate the maintenance of the elites' rule. Among other things, some alleviation of external pressures frees resources for the consolidation of domestic control."

The central argument in this chapter has been that the international environment has played a pivotal role in determining the dynamics of Arab-Israeli relations, especially in terms of the level of conflict and cooperation. Bipolarity facilitated and enabled sustained conflict by lowering the costs to the regional states, because the great powers provided military and economic assistance, on the one hand, and political assurances that reduced the potential costs, and thus the risks, of conflictual behavior, on the other hand. To the extent that there were changes at the regional and domestic levels—respectively the evolution of mutual deterrence and the strengthening of the states—that ameliorated the conflict, they were to a great extent influenced by the bipolar competition.

The movement toward peace was in turn a result of a change in the international environment and not a change in domestic politics. To highlight this point, some examples of simplified preference structures may be useful. Assume that the underlying preference structure of the Arab actors is as follows: destroy Israel through war > regain territories through war > regain territories through peace > concede territories to Israel with peace. The first option was foreclosed by Israel's strength, and the second, which was pursued in 1973, has been eliminated by the change in the international environment. No change in preferences is necessary to explain the change in Arab policies. Adding domestic goals, such as liberalization, and positing that these have led to a shift in preferences favoring peace does not help much. Because the impetus for liberalization is more external than internal, the relationship between liberalization and peace may be the opposite of that hypothesized. For example, in an analysis similar to Solingen's (this volume), Janice Stein (1993) argues that peace with Israel and improved relations with the United States were necessary to strengthen Egypt's liberalization in the 1970s. An alternative explanation is that with the Soviet Union either unwilling or unable to provide the political, military, and economic support Sadat required to strengthen his domestic position, liberalization and peace with Israel were necessary for improved relations with the United States. Although both explanations posit that the underlying motivation was Sadat's desire to enhance his domestic position, the former contends that liberalization was strategic, while peace and improved relations with the United States were tactical, and the latter holds that improved relations were strategic, while liberalization and peace were tactical. To the extent that the peace has remained cold and the liberalization at best superficial, the latter appears to be consistent with the evidence.

Nor is the case of Israel more straightforward. Assume that Israel's preference structure is as follows: keep occupied territories with peace > keep with war > cede with peace > cede with war. Although an Arab war option may not exist, to the extent that the *intifada* constituted a quasi-war it made the first two options more onerous for Israel. It can be argued that this preference structure is characteristic only of that part of the population supporting the Likud, and that supporters of Labor have a different preference structure, for example: cede with peace > keep with peace > keep with war > cede with war.[23] If such is the case, then the 1992 elections brought about a preference shift. And if the simplification is relaxed by bringing in domestic goals, for example, immigrant integration, then the extent of the shift becomes more apparent. Yet to the extent that the election result was influenced by circumstantial events and especially by American policy, the shift was caused by environmental changes.

The emphasis on environmental conditions is certainly not cause for pessimism concerning the strength of the transition or its likelihood to generate a transformation. The longer the current international system, at least as it impacts and is perceived in the Middle East, continues, the greater the likelihood that the transition can be sustained and that a transformation can take root via a change in the preferences of the regional actors. This is not to say that domestic political events could not serve significant and even debilitating blows to the transition. To the extent that revolutions generally tend to create international instability, in part because the new regimes may seek to use an external threat to solidify their control (Maoz 1989; Walt 1992), and to the extent that a revolution in the Middle East would likely be led by groups hostile to peace, the transition would be endangered. Nor is it clear

23. Whether this second preference structure, rather than the first, represents that of the Labor Party is open to doubt. In an interview for Israel's Independence Day, Prime Minister Yitzhak Rabin was characteristically blunt: "I look for ways to attain a goal that I believe will solve the Palestinian-Israeli conflict. I and Labor determined that we do not want a binational state. *I believe the people of Israel have a right to the entire Eretz Yisra'el* [Land of Israel]. Yet, in the current reality what I want is: A Jewish state inside and on most of the territory of Eretz Yisra'el with a Palestinian entity which is less than a state alongside it" ("Special Independence Day Interview," Jerusalem Qol Yisra'el, 29 April 1995, translated in FBIS-NES-95-083, 1 May 1995, 31; emphasis added).

that the process of democratization is necessarily any more stabilizing, for many of the same reasons (Mansfield and Snyder 1995); indeed, some analysts of the Arab world suggest that forces opposed to peace are likely to have greater influence in the wake of democratization (Hudson 1995).[24]

What it *is* to say is that the longer the extant international system continues to create incentives for cooperation and, over time, benefit those domestic actors whose interests are served by peace, the more likely a transformation. Nor is continued American dominance required. Rather, to the extent that the regional actors "realize that they can no longer compel foreign aid . . . [they] must reassess their interests, purposes, and possibilities" (Lewis 1992, 109). Left alone, in a world interested in commerce rather than conflict, and facing domestic needs, the Arabs and Israelis can opt to adjust and adapt and take advantage of the corresponding gains, for which peace is necessary, or on their own pay the costs of continued conflict. The choice is stark: between a genesis of a new regional order or, as the title of the book from which the quote opening this chapter is drawn puts it, Armageddon in the Middle East.

24. As to the likelihood of democratization in the region, notwithstanding progress in Jordan, the prospects are not bright: the specter of Algeria is haunting. On democratization, see Sayyid 1991; Norton 1993; Richards 1993; Ibrahim 1993.

13

Rethinking African Regional Security

Edmond J. Keller

In the international relations literature, Africa is generally considered to be a region where the member states face no external threats from each other, and therefore a region without a "security dilemma."[1] In the postcolonial era, Africa has generally been viewed by outsiders as an area where external threats were not the problem. To the extent that security is considered a problem on the continent, students of international affairs generally view this as the result of domestic conflict and individual insecurities (Jackson 1992, 93). Over the past two decades factors such as drought, famine, and internal wars have often led to human dislocations within African states as well as across their borders. However, it must be emphasized that in Africa's recent political history the incidence of interstate conflict has been much less common than domestic conflict. The reasons normally given for the generalized absence of problems of regional security include the following:

1. A security dilemma exists when threats or perceived threats to a country's sovereignty might force its leadership to enter into regional or extraregional alliances in an effort to ensure the security of its citizens and territory.

1. *African states tend to be resource-poor.* This condition explains why they seldom challenge the territorial integrity of their neighbors. They cannot afford to. This also makes them of little interest to non-African actors. As Brian Job (1992b, 17) has noted, to the extent that a threat exists, it is normally from autocratic regimes themselves rather than from some outside force.
2. *Third World countries like those found in Africa tend to be artificial creations,* cobbled together during the processes of colonization or decolonization. Consequently, regimes in those regions tend to lack the popular support that would be needed to act efficaciously in regional matters (Job 1992b, 17).
3. *African states tend to be relatively weak,* and are, therefore, unlikely to see the need to enter into regional security arrangements with their neighbors.

For the purposes of this discussion, the term "region" refers to a geographic area (e.g., Africa, Asia, Latin America). Before a region becomes a relevant arena for security purposes, the states in the area have to perceive themselves as being interdependent relative to security (Morgan, this volume; Job, this volume). States that perceive a mutual interest in protecting their national security through entering into regional security arrangements are, when the right circumstances obtain, prime candidates for forming "regional security complexes."[2] States in regions may belong to regional complexes that transcend the region, but they may also belong complexes that are regionally specific.

Regional security complexes are inspired by what Lake refers to as "security externalities," situations or factors emanating from outside a country or region that threaten national or regional security (Lake, this volume). Some security externalities are relevant only at the subregional level, but others encompass whole regions and give rise to regional security complexes. In Africa, domestic insecurities have increasingly come to present dilemmas for specific subregions, and some have generated continent-wide efforts to achieve collective security.

States might want to unite against a threat external to the region, or they might simply want to keep lines of communications open because this

2. Buzan (1991) defines "security complexes" as groups of states whose primary security concerns are perceived to be closely linked, creating a situation of interdependence among the states. This interdependence could originate in the competition among rivals, or it could emanate in a need to improve the comparative position of member states vis-à-vis external actors.

might reduce the possibility of conflict among themselves (Buzan 1992, 169). Buzan suggests that the Organization of African Unity (OAU) falls short of being a security complex, since that organization's main mission has historically been to uphold the territorial integrity of its sovereign member states against the claims of others. However, he goes on to suggest that, based on the peacekeeping efforts of the Economic Community of West African States Cease-fire Monitoring Group (ECOMOG) in Liberia, it is more likely that Africa will in the future see more successful subregional security complexes (Buzan 1992, 184).

In recent years the OAU has taken steps to expand its role, and is now attempting to develop a capacity for managing regional insecurities even when they sprout from domestic conflicts.[3] The organization has aspirations of becoming the focus of a large regional order, but the reality of the situation is that the process has moved much faster and further at the subregional level. What seems to be emerging are loosely knit subregional multilateral collective security arrangements with an emphasis on cooperative security. In other words, subregional security-management complexes are "nested" within the context of an aspiring continental security complex; and the subregional institutions sometimes act on behalf of or in concert with the OAU security-management apparatus.

Africa could be conceived as being divided into at least four subregional complexes: North Africa, or the Maghreb; northeastern Africa, or the Horn; southern Africa; and West Africa. Each of these subregions has had a different historical experience, and to a large extent current subregional security dilemmas and security complexes can be linked to their respective pasts.

The states of North and northeastern Africa possess their own security complexes but at the same time belong to "nodes of security interdependence" linking them both to a Middle East security complex (Buzan 1992, 182). For the purposes of this essay, when the term "Africa" is used, it refers to sub-Saharan Africa, rather than to the entire continent. However, North African states are significant players in the deliberations concerning the development of a continental security-management arrangement.

Patrick Morgan (this volume) offers a catalogue of ideal types of

3. The OAU is attempting to assume leadership in the development of a continent-wide capacity for conflict prevention, conflict resolution, and peacekeeping. The thinking behind this project is that "[t]he security, stability of every African country affects every other African country" (African Leadership Forum 1992). At the same time, it is clear that, should it be successful, it is going to have to approach the security problem from a subregional perspective and rely upon subregional security organizations in order to be effective.

security-management arrangements within regional security complexes. At one end of the continuum we find a regional balance of power, and at the other we find states in a region that are for all intents and purposes totally integrated. In between are great-power concerts, which involve great powers maintaining regional security by accepting their mutual responsibility to do so; pluralistic security communities, which involve states that are not totally integrated but have a common understanding that no member will act violently against any other members; and multilateral collective security-management arrangements. By joining into an arrangement such as the latter, the signatories agree to enforce peace and security in the region collectively, even if this involves armed intervention into a domestic or regional dispute.

In Africa, most member states of the OAU recognize that, more than at any other time in the postindependence era, they all confront subregional security dilemmas. Particularly, domestic insecurity in one state has a high potential to have a destabilizing effect in neighboring states, and therefore new approaches need to be developed to prevent such problems and to manage them if they erupt. However, there is reason to question the viability of a continent-wide security-management arrangement for Africa. In the first place, the continent is huge, almost three times the size of the United States, and its states tend to be poor, weak, and underdeveloped. Second, significant state-to-state relations outside of the respective subregions are relatively recent, and the interdependence of all states on the continent and the need to develop cooperative security arrangements are only slowly becoming widely accepted.

The purpose of this essay is twofold. First, I want specifically to challenge the assumption of scholars who argue that Africa is not characterized by a regional security dilemma (Jackson 1992). Although it seems to make sense to contend that Africa's security problems emanate from origins other than, let us say, the countries of Western Europe or the Americas, it is quite another to argue that African leaders do not perceive a regional security problem. Here I argue quite the contrary. Second, the essay attempts to make the case for more scholarly attention to state-to-state relations within regions and subregions and for analyses focusing on regional-subregional relations and on the relationship of individual states with regional and subregional organizations. Attempts to apply general theories of international relations to regional problems in areas like Africa often serve to hinder insightful and textured understanding of issues rooted in the idiosyncrasies of the area in question.

In some cases, the character of Africa's regional security problems is not *sui generis,* but in fact is fundamentally similar to that found in parts of the world such as Bosnia or India. For example, domestic inter- or intraethnic, religious, or regional tensions in certain areas have in recent years become transnationalized, resulting in security dilemmas that have drawn the attention of subregional, regional, and international actors in efforts to manage conflict. Because of the very artificial, multiethnic, and multicultural nature of modern African nation-states, they are vulnerable to domestic conflict that can grow into regional security problems. Domestic conflicts that spill across borders represent security problems for states in all parts of the world.

As alluded to above, international politics in Africa, particularly as it involves relations among African states, is at a relatively early stage of development. For example, in only a few instances have independent African states invaded the territory of neighbors for the purpose of territorial aggrandizement. Exceptions include Libya's incursion into Chad, and Somalia's incursion into the Ogaden region of Ethiopia. Historically, in the early stages of international politics in Europe and the Middle East, states invaded their neighbors with the intention of seizing access to valued resources or in order to expand the aggressors' political community.

The rarity of interstate conflict in Africa is in part due to the recency of the creation of independent African states, and in part due to the fact that, until recently, domestic conflicts had been relatively low in intensity and had not spilled over their borders. However, with advances in communications technology, the increasing availability of weapons of mass destruction as well as small arms, and the internationalization of regional politics, African security dilemmas have become manifest.

In Africa, domestic conflicts in Liberia, Sudan, Somalia, Mozambique, and now Rwanda, to name only a few of the more salient cases, have created refugee flows and flows of armed rebels across national borders, thus regionalizing and even internationalizing what were once thought to be domestic conflicts (Weiner 1992). Therefore, leaders in Africa as well as in the international state system have begun to reconsider such issues as the notion of state sovereignty and the norms governing external intervention to address domestic conflicts. It is now clear that before African states can adequately approach their development problems, they are going to have to reduce domestic insecurities that have a high propensity to become regionalized and even internationalized.

In order for us to appreciate the regional security dilemmas of Africa, we have to understand (1) the historical origins of contemporary African states; (2) the impact of the Cold War and its demise on some of Africa's most intractable problems of regional security; (3) the manner in which the UN has historically dealt with domestic as well as regional conflict in Africa; (4) the motivation for the creation of the Organization of African Unity and its subsequent activities in the areas of conflict management; and (5) the relative effectiveness of those activities.

The Origins of Africa's Regional Insecurity Dilemma

THE COLONIAL INHERITANCE

The states of contemporary Africa are largely multiethnic, artificial creations, the products of the European scramble for Africa in the late 1880s. In the regions they claimed, the colonial powers divided the peoples they found according to administrative convenience rather than with respect to precolonial sociopolitical arrangements. Consequently, during the colonial period, African peoples most often found themselves thrown together in their particular regions with other ethnic groups with whom they had had little, if any, prior political relationships. For example, Kenya comprises more than 40 distinct ethnic groups, Eritrea 9, and Tanzania 120. Similar patterns can be found in most of Africa's contemporary states.

In an effort to cast off the yoke of European colonialism after the Second World War, nationalist leaders in Africa accepted the fiction of an inherent national unity based upon the states created during the colonial period (Davidson 1992). The slogan in many places became "We must die as tribes so that we can be born as a nation." While most African societies have come to accept the legitimacy of colonially created states, in some cases groups claiming the right to national self-determination have risen to challenge such arrangements. Therefore, in addition to being preoccupied with asserting their hegemony and sovereignty, some modern African states have had to be preoccupied with ensuring and maintaining the territorial integrity of their respective polities (Young 1988, 31).

In the lexicon of international affairs, the term "security" generally refers to the insulation of a state from threats emanating from outside its borders. Individual states exist in regions, and internal disputes such as civil wars can have a dramatic effect upon their collective, regional security. This threat can be a military one, but in Africa it often boils down to a wide variety of deprivations (e.g., drought, disease, pestilence). For example, drought and famine in Ethiopia in the mid-1980s created refugee flows across that country's borders with Kenya and Sudan (Keller 1992). If domestic problems spill over into a neighboring state and threaten the ability of that state to meet the basic needs of its own citizens, then the problems have been regionalized. However, in most cases it is armed conflict within neighboring states that has, in recent years, created refugee and arms flows that in turn heightened the instability and insecurity of entire regions. Take, for example, the anarchy that has been raging in Liberia since 1989, in Somalia since 1990, and most recently the troubles in Rwanda.

Africa, as a region, has historically perceived a vested interest in maintaining the collective security of the continent and its various regions, and the national security of individual member states. The OAU was specifically founded in 1963 in order to provide a vehicle for the effective resolution of disputes and violations of the territorial integrity of member states.

Within Africa, the artificial nature of colonially created states has always caused leaders to fear the balkanization of their states, particularly as a consequence of the actions of secessionists or irredentists. This can clearly be seen in the fact that the territorial integrity of member states is enshrined in Chapter III (3) of the OAU Charter. This principle was reaffirmed in a resolution of that organization in 1964, at a summit of the heads of its member states in Cairo, Egypt. The principle of *uti posside juris* was adopted by the body, and it was asserted that the colonial boundaries inherited by individual states at independence should remain inviolable (Amate 1986). This move was seen by most African leaders as a hedge against secessionism and irredentism. At the same time, it was an effort by the majority of the member states to avoid dealing directly with already existing disputes involving Somalia and Ethiopia, Somalia and Kenya, and Ethiopia and the former Italian colony, Eritrea.[4]

The Eritrean war of national liberation, which culminated after thirty years in 1991, had similar roots. Eritrean nationalists claimed that their right

4. Although at the time of the creation of the OAU a border dispute involving Algeria and Morocco also existed, the North African region, as noted earlier, is in political terms much more a part of the Arab world than it is a part of the African region as I use that term here. In addition to the OAU, Arab regional organizations have also had influence in the course of this dispute. For this reason the border claims of Morocco and Algeria are not considered in this analysis. I concentrate on sub-Saharan Africa.

to self-determination was denied them by imperial Ethiopia when it violated the terms of a UN-sponsored federation involving the two countries (Habte Selassie 1989).

Various incidents involving Somali irredentists are based on the desire of ethnic Somalis living in Ethiopia's Ogaden region to be united with others in the Somali nation, which they claim was illegitimately partitioned during the colonial period (Laitin and Samatar 1987).

Some problems of regional security in Africa are fairly recent, being the product of civil wars and local rebellions that stop short of possessing revolutionary objectives. Others are long-standing problems that can be traced to the colonial legacy. In either case, the Cold War and its immediate aftermath greatly affected the persistence, scope, and intensity of such civil conflicts. Stein and Lobell (this volume) present evidence that the bipolar nature of the international system at the height of the Cold War and the ideological competition between the two superpowers had the effect of globalizing what had been only local disputes. Nowhere was this more evident than in parts of Africa. William Zartman (1989, 5) has further noted that before the height of the Cold War, African conflicts often lasted only until the exhaustion of current military stocks. But, since then, such conflicts, particularly in the Horn and southern Africa, have tended to be protracted.

The Cold War and Regional Security in Africa

THE SOVIET UNION AND THE UNITED STATES

The Cold War competition between the United States and the former Soviet Union in Africa, as in other parts of the Third World (Stein and Lobell, in this volume), greatly contributed to several of the incidents of militarily based regional conflict. This can be clearly seen when we compare the experiences of the territorial dispute between Ethiopia and Somalia, the Eritrean war of national liberation, and the various conflicts in southern Africa that escalated after 1975. The roots of each of these conflicts are historic, but a new dimension was added during the Cold War.

Throughout the 1980s, the superpowers were heavily involved in supporting clients in the Horn of Africa. Over a thirteen-year period Soviet military assistance to Ethiopia is estimated to have been as high as \$11 billion (Henze 1990, 105).

Following its 1977 break with Ethiopia, its client of twenty-three years, the U.S. administration of President Jimmy Carter embarked upon an "encirclement strategy," attempting to contain Soviet expansion in the Horn and Middle East by engaging in military alliances with Ethiopia's neighbors: Egypt, Sudan, Kenya, Somalia, and Oman. In addition to assisting these countries in upgrading their military facilities and capabilities, joint military exercises became common. The territories of U.S. clients in the Horn were used as staging grounds for the U.S. Rapid Deployment Force, which was designed to facilitate the efficient projection of U.S. military power into the Middle East and Persian Gulf (Jackson 1982, 32). These developments caused Soviet clients in the region, Ethiopia and South Yemen, to come together in a show of solidarity and to resolve jointly to repulse any efforts on the part of the United States or its proxies to intervene in their affairs. The resulting tensions continued for almost a decade, and did not begin to abate until the Cold War began its meltdown in the mid-1980s.

In the process of pursuing what they felt to be their own vital interests, the superpowers contributed to an escalation of a regional arms race in the Horn. The Soviets and Americans jockeyed to check one another; the Ethiopians and Somalis tried to outfox each other. The consequences were momentous. The size of the Ethiopian armed forces grew from 54,000 in 1977 to more than 300,000 a decade later. By 1991, the Ethiopian army was estimated to be over 600,000 strong. Somalia's army swelled from about 32,000 in 1977 to 65,000 in 1987 (International Institute for Strategic Studies 1976–77, 1989–90). The growth of the military of Sudan was less dramatic, but internally, military activities over the decade of the 1980s grew significantly as the Ethiopian-supported Sudan People's Liberation Army was able to capture and control large portions of Southern Sudan.

Over the same period, Ethiopia's defense budget grew from $103 million to almost $472 million. Between 1977 and 1985 Somalia's defense expenditures rose from $36 million to $134 million, and Sudan's from $237 million to $478 million. This level and pattern of growth in military expenditures could not have taken place if the countries of the Horn had not been able to rely upon superpower patrons for ever-increasing levels of military assistance.

Ironically, the desire for more and more arms on the part of the countries in the region seems to have been more inspired by internal conflicts than by the need to protect the border zones of each country. The catastrophic defeat of the Somali army and the irredentist Western Somali Liberation Front in the Ogaden War of 1977–78 caused internal opposition to surface against

Somali president Siad Barre. Over the next decade, the internal crisis escalated until the whole country was affected. The Barre regime was forced to abdicate in January 1991, and the Somali state was plunged into anarchy. The possible level of destruction was dramatically heightened by the availability of heavy as well as light arms and equipment left over from the largess of the superpowers during the Cold War.

The decade of the 1980s also witnessed an increase in the capacity and efficiency of the Eritrean national liberation movement. After having been routed by the Ethiopian army in the late 1970s, the Eritrean People's Liberation Army (EPLA) was able to regroup and, by 1987, began to make serious inroads toward liberating Eritrea from Ethiopian control. The success of the EPLA was enhanced by the fact that the Tigre People's Liberation Front (TPLF) and the Ethiopian People's Democratic Movement formed a united front, the Ethiopian People's Revolutionary Democratic Front (EPRDF). The EPRDF, operating inside the Ethiopian central highlands and with the logistical and tactical support of the EPLA, was able by 1991 to capture huge tracts of territory and totally to demoralize the Ethiopian army. In May of 1991, Ethiopia's president Mengistu Haile Mariam fled into exile, and his army of six hundred thousand totally collapsed. The EPRDF rebels were able to seize control of Ethiopia's capital, Addis Ababa, without any significant resistance.

By 1987, evidence existed that the Soviet Union was backing away from the Brezhnev policy of spreading the Soviet model throughout the Third World, and was interested in supporting political resolutions to internal wars in client states. Consequently, a combination of economic realities and Soviet pressure eventually encouraged Mengistu to retreat partially from his regime's dogmatic statist development strategy. By late 1989, Ethiopia was witnessing a cooling not only in Soviet support of its revolution, but also in support from allies such as East Germany and South Yemen, which were involved in their own process of political opening. The net result was that the Ethiopian regime could no longer rely upon its superpower sponsor for the assistance it needed to repress internal opposition. Ultimately, the regime collapsed. However, a power vacuum was averted because the forces of the EPRDF, with international support, were able to assume power and prevent the country from falling into anarchy, as had been the case in Somalia.

Solingen (this volume) has found that intractable coalitional strife within a ruling group, or no coalition at all, is the worst scenario for regional conflict. Internal conflicts that manifest themselves in fractious coalitional strife have the potential of spilling over into neighboring states. In the case of

Somalia and Ethiopia, the internal conflicts did not result in interstate disputes, simply because the two countries did not have the capacity to maintain war on two fronts—domestic and regional. However, a regional security dilemma was created for both countries by the uncontrolled flow of refugees into and out of their territories as well as the free flow of arms in both directions.

Regional security in southern Africa had been a problem ever since the early 1960s, when wars of national liberation erupted in the Portuguese colonies of Angola and Mozambique, and since black opposition parties in South Africa such as the African National Congress (ANC) and the Pan-African Congress (PAC) were banned and driven underground. For more than two decades the Portuguese, with tacit support from NATO allies, doggedly attempted to hold on to their southern African colonies. Rebel groups came to rely upon the Soviet Bloc for military and political support against Portuguese colonialism. Given the unstable conditions in the neighboring Portuguese colonies, South Africa entered the fray in an effort to prevent conflicts in Angola and Mozambique from spilling into Namibia and eventually South Africa itself. South Africa initially supported the Portuguese, but later engaged in military actions in Mozambique and Angola for purely defensive reasons. After 1975, it came to fear that independent and stable Angola and Mozambique might make it easier for black liberation movements to wage war in South Africa itself.

Independent Angola and Mozambique quickly assumed active involvement in the Frontline African States organization, formed to press for the complete independence of all countries in the region. Whereas South Africa throughout the 1960s had periodically invaded or infiltrated black states in the region in an effort to undermine the planning and training of the armies of the ANC and PAC, after 1975 it projected its military into southern Angola and supported a destabilization campaign in Mozambique (Flannigan 1992). The presence in Angola was largely to crush the army of the Southwest African People's Organization (SWAPO), fighting for the independence of Namibia, and to support the effort of Jonas Savimbi's National Union for the Total Independence of Angola (UNITA) to overthrow the Marxist government in Luanda. The net effect of the military activities of South Africa in its efforts to maintain domestic order and security was an exacerbation of regional insecurity. This did not begin to change until the effects of the international sanctions and disinvestment initiated in the mid-1980s against South Africa began to have their effect. The international community had placed nominal sanctions against South Africa as early as the 1960s, but they were ineffective. The latest sanctions, coupled with enlightened white leadership in South Africa, led to a reduction in that country's efforts to destabilize neighboring countries.

South Africa feared a Communist threat from its black-ruled neighbors. The threat posed by South Africa forced countries like Mozambique and Angola to turn to Marxist patrons for military, political, and economic assistance. Except for quietly providing military support to UNITA following the political ascendancy of the MPLA (Popular Movement for the Liberation of Angola) in the mid-1970s, the United States did not begin to become a major player in the region until the U.S. Congress passed the Comprehensive Anti-Apartheid Act in 1986. Following this, South Africa was pressured by the United States to find a political solution to its problems.

Despite these clear threats to regional security involving interstate conflict, most insecurity in Africa is domestic in origin. Yet, these domestic conflicts have contributed to regional insecurity, and will continue to do so in the foreseeable future. This is a particularly grave problem for Africa because major outside actors have, since the end of the Cold War, become reluctant to intervene in the region. Lake (this volume) and Papayoanou (this volume) argue that the big powers no longer have an interest in competing for clients in the developing world, and are more likely to intervene and to be interested in minimizing conflicts in their own regions. The "distant partners" of the major powers are today far fewer, and presently none is to be found in Africa.

BRITAIN AND FRANCE

Even though we could not consider Britain and France superpowers in the strictest sense of the word, they are important in Africa because of their significant roles as the former primary colonizing powers on the continent and because of their continuing interests there. The role of Britain in its former African colonies since 1964 has been indirect at best, involving military training for African officers and private arms sales to African governments. In 1964 Britain intervened in Tanzania, Kenya, and Uganda to put down mutinies against newly independent governments. The most obvious involvement of Britain in Africa during the postindependence period has been via private business activities and bilateral aid arrangements. Given this pattern, Britain appears to be of little relevance to a discussion of the role of external actors in regional security matters during the Cold War in Africa.

In contrast to Britain, France has until recently been extremely active in carving out a role for itself in Africa through its economic as well as military activities. The disengagement of Britain and Belgium from active military involvement in Africa after the independence era by default left France the only European actor in the region willing to accept an interventionist role. In the early 1960s, France intervened to prop up regimes in the Congo, Cameroon, Gabon, Mauritania, Niger, and Chad. However, the French military presence on the continent dropped from 60,000 in 1960 to around 5,000 by the late 1960s. Also, direct military intervention in African domestic and regional affairs became less common. One particularly bold and controversial intervention to remove an African head of state occurred in 1979 in the Central African Republic (Smock 1993, 5).

In the 1970s and 1980s France extended its involvement beyond francophone Africa. Sheldon Geller argues (1992, 111) that this was in part because France felt it had a historic mission to be the most active European power in Africa and also to counter the expansion of the two superpowers on the continent. France seems most interested in maintaining political stability so as to protect French economic interests. This is one reason the leadership in France provided for restoring order in Zaire's Shaba province in 1977 and 1978, for intervening in Chad to halt Libyan expansionism between 1977 and 1980; and for attempting more recently to prop up the failed Hutu-dominated government in Rwanda before that government's overthrow in early 1994. However, for the most part, during and after the administration of President François Mitterand, France sharply curtailed its tendency to intervene militarily in African affairs.

Modalities of Conflict Management in Africa

Donald Rothchild (1996, 228) has noted that almost half (sixteen) of the thirty-five internal wars being waged throughout the world, with battle deaths exceeding one thousand per year, are currently taking place in Africa. The Cold War is over, and the superpowers are no longer there to step in to support one regional client or the other. Africa is generally being left to its own devices. The realities of the situation have encouraged African leaders to reconsider seriously the norms of external intervention for the purpose of settling domestic disputes. In the process the notion of state sovereignty is also being reexamined.

UN MODALITIES

The United Nations, like the OAU, has historically supported the idea of the inviolability of the national boundaries of African states that existed at the time of independence. Consequently, it has been unwilling to become involved in adjudicating boundary disputes between neighboring states. On the other hand, in cases where it was perceived that in certain territories the right of the people to self-determination was being denied, the UN has consistently engaged in diplomatic efforts to secure that right. For example, in the case of Namibia, after years of diversionary tactics and foot-dragging on the part of South Africa, the UN was able to negotiate a cease-fire between the protagonists, to establish a peacekeeping presence in the country, and to organize and supervise multiparty elections that led to Namibian independence in 1990. On the other hand, the UN and the OAU refused to recognize the right of the people of the former Italian colony, Eritrea, to self-determination until the forces of the Eritrean People's Liberation Front had vanquished the Ethiopian army on the battlefield in 1991. Only then did the UN agree to oversee the referendum that led to the creation of the independent state of Eritrea in 1993.

When, after a prolonged period of domestic instability in the Congo in the early 1960s, the UN decided to commit troops in an effort to restore peace, many observers seemed to believe that this action would serve notice that the organization would intervene anywhere on the continent where a Communist threat was perceived. However, the Congo operation proved to be unique and was never repeated. The Soviet Union, for example, acquired significant clients in Africa in the mid-1970s without UN objection. Even when internal conflicts threatened to dismember African states, the OAU seemed more concerned than the UN. I return to this point below, but for now the important point is that the UN as an organization finds it difficult to mediate disputes involving member states, particularly those disputes that are at a very intense stage or those that have proved intractable. Touval (1994) suggests that the problem is ingrained in all international organizations.

Despite its record in this area, in the 1990s the UN began to rethink the notion of state sovereignty and the norms of intervention in domestic disputes. Iraq's repression of its Kurdish minority following the Gulf War in 1991 prompted the passage of UN Resolution 688 authorizing direct UN intervention into Iraq's internal affairs in order to protect the Kurds. This was a clear indication of the international consensus on the legitimacy of external collective action to halt domestic oppression as well as external aggression (Stremlau 1991, 659).

As the decade of the 1990s unfolded, the UN came to link food insecurity with regional conflict. In the spring of 1992 the organization committed peacekeeping troops to Somalia in an operation called UNISOM I. The primary motivation was humanitarian. The force was to clear the way for desperately needed food deliveries to an estimated 1.5 million Somalis threatened by war-induced famine. By December 1992, the idea of using UN peacekeepers in the Somali humanitarian effort had gained broad support in the UN, and the Security Council unanimously passed a resolution authorizing the deployment of a U.S.-led military force, UNITAF, to protect relief workers as they attempted to reach at-risk populations. Whereas the United States defined its role in strictly humanitarian terms, UN secretary-general Boutros-Ghali envisioned a wider role for UN forces: to disarm the armies of local warlords and to create an enabling environment for the restoration of a Somali national government. By May 1993 the United States declared its humanitarian mission a success and withdrew most of its 30,000 troops from the operation. However, a small contingent of U.S. soldiers remained under UN command in Somalia until March 1994 (Fromuth 1993). By the end of 1994, all UN forces were being withdrawn from the country; the international body had chosen to leave the processes of state reconstruction and political reconciliation to local and regional actors.

The lessons of UN involvement in the Somali humanitarian mission indicate that such actions are unlikely to remain strictly humanitarian and that political problems are invariably much more intractable than humanitarian ones. Within the UN community there appears to be a growing consensus that domestic conflicts that spill over borders cannot be ignored. At the same time, there is no agreement that it should be the UN itself that intervenes. Consequently there is emerging support for the strengthening, with the assistance of multilateral and bilateral donors, of regional conflict-management capacities. This thinking not only applies to regional and domestic conflicts in Africa. For example, Pervin (this volume) suggests that a modified concert seems to be developing in the Middle East because outside actors such as the UN and the major powers are now more interested in letting regional actors find their own solutions to their problems. Morgan (this volume) suggests that to the extent that the major powers will in the future be interested in regional or domestic conflicts in places where they have no direct interests, they will tend to encourage the pursuit of regional conflict-prevention and -resolution efforts.

OAU MODALITIES

African states are increasingly defining domestic conflicts that spill across borders in collective security terms. There has always been an inclination for African states to intervene collectively in some of the more serious conflicts, but there has not always been the capacity. The first major OAU peacekeeping effort of an inter-African force occurred in Chad in 1981–82. From the very beginning the action seemed doomed to failure. It was underfinanced and plagued by logistical problems. The OAU turned to the UN for assistance, but was refused on the grounds that it was inappropriate for the organization to make extensive financial or operational contributions to an effort that would not be carried out under the UN's own political authority and military direction. Ultimately, the burden of the Chad mission was borne mostly by OAU member states.

The most successful inter-African peacekeeping effort to date has been that mounted by the Economic Community of West African States (ECOWAS), the ECOWAS Cease-Fire Monitoring Group (ECOMOG). Nigeria took the lead in establishing this force in the summer of 1990 for the purpose of restoring peace and order in Liberia, which was at the time gripped in a bloody civil war. The novelty of ECOMOG lay in its regional origin and character, not in the mission it undertook. After five years of "peacekeeping," the West African units of ECOMOG were augmented by troops from three East African countries. Some semblance of order was briefly restored in 1995, and preparations began for multiparty elections. However, before these efforts could bear fruit, Liberia again erupted into intense civil war, proving ECOMOG powerless to manage a conflict of such intensity. The war was again brought directly to the capital city of Monrovia in the spring of 1996, resulting again in massive human dislocation and refugee flows by land and sea.

The ECOMOG operation in Liberia has set a precedent, and its limited and fleeting success has fueled new discussion about the possibility of a permanent inter-Africa military to be deployed for the purposes of peacekeeping and peacemaking. This would represent a radical departure from past practice.

Although it was founded to manage conflict among member states and to represent their interests in international forums, the OAU has historically played more of a reactive role in addressing threats to national and regional security. The Commission of Mediation, Conciliation, and Arbitration is theoretically responsible for settling disputes between member states, but it has historically left that task to various ad hoc commissions and committees of the organization and to eminent persons. Moreover, the commission does not have a mandated role in conflict prevention. It is responsible exclusively for addressing interstate conflicts only after they have erupted; it has no role in the mediation of what are determined to be internal conflicts.

The manner in which the OAU has historically dealt with the border dispute between Ethiopia and Somalia is instructive. The first time the organization considered the problem was on the occasion of the second meeting of the OAU Council of Ministers in 1964. At the time, the UN deferred to the OAU to settle the dispute in this forum. The two adversaries were allowed to plead their respective cases. The Somalis claimed that Ethiopia's Ogaden region was a part of historic Somalia and that it had been acquired by Ethiopia in a colonial "landgrab." This claim rested on the assumption that the dispute predated the establishment of the OAU and the adoption of its charter. Ethiopia rejected this claim, arguing that the Ogaden was a part of historic Ethiopia.

Rather than settle the dispute once and for all, the OAU Council of Ministers merely appealed to Ethiopia and Somalia to abide by the OAU Charter and to settle their differences peacefully. Until 1973, the OAU refrained from again becoming involved in the dispute. It became involved again only when hostilities between the two neighbors reemerged. A good-offices committee was appointed, and it was able to arrange a short-lived and tenuous peace.

The first part of the 1970s witnessed the height of the Somali Revolution, and Somali nationalism took on an increasingly aggressive cast. In the context of this heightened sense of Somali nationalism, the desire to recover the "lost" Somali clans became more intense than ever before and was at the root of the Ogaden War of 1977–78. An OAU good-offices committee was again set up, but this time it failed. The dispute was temporarily settled on the battlefield, since the Ethiopians, with the assistance of their Eastern-bloc allies, were able to reestablish control over the Ogaden.

Ironically, the border dispute between Somalia and Ethiopia achieved a tentative resolution through the facilitation of the subregional technical organization, the Intergovernmental Authority on Drought and Development (IGADD). This organization was formed in 1986 by the governments of Djibouti, Ethiopia, Kenya, Somalia, Sudan, and Uganda for the purpose of providing a subregional approach to the problems of drought and famine. At the first IGADD summit in Djibouti, Ethiopia and Somalia agreed to begin direct talks to resolve their border problems.

Ad hoc committees of the OAU have been equally ineffective in conflict resolution. They have no enforcement authority, and can only appeal to the disputing parties to adhere to OAU principles.

New Directions?

What has been made abundantly clear by the continuing armed conflicts in Somalia, Sudan, Liberia, and Angola, as well as the anarchy now raging in Rwanda, is that Africa will have to find new ways of addressing both domestic and regional conflicts. New institutions have to be developed in order to avert such debilitating conflicts and to resolve them once they erupt. Such a realization was reinforced between 1990 and 1996 by the actions of the activist UN secretary-general Boutros Boutros-Ghali, who, much more than any of his recent predecessors, envisioned an interventionist role for the UN, and by the visionary leadership of OAU secretary-general Salim Ahmed Salim.

The situation in modern Africa, as it pertains to development of a collective security-management system, is unique. The threat to individual African states, as well as to Africa as a whole, is less external to the continent and less military than it is economic, environmental, and social. Economic insecurity results both from the disadvantageous position of African states in the world economic system, a position that is a part of the colonial legacy, and from official corruption and poor public management of the economy. Environmental insecurity is not only rooted in a long history of poor environmental management but also in periodic drought and famine, uncontrolled population growth, and low technological capacities for addressing serious environmental problems such as deforestation, desertification, and soil erosion. The social threats to African security include poverty, inadequate educational opportunities, gender and ethnic inequities, inadequate health care, malnutrition, and overall underdevelopment. The withdrawal of the superpowers and other rich and powerful states from significant involvement in the pursuit of development and politico-military stability on the continent has made African states vulnerable to implosion, creating a potential for subregional and even regional security dilemmas. These are the types of forces that seem to be driving the quest in Africa today for collective security-management systems.

In 1991, the African Leadership Forum, the OAU, and the UN Economic Commission for Africa cosponsored a historic conference at Kampala, Uganda, to discuss the continent's problems. The five hundred conferees agreed that their countries are interdependent and that their respective national security situations were intertwined with regional security throughout the continent. In other words, many African leaders are now of the opinion that the security, stability, and development of every African country affects every other African country, and that Africa cannot hope to make progress toward development or democracy without creating the conditions and institutions necessary for lasting solutions to its security and stability problems. The final report of the gathering proposed the establishment of the permanent Conference on Security, Stability, Development, and Cooperation (CSSDCA).[5]

The Kampala Document called for the establishment of continental peacekeeping machinery, and for the drastic lowering of military expenditures by African states. This theme was picked up by the OAU's Salim, and for the first time African leaders are confronting regional security issues and seriously considering how they might cooperate to reduce interstate as well as domestic conflicts and, in the process, create conditions conducive to democracy and sustained development.

At the 1992 OAU summit in Dakar, Senegal, Salim proposed an "OAU Mechanism for Conflict Prevention and Resolution." The following year, the African heads of state at their annual summit formally approved the establishment of this mechanism, even though it implied that member states might on occasion have to surrender their sovereignty in the interest of regional security. Early indications are that the member states of the OAU have not adopted an attitude conducive to the establishment of a Wilsonian multilateral collective security-management system. In other words, it is not clear whether the notions of state sovereignty and the norms of intervention will indeed be altered in the process of implementing this mechanism.

The resolution establishing the mechanism states: "The Mechanism will be guided by the objectives and principles of the OAU Charter; in particular, the sovereign equality of Member States, noninterference in the internal affairs of States, the respect of the sovereignty and territorial integrity of Member States, their inalienable right to independent existence, the peaceful settlement of disputes as well as the inviolability of borders inherited from

5. It is important to note that CSSDCA is largely an informal effort, privately funded, and with no official authority. Talks continue, but the plan has yet to be implemented. In fact, the idea has been co-opted by the OAU.

colonialism. It will also function on the basis of the consent and rely on the cooperation of the parties to a conflict" (African Leadership Forum 1992).

The primary objective of the mechanism is said to be "the anticipation and prevention of conflicts." In situations where conflicts have occurred, the mechanism is supposed to be responsible for undertaking peacemaking and peace-building activities. In cases of severe conflict, there is a provision for OAU cooperation with the United Nations.

Despite the ambiguities in the language of the resolution creating the mechanism, it greatly broadens the role of the OAU Secretariat and the secretary-general in coordinating inter-Africa peacekeeping efforts. The mechanism is built around a "central organ" headed by the secretary-general of the OAU. This new institution is the OAU's Bureau of the Assembly of Heads of State and Government, elected annually, comprising a chairman and eight other members representing Africa's five regions, including North Africa. The bureau is empowered to act on behalf of heads of state in sanctioning any deployment of peacekeeping forces. In addition, the office of the secretary-general is strengthened by the creation of an "early-warning system" to monitor and analyze trends. The secretary-general can also rely upon a committee of eminent persons to engage in preventive diplomacy and upon the advice of African military and technical experts. Salim envisions that each African military will have specially trained units that could be deployed under OAU command.

A special fund has been established for the mechanism. It is made up of funds from the regular appropriations of the OAU and voluntary contributions from member states and from other sources within Africa. There are also provisions for receiving resources from outside Africa.

The United States is one of those extracontinental actors working with the OAU as well as with subregional organizations such as ECOWAS and IGADD to help them implement plans and procedures for enhanced African conflict prevention, peacemaking, and peacekeeping capabilities. Legislation in the form of H. R. 4541, the *African Conflict Resolution Act,* calls for the provision of material and technical assistance to help institutionalize conflict-resolution capabilities in Africa. This aid is to be provided to the OAU, subregional organizations, and national governments. Also, it provides for education and training in conflict resolution and peacekeeping for civilian and military personnel, and the strengthening of the mediation and reconciliation capacities of nongovernmental organizations in Africa. The projected cost over a four-year period is $60 million (U.S. House 1994).

There are a host of possible obstacles to the long-term viability of the mechanism. Even though bilateral and multilateral donors have made contributions to the mechanism's fund, a chief obstacle continues to be funding. At its 1995 summit, the OAU made some tentative strides toward addressing some of its funding needs. The secretary-general was able to pressure a number of member states to pay dues that were in arrears, resulting in a $20 million infusion into the OAU coffers. A second major potential obstacle is the problem of commitment. At the Addis Ababa summit, however, all but a few leaders in attendance agreed to place their armed services on standby for possible intervention in increasingly unstable Burundi. These actions were preceded by the establishment of the Cairo Center for African Crisis Solving, which hosted a one-month training course on conflict prevention and management for twenty-eight military officers from fourteen African countries (Agence France Presse 1995).

Third, a related problem of commitment has to do with the depth of the new thinking in Africa on the norms of external intervention in domestic matters. Will the OAU mechanism be able to assert its assigned authority when crises emerge, or will it be obstructed by states who feel targeted? While African leaders seem to agree that the mechanism is needed, it is not clear just how most would respond if the OAU decided to intervene to manage disputes in their own countries.

In any case, the decision to intervene is not likely to be easily taken. However, when the OAU does decide to intervene, militarily at least, it might feel more confident intervening in smaller and weaker countries and might be least likely to intervene in larger and stronger states that are highly unstable but still coherent (e.g., Sudan, Nigeria). In states that have descended into chaos, intervention options for the OAU may be limited to the domain of humanitarian aid.

In the case of the most severe domestic conflicts occurring in subregions, the OAU has begun to work through subregional organizations such as ECOMOG in Liberia and IGADD in the mediation of the conflict in Sudan. However, experience has shown that good intentions are not enough. Neither IGADD nor ECOMOG has been able successfully to manage intense internal conflicts in their subregions, mainly because of limited resources available and the high level of mistrust among the protagonists.

Despite the obvious limitations of regional and subregional approaches in dealing with domestic conflicts that have become, or have the potential to become, the source of regional security dilemmas, Africa seems to have little alternative but to cultivate such approaches. The development of new mechanisms and modalities for collective security management will not be easy, but such new approaches must be found.

Conclusion

African states are confronted with subregional security dilemmas that are largely domestic in origin. Internal conflicts that grow from the colonial legacy of artificially created nation-states have in some subregions been exacerbated by the widespread availability of weapons of war left over from the Cold War. Throughout the continent domestic conflicts are increasingly spilling across borders, resulting in human dislocation, arms flows, and food insecurity. Such conditions strain the resources of already impoverished African countries and prevent progress toward democracy and self-sustained development. Such problems are now being seen as not only subregional but regional security dilemmas that demand the development of interlocking collective security-management systems linking the OAU with subregional organizations having common collective security interests.

Traditional modalities for addressing subregional as well as domestic conflicts in Africa are widely recognized as being inadequate under present circumstances. Both the UN and the OAU are now in the process of rethinking the notions of state sovereignty and the norms governing multilateral external intervention for the purpose of resolving these conflicts. This new thinking was inspired in part by the changes in the world order following the collapse of Communism and the end of the Cold War, and in part by the emergence of liberalizing regimes throughout the continent.

The OAU has established the Mechanism for Conflict Prevention, Management, and Resolution. Significantly, this new body is mandated to engage in preventive diplomacy in efforts to avert debilitating domestic and interstate conflicts. Should the OAU succeed in setting up an effective procedure for preventive diplomacy, this will represent a major breakthrough on behalf of African regional security.

14

ASEAN and the Southeast Asian Security Complex

Yuen Foong Khong

The "Southeast Asian security complex," according to Barry Buzan, "is composed of nine states sharply divided into two groups: a Communist-led Soviet-aligned, and Vietnamese-dominated group of three (Vietnam, Laos, Kampuchea); and a non-Communist, Western-orientated group of six, organized since 1967, in the Association of Southeast Asian Nations (Malaysia, Singapore, Philippines, Indonesia, Thailand, and since 1984, Brunei)." This "local pattern of security relations" has undoubtedly been "penetrated and distorted" by the United States, the Soviet Union, and China, but these major powers remain outside the complex because the local pattern "reflects an independently rooted regional security dynamic." Buzan believed that "[t]his local pattern looks stable, and seems likely to define the internal dynamics of the Southeast Asian security complex for the foreseeable future" (1988, 4–9).

How things have changed! The shelf life of Buzan's article and of his effort to apply an admittedly promising concept to Southeast Asian security affairs was approximately a year. During 1988–89, Vietnam began withdrawing its troops from Cambodia. Soon thereafter, the Berlin Wall crumbled. In 1991, the Soviet Union imploded. In the same year, the Paris agreements were signed: with the Vietnamese troops gone, the political future of Cambodia would be decided by United Nations–sponsored elections. In 1992, the idea for an ASEAN-based multilateral forum for discussing Asia-Pacific security would be mooted; in 1994, the ASEAN Regional Forum came to fruition. Instead of a local pattern of a "Soviet-aligned and Vietnamese-dominated group" facing off—or existing in a state of enmity—against a Western-oriented ASEAN, we are witnessing the gradual and amiable absorption of the "Vietnamese-dominated" group into ASEAN. By the dawn of the twenty-first century, the Southeast Asian security complex will comprise the ASEAN-10 (ASEAN, Vietnam, Laos, Cambodia, and Myanmar); the security pattern characterizing the complex, in all likelihood, will be one of amity.

It is not my intention to single out Buzan for failing to anticipate the end of the Cold War and its attendant consequences. Virtually no international relations specialist foresaw them. Most analyses of Southeast Asia published before 1990 assumed the enduring relevance of Soviet power and the continuation of Soviet-Chinese and Soviet-U.S. rivalries via proxies in the Third World. Given these assumptions, it would be quite natural to define the Southeast Asian security complex in terms of Indochinese-ASEAN enmity and to expect that dynamic to endure (Buzan 1988, 12–13).

The chief promise of the security-complex notion, in my view, lies in its utility for *ex ante* identification of the central players and security issues in a given region. If the criteria for inclusion and a typology of security dynamics can be properly specified, the notion should give us some analytic purchase on how new disturbances might impinge on the region. Yet such clues about the security dynamics of post–Cold War Southeast Asia are hard to find in Buzan's account of the Southeast Asian complex. I suspect, with hindsight to be sure, that Buzan's privileging of enmity over amity in his search and characterization of security complexes might have done his analysis a disservice. For Buzan (1988, 2), "the identification of security complexes tends to rest more on patterns of enmity, fear and rivalry, than it does on patterns of amity, trust and co-operation" (cf. Buzan 1991, 189–94, where amity and enmity are given equal emphasis).[1] The emphasis on enmity and fear led to the ele-

1. Ultimately, this privileging of fear and rivalry over trust and cooperation can be attributed to Buzan's measured affection for realism. See Buzan 1996 for a thoughtful defense of realism against its detractors.

vation of the Indochina-ASEAN divide as the principal axis, and to the issue of Vietnamese occupation of Cambodia as the "principal variable" (or bone of contention), within the Southeast Asian security complex. It also accentuated the role of the Soviet Union and China in defining the dynamics of the complex (Buzan 1988, 7–12).

While this characterization captured a key reality of the day, it gave short shrift to the pattern or process that turned out to be more enduring and relevant for the 1990s and beyond: the transformation of intra-ASEAN security relations from enmity, fear, and rivalry to amity, trust, and cooperation. Understanding and appreciating this alternative pattern within the complex would have afforded one more analytic purchase: it would have identified ASEAN and its modalities as being central to the construction of order among formerly contentious Southeast Asian states, and it would also have raised the question whether "ASEAN's way" might have relevance for the non-ASEAN states in Southeast Asia. This lament about the analytical costs of neglecting ASEAN's evolution in security matters is not based entirely on hindsight: ASEAN's founding charter in 1967 explicitly left it open to ascension by the other Southeast Asian states, and ASEAN's Treaty of Amity and Cooperation (1976) articulated a norm-based code of diplomatic conduct for all of Southeast Asia.

This chapter therefore focuses on the ASEAN side of the Southeast Asian security complex, the side that not only has extended its strategic arms to Vietnam, Laos, Cambodia (and soon Myanmar), but also has been a prime mover of new strategic initiatives for the complex and beyond. Today's Southeast Asian security complex is ASEAN-based and ASEAN-dominated. To understand how it came to be, to obtain a sense of the complex's operating security dynamic, and to anticipate its future promise and problems, this chapter provides an analysis of the evolution of security relations among the original ASEAN-5 (Malaysia, Singapore, Philippines, Indonesia, and Thailand).[2]

My theme is that interstate relations among the ASEAN-5 have evolved in the direction of a pluralistic security community, albeit a nascent one (cf. Morgan, this volume; see also Weatherbee 1984; Acharya 1991; Djiwandono 1991). As defined by Deutsch and his colleagues (1957, 5–6), the term "pluralistic security community" refers to "a group of states whose members share 'dependable expectations of peaceful change' in their mutual relations

2. For the sake of convenience, I use the term "the ASEAN-5" to refer to Malaysia, Indonesia, Philippines, Thailand, and Singapore, both before and after they joined ASEAN. Brunei became the sixth member of ASEAN in 1984.

and rule out the use of force as a means of problem solving" (cf. Acharya 1991, 159). While there is a norm against the use of force to settle disputes among the ASEAN states, it would be too much to suggest that these states have completely ruled out the use of force against each other. For this and other reasons I have discussed elsewhere, ASEAN has not completely met the criteria advanced by Deutsch and his colleagues and elaborated by others. Hence the necessity of qualifying the term "security community" with the adjective "nascent." This chapter does not dwell on the differences between ASEAN as a nascent and as a full-fledged security community (see discussion in Khong 1994); instead, it traces the evolution of the common identity, or "we-feeling," that Deutsch and his colleagues (1957, 123–30) deemed so essential to the making of security communities. Previous discussions of ASEAN as a security community have not explicitly traced the development of this sense of "we-ness" or regional identity among the ASEAN countries.[3]

I suggest that the evolution of this sense of we-ness can best be understood by breaking down ASEAN's history into four periods: before 1967, 1967–76, 1976–89, and 1989 to the present. Attempts at regional organization along security, economic, or cultural lines before 1967 tended to be stillborn; the unrestrained pursuit of national interests and the lack of consciousness of community characterized this period. Nascent stirrings of a sense of we-ness may be observed in the 1967–76 period; these stirrings were brought about by a change of political regime in Indonesia, security interdependence, and the institution of ASEAN.

The consolidation of the "ASEAN spirit" occurred in the next phase, 1976 to 1989, principally because of a perceived external threat, the security threat emanating from Vietnam. In the first three phases, economic interdependence and transactions did not play a vital role in generating and sustaining the ASEAN spirit. In the most recent phase, 1989–96, economic considerations have become more salient in enhancing the ASEAN spirit; however, that spirit is still primarily sustained by new security institutions and practices. Realist predictions about the splintering of the ASEAN community in the post–Cold War era have not been confirmed; on the contrary, the ASEAN community seems to be moving forward on all fronts.

In focusing on the development and consolidation of the ASEAN spirit, or we-feeling, my analysis would seem to privilege the cognitive aspects of the

3. The second necessary condition for qualifying as a pluralistic security community is "compatibility of major values" among potential members. See Deutsch et. al. 1957, 123–29; cf. Khong 1994.

Southeast Asian security complex (Job, this volume). However, as the editors emphasize, and as the ensuing analysis indicates, the security externalities so central to Lake's notion of regional systems are difficult to separate from the development of the collective self-understandings underpinning ASEAN. The case of ASEAN reinforces Lake and Morgan's observation that "common conceptions absent interactions are not likely to be sustained, and dense interactions are likely to produce a perception of common destiny or 'regionness'" (this volume, 12).

Regional Conflict in the Pre-ASEAN Years

Among the original ASEAN-5, only Thailand was exempt from being colonized. The Philippines, Indonesia, Malaya, and Singapore were American, Dutch, and British colonies respectively. The Philippines became independent in 1946, Indonesia in 1949, Malaya in 1957, and Singapore in 1963. Indonesia was the only country that had to fight (militarily) for its independence; that experience would influence its foreign policy in later years. The ethnic makeup of each of these new states was extremely diverse, with Indonesian/Malay Muslims forming the majority in Indonesia and Malaya, and with the commercially prominent Chinese and Indians in the minority. Singapore, on the other hand, was predominantly Chinese, with a small percentage of Malays and Indians.

The checkered past and heterogeneity of these new states made many observers of the region pessimistic. The prospects for peace and security in the region were considered to be dim. Unsettled boundaries—in the wake of the colonizers' hasty retreat—became issues of contention among the new states. Also, many of the ASEAN-5 governments faced internal challenges to their rule, whether from Communist guerrillas, disaffected ethnic groups, or from irredentist and secessionist movements. Even more important, all these insurrections had *negative local spillover* effects that threatened neighborly amity. In 1962, for example, the Philippines made repeated claims on Sabah (which became part of Malaysia in 1963); this dispute with Malaysia remains till this day. Malaysia was also accused of aiding Muslim secessionists in southern Philippines; Malaysia in turn expressed outrage at Filipino attempts to infiltrate saboteurs into Sabah. Thailand was suspicious of Malaysian overtures to Muslim secessionists in southern Thailand, and Malaysia resented Thailand's lax attitude toward Malaysian Communist guerrillas seeking sanctuary in southern Thailand.

The most ominous event in the region was Indonesia's decision to launch a military confrontation (*konfrontasi*) against Malaysia in 1963. For ideological and domestic political reasons, President Sukarno of Indonesia objected to Sabah and Sarawak's (former British Borneo territories contiguous with Kalimantan Indonesia) merger with Malaya (to form, together with Singapore, Malaysia) and sought to prevent this "neocolonialist plot" by military force (Weinstein 1969). The confrontation lasted until 1966.

Meanwhile, Singapore's inclusion in the federation of Malaysia was making ethnic tensions between the Malays and the Chinese in Malaysia unbearable. Singapore was expelled from the federation in 1965. Malaysia-Singapore tensions remained high throughout much of the 1960s and 1970s. In 1968, Singapore-Indonesian relations were seriously strained when the former rejected Indonesian pleas for clemency and executed two Indonesian commandos for their *konfrontasi* activities. Singapore's actions set off riots in Jakarta and demands for teaching Singapore a lesson.

During this period, three attempts aimed directly or indirectly at alleviating these negative externalities can be discerned. SEATO, or the Southeast Asian Treaty Organization, was a United States–led military alliance created in 1954 to draw the line against Communist expansionism in Southeast Asia. SEATO may therefore be seen as a traditional balance-of-power approach—via external alliances—to regional security (Morgan, this volume). Thailand and the Philippines became members. Since Malaya and Singapore were British colonies then, they were not SEATO members; nor did they join upon achieving independence. Indonesia also refused to join. The externality that was SEATO's purpose to contain—the spread of Communism from Indochina to non-Communist Southeast Asia—was indeed the most pressing security issue confronting Malaya, Singapore, and Indonesia. But from the perspective of these new states, SEATO bore too heavily the imprint, if not imposition, of an external actor, the United States. Already there was a vague and inchoate sense that their problems might be better dealt with by something more local or indigenous. With more non–Southeast Asian states than Southeast Asian states as members, SEATO never had much regional integrity; nor was it explicitly invoked during the Vietnam War. It died a natural death in 1977.

The other two experiments in regionalism were indeed more local. The Association of Southeast Asia (ASA) was formed in 1961 with Thailand, Malaya, and the Philippines as members. What the members had in common was their hostility toward Communism and vague notions of forging an indigenous alternative to externally directed alliances such as SEATO. To be sure, the ASA had no illusions about being a military alliance; it was merely an early attempt to try out the possibilities of a political-economic form of regionalism. Two years later another regional organization, Maphilindo, comprising Malaya, Philippines, and Indonesia, was formed; it sought to capitalize on the ethno-linguistic commonalities of the Malay race present in each of these states (Solidum 1974). Yet whatever emerging spirit of cooperation the ASA and Maphilindo may have nurtured could not withstand the assertion of the sovereign self-interests of Malaya, Philippines, and Indonesia.

In 1963, the former British Borneo territories of Sabah and Sarawak, and Singapore, merged with Malaya to form the federation of Malaysia. The formation of Malaysia engendered one of the most serious territorial disputes in postcolonial Southeast Asia. To maintain the Malay character of Malaysia, the inclusion of Singapore was to be balanced by the addition of Sabah and Sarawak. From the perspective of Indonesia and the Philippines, Sabah and Sarawak could just as well be part of Indonesia or the Philippines. The Philippines claimed Sabah on the grounds that it was leased, not ceded, to the British by the Sultan of Sulu, who had since bequeathed his territorial possessions to Manila.

President Sukarno of Indonesia argued that Britain and Malaya did not consult Indonesia and the people of Sabah and Sarawak in the decision to include the latter in the federation of Malaysia, the implication being that the people of Sabah and Sarawak would prefer to merge with Indonesia than with Malaya. Sukarno decided to launch a military campaign to "crush" the newly formed Malaysia (Mackie 1974). For Sukarno, Malaya and Singapore were "inauthentic" to begin with because they had not used force to eject their colonial masters; they remained "neocolonies" through which Britain would exert its influence in the region.

Indonesia under Sukarno gave precedence to such highly nationalistic, anti-imperialistic campaigns over the more mundane details of economic planning. Sukarno found it useful to deflect domestic crises and challenges to his authority via foreign adventures: hence the fight against the Dutch for Irian Jaya despite reservations by his closest advisers, and the military confrontation against Malaysia (Vatikiotis 1994, 2–4; Weinstein 1969). In so doing, however, Sukarno found himself moving increasingly closer to the Indonesian Communist Party (Partai Komunis Indonesia, or PKI), to the consternation of important segments of the Indonesian military.

The point to be made is that unsettled borders and territorial disputes, coupled with a restive and nationalistic Indonesia under Sukarno, made neighborly amity between Malaysia, Indonesia, and the Philippines difficult; neither the ASA nor Maphilindo was intended, or had the institutional capacity, to moderate these disputes. In fact both the ASA and Maphilindo fell victims to these disputes: they became defunct in 1963 and 1966 respectively.

For the international relations of the region, the most critical event during this period was the 1965 coup in Indonesia and the subsequent removal of Sukarno as president. The details of the coup and its aftermath—involving the loss of up to three hundred thousand Indonesian lives, some of them suspected or real Communists, others innocent—have been analyzed by others (Sundhaussen 1982; Schwarz 1994). A major reason for the coup, according to these analyses, was divisions within the military over political ideology, foreign policy, and the economy. The faction that won, led by General Suharto, was anxious to reverse Sukarno's drift toward the PKI, end Indonesia's confrontation with Malaysia, and restore economic stability. They began pursuing these policies soon after the coup, even though Sukarno was nominally still president.

One of the first foreign-policy changes undertaken by Indonesia was to allow the new foreign minister, Adam Malik, to negotiate an end to *konfrontasi* and to ease Indonesia back into being a responsible member of the region. With the help of Thai foreign minister Thanat Khoman, Malik devoted his efforts to creating a new regional arrangement in which Indonesia could reassure its neighbors as well as learn to cooperate with them. That arrangement was ASEAN. When Suharto finally replaced Sukarno as president in 1968, Indonesia became one of ASEAN's most enthusiastic members.

Although it would have been difficult to tell in the late 1960s whether Suharto and his supporters constituted a coalition favoring economic liberalization, hindsight indicates that they did. Suharto rejected Sukarno's fiery brand of political and economic nationalism in favor of a lower political profile and economic liberalization for Indonesia. Advised by a group of Western-trained Indonesian neoclassical economists, Suharto moved to curb inflation, stabilize the rupiah, repair ties with the international financial community, and invite foreign investment (Schwarz 1994, chap. 2). Indonesia's post-1965 support for regional order and its gradual movement toward economic liberalization thus lend support to Etel Solingen's argument (in this volume) about the positive relationship between liberalizing coalitions and regional order.

1967–1976: ASEAN's First Decade

Much misunderstanding of ASEAN has been caused by cursory readings of its founding charter. That charter, widely known as the Bangkok Declaration, explicitly downplays political-security cooperation and emphasizes instead economic, cultural, and social cooperation. As the declaration puts it, ASEAN aims to "accelerate the economic growth, social progress and cultural development in the region through joint endeavors . . . in order to strengthen the foundation for a prosperous and peaceful community of Southeast Asian Nations" (Sukrasep 1989, app. A).

The apparent omission of political aspirations in the declaration and ASEAN's opaque style have led many analysts to view ASEAN as an economic organization along European Community lines and a failed one at that. A closer reading of the founding charter, however, reveals references to security-related aims. Thus the declaration stipulates that member countries are also "determined to ensure their stability and security from external interference" as well as to "promote peace and stability through abiding respect for peace and the rule of law in the relationship among countries of the region" (Sukrasep 1989, app.).

ASEAN's methods and goals were explicitly multifaceted: economic growth, social progress, cultural development, regional peace and stability were to be pursued via joint endeavors. The founding document assumed the inseparability of these goods and the idea was that each of these sectors had the potential for positive spillover effects or synergistic interactions. Thus ASEAN was not just a regional economic organization along European Community lines; nor was economic integration ever a goal. It was also not a military alliance like NATO. In the terminology of post–Cold War writings on Southeast Asia's security, ASEAN may be said to have acted, right from the start, on a notion of "comprehensive security" (Dewitt 1994). Security was not seen in purely military or deterrence terms; economic resilience, dialogues, cultural exchanges, and diplomatic reassurances were all seen as contributing to the overall sense of security.

From experience, the leaders knew that threats like *konfrontasi* and suspicions about one's neighbors aiding disenchanted ethnic or separatist groups within one's borders were destabilizing; such threats did not just divert valuable resources away from economic activities to military spending, for the insecurity they engendered was not conducive to attracting foreign investment. This train of thought can be seen in the statement of Adam Malik, foreign minister of Indonesia, and one of the major figures in the founding of ASEAN. Malik's recollection is unusually thorough and informative, and for that reason is worth quoting at length: "Although from the outset ASEAN was conceived as an organization for economic, social and cultural cooperation . . . it was the fact that there was a convergence in the political outlook of the five prospective member-nations, both with regard to national priority objectives as on the question of how best to secure these objectives in the emergent strategic configuration of East Asia, which provided the main stimulus to join together in ASEAN." Malik elaborated on what he meant by common political outlook and the strategic configuration in the following way: "By the time of ASEAN's birth, the nations of Southeast Asia were all intent on restoring stability and ensuring progress for their region, after centuries of stagnation and strife . . . the shaping of a coordinated approach among the nations of Southeast Asia toward the problems of peace, stability and development had therefore become an urgent necessity. . . . *There was early recognition that meaningful progress could only be achieved by giving first priority to . . . rapid economic development. It was also realized that, to this end, policies should be consciously geared toward safeguarding this priority objective, not only in purely economic terms but simultaneously also to secure the essential conditions of peace and stability. . . . Phrased differently, the Southeast Asian countries must develop the capacity to live with a minimum degree of internal disturbance and external interference, so as to enable the establishment of relative peace and stability, without which national development becomes practically impossible*" (CSIS 1974, 161–62).

While helpful in providing some standard against which future achievement may be measured, founding declarations and post hoc recollections are no substitutes for results. In the economic field, ASEAN's achievements were meager in its first decade; the next phase (1976–89) witnessed some minor improvements, but the overall results remained unimpressive. Thus Michael Antolik's assessment (1990, 4) of ASEAN in its first two decades is right on the mark: "ASEAN . . . has succeeded in carrying out only two joint industrial projects. Trade tariffs . . . have been lowered, but only slightly," and overall, "progress toward economic cooperation has been limited."

ASEAN's inability to cooperate on economic matters should not be surprising, since, until recently, the ASEAN economies were in varying stages of economic development. For much of the 1960s and 1970s, they were also competing against one another as exporters of primary commodities. In the mid-1970s, however, Thailand, Malaysia, and Indonesia switched from import substitution to export-led growth. As a result of that switch, the

ASEAN economies have acquired some complementary characteristics; they have also developed a stake in a liberal world economy, which has in turn encouraged them to coordinate the opening of their economies. The story of increasing intra-ASEAN and ASEAN–Asia-Pacific economic cooperation in the 1990s is relevant to an understanding of order in the Southeast Asian security complex but because of space considerations is not examined here (see Khong 1995b).

The point to be made is that the sense of collective identity central to the building of security communities did not originate from intensive economic interaction or interdependence. The lack of success in economic cooperation during ASEAN's first decade was more than made up by achievements in political-security cooperation. It is here that the inklings of a regional consciousness or solidarity may be found.

The territorial, ethnic, and ideological disputes that pitted one ASEAN state against another indicated to the region's leaders how interdependent their security was. As mentioned earlier, virtually all the ASEAN-5 faced internal threats, and most of these threats had a regional dimension. Three of the most vexing of these threats are discussed briefly here. The first of these is the Communist insurgency in Malaya, which was Malaya's and (since 1963) Malaysia's chief security threat. The most serious fighting between the Communist guerrillas and government forces occurred in the 1948–60 period, but the threat was not extinguished until the late 1970s.

Throughout the 1960s, guerrillas belonging to the Malayan Communist Party were able to stage raids against government forces in northern Malaysia. After each attack, they would retreat to sanctuaries along the Thai border. Without Thai cooperation, Malaysian soldiers could not engage in hot pursuit into Thai territory. The Communist guerrillas were protected. Thai cooperation did not come readily, but after intensive negotiations, it did materialize in the form of joint Thai-Malaysian border patrols. Eventually, Thailand also permitted Malaysia to conduct limited hot-pursuit activities in Thai territory. These acts of security coordination predated ASEAN; they were further institutionalized after the creation of ASEAN. To be sure, there is an important element of tit for tat in Thai-Malaysian security cooperation. Thailand's cooperation was also based on Malaysia's reciprocating by withholding support for Thai Muslim secessionists in southern Thailand (Chan 1986; Leifer 1989; Antolik 1990).

More significantly, the existence and modalities of ASEAN moderated two of the major problems that bedeviled the region in the earlier period: Indonesia's ambitions and the Philippines' claim to Sabah. Sukarno's "regional overstretch" and his lack of interest in, and mishandling, of the Indonesian economy precipitated his downfall. President Suharto was determined to avoid his predecessor's ruinous course by negotiating an early end to *konfrontasi.* In 1966, Indonesia and Malaysia signed an agreement ending *konfrontasi;* a year later, with Indonesia, Malaysia, and Thailand playing lead roles, ASEAN was founded.

Indonesia was enthusiastic about ASEAN because Suharto and Adam Malik were determined to take Indonesian foreign policy in a new direction. Indonesia would desist from its revolutionary rhetoric, refrain from throwing its weight around, and would behave like a good neighbor. ASEAN and its provisions on regional cooperation facilitated Malik's efforts at taming elements of Indonesian society bent on pursuing a Sukarno-style foreign policy. ASEAN was also provided the institutional locus through which Indonesia could reassure its neighbors and through which third-party mediation would be deemed unthreatening.

Indonesia's new approach to the region was felt immediately. As Mohd. Ghazali Shafie, former foreign minister of Malaysia,' has pointed out, Indonesia's reconciliation with Malaysia was guided by "the spirit of '*berkampung*' or to be in togetherness which emphasizes that problems or differences . . . should be managed through consensual consultations (*New Straits Times,* 4 June 1994). With reconciliation, Indonesia did not only accept Sabah and Sarawak's inclusion in Malaysia, it was also willing, in due course, to cooperate on joint Malaysian-Indonesian military patrols along the borders of Kalimantan to suppress Communist insurgents.

The Philippine claim to Sabah (part of Malaysia since 1963), although not completely solved to this day, has also been greatly moderated by the institution and spirit of ASEAN. Manila's claim is that Sabah (formerly North Borneo) was leased, not ceded, to Britain by the Sultan of Sulu. As such, when Britain left Sabah, the territory ought to have reverted to the Philippines, the "reversionary heir of the Sultan of Sulu" (Thongswadi 1979; also see Lau 1974). Britain, however, based its actions on the title to North Borneo it obtained from the Sultan of Brunei in 1877, and felt that the territory was its to dispose, and it decided in favor of Malaya. The Philippines-Malaysia dispute is thus one of those colonial legacies bequeathed to its former colonies by Britain.

The Philippines claimed Sabah in 1962, when it learned that Sabah was to become part of the Malaysian federation. The claim strained Philippines-Malaysian ties to the point where diplomatic relations were abrogated for the next three years (1963–66). Relations were restored in 1966, and the issue became dormant until 1968. In March 1968, it was discovered that Muslims from the southern Philippines were being trained in guerrilla tactics on Corregidor Island for the purpose of infiltrating into Sabah. Malaysia saw this program as "a Philippine threat to use force to settle the dispute" (Thongswadi 1979, 148).

At this point, two ASEAN members intervened. Indonesia and Thailand offered to mediate the dispute; they took the initiative of inviting the two parties to meet, at first in Indonesia, and then in Bangkok (Thongswadi 1979). A "cooling-off" period was announced, and the dispute was prevented from spiraling out of control. As Tarnthong Thongswadi puts it, "ASEAN [had] successfully used a face-saving agreement" to suspend the dispute (149).

President Suharto of Indonesia had sought to help the two parties resolve the issue. Indonesian emissaries visited Manila in 1973, carrying an appeal from President Suharto to President Marcos to drop the claim on Sabah in the interests of ASEAN solidarity. Suharto continued to raise the Sabah issue in follow-up meetings with Marcos in 1978 and 1979 (Solidum 1982). By then President Marcos had promised to take "definite steps" to end the dispute.

Reconciliation between Malaysia and the Philippines was greatly facilitated by the institutional context of ASEAN, which made third-party mediation legitimate and unthreatening. Suharto's intervention, for example, was consultative and sought to move Malaysia and the Philippine toward a consensus. From such experiences, a set of procedural norms for the conduct of regional relations began to emerge. Norms such as *musjawarah* (consultation) and *mufakat* (consensual decision making) became part of the "ASEAN style."

Perhaps the most critical norm—unstated but understood—permeating these efforts at conflict management was the proscription against calling in outside powers such as the United States, China, or Japan. To be sure, all the ASEAN countries were spiritually and economically aligned with the West. Yet Malaysia never saw SEATO as relevant to solving its Communist insurgency problem, nor did it invite the United States to help stem the insurrection. Similarly, the Philippines might have found it useful to involve the United States in its dispute over Sabah with Malaysia; yet it abstained from taking that road.

This aversion to "external interference" (as Adam Malik put it) was primarily a reaction to the Vietnam War, then raging in ASEAN's front yard. From the Vietnam War, the ASEAN states deduced the lesson that involving external powers, while the Cold War was on, in their intrastate or interstate disputes would only exacerbate those disputes. This interest in fending off great-power involvement was explicitly articulated in ASEAN's 1971 declaration calling for making Southeast Asia a Zone for Peace, Freedom, and Neutrality (ZOPFAN). The idea was for the great powers—the United States, Russia, and China—to minimize their involvement in the region and to guarantee its neutrality so that the Southeast Asian states would be left on their own to work out their differences as well as to cooperate on economic and security matters. More an aspiration than a reality, ZOPFAN reflected ASEAN's desire to insulate the region from some of the traditional variants of international politics such as hegemony by one state (the United States or Indonesia) or bipolarity (whether United States–China or China-Japan). In seeking great-power guarantees, ASEAN seemed to be seeking their cooperation in keeping the peace in Southeast Asia, but as far as ASEAN was concerned, the emphasis was on allowing Southeast Asians to work out their own problems.

Omitted from the discussion so far are the institutional structures of ASEAN that have made possible "habits of dialogue" and functional cooperation among its members. The institutional mechanisms include (1) an annual meeting of the foreign ministers (annual ministerial meeting, or AMM); (2) national secretariats in each of the capitals, although an overarching ASEAN secretariat was formed in Jakarta in 1982; (3) various standing and ad hoc committees dealing with ASEAN issues; and (4) heads-of-state summits.

With the exception of the AMM, the structures above were not fully used during ASEAN's first decade. ASEAN had rejected any "great leap forward" in initial years because, as Singapore's foreign minister S. Rajaratnam put it, that would have been "the last leap forward." As he saw it, "ASEAN had quite correctly chosen to move forward through a series of small steps" (cited in Broinowski 1982, 21). Malaysia's deputy prime minister, Tun Ismail, also saw wisdom in this approach. He wrote then that despite ASEAN's modest beginnings, "the constant contact and communication between our officials has helped to develop a habit of co-operation and a sense of solidarity which will in turn help us when we move forward toward wider areas of co-operation" (cited in Broinowski 1982, 22). By the mid-1970s however, ASEAN was ready to move forward, and its institutional structures swung into full gear. The first heads-of-state summit was held in Jakarta in 1976, and it resulted in the important Treaty of Amity and Cooperation (TOFAC). (The significance of the treaty is discussed below.)

Equally important but more novel was the initiation of the postministerial conferences (PMCs), so called because they occur after ASEAN's AMMs. At the PMCs, the ASEAN foreign ministers would meet with their counterparts ("dialogue partners") from the United States, European Community, Japan, Korea, Australia, and New Zealand to discuss economic and security issues. These high-level consultations began in 1974 and have become an annual fixture of ASEAN's diplomacy. Because the PMC's most significant accomplishments occurred in the late 1970s, I will defer discussion of the PMCs until later.

Between 1967 and 1975, therefore, the ASEAN states used a variety of bilateral and multilateral means to attenuate the dilemmas engendered by their security interdependence. The result of these dialogues, consultations, and movement toward consensus was a nascent sense of collective identification. As Ghazali bin Shafie puts it, it was a sense of *berkampung,* or togetherness. This sense, it should be emphasized, was based primarily on security, not economic, cooperation. Compared to the pre-1967 period, a semblance of order may be said to have prevailed.

1976–1989: Solidarity Against Vietnam

If the emerging sense of collective identification in ASEAN's early years was a result of intraregional security interdependence and mitigating negative security externalities, the consolidation of that identity in the next decade was an indirect result of an external shock: the victory of Communism in Indochina. In April 1975, the Khmer Rouge took over Cambodia; one month later, North Vietnamese tanks rolled into Saigon, thus accomplishing Ho Chi Minh's thirty-year dream of uniting North and South Vietnam. Anti-Communist as they were, the ASEAN states responded calmly, at least initially. In 1976, the first ASEAN heads-of-state summit was held in Bali, Indonesia. An important outcome of the meeting was the Treaty of Amity and Cooperation. The treaty is perhaps one of the most important developments in the history of ASEAN because it stipulates a norm-based code of conduct for regional relations as well as the use of an institutional mechanism for settling disputes peacefully. The treaty codified norms and procedures that were already in use. As Sheldon Simon (1982, 38) put it, "ASEAN mediation [based on consultative methods and adherence to certain norms] over Sabah proved so successful that the procedure was written into treaties on settlement of intra-ASEAN conflict signed at the Bali Summit of 1976." Among the most important norms and principles enunciated by the treaty and which were to guide signatories in the conduct of their relations with one another were "mutual respect for the independence, sovereignty . . . territorial integrity of all nations"; "non-interference in the internal affairs of one another"; "settlement of differences or disputes by peaceful means"; and "renunciation of the threat or use of force" (Sukrasep 1989, app. B).

The treaty was ASEAN's response to the ending of the second Indochina war. A victorious Vietnam, with its enormous military capability and Soviet backing, was perceived by most ASEAN states as a potential threat. The worry was partly that Vietnam would pose a direct military threat to Thailand and partly that a united and strong Vietnam might introduce uncertainty and instability into the security equation in the region. The treaty was a typically ASEAN way of dealing with the problem: it ratified the norms that the ASEAN states had found helpful in regulating their relations with one another, and it held out the possibility that others in the area (read Indochina) who subscribed to these norms could join in the treaty and eventually join ASEAN.

Vietnam dismissed this attempt by ASEAN to stipulate a code of conduct for regional relations. During the Vietnam War, North Vietnam had derided ASEAN as an imperialist plot aimed against it; now that it had won, there was even less of a need to take ASEAN seriously. Vietnam went on to invade Cambodia in 1978, and ASEAN spent the next decade responding to this violation of regional norms by seeking the diplomatic and economic isolation of Vietnam. ASEAN kept the diplomatic heat on Vietnam, so to speak, at a time when the United States sought to minimize its dealings with Southeast Asia. Beginning in 1979, ASEAN diplomats worked to keep the Cambodian problem high on the United Nations agenda, urging the international community not to recognize the credentials of the "puppet regime" set up by Vietnam in Cambodia or to provide reconstruction aid to Vietnam through international agencies as long as its troops still occupied Cambodia (Chan 1986).

ASEAN's strategy of isolating Vietnam is a good test case of the importance of norms and of ASEAN solidarity. A norm dear to ASEAN and that ASEAN hoped would regulate regional relations—respect for the territorial integrity and sovereignty of neighbors—had been violated by Vietnam. However, ASEAN's solidarity and its ability to continue with its consultative ways and to create consensus were severely tested by the policy of isolating Vietnam. This was because these procedures—based on the idea of a collective interest and identity—conflicted with Malaysia's and Indonesia's perception of their strategic interests. Although Malaysia and Indonesia initially abided by the ASEAN norms of consultation and consensus in their approach to the Cambodian crisis, and although they also accommodated Thailand (the frontline state) and Singapore by taking a hard line toward Vietnam, they had occasion to reconsider in 1980.

Both Malaysia and Indonesia saw China as a greater threat to Southeast Asia than Vietnam. But ASEAN's policy against Vietnam required China's help to keep the pressure on Vietnam at the Vietnamese-Chinese border and to support the Cambodian resistance against Vietnam. It was also necessary to count on China's diplomatic weight in the United Nations. China, for its own strategic reasons, was glad to oblige. Over time, Malaysia and Indonesia worried that ASEAN's policy would prolong the Cambodian crisis and weaken Vietnam severely. While they would have liked Vietnam to withdraw from Cambodia, they preferred to see a Vietnam that was strong enough to play a balancing role against China. They did not want inadvertently to help China "bleed Vietnam into submission," because that would give China incentive to assert its power in Southeast Asia (Antolik 1990, 132).

This line of thinking, consistent with what balance-of-power theorists might expect (Walt 1987), caused Indonesia and Malaysia nearly to break ranks with the rest of ASEAN on the Cambodian issue. They adopted a more conciliatory approach toward Vietnam in order to avoid increasing Chinese influence in Southeast Asia (Weatherbee 1985). But their defection was short-lived; soon Indonesia and Malaysia abandoned their approach and "adjusted" their policy toward ASEAN's. The importance of keeping to the norms of (intra-ASEAN) consultation, accommodation, and consensus goes a long way toward explaining Indonesia and Malaysia's decision to subsume their individual interests in favor of maintaining ASEAN solidarity. As Jorgensen-Dahl (1982, 169) puts it, norms such as *musjawarah* and *mufakat*, by functioning as the "principal mode of negotiation [within ASEAN] . . . have become internalized to the extent that the calculations the members make with regard to what is possible are limited or circumscribed by what they can adapt to the prevalent style of negotiation." In other words, Malaysia and Indonesia were reluctant to pursue their independent ways and were willing to sacrifice their short-term strategic interests because they were constrained by norms of decision making and negotiations that they had accepted and internalized.

ASEAN's willingness to take the initiative on Cambodia and its ability to keep its solidarity have impressed many. What ASEAN wanted (the withdrawal of Vietnamese troops from Cambodia) and its template for a solution (an independent Cambodia under some form of international guarantees) were both eventually achieved (cf. Job, this volume). Interestingly, with the end of the Cold War, with Vietnam's withdrawal from Cambodia, and with the ascendancy of moderates in Vietnam interested in economic renovation, Vietnam was ready to take ASEAN and its norms more seriously. In 1990, Vietnam and Laos asked for observer status in ASEAN deliberations; in 1992, they signed the TOFAC, thus agreeing to abide by ASEAN's norms and code of conduct for regional relations. Vietnam's rapprochement with ASEAN, like that of post-Sukarno Indonesia, seems consistent with Solingen's point (this volume) about liberalizing coalitions and regional order.

1989–1996: Institutional Deepening and Expansion

In the aftermath of ASEAN's success—no doubt aided by the end of the Cold War—in pressuring Vietnam to leave Cambodia and thereby making a solution to the Cambodian problem possible, some have predicted that ASEAN would lose its raison d'être and that its solidarity and cohesion would be weakened. Thai prime minister Chatichai Choonhavan's eagerness to turn the "battlefields [of Indochina] into market places" and to promote Thailand as the gateway to that economic market seemed to confirm such predictions, since his policy could be interpreted as Thailand's attempt to pursue an independent course once ASEAN's utility had diminished. This led some observers to suggest that Thailand's geopolitical interests lay with the Indochinese states and that ASEAN would splinter along Thailand-Indochina and Malaysia-Indonesia-Singapore lines (Simon 1992, 112).

The reverse happened. Chatichai's unilateral pursuit of Thailand's economic and security interests was an aberration. After Vietnam pulled out from Cambodia, ASEAN, instead of splintering, moved in the direction of deeper institutionalization and expansion on the security as well as economic fronts. Two concurrent developments have done much to redefine the nature of the Southeast Asian security complex, its relations with external actors, and its regional order.

The first is the expansion of ASEAN. For twenty years, Vietnam had dismissed ASEAN as a SEATO in disguise or worse; in that sense Barry Buzan's expectation of continued Vietnamese-ASEAN enmity as the defining characteristic of the complex had solid historical foundation. But the global strategic situation underwent such fundamental changes that by the 1990s Vietnam was ready to apply to join ASEAN. In July 1995, it was formally admitted as ASEAN's seventh member. Laos, Cambodia, and Myanmar are to become full members in 1997 or 1998. The Southeast Asian security complex of the late 1990s—the ASEAN-10—is essentially ASEAN writ large over the geographical expanse of what is commonly accepted as Southeast Asia. The amity that has characterized security relations between the original ASEAN-5 since the 1970s should spill over to the new members and continue to define the security dynamic of the enlarged complex. One would expect the TOFAC norms and decision-making procedures that have governed interstate relations in ASEAN—and that have been instrumental in shaping regional peace and order—will continue to be observed.

The second development that bears on the ASEAN-10 security complex and regional order is the advent of the ASEAN Regional Forum (ARF). Building on and modeled after ASEAN's postministerial conference (PMC), the ARF brings together the foreign ministers of ASEAN, ASEAN's dialogue partners—the United States, Japan, Canada, the European Union, South Korea, Australia, and New Zealand—and Russia, China, Vietnam, Laos, Cambodia, and Papua New Guinea for multilateral discussions of Asia-Pacific security issues.[4] Three meetings have been held so far, each preceded by extensive staff work by senior officials. The actual ARF sessions have been informal, restricted to the top principals, with consultations and consensus building being very much the order of the day: in other words, they have been very "ASEAN."

Among the issues taken up are nuclear proliferation on the Korean peninsula, competing claims in the South China Sea, confidence-building measures (CBMs), and the exchange of defense white papers to increase military transparency in the region. In the second meeting in Brunei (1995), working groups on CBMs (chaired by Indonesia and Japan), peacekeeping (chaired by Malaysia and Canada), and search-and-rescue cooperation (chaired by Singapore and the United States) were established. A concept paper, outlining the ARF's future trajectory was also adopted. The paper envisaged security cooperation to unfold in three stages, beginning with CBMs, followed

4. In 1996, India and Myanmar became members of the ARF. Britain and France have expressed interest in participating in the ARF as individual states, separate from their European Union representation.

by the development of preventive diplomacy, and culminating in the elaboration of approaches to conflicts. A substantive result of the Brunei meeting was China's willingness to discuss the South China Sea dispute multilaterally with ASEAN.

Three meetings later, the ARF has become an institution linking the Southeast Asian security complex with that of Northeast Asia and the South Pacific, while including almost all of the other major actors in the Asia-Pacific. It is of course the only such security institution in the Asia-Pacific. The ARF should not be viewed as an "ASEAN security community" writ large. The number of major powers involved in the ARF and their suspicions about one another make it premature to dismiss the possibility that they may still resort to force to settle disputes. More important, despite ASEAN's enviable record, it is still a pluralistic security community in its nascent stages. ASEAN's solidarity is palpable and has grown from strength to strength in the last thirty years, but ASEAN has yet to reach a stage where mutual trust is so strong that using force against member states is unthinkable. The recent incorporation of the Indochinese states into ASEAN suggests that the original bases of ASEAN's "we-feeling" can no longer be taken for granted and that they may need to be periodically reiterated, if not renegotiated, as part of the ASEAN myth.

Analysts are split over the question whether the ARF will play a significant role in the management of post–Cold War order in the Asia-Pacific. Realists informed by changing power distributions and patterns of enmity doubt that such a motley institution will have the wherewithal to deal with a rising China or Japan (Buzan and Segal 1994). Others are more optimistic, focusing as they do on the ability of the ARF to facilitate cooperation, as well as its potential to help rising powers define their interests in sociable ways (Khong 1995a, 1995b). It is too early to tell who is right. Perhaps a more meaningful assessment will be possible when the ARF reconvenes in Bangkok (site of the inaugural meeting) six to eight years from now. If the ARF is still around, if most East Asians feel as secure as they did in the early 1990s, if the ARF has helped prevent rivalry in the South China Sea from degenerating into warfare, and if ARF-sponsored CBMs have checked an arms race, then it may be proclaimed a success. Conversely, if the ARF dies (as did the Association of Southeast Asia, Maphilindo, and SEATO), if arms racing has become a permanent feature of the East Asian military landscape, perhaps because of violent contentions in the South China Sea, then one must conclude that the ARF has failed.

Conclusion

A growing literature has attributed the modicum of order evident in the ASEAN portion of the Southeast Asian security complex to the institution of ASEAN in general and to ASEAN's evolution in the direction of a pluralistic security community in particular. This chapter has sought to refine and elaborate upon this hypothesis by focusing on a critical variable in the making of security communities: the process by which the states come to identify with each other positively and to begin defining their interests with some regard for the other (see Wendt 1994, 386).

Before the formation of ASEAN, negative externalities in the form of ambiguous boundaries, Communist insurgencies, and ethnic conflicts—all with transborder spillover effects—indicated to Malaysia, Indonesia, Philippines, Thailand, and Singapore their regional interconnections and security interdependence. However, as long as Indonesia, the subcomplex's potential hegemon, was led by a leader (Sukarno) who aspired to leadership on a larger stage (e.g., the nonaligned movement), there was not much room for the development of a strong regional consciousness. It was only with Sukarno's departure from the scene that the ASEAN-5 began working toward some form of collective identity. ASEAN was the most important institutional manifestation of that effort. The first decade of ASEAN's existence saw the slow but gradual growth of the ASEAN spirit. This identification with one another facilitated security cooperation, and successful cooperation in turn enhanced the feeling of solidarity. In the second decade, ASEAN solidarity was tested by differing perceptions (within ASEAN) of the Vietnamese threat, but ASEAN emerged intact and strengthened.

By the late 1980s, the security interdependence and cooperation that had been the major impetus behind ASEAN's collective identification also allowed it to reach wider and higher in the form of the ARF. As ASEAN moves toward expanding its membership and reaches out to nest itself in larger multilateral organizations such as the ARF and APEC, it is conceivable that the spirit of togetherness engendered by ASEAN's cooperative ventures in the previous three decades may come under strain. Indeed, notions like the ASEAN-10 and the emergence of institutions like the ARF also suggest that the security dilemmas and disputes of the 1990s—such as rival claims in the South China Sea, nuclear proliferation on the Korean peninsula, and the regional consequences of a strong China—will not be restricted to, or center around, ASEAN or the Southeast Asian security complex. The complex will be implicated in a major way in most of these issues, but the negotiation and resolution of these issues will involve interactions between (1) different security complexes (such as Northeast Asia, Southeast Asia, and the South Pacific), and (2) these complexes and external powers such as the United States. In the short term, these new security dynamics are unlikely to erode ASEAN's collective identity; their medium- to long-term impact, however, is harder to assess. Some ASEAN members, concerned about the centrifugal forces impinging on ASEAN's core identity, have lamented that "[w]hen we [in ASEAN] put on our ARF or APEC suits, some of us seem to be transformed" (*Far Eastern Economic Review,* 29 December 1994). Some transformation will probably be inevitable as ASEAN adapts to its expansion and its participation in numerous multilateral forums; the question is whether enough of the ASEAN spirit can be retained to nurture the nascent pluralistic security community that has been so helpful in providing a modicum of order for the ASEAN states.

Part V

Conclusion

15

Building Security in the New World of Regional Orders

David A. Lake and Patrick M. Morgan

At the end of the Cold War and during the Persian Gulf War, political leaders and commentators alike trumpeted the possibilities for a new world order. Many envisioned a revitalized United Nations and more effective global management of peace and security. Subsequent events in Somalia, Bosnia, Chechnya, Rwanda, and elsewhere have tarnished these once bright hopes for global security. Indeed, many now fear growing disorder and a retreat by the United States into isolationism.

Both the global euphoria and global disillusionment of the post–Cold War era are misplaced. In the preceding chapters, we have tried to show that efforts to cope with conflict and to promote security are frequently occurring within regional security complexes, rather than at the global level. While some issues will undoubtedly continue to be managed at the global level, states increasingly are turning to regional orders for managing conflict.

Rather than a new world order, we are witnessing today a wide variety of new regional orders. As the chapters demonstrate, regional security complexes differ both in their characteristics and in the orders that are evolving within them. While some regional security complexes remain rooted in traditional balance-of-power mechanisms, others are beginning to explore various forms of collective security management and even pluralistic security communities. Both optimists and pessimists today can find confirming evidence for their presumptions in different regions. This suggests, perhaps more than anything else, that to understand security affairs in the contemporary world requires a nuanced and variegated approach, one that takes differences between regional security complexes explicitly into account.

Understanding Regional Orders

The essays in Part II of this volume suggest three major determinants of the regional orders observed in the new, post–Cold War world: regional systems, domestic political coalitions, and the international system, including how the area was embedded into the Cold War, the unique way in which the Cold War ended, and the present motivations of the great powers for regional intervention. The chapters in Part IV, to a greater or lesser degree, confirm the importance of these factors.

In the regional security complex centered on Southeast Asia, dense regional externalities have helped political leaders identify their common interests and facilitated the development of an effective institution for cooperation (Khong, this volume). Likewise, in Africa, an emerging insecurity dilemma is prompting the development of a nascent collective security system (Keller, this volume). Despite these examples, however, it does not follow from the cases examined here that denser externalities always motivate states to adopt "higher" or more cooperative regional orders. Among the Soviet successor states, for instance, dense local externalities have nonetheless produced—or at least coexist with—a hegemonic regional order (Roeder, this volume). While the concept of local externalities may be helpful in identifying the extent and nature of a regional security complex, they are clearly only one of many causal variables that shape a regional order. At the very least, analysts must examine how relevant externalities coexist and possibly interact with other factors.

Within regional security complexes, the political structure of each area is a major constraint on the type of regional order adopted. The overriding—even primordial—importance of this variable is demonstrated most clearly in Latin America and the former Soviet states (Mares and Roeder, respectively). In these two regional security complexes, the dominant position of one state, the United States or Russia, both conditions the nature of political relations and inhibits the emergence of more cooperative orders that might constrain and possibly emerge as competitors to these hegemonic states at some future date. As noted in the first chapter to this volume, and in the chapters by Mares and Roeder, the role of these dominant states is a double-edged sword: on the one hand, they can provide a measure of stability in the regional security complex; on the other hand, they simultaneously pose the most serious threats to the security of others. Perhaps ironically, the least progress in moving beyond traditional power-balancing strategies has occurred in the two regional security complexes dominated by the Cold War superpowers; at present there seems little prospect this will change.

These "hegemonic" outcomes contrast in interesting ways with those in the Middle East security complex, where Israel is a regional power that cannot be defeated by others but nonetheless lacks the ability to dominate the area, and East Asia, where the four great powers of China, Japan, the United States, and Russia all compete and cooperate within the regional security complex. In both, although power balancing remains the default strategy, countries are exploring and beginning to develop more cooperative orders. Finally, in both the African and Southeast Asian regional complexes, multipolarity has prompted states to develop in varying degrees multilateral cooperative security organizations and, possibly in the case of ASEAN, a regional pluralistic security community. The structure of the regional system appears to set the basic parameters within which states can pursue their interests. While multipolar distributions of power are not necessarily conducive to more cooperative orders, this does appear to be the case in several regional security complexes—suggesting either that the appraisals of some analysts are overly pessimistic (Mearsheimer 1990) or that regional multipolarity differs in some important but as yet poorly understood ways from its global counterpart.

Domestic political coalitions also appear important for regional conflict management. Etel Solingen (this volume) differs from other "second-image" analysts by recognizing that, at least in security affairs, the domestic regime itself does not drive variations in policy but that the internal regimes of states together can influence the regional order. Two or more strong, economically liberalizing states are most likely to pursue cooperative security policies. Although not a major theme of Solingen's chapter, postwar Europe may be the paramount case of a cluster of liberalizing states deeply intent on the cooperative management of security affairs. Southeast Asia also provides important support for Solingen's thesis; here, liberalizing coalitions within nearly all of the states have come together to build and support a more cooperative regional order. This has also been a factor behind the emergence of a nascent East Asian concert and, in turn, will help keep the United States deeply rooted in the regional security complex. Paul Papayoanou complements this argument, and focuses on the crucial role of the great powers in regional intervention; where the great powers possess deep economic ties with members of the regional security complex, their attempts to balance power within the area will be more credible and, therefore, effective.

Yet, domestic political coalitions are, like regional systems, facilitative rather than deterministic. In the Soviet successor states and Latin America, for example, the nature of the coalitions in power and the type of regional order that is emerging do not correlate tightly. In Africa, while it has perhaps not experienced the extremes in economic and political orientations found in other regions, and in the Middle East, efforts at collective security have emerged despite the presence of decidedly mixed regimes.

Finally, how the regional security complex was and is today embedded into the larger international system is also important. As Arthur Stein and Steven Lobell argue, how a particular complex was integrated into the Cold War and the way in which the superpower competition ended have influenced the regional security agenda. In many ways, the end of the Cold War was a common exogenous shock to all regions—and the shift to regional security management is driven by this factor. Nonetheless, the response of different areas varies by the way in which the regional security complex was subsumed within that previous conflict. Obviously, conflict management among the Soviet successor states has changed more dramatically than in Latin America; the Cold War ended not with a political condominium between the two superpowers but with the internal collapse of one side—accompanied by its political delegitimation and the need for extensive political and economic reconstruction in its sphere of influence. Middle Eastern states, able to engage in high levels of conflict during the Cold War by drawing in outside powers and resources, have moved toward more conciliatory relations in the new, unipolar world. Many of the more radical regimes have lost their external support and, in turn, some of their political legitimacy, and the moderates have recognized more fully the benefits of compromise. Although East Asia had already become more multipolar by the end of the Cold War, it is also coping with the collapse of the Soviet Union, rising tensions between the United

States and Japan and China, and the consequences of a more fluid political environment in the area.

In Africa, which was less deeply integrated into the Cold War than, say, the Middle East, the states of the region are primarily coping with the large residue of weapons built up during the superpower race for influence and the diminished incentives for outside powers to offer assistance. This is particularly true in the Horn of Africa. Among the states of Southeast Asia, interestingly, cooperation emerged in part as a reaction against the Cold War and the destructive conflicts arising from it that threatened to unfold within the area and that actually did unfold in Indochina. The end of the Cold War has not altered the basic nature of the complex, but has allowed the states of the region to pursue the integration of their own cooperative regional order into the broader Asia-Pacific environment.

What we do not see these days is as significant as what we have just described. We do not see security pursued within and through the same kinds of relationships and practices in all parts of the world. In marked contrast to the Cold War era, we do not see global political considerations leading to the consistent imposition of global issues, institutions, or orders on all regional security complexes. We do not even see the end of the Cold War affecting different complexes in similar ways. As a result, we cannot explain what unipolarity, multipolarity, or some other arrangement of the global system will mean at and for the regional level, even when actors of global stature are immersed in a regional security complex. What we do see is a rich mosaic of regional security complexes and regional orders.

This has two important theoretical implications. First, as highlighted in Chapter 1, to understand contemporary world politics, we must undertake the comparative study of the international politics of regions. This does not mean treating each region as unique. Rather, it means identifying and understanding the dimensions along which regions vary. Second, general theories of international politics, developed largely at the global level, will not be consistently appropriate or helpful in explaining regional order. While theories drawn from the global level may sometimes provide insight into regional relations, they may at other times prove equally misleading. Great care must be taken in applying general theories of international relations to regional relations. The regional level must be both studied on its own and, in turn, integrated into the broader study of international relations and foreign policy.

A very important direction for future research, as noted in Chapter 1, is the study of the interaction between the causal processes discussed earlier.

For instance, the local externalities emphasized by Lake are obviously a function both of decisions taken by domestic regimes and of strategic interactions within the broader international environment. The varying policies countries choose to pursue can create greater or smaller regional externalities. Likewise, as Lake notes in Chapter 3 (see also Stein and Lobell, this volume), the Cold War globalized many local spillovers; it is not so much that the nature of the local externalities has changed in recent years but rather that the externalities that exist are now more independent of global politics.

Similarly, the liberalizing coalitions central to Solingen's argument may actually be endogenous to the regional system; in Roeder's view (this volume), for instance, political leaders assemble the domestic coalition, in conjunction with resources from the dominant regional power, that is most likely to ensure their own political survival. Political coalitions may not be fixed, but rather the outcome of regional political interactions. Even in a second-image argument as sophisticated as Solingen's, much still depends upon the broader regional and global systems.

International politics as a whole is a seamless web of strategic interactions among different actors (see Lake and Powell 1995). Much interesting and important work has proceeded through conceptual experiments that focus on varying one characteristic while explicitly or implicitly holding other factors constant. For much of the foreseeable future, these sorts of conceptual experiments will continue to define the state of the art in the field of international relations. Our focus on regional security complexes adds another layer of complexity in these strategic interactions, another layer of possible conflict and cooperation as actors seek their desired ends. But focusing on regions does not by itself integrate the levels of analysis.

Politics at the regional level is becoming increasingly important to states as they seek security in the post–Cold War world. Analysis pitched at the level of the global system, as a result, will have less explanatory power than before. Regions will and must become a greater focus of our attention as we seek to unravel, understand, and possibly influence the choices states make. As noted, however, we must also aspire to create better theories that explicitly capture the interaction of domestic, regional, and global politics. The studies in this volume point in several interesting directions on this score, highlighting the endogenous nature of domestic coalitions, externalities, and global systems.

Many chapters also highlight the important interaction between the material constraints that shape the choices of actors and the cognitive constructions actors use to order and interpret their environment. Material conditions matter most in extremely "tight" systems of constraints or over the long run, as systems select out through evolutionary processes certain types of behaviors or kinds of actors. Constructed identities and interests may often matter, but will prove poor guides to policy or behavior if they are consistently at variance with the underlying reality. Future research needs to identify more clearly how constraints and cognition interact to produce regional security complexes and orders—as well as how they define the choices available to decision makers.

American Foreign Policy in a World of Regional Orders

The perspective developed in this volume is of more than theoretical interest. It implies a necessity to refocus the design and implementation of foreign policy and provides a means for achieving this analytic shift. This is especially important for the United States in the current era.

During the Cold War, the United States, not inappropriately, thought in global terms and played the game of international politics on a global scale. Events in one area were understood as linked to events everywhere, if only through their effects on national reputation. Rightly or wrongly, the hallmarks of American policy across many areas of the globe were consistency, clarity, and precedent—all pursued in the name of global deterrence of a single, hostile adversary. Today, the primary challenge before the United States is to adapt to the new regionalism in security affairs and adjust its policy to the varying needs of differing regions. To meet this challenge, the United States must—while acknowledging the continuing importance of consistency in global affairs—achieve a greater degree of regional flexibility in its foreign-policy objectives, principles, and policies.

The United States is deeply embedded in several different regional security complexes, and possesses greater or lesser interests in several more. It is an integral member of the European, Latin American, and East Asian regional security complexes. It is a prominent, if geographically separated, member of the Middle East regional security complex. It follows events in Southeast Asia, South Asia, Africa, and elsewhere with interest, and intervenes occasionally in the affairs of each of these regions. The United States cannot readily retreat from these commitments and responsibilities. At the same time, it cannot impose a false consistency on developments in differing regions of the world. The United States must think and act regionally, not globally. American definitions of the national interest must be more plural than singular; foreign-policy principles must be flexible; and policies must be tailored to fit specific regional needs and developments.

In the midst of this flexibility, consistency must nonetheless be maintained through a general frame of reference. Parallel to our discussion of theories of regions, we do not mean to champion here the view that foreign policy must always respond primarily to unique peoples and their singular cultures and histories. We have tried instead to suggest a typology of regional orders that applies to all regional security complexes. The variation comes in the typology and in the values of the causal variables of regional systems, domestic political coalitions, and the international system. United States foreign policy must respond, in a flexible fashion, to this variation.

An illustration may help make the point. The United States, it is now commonly averred, should champion multilateralism as the foreign-policy strategy best able to manage security in a way that is consistent with American values and interests (Ruggie 1996). In the European security complex, of which the United States is an important member, and particularly in the Western and the (newly defined) central European complexes, multilateralism is the cornerstone of the contemporary regional order. NATO is no longer a classic balance-of-power alliance, but is evolving into a collective security organization that is prepared to undertake regional peacekeeping or peace-enforcing interventions. There are also efforts under way to enlarge NATO and to establish links with nonmembers under which these new operations could be performed in conjunction with nonmembers' forces. This is meant to bulwark continued construction of the pluralistic security community in Europe, which remains the ultimate objective. Even recognizing the limitations of multilateralism (see Job, this volume), it is highly appropriate that the United States concentrate on supporting these endeavors and on building further links of its own to the European order. A policy seeking to restore a balance of power as the true guarantee of European security or one seeking a true great-power concert would violate the objectives of the regional governments and clash with the extant regional order.

On the other hand, in the East Asian security complex, to which the United States also belongs, multilateral security management is in its infancy, and no evidence of political integration can be found. Most governments remain wedded to the balance of power. There are some efforts to move toward limited forms of cooperative security management, notably in the direction of a great-power concert, but they are still preliminary (Shirk, this volume). Thus, when the United States has vigorously endorsed multilateralism in East Asia on economic matters, others suspect that it may press for similar steps on security matters—a course viewed by many in East Asia with misgivings because they see it as out of sync with the regional order. And when the United States advocates multilateralism in security affairs, many fear that it is really preparing to abandon its present responsibilities in the regional power-balancing system. For the United States to pursue multilateralism in East Asia out of a broad commitment to this principle would appear unwise at present.

In the Middle East, the United States participates deeply in a regional security complex that also remains dependent upon power-balancing, although a nascent concert may be forming among some regional powers (Pervin, this volume). Despite or alongside the agreements Israel has with some of its neighbors and the PLO, considerations of relative military power are deemed crucial to order and stability. In the Middle East, the United States contributes directly to the balance of power—through American and Israeli military superiority vis-à-vis Iran, Iraq, Syria, and Libya. The American contribution is believed crucial for order and stability by many states. While some recourse to multilateralism might arise in connection with a general settlement in the Middle East, the relevant actors seem a long way from this at the moment. For the United States to treat this area with the same approach it is using in Europe would also be inappropriate.

A second illustration yields similar conclusions. Even advocates of enlarging NATO acknowledge that in the absence of a threat from the Soviet Union, and if peace continues to flourish in most of Europe, the United States should draw down its forces and limit its direct military engagements in that region. Likewise, in the Soviet successor states and South Asia there is no ready role for U.S. forces. In these hegemonic regional security complexes, the United States would be well advised simply to encourage stability by applauding moderation by all parties and discouraging the acquisition of nuclear weapons by members who dislike the hegemon. In East Asia, on the other hand, where power balancing is widely seen as the basis for order and stability and where the U.S. contribution to that distribution is central, a sharp reduction in American forces might well prove disastrous. And in the Middle East, where American military aid is considered crucial, a substantial reduction in U.S. involvement in the region would also be counterproductive.

Once again, looking for a single set of principles or policies—in this case, the scaling back of military commitments—ignores relevant regional variations and promises to reduce, rather than enhance, American security.

By extension the same is true for other foreign-policy values and strategies, such as promoting democracy and human rights, restraining arms sales, and intervening in domestic conflicts. In some regional security complexes, these actions will make much more sense than in others. In turn, the pursuit (or neglect) of any of these in one complex should not be taken as setting a precedent for American policy in others. This may eventually turn out to be true even for nuclear proliferation, a problem the United States continues to tackle through a global policy because of the perceived importance of reputational concerns in inhibiting countries from developing such weapons.

This discussion implies an additional analytic challenge for American foreign policy. If the management of security in regions varies a good deal, and for good reasons, then the United States needs to decide what security-management arrangement it considers feasible and appropriate in each region. Whether one agrees with the specific arguments developed in this volume, meeting this challenge requires an analysis similar to the one undertaken here. Any analysis would need a typology of regional orders, a means to detect where specific regional security complexes fall on the typology and the direction (if any) in which they are moving, and an examination of the factors propelling states to move toward a particular regional order. Only then could the United States, or others, begin designing policies to shift existing security-management arrangements in more favorable directions.

A thoroughly consistent strategy for global order is appropriate only if the critical components of the security complex are global in nature, dimensions, and location—such as in global multilateral institutions, a global great-power concert, or a global balance of power—or if the management of peace and security is best pursued in the same basic fashion in all regions. We suggest in this volume that neither is true now and neither is likely to be true in the foreseeable future.

The changes required in American policy are not drastic. Even in the Cold War, the United States successfully adapted general principles and objectives to regional and local situations—albeit always within the overriding objective of the containment of Communism. Thus, the preference for democracy was frequently set aside in favor of bolstering anti-Communist regimes, just as the desire for non-Communist systems was relaxed to permit associating with some Communist regimes that were at odds with the Soviet Union. These days, the United States is also not lacking a capacity for pragmatic flexibility on a case-by-case basis. Universalistic rhetoric about democracy is not decisive in many instances of economic assistance, military aid, and arms sales. Isolation and containment of Iraq and Iran coexists with steps toward normal diplomatic and commercial relations with North Korea.

What is needed, therefore, is to put flexibility on a sound and consistent analytical basis by recognizing where, with the passing of the Cold War, the crux of successful security management is located today. Using the regional perspective offered in this volume will not make everything simple. It is never easy to characterize regional orders—they are multifaceted and complicated. Regional security complexes are also potentially quite fluid, as suggested by the recent history of Europe. However, the task of managing security relations within the new world of regions cannot be avoided. Otherwise, the degree of consistency achieved will be counterproductive in all too many instances, while the flexibility that remains will readily deteriorate into ad hoc reactions to events beyond our control.

References

Abdel-Latif, Omayma. 1995. "Saudi *Fatwa* Triggers Controversy." *Al-Ahram Weekly,* 5–11 January, 3.

Abu-Amr, Ziad. 1993. "Hamas: A Historical and Political Background." *Journal of Palestine Studies* 22 (4): 5–19.

ACDA (see U.S. Arms Control and Disarmament Agency).

Acharya, Amitav. 1991. "The Association of Southeast Asian Nations: 'Security Community' or 'Defence Community'?" *Pacific Affairs* 64:159–77.

———. 1992a. "Regionalism and Regime Security in the Third World: Comparing the Origins of the ASEAN and the GCC." In *The Insecurity Dilemma: National Security of Third World States,* edited by Brian L. Job. Boulder, Colo.: Lynne Rienner.

———. 1992b. "Regional Military-Security Cooperation in the Third World: A Conceptual Analysis of the Relevance and Limitations of ASEAN (Association of Southeast Asian Nations)." *Journal of Peace Research* 29:7–21.

———. 1993. "A New Regional Order in South-East Asia: ASEAN in the Post–Cold War Era." Adelphi paper no. 279. International Institute of Security Studies. London: Brassey's Inc.

———. 1994. *An Arms Race in Post–Cold War Asia?* Singapore: Institute of Southeast Asian Studies.

Adler, Emanuel. 1991. "Cognitive Evolution: A Dynamic Approach for the Study of International Relations and Their Progress." In *Progress in Postwar International Relations,* edited by Emanuel Adler and Beverly Crawford. New York: Columbia University Press.

———. 1992. "Europe's New Security Order: A Pluralistic Security Community." In *The Future of European Security,* edited by Beverly Crawford. Berkeley: Center for Germany and European Studies, University of California, Berkeley.

Adler, Emanuel, and Michael N. Barnett. 1994. "Security Communities." Paper presented to the annual meeting of the American Political Science Association (1–4 September), New York.

Adomeit, Hannes. 1995. "Russia as a 'Great Power' in World Affairs: Images and Reality." *International Affairs* 71:35–68.

African Leadership Forum (ALF). 1992. *The Kampala Document: Toward a Conference on Security, Stability, Development, and Cooperation in Africa.* New York: African Leadership Forum.

Agence France Presse. 1995. "OAU Rapid Deployment Force." June 27.

Aggarwal, Vinod K. 1985. *Liberal Protectionism: The International Politics of Organized Textile Trade.* Berkeley and Los Angeles: University of California Press.

Ajami, Fouad. 1978–79. "The End of Pan-Arabism." *Foreign Affairs* 87:355–75.

Al-Ahram Centre for Political and Strategic Studies. 1994. *The Arab Strategic Report 1992.* Cairo: Al-Ahram Center.

Al-Ahram Weekly 1995. "Pacifying the Environment." 23–29 March, 3.
Alagappa, Muthiah. 1991. "Regional Arrangements and International Security: An Evaluation of ZOPFAN." In *Beyond the Cold War in the Pacific,* edited by Miles Kahler. San Diego: Institute on Global Conflict and Cooperation, University of California, San Diego.
———. 1995. "Regionalism and Conflict Management." *Review of International Studies* 21(4): 359–88.
Alan, Ray. 1953. "Palace Politics in the Damascus Oasis." *Commentary* 14 (2): 149–58.
Alchian, Armen A. 1950. "Uncertainty, Evolution, and Economic Theory." *Journal of Political Economy* 58:211–21.
Alexander, Robert J., ed. 1973. *APRISMO.* Kent, Ohio: Kent State University Press.
Allison, Roy, and Phil Williams. 1990. "Superpower Competition and Crisis Prevention in the Third World." In *Superpower Competition and Crisis Prevention in the Third World,* edited by Roy Allison and Phil Williams. Cambridge: Cambridge University Press.
Amate, C.O.C. 1986. *Inside the OAU.* New York: St. Martin's Press.
Ames, Barry. 1987. *Political Survival: Politicians and Public Policy in Latin America.* Berkeley and Los Angeles: University of California Press.
Amsden, Alice H. 1989. "The State and Taiwan's Economic Development." In *Bringing the State Back In,* edited by Peter B. Evans, Dietrich Rueschemeyer, and Theda Skocpol. Cambridge: Cambridge University Press.
Anderson, Jeffrey J. 1995. "The State of the (European) Union: From the Single Market of Maastricht, from Singular Events to General Theories." *World Politics* 47:441–65.
Anderson, Lisa. 1987. "The State in the Middle East and North Africa." *Comparative Politics* 20:1–18.
Anderson, M. S. 1966. *The Eastern Question, 1774–1923.* New York: Macmillan.
Annals. 1991. "Resolving Regional Conflicts: International Perspectives." Vol. 518.
Antolik, Michael. 1990. *ASEAN and the Diplomacy of Accommodation.* Armonk, N.Y.: East Gate Books.
Arad, Ruth W., and Seev Hirsch. 1981. "Peacemaking and Vested Interests: International Economic Transactions." *International Studies Quarterly* 25 (3): 439–68.
Arad, Ruth W., Seev Hirsch, and Alfred Tovias. 1983. *The Economics of Peacemaking: Focus on the Egyptian-Israeli Situation.* New York: St. Martin's Press.
Arian, Asher. 1994. "Israeli Security and the Peace Process: Public Opinion in 1994." Jaffee Center for Strategic Studies Memorandum no. 43, Tel Aviv.
Arian, Asher, and Michal Shamir. 1995. "Two Reversals: Why 1992 Was Not 1977." In *The Elections in Israel, 1992,* edited by Asher Arian and Michal Shamir. Albany: State University of New York Press.
Asad, Hafez al-. 1994. "Al-Asad Addresses People's Assembly." Damascus Syrian Arab Television, 10 September 1994, as translated in Foreign Broadcast Information Service–NES-94-176, 12 September 1994, 41–48.
Asahi Shimbun. 1995. "Constitution and International Cooperation" (editorial). 9 May, 5.
Avidan, Dan. 1994. "Egyptian Official Views Syrian Stand." *Davar,* 1 August, as cited in Foreign Broadcast Information Service–NES-94-147, 1 August, 4.
Axelrod, Robert. 1984. *The Evolution of Cooperation.* New York: Basic Books.

Ayoob, Mohammed. 1986. "Regional Security and the Third World." In *Regional Security in the Third World: Case Studies from Southeast Asia and the Middle East,* edited by Mohammed Ayoob. London: Croom Helm.

———. 1989. "The Third World in the System of States: Acute Schizophrenia or Growing Pains?" *International Studies Quarterly* 33 (1): 67–79.

———. 1991. "India as a Regional Hegemon: External Opportunities and Internal Constraints." *International Journal* 46:420–48.

———. 1992. "The Security Predicament of the Third World State: Reflections on State Making in a Comparative Perspective." In *The Insecurity Dilemma: National Security of Third World States,* edited by Brian L. Job. Boulder, Colo.: Lynne Rienner.

———. 1995. *The Third World Security Predicament: State Making, Regional Conflict, and the International System.* Boulder, Colo.: Lynne Rienner.

Azar, Edward, Paul Jureidini, and Ronald McLaurin. 1978. "Protracted Social Conflict: Theory and Practice in the Middle East." *Journal of Palestine Studies* 8: 41–60.

Azar, Edward, and Chung-in Moon. 1988. "Rethinking Third World National Security." In *National Security in the Third World,* edited by Edward Azar and Chung-in Moon. Aldershot: Edward Elgar.

Bailey, Clinton. 1984. *Jordan's Palestinian Challenge, 1948–1983.* Boulder, Colo.: Westview Press.

Bailey, Samuel L. 1967. *Labor, Nationalism, and Politics in Argentina.* New Brunswick, N.J.: Rutgers University Press.

Ball, Desmond. 1993. "Strategic Culture in the Asia-Pacific Region." *Strategic Studies* 3 (1): 44–74.

———. 1993–94. "Arms and Affluence: Military Acquisitions in the Asia-Pacific Region." *International Security* 18 (3): 78–112.

Ball, Nicole. 1988. *Security and Economy in the Third World.* Princeton: Princeton University Press.

Banks, Jeffrey S. 1991. *Signaling Games in Political Science.* Chur: Harwood Academic Publishers.

Baram, Amatzia. 1990. "Territorial Nationalism in the Middle East." *Middle Eastern Studies* 26:425–48.

Barnds, William. 1972. *India, Pakistan, and the Great Powers.* New York: Praeger.

Barnett, Michael N. 1990. "High Politics Is Low Politics: The Domestic and Systemic Sources of Israeli Security Policy, 1967–1977." *World Politics* 42 (4): 529–62.

———. 1991. "From Cold Wars to Resource Wars: The Coming Decline in U.S.-Israeli Relations?" *Jerusalem Journal of International Relations* 13 (3): 99–119.

———. 1992. *Confronting the Costs of War: Military Power, State, and Society in Egypt and Israel.* Princeton: Princeton University Press.

Barnett, Michael N., and Jack S. Levy. 1991. "Domestic Sources of Alliances and Alignments: The Case of Egypt, 1962–73." *International Organization* 45 (3): 369–96.

Bar-Siman-Tov, Yaacov. 1980. *The Israeli-Egyptian War of Attrition, 1969–1970.* New York: Columbia University Press.

Belokrenitsky, Vyacheslav Ya. 1994. "Russia and Greater Central Asia." *Asian Survey* 34:1093–108.

Bemis, Samuel F. 1955. *A Diplomatic History of the United States.* Rev. ed. New York: Holt.

Ben-Dor, Gabriel. 1983. *State and Conflict in the Middle East: Emergence of the Postcolonial State.* New York: Praeger.

Bergsten, Fred. 1973. "The Threat from the Third World." *Foreign Policy* 11: 102–24.

Betts, Richard. 1993–94. "Wealth, Power, and Instability: East Asia and the United States After the Cold War." *International Security* 18 (3): 34–77.

Bialer, Seweryn. 1986. *The Soviet Paradox: External Expansion, Internal Decline.* New York: Knopf.

Binder, Leonard. 1958. "The Middle East as a Subordinate International System." *World Politics* 10:408–29.

Black, J. L. 1986. *Origins, Evolution, and Nature of the Cold War.* Santa Barbara, Calif.: ABC-CLIO.

Blechman, Barry. 1972. "The Impact of Israel's Reprisals on Behavior of the Bordering Arab Nations Directed at Israel." *Journal of Conflict Resolution* 16:155–81.

Boals, Kay. 1973. "The Concept 'Subordinate International System': A Critique." In *Regional Politics and World Order,* edited by Richard A. Falk and Saul H. Mendlovitz. San Francisco: W. H. Freeman.

Bondarevsky, Grigory, and Peter Ferdinand. 1994. "Russian Foreign Policy and Central Asia." In *The New States of Central Asia and Their Neighbors,* edited by Peter Ferdinand. New York: Council on Foreign Relations Press.

Boulding, Kenneth. 1963. *Conflict and Defense: A General Theory.* New York: Harper Torchbooks.

Boutros-Ghali, Boutros. 1992. *Agenda for Peace.* New York: United Nations.

Brand, Laurie. 1991. "Liberalization and Changing Political Coalitions: The Bases of Jordan's 1990–1991 Gulf Crisis Policy." *Jerusalem Journal of International Relations* 13 (4): 1–46.

Brecher, Michael. 1963. "International Relations and Asian Studies: The Subordinate State System of Southern Asia." *World Politics* 15:213–35.

Brecher, Michael, and Jonathan Wilkenfeld. 1991. "International Crises and Global Instability: The Myth of the 'Long Peace.'" In *The Long Postwar Peace,* edited by Charles W. Kegley. New York: HarperCollins.

Breslauer, George. 1979. "Soviet Policy in the Middle East, 1967–1972: Unalterable Antagonism or Collaborative Competition." In *Managing U.S.-Soviet Rivalry: Problems of Crisis Prevention,* edited by Alexander L. George. Boulder, Colo.: Westview Press.

Breslauer, George W., and Philip E. Tetlock, eds. 1991. *Learning in U.S. and Soviet Foreign Policy.* Boulder, Colo.: Westview Press.

Broinowski, Alison, ed. 1982. *Understanding ASEAN.* London: Macmillan.

Brown, L. Carl. 1984. *International Politics and the Middle East: Old Rules, Dangerous Game.* Princeton: Princeton University Press.

———. 1991. "Nasser and the June 1967 War: Plan or Improvisation?" In *A Question of Understanding,* edited by S. Seikaly, R. Baalbaker, and P. Dodd. Beirut: American University of Beirut.

Brynen, Rex. 1991. "Palestine and the Arab State System: Permeability, State Consolidation, and the *Intifada.*" *Canadian Journal of Political Science* 24:595–621.

———. 1992. "Economic Crisis and Post-Rentier Democratization in the Arab World: The Case of Jordan." *Canadian Journal of Political Science* 25:69–97.

Brzezinski, Zbigniew K. 1967. *The Soviet Bloc: Unity and Conflict.* Rev. and enlarged ed. Cambridge, Mass.: Harvard University Press.

Buchanan, J. M., R. D. Tollison, and G. Tullock, eds. 1980. *Toward a Theory of the Rent-Seeking Society.* College Station: Texas A & M University Press.

Bueno de Mesquita, Bruce, and Randolph M. Siverson. 1995. "War and the Survival of Political Leaders: A Comparative Study of Regime Types and Political Accountability." *American Political Science Review* 89:841–55.

Bull, Hedley. 1977. *The Anarchical Society: A Study of Order in World Politics.* New York: Columbia University Press.

Bunce, Valerie. 1985. "The Empire Strikes Back: The Transformation of the Eastern Bloc from a Soviet Asset to a Soviet Liability." *International Organization* 39: 1–46.

———. 1987. "Soviet Decline as a Regional Hegemon: The Gorbachev Regime and Reform of Eastern Europe." Paper presented at the annual meeting of the American Political Science Association (3–6 September), Chicago.

Burant, Stephen R. 1993. "International Relations in a Regional Context: Poland and Its Eastern Neighbours (Lithuania, Belarus, and Ukraine." *Europe-Asia Studies* 45:395–418.

Burns, E. Bradford. 1966. *The Unwritten Alliance.* New York: Colombia University Press.

Burr, Robert N. 1965. *By Reason or Force.* Berkeley and Los Angeles: University of California Press.

Buzan, Barry. 1983. "Regional Security as a Policy Objective: The Case of South and Southwest Asia." In *The Great Game: Rivalry in the Persian Gulf and South Asia,* edited by Alvin Z. Rubinstein. New York: Praeger.

———. 1986. "A Framework for Regional Security Analysis." In *South Asian Insecurity and the Great Powers,* edited by Barry Buzan and Gowher Rizvi. London: Macmillan.

———. 1988. "The Southeast Asian Security Complex." *Contemporary Southeast Asia* 10 (1): 1–16.

———. 1991. *People, States, and Fear: An Agenda for International Security Studies in the Post–Cold War Era.* 2d ed. Boulder, Colo.: Lynne Rienner.

———. 1992. "Third World Regional Security in Structural and Historical Perspective." In *The Insecurity Dilemma: National Security of Third World States,* edited by Brian L. Job. Boulder, Colo.: Lynne Rienner.

———. 1993. "From International System to International Society: Structural Realism and Regime Theory Meet the English School." *International Organization* 47 (3): 327–52.

———. 1996. "The Timeless Wisdom of Realism?" In *International Theory: Positivism and Beyond,* edited by Steve Smith, Ken Booth, and Marysia Zalewski. Cambridge: Cambridge University Press.

Buzan, Barry, Charles Jones, and Richard Little. 1993. *The Logic of Anarchy: Neorealism to Structural Realism.* New York: Columbia University Press.

Buzan, Barry, Morten Kelstrup, Pierre Lemaitre, Elzbieta Tromer, and Ole Waever. 1990. *The European Security Order Recast: Scenarios for the Post–Cold War Era.* London: Pinter.

Buzan, Barry, and Gerald Segal. 1994. "Rethinking East Asian Security." *Survival* 36 (2): 3–21.

Buzan, Barry, and Ole Waever. 1992. "Framing Nordic Security: European Scenarios for the 1990s and Beyond." In *Nordic Security in the 1990s: Options in the Changing Europe,* edited by Jan Oberg. London: Pinter.

Campbell, Kurt. 1987–88. "Southern Africa in Soviet Foreign Policy." International Institute for Strategic Studies Adelphi paper, London.

Cantori, Louis, and Steven Spiegel, eds. 1970a. *The International Politics of Regions: A Comparative Approach.* Englewood Cliffs, N.J.: Prentice Hall.

———. 1970b. "Introduction: The Subordinate System." In *The International Politics of Regions: A Comparative Approach,* edited by Louis Cantori and Steven Spiegel. Englewood Cliffs, N.J.: Prentice Hall.

Caporaso, James. 1993. "International Relations Theory." In *Multilateralism Matters: The Theory and Praxis of an Institutional Form,* edited by John Ruggie. New York: Columbia University Press.

Cardoso, Eliana, and Ann Helwege. 1991. "Populism, Profligacy, and Redistribution." In *The Macroeconomics of Populism in Latin America,* edited by Rudiger Dornbusch and Sebastian Edwards. Chicago: University of Chicago Press.

Cervo, Amado Luiz, and Clodoaldo Bueno. 1992. *História da política exterior do Brasil.* São Paulo: Editora Atica.

Chan, Heng Chee. 1986. "ASEAN: Subregional Resilience." In *Security Interdependence in the Asia Pacific Region,* edited by James Morley. Lexington, Mass.: Lexington Books.

Chan, Steve. 1984. "Mirror, Mirror on the Wall: Are the Freer Countries More Pacific?" *Journal of Conflict Resolution* 28 (4): 617–48.

———. 1988. "Defense Burden and Economic Growth: Unraveling the Taiwanese Enigma." *American Political Science Review* 82:913–20.

Cheung, Tai Ming. 1996. "The Interaction Between Economics and Security for China's External Relations." In *Power and Prosperity: Economics and Security Linkages in Asia-Pacific,* edited by Susan L. Shirk and Christopher P. Twomey. New Brunswick, N.J.: Transaction Publishers.

Child, Jack. 1980. *Unequal Alliance: The Inter-American Military System, 1938–78.* Boulder, Colo.: Westview Press.

CLADDE (Latin American Center for Defense and Disarmament), ed. 1988. *Estudio estrategico de America Latina,* vol. 2, *Limitacion de armamentos y confianza mutua en America Latin.* Santiago: Ediciones Chile América.

Coase, Ronald. 1960. "The Problem of Social Cost." *Journal of Law and Economics* 3:1–44.

Cobban, Helena. 1984. *The Palestine Liberation Organization: People, Power, and Politics.* Cambridge: Cambridge University Press.

Cohen, Raymond. 1990. *Culture and Conflict in Egyptian-Israeli Relations: A Dialogue of the Deaf.* Bloomington: Indiana University Press.

———. 1994. "Culture Gets in the Way: Negotiations Across the Golan Heights." *Middle East Quarterly* 1 (3): 45–53.

Cohen, Saul. 1991. "Global Geopolitical Change in the Post–Cold War Era." *Annals of the Association of American Geographers* 81:551–80.

———. 1994. "Geopolitics in the New World Era: A New Perspective on an Old Discipline." In *Reordering the World: Geopolitical Perspectives on the Twenty-First Century,* edited by George Demko and William Wood. Boulder, Colo.: Westview Press.

Cohen, Stephen P. 1994. "A Not-So-Odd Mideast Couple." *New York Times,* 25 August, A21.

Combs, John. 1983. *American Diplomatic History: Two Centuries of Changing Interpretations.* Berkeley and Los Angeles: University of California Press.

Connell-Smith, Gordon. 1974. *The United States and Latin America.* New York: Wiley.

Cooper, Andrew F., Richard A. Higgott, and Kim R. Nossall. 1993. *Relocating Middle Powers: Australia and Canada in a Changing World Order.* Vancouver: University of British Columbia Press.

Cooper, Richard. 1968. *The Economics of Interdependence: Economic Policy in the Atlantic Community.* New York: Columbia University Press.

Copson, Raymond, and Richard Cronin. 1987. "The 'Reagan Doctrine' and Its Prospects." *Survival* 29:40–55.

Cornes, Richard, and Todd Sandler. 1986. *The Theory of Externalities, Public Goods, and Club Goods.* New York: Cambridge University Press.

Cottam, Martha L. 1994. *Images of Intervention.* Pittsburgh: University of Pittsburgh Press.

Council on Foreign Relations (CFR). 1995. *The Casablanca Report.* New York: Council on Foreign Relations.

Cowell, Alan. 1993. "Turkey Loses Its Allure as a Patron in Central Asian Nations." *New York Times,* 4 August, A3.

Cowhey, Peter F. 1990. "'States' and 'Politics' in American Foreign Policy." In *International Trade Policies: Gains from Exchange Between Economics and Political Science,* edited by John S. Odell and Thomas D. Willett. Ann Arbor: University of Michigan Press.

Cox, Robert W. 1986. "Social Forces, States, and World Orders: Beyond International Relations Theory." In *Neorealism and Its Critics,* edited by Robert O. Keohane. New York: Columbia University Press.

Crystal, Jill. 1994. "Authoritarianism and Its Adversaries in the Arab World." *World Politics.* 46: 262–89.

CSIS (Center for Strategic and International Studies, Jakarta). 1974. "Regional Cooperation in International Politics." In *Regionalism in Southeast Asia.* Jakarta: CSIS.

Damrosch, Lori Fishler, ed. 1993. *Enforcing Restraint: Collective Intervention in Internal Conflicts.* New York: Council on Foreign Relations Press.

David, Steven R. 1989. "Why the Third World Matters." *International Security* 14: 50–85.

———. 1991a. *Choosing Sides: Alignment and Realignment in the Third World.* Baltimore: Johns Hopkins University Press.

———. 1991b. "Explaining Third World Alignment." *World Politics* 43:233–56.

Davidson, Basil. 1992. *Black Man's Burden: Nationalism and the Curse of the Nation-State in Africa.* New York: Random House.

Dawisha, Adeed. 1980. *Syria and the Lebanese Crisis.* New York: St. Martin's Press.

Dawn, C. Ernest. 1968. "The Egyptian Remilitarization of Sinai, May 1967." *Journal of Contemporary History* 3:201–24.

Dehio, Ludwig. 1962. *The Precarious Balance.* New York: Knopf.

De Luca, Anthony. 1977. "Soviet American Policy and the Turkish Straits." *Political Science Quarterly* 92:503–24.

Deng, Francis, et al. 1996. *Sovereignty as Responsibility: Conflict Management in Africa.* Washington, D.C.: Brookings Institution.

Denoon, David B. H. 1993. *Real Reciprocity: Balancing U.S. Economic and Security Policy in the Pacific Basin.* New York: Council on Foreign Relations Press.

Deutsch, Karl, et al. 1957. *Political Community and the North Atlantic Area: International Organization in the Light of Historical Experience.* Princeton: Princeton University Press.

Dewitt, David. 1994. "Comprehensive, Common, and Cooperative Security." *Pacific Review* 7 (1): 1–15.

Dewitt, David, David Haglund, and John Kirton. 1993. *Building a New Global Order: Emerging Trends in International Security.* New York: Oxford University Press.

Diab, M. Zuhair. 1994a. "Have Syria and Israel Opted for Peace?" *Middle East Policy* 3 (1): 77–90.

———. 1994b. "The Prospects for Peace Between Israel and Syria: A Syrian View." In *Israel at the Crossroads: Challenge of Peace,* edited by Efraim Karsh and Gregory Mahler. London: British Academic Press.

———. 1995. "An Arms Control Regime for an Arab-Israeli Settlement." In *Practical Peacemaking in the Middle East: Arms Control and Regional Security,* edited by Steven Spiegel and David J. Pervin. New York: Garland Publishing.

Diehl, Paul. 1993. *International Peacekeeping.* New Haven: Yale University Press.

Dishon, Daniel, and Bruce Maddy-Weitzman. 1984. "Inter-Arab Relations." In *Middle East Contemporary Survey,* vol. 6, *1981–82,* edited by Colin Legum, Haim Shaked, and Daniel Dishon. New York: Holmes & Meier.

di Tella, Guido, and D. Cameron Watt, eds. 1990. *Argentina and the Great Powers, 1939–46.* Pittsburgh: University of Pittsburgh Press.

Djiwandono, J. Soedjati. 1991. *ASEAN: An Emerging Regional Security Community?* Center for Strategic and International Studies, paper M61/91, Jakarta.

DOD (see U.S. Department of Defense).

Dominguez, Jorge I. 1984. "Ghosts from the Past: War, Territorial and Boundary Disputes in Mainland Central and South America Since 1960." Typescript, Department of Government, Harvard University.

———. 1989. *To Make the World Safe for Revolution: Cuba's Foreign Policy.* Cambridge: Harvard University Press.

Doran, Charles. 1989. "Globalist-Regionalist Debate." In *Intervention in the 1980s: U.S. Foreign Policy in the Third World,* edited by Peter Schraeder. Boulder, Colo.: Lynne Rienner.

———. 1991. "Conflict and Cooperation: Between the Cold War and the Gulf." *Annals of the American Academy of Political and Social Science* 518 : 155–64.

Douglas, Roy. 1977. *In the Year of Munich.* London: Macmillan.

Doyle, Michael W. 1986. "Liberalism and World Politics." *American Political Science Review* 80 (4): 1151–69.

Druckman, Daniel. 1980. "Social-Psychological Factors in Regional Politics." In *Comparative Regional Systems,* edited by Werner Feld and Gavin Boyd. New York: Pergamon Press.

Dulles, Foster Rhea. [1965] 1971. *Prelude to World Power.* New York: Macmillan.

Dunlop, John B. 1993–94. "Russia: Confronting a Loss of Empire, 1987–1991." *Political Science Quarterly* 108 : 603–34.

Eggertsson, Thráinn. 1990. *Economic Behavior and Institutions.* New York: Cambridge University Press.

Eichengreen, Barry. 1989. *Elusive Stability*. New York: Cambridge University Press.

———. 1992. *Golden Fetters*. New York: Oxford University Press.

Einaudi, Luigi. 1991. "La política hemisferica de Estados Unidos en la decada actual." *Fuerzas Armadas y Sociedad* 6 (1): 28–29.

Eisenstadt, Michael. 1992. *Arming for Peace? Syria's Elusive Quest for "Strategic Parity."* Washington, D.C.: Washington Institute for Near East Policy.

EIU. 1995. *Syria: A Country Report* (2d quarter).

El-Din, Gamal Essam. 1995. "Protests Greet Israeli Visitors." *Al-Ahram Weekly*, 23–29 March, 2.

Elon, Amos. 1995. "One Foot on the Moon." *New York Review of Books*, 6 April, 32–36.

Elrod, Richard. 1976. "The Concert of Europe: A Fresh Look at an International System." *World Politics* 28 (2): 159–74.

English, Adrian J. 1984. *Armed Forces of Latin America*. London: Jane's.

English, Adrian J., with Anthony Watts. 1982. *Battle for the Falklands*, vol. 2, *Naval Forces*. London: Osprey.

Evans, Peter B., Harold K. Jacobson, and Robert D. Putnam, eds. 1993. *Double-Edged Diplomacy: International Bargaining and Domestic Politics*. Berkeley and Los Angeles: University of California Press.

Evron, Yair. 1987. *War and Intervention in Lebanon: The Israeli-Syrian Deterrence Dialogue*. Baltimore: Johns Hopkins University Press.

———. 1994. "Gulf Crisis and War: Regional Rules of the Game and Policy and Theoretical Implications." *Security Studies* 4 (1): 115–54.

Fairbank, John K., ed. 1968. *The Chinese World Order: Traditional China's Foreign Relations*. Cambridge, Mass.: Harvard University Press.

———, ed. 1972. *The United States and China*. Cambridge, Mass.: Harvard University Press.

Faksh, Mahmud. 1993. "Asad's Westward Turn: Implications for Syria." *Middle East Policy* 2 (3): 49–61.

Falk, Richard, and Saul Mendlovitz, eds. 1973. *Regional Politics and World Order*. San Francisco: W. H. Freeman.

Far East Economic Review (FEER). 1994. December 29.

Fawcett, Louise L'estrange. 1992. *Iran and the Cold War: The Azerbaijan Crisis of 1946*. Cambridge: Cambridge University Press.

Fearon, James D. 1995. "Rational Explanations for War." *International Organization* 49:379–414.

Feigenbaum, Harvey B., and Jeffry R. Henig. 1994. "The Political Underpinnings of Privatization: A Typology." *World Politics* 46:185–208.

Fein, Aharon. 1995. "Voting Trends of Recent Immigrants from the Former Soviet Union." In *The Elections in Israel, 1992*, edited by Asher Arian and Michal Shamir. Albany: State University of New York Press.

Feis, Herbert. 1967. *Churchill, Roosevelt, and Stalin*. Princeton: Princeton University Press.

Feld, Werner J., and Gavin Boyd, eds. 1980. *Comparative Regional Systems: West and East Europe, North America, the Middle East, and Developing Countries*. New York: Pergamon Press.

Fellner, William. 1965. *Competition Among the Few*. New York: Augustus M. Kelley.

Fiqi, Mona el-. 1995. "Cairo Fair: The Politics of Business." *Al-Ahram Weekly*, 23–29 March, 3.

Flannigan, William. 1992. *A Complicated War.* Berkeley and Los Angeles: University of California Press.

Flynn, Gregory, and David J. Scheffer. 1990. "Limited Collective Security." *Foreign Policy* 80:77–101.

Fontana, Andres, and Augusto Varas. 1992. "Percepciones y opiniones sobre las fuerzas armadas en Argentina y Chile: Analisis comparativo de dos estudios." *Fuerzas Armadas y Sociedad* 7 (2): 30–35.

Foye, Stephen. 1993. "End of CIS Command Heralds New Russian Defense Policy?" *RFE/RL Research Report* 2 (2 July): 45–49.

Francis, Michael J. 1977. *The Limits of Hegemony.* Notre Dame, Ind.: University of Notre Dame Press.

Freedman, Robert. 1975. *Soviet Policy Toward the Middle East Since 1970.* New York: Praeger.

———. 1990. "The Superpowers and the Middle East." In *Superpower Competition and Crisis Prevention in the Third World,* edited by Roy Allison and Phil Williams. Cambridge: Cambridge University Press.

Friedberg, Aaron. 1993–94. "Ripe for Rivalry: Prospects for Peace in a Multipolar Asia." *International Security* 18:5–33.

Frieden, Jeff. 1988. "Sectoral Conflict and U.S. Foreign Economic Policy, 1914–1940." In *The State and American Foreign Economic Policy,* edited by G. John Ikenberry, David A. Lake, and Michael Mastanduno. Ithaca: Cornell University Press.

Friedman, James W. 1971. "A Noncooperative Equilibrium for Supergames." *Review of Economic Studies* 38:1–12.

———. 1977. *Oligopoly and the Theory of Games.* Amsterdam: North-Holland Publishing.

Frohmann, Alicia. 1989. "De contadora al grupo de los ocho: El reaprendizaje de la concertación política regional." *Estudios Internacionales* 22 (87): 365–427.

Fromouth, Peter. 1993. "The Making of a Security Community: The UN After the Cold War." *Journal of International Affairs* 46 (2): 341–66.

Fudenberg, Drew, and E. Maskin. 1986. "The Folk Theorem in Repeated Games with Discounting or Incomplete Information" *Econometrica* 54:533–54.

Fukuyama, Francis. 1989. "The End of History?" *National Interest* 25:3–18.

Fuller, Elizabeth. 1993. "Russia's Diplomatic Offensive in the Transcaucasus." *RFE/RL Research Report* 2 (1 October): 30–34.

Funabashi, Yoichi. 1991–92. "Japan and the New World Order." *Foreign Affairs* 70 (5): 58–74.

Fusfield, Daniel R. 1988. *Economics: Principles of Political Economy.* 3d ed. Glenview, Ill.: Scott, Foresman.

Gaddis, John Lewis. 1982. *Strategies of Containment: A Critical Appraisal of Postwar American National Security Policy.* New York: Oxford University Press.

———. 1986. "The Long Peace: Elements of Stability in the Postwar International System." *International Security* 10:99–142.

———. 1987. *The Long Peace: Inquiries into the History of the Cold War.* New York: Oxford University Press.

Gallicchio, Marc. 1988. *The Cold War Begins in Asia: American East Asian Policy and the Fall of the Japanese Empire.* New York: Columbia University Press.

Gamba, Virginia. 1987. *The Falklands/Malvinas War.* Boston: Allen & Unwin.

Gannon, Francis X. 1982. "Globalism Versus Regionalism: U.S. Policy and the OAS." *Orbis* 26:195–221.
Gardner, Lloyd. 1993. *Spheres of Influence: The Great Powers Partition Europe: From Munich to Yalta.* Chicago: Ivan R. Dee.
Garthoff, Raymond. 1994. *The Great Transition: American-Soviet Relations and the End of the Cold War.* Washington, D.C.: Brookings Institution.
Gause, F. Gregory. 1991. "Revolutionary Fevers and Regional Contagion: Domestic Structures and the 'Export' of Revolution in the Middle East." *Journal of South Asian and Middle Eastern Studies* 14 (3): 1–23.
———. 1992. "Sovereignty, Statecraft, and Stability in the Middle East." *Journal of International Affairs* 45:441–69.
Geddes, Barbara. 1994. *Politician's Dilemma: Building State Capacity in Latin America.* Berkeley and Los Angeles: University of California Press.
Geller, Sheldon. 1992. "All in the Family: France in Black Africa, 1958–1990." *Asian and African Studies* 26 (2): 109–23.
George, Alexander. 1983. "Crisis Prevention Reexamined." In *Managing U.S.-Soviet Rivalry: Problems of Crisis Prevention,* edited by Alexander George. Boulder, Colo.: Westview Press.
Gerges, Fawaz. 1995. "Egyptian-Israeli Relations Turn Sour." *Foreign Affairs* 74 (3): 69–78.
Ghani, Husayn 'abd-al. 1995. "Egypt's Musa on Ties, NPT, Peace Process." *Al-Hayah,* 18 March, as cited in Foreign Broadcast Information Service–NES-95-057, 24 March, 17–20.
Ghazali bin Shafie Muhammed. 1994. "Partnership in Spirit and Togetherness." *New Straits Times* (Malaysia), 4 June.
Gilpin, Robert. 1970. "The Politics of Transnational Economic Relations." In *Transnational Relations and World Politics,* edited by Robert O. Keohane and Joseph S. Nye Jr. Cambridge, Mass.: Harvard University Press.
———. 1987. *The Political Economy of International Relations.* Princeton: Princeton University Press.
Glassman, Jon. 1975. *Arms for the Arabs.* Baltimore: Johns Hopkins University Press.
Goble, Paul. 1992. "Forget the Soviet Union." *Foreign Policy* 86:56–65.
———. 1993. "Russia and Its Neighbors." *Foreign Policy* 90:79–88.
Gochman, Charles S., and Zeev Maoz. 1984. "Militarized Interstate Disputes, 1816–1976." *Journal of Conflict Resolution* 28 (4): 585–616.
Golan, Galia. 1991. "Superpower Cooperation in the Middle East." In *The Cold War as Cooperation,* edited by Roger E. Kanet and Edward A. Kolodziej. Baltimore: Johns Hopkins University Press.
Goldberg, Joyce S. 1986. *The Baltimore Affair.* Lincoln: University of Nebraska Press.
Goldgeier, James, and Michael McFaul. 1992. "A Tale of Two Worlds: Core and Periphery in the Post–Cold War Era." *International Organization* 46:467–91.
Goldman, Emily O. 1994. *Sunken Treaties: Naval Arms Control Between the Wars.* University Park: Pennsylvania State University Press.
Goltz, Thomas. 1993. "Letter from Eurasia: The Hidden Russian Hand." *Foreign Policy* 92:92–116.
Goose, Stephen, and Frank Smyth. 1994. "Arming Genocide in Rwanda." *Foreign Affairs* 73 (5): 97–108.

Gordon, Michael. 1974. "Domestic Conflict and the Origins of the First World War." *Journal of Modern History* 46:191–226.
Gourevitch, Peter. 1978. "The Second-Image Reversed: The International Sources of Domestic Politics." *International Organization* 32:881–911.
———. 1986. *Politics in Hard Times: Comparative Responses to International Economic Crises.* Ithaca: Cornell University Press.
Gowa, Joanne. 1994. *Allies, Adversaries, and International Trade.* Princeton: Princeton University Press.
Gowa, Joanne, and Edward Mansfield. 1993. "Power Politics and International Trade." *American Political Science Review* 87:408–20.
Granot, Oded. 1994. "Musa Interviewed on Ties with Israel." *Maariv (Sof Shavua supplement),* 25 November, as cited by Foreign Broadcast Information Service–NES-94-228, 28 November, 19–22.
Greenberg, Joel. 1994. "Settlement Vows Fight on Peace Plan." *New York Times,* 21 February, A4.
———. 1995. "Zofar Journal: Israel's Crops in Jordan's Fields? It Must Be Peace." *New York Times,* 28 March, A4.
Greenhouse, Steven. 1995. "Rabin Tells U.S. Lawmakers Aid Cuts Would Hurt Peace Efforts." *New York Times,* 9 May, A7.
Gros Espiell, Hector. 1986. *Conflictos territoriales en Iberoamerica y solucion pacifica de controversias.* Madrid: Ediciones Cultura Hispánica.
Gruner, Wolf. 1992. "Was There a Reformed Balance of Power System of Cooperative Great Power Hegemony?" *American Historical Review* 97:725–32.
Gurr, Ted Robert, Keith Jaggers, and Will H. Moore. 1994. Updated version by Keith Jaeggers. *Polity II.* Boulder: University of Colorado.
Haas, Ernst. 1958. *The Uniting of Europe: Political, Social, and Economic Forces.* Stanford: Stanford University Press.
———. 1990. *When Knowledge Is Power: Three Models of Change in International Organizations.* Berkeley and Los Angeles: University of California Press.
Haas, Michael. 1989. *The Pacific Way: Regional Cooperation in the South Pacific.* New York: Praeger.
Haberman, Clyde. 1995a. "Now, the Tough Issue: Palestinian Refugees." *New York Times,* 9 March, A3.
———. 1995b. "Israel Suspends Its Plan to Seize Land in Jerusalem." *New York Times,* 23 May, A1.
Habte Selassie, Berekat. 1989. *Eritrea and the United Nations.* Trenton, N.J.: Red Sea Press.
Hagan, Joe. 1984. "Development and the Evolving Foreign Policy Orientations of Middle East Regimes." *Journal of Asian and African Studies* 19:240–62.
Haggard, Stephan, and Robert R. Kaufman, eds. 1992. *The Politics of Economic Adjustment.* Princeton: Princeton University Press.
Haglund, David G. 1984. *Latin America and the Transformation of U.S. Strategic Thought, 1936–1940.* Albuquerque: University of New Mexico Press.
Haley, P. Edward, and Lewis Snider, eds. 1979. *Lebanon in Crisis: Participants and Issues.* Syracuse, N.Y.: Syracuse University Press.
Halliday, Fred. 1995. "The Empires Strike Back? Russia, Iran, and the New Republics." *World Today* 51:220–22.
Hampson, Fen Osler, and Brian S. Mandell. 1990. "Managing Regional Conflict:

Security Cooperation and Third Party Mediators." *International Journal* 45: 191–201.

Handel, Michael. 1982. "Does the Dog Wag the Tail or Vice Versa? Patron-Client Relations." *Jerusalem Journal of International Relations* 6:24–35.

Hannah, John. 1989. *At Arms Length: Soviet-Syrian Relations in the Gorbachev Era.* Washington, D.C.: Washington Institute for Near East Policy.

Hannan, Michael, and John Freeman. 1977. "The Population Ecology of Organizations." *American Journal of Sociology* 82:929–64.

Harik, Ilya. 1990. "The Origins of the Arab State System." In *The Arab State,* edited by Giacomo Luciani. Berkeley and Los Angeles: University of California Press.

Harkavy, Robert. 1977. *Preemption and Two-Front Conventional Warfare: A Comparison of 1967 Israeli Strategy with the Pre–World War One German Schlieffen Plan.* Jerusalem Papers on Peace Problems, no. 23. Jerusalem: Leonard David Institute of the Hebrew University.

Haskel, Barbara G. 1980. "Access to Society: A Neglected Dimension of Power." *International Organization* 34 (1): 89–120.

Hedges, Chris. 1995. "In Cairo, Israel and Arabs Back Peace Talks." *New York Times,* 3 February, A1.

Henkin, Louis, et al. 1989. *Right v. Might; International Law and the Use of Force.* New York: Council on Foreign Relations Press.

Henze, Paul. 1992. "Ethiopia in Transition." *Ethiopian Review,* July, 5–8.

Herbst, Jeffrey. 1990. "War and the State in Africa." *International Security.* 14 (4): 117–39.

Herring, George. 1977. "The Truman Administration and the Restoration of French Sovereignty in Indochina." *Diplomatic History* 1:97–117.

Hess, Gary. 1974. "The Iranian Crisis of 1945–46 and the Cold War." *Political Science Quarterly* 89:117–46.

———. 1987. *The United States' Emergence as a Southeast Asian Power, 1940–1950.* New York: Columbia University Press.

Heydemann, Steven. 1992. "The Political Logic of Economic Rationality: Selective Stabilization in Syria." In *The Politics of Economic Reform in the Middle East,* edited by Henri J. Barkey. New York: St. Martin's Press.

———. 1993. "Taxation Without Representation: Authoritarianism and Economic Liberalization in Syria." In *Rules and Rights in the Middle East: Democracy, Law, and Society,* edited by Ellis Goldberg, Reset Kasaba, and Joel Migdal. Seattle: University of Washington Press.

Hilton, Stanley E. 1991. *Brazil and the Soviet Challenge.* Austin: University of Texas Press.

Hinnebusch, Raymond. 1993a. "Asad's Syria and the New World Order: The Struggle for Regime Survival." *Middle East Policy* 2 (1): 1–14.

———. 1993b. "State and Civil Society in Syria." *Middle East Journal* 47:229–57.

———. 1995. "Syria: The Politics of Peace and Regime Survival." *Middle East Policy* 3 (4): 74–87.

Hinsley, F. H. 1963. *Power and the Pursuit of Peace: Theory and Practice in the History of Relations Between the States.* Cambridge: Cambridge University Press.

Hirschman, Albert O. [1945] 1980. *National Power and the Structure of Foreign Trade.* Berkeley and Los Angeles: University of California Press.

———. 1982. *Shifting Involvements: Private Interest and Public Action.* Princeton: Princeton University Press.

Holmes, Steven. 1994. "Office in Grenada Closing, U.S. Says: Embassy No Longer Needed as Strategic Role Wanes." *New York Times,* 2 May, 1994, A1.

Holsti, Kalevi J. 1991. *Peace and War: Armed Conflicts and International Order, 1648–1989.* Cambridge: Cambridge University Press.

———. 1992. "International Theory and War in the Third World." In *The Insecurity Dilemma: National Security of Third World States,* edited by Brian L. Job. Boulder, Colo.: Lynne Rienner.

———. 1995. "War, Peace, and the State of the State." *International Political Science Review* 16 (4): 319–39.

Hoon, Shim Jae. 1994–95. "Silent Partner." *Far Eastern Economic Review,* 29 December–5 January, 14.

Hubbard, Michael, Nicoletta Merlo, Simon Maxwell, and Enzo Caputo. 1992. "Regional Food Security Strategies: The Case of IGADD in the Horn of Africa." *Food Policy* 17 (1): 7–22.

Hudson, Michael. 1984. "Public Opinion, Foreign Policy, and the Crisis of Legitimacy in Arab Politics." *Journal of Arab Affairs* 5 (2): 131–60.

———. 1992. "The Middle East Under *Pax Americana:* How New, How Orderly?" *Third World Quarterly* 13:301–16.

———. 1995. "Democracy and Foreign Policy in the Arab World." In *Democracy, War, and Peace in the Middle East,* edited by David Garnham and Mark Tessler. Bloomington: Indiana University Press.

Huntington, Samuel P. 1957. *The Soldier and the State.* New York: Vintage.

Hurewitz, J. C. 1973. "Super Power Rivalry and the Arab-Israeli Dispute: Involvement or Commitment?" In *The U.S.S.R. and the Middle East,* edited by Michael Confino and Shimon Shamir. Jerusalem: Israel University Press.

Hurrell, Andrew. 1992. "Latin America in the New World Order: A Regional Bloc of the Americas?" *International Affairs* 68:121–39.

———. 1995. "Explaining the Resurgence of Regionalism in World Politics." *Review of International Studies* 21 (4): 331–58.

———. 1996. "An Emerging Security Community in South America?" Paper presented at the annual convention, International Studies Association, April.

Hurrell, Andrew, and Louise Fawcett. 1995. *The Resurgence of Regionalism in World Politics.* New York: Oxford University Press.

Hussein, King. 1990. "Speech to the Fourth Summit of the Arab Cooperation Council." Amman, Jordan, 24 February, as cited in Foreign Broadcast Information Service–NES-90-039, 27 February, 5–7.

———. 1994a. "King Addresses Army on Peace, Rights." *Al-Aswaq* (Amman) 16 July, as cited in Foreign Broadcast Information Service–NES-94-137, 18 July, 50–52.

———.1994b. "King Remarks on Peace Talks, Meeting Rabin." Jordan Television Network, 9 July, as cited in Foreign Broadcast Information Service–NES-94-132, 11 July, 61–65.

Hussein, Saddam. 1990. "Speech to the Fourth Summit of the Arab Cooperation Council." Amman, 24 February, as cited in Foreign Broadcast Information Service–NES-90-039, 27 February, 1–5.

Hyman, Anthony. 1993. "Moving out of Moscow's Orbit: The Outlook for Central Asia." *International Affairs* 69:289–304.
Ibrahim, Saad Eddin. 1993. "Crises, Elites, and Democratization in the Arab World." *Middle East Journal* 47:292–305.
Ibrahim, Youssif. 1995. "Muslims Argue the Theology of Peace with Israel." *New York Times*, 31 January, A9.
Igarashi, Takeshi. 1995. "To Gain Credibility from Asians." *Asahi Shimbun*, 9 May, 4.
Indyk, Martin. 1993. "The Clinton Administration's Approach to the Middle East." In *Challenges to U.S. Interests in the Middle East: Obstacles and Opportunities.* Washington, D.C.: Washington Institute for Near East Policy.
International Institute for Strategic Studies. 1976–77, 1989–90. *The Military Balance.* London: International Institute for Strategic Studies.
———. 1995. *The Military Balance, 1995–96.* Oxford: Oxford University Press.
International Monetary Fund. 1994. *Direction of Trade Statistics Yearbook.* Washington, D.C.: International Monetary Fund.
Iriye, Akira. 1974. *The Cold War in Asia: A Historical Introduction.* Englewood Cliffs, N.J.: Prentice Hall.
———. 1994. "The United States and Japan in Asia." In *The United States, Japan, and Asia, Challenges for U.S. Policy,* edited by Gerald L. Curtis. New York: W. W. Norton.
Irwin, Zachary. 1991. "Israel: An Aspiring Hegemon." In *Regional Hegemons: Threat Perception and Strategic Response,* edited by David Myers. Boulder, Colo.: Westview Press.
Ispahani, Mahnaz Zehra. 1984. "Alone Together: Regional Security Arrangements in Southern Africa and the Arabian Gulf." *International Security* 8:152–75.
Jackson, Henry F. 1982. *From the Congo to Soweto: U.S. Foreign Policy Toward Africa Since 1960.* New York: William Morrow.
Jackson, Robert H. 1990. *Quasi-States: Sovereignty, International Relations, and the Third World.* Cambridge: Cambridge University Press.
———. 1992. "The Security Dilemma in Africa." In *The Insecurity Dilemma: National Security of Third World States,* edited by Brian L. Job. Boulder, Colo.: Lynne Rienner.
———. 1993. "Armed Humanitarianism." *International Journal* 48 (4): 579–606.
Jervis, Robert. [1970] 1989. *The Logic of Images in International Relations.* New York: Columbia University Press, Morningside Edition.
———. 1978. "Cooperation Under the Security Dilemma." *World Politics* 30 (2): 167–214.
———. 1979. "Systems Theories and Diplomatic History." In *Diplomacy,* edited by Paul Gordon Lauren. New York: Free Press.
———. 1980. "The Impact of the Korean War on the Cold War." *Journal of Conflict Resolution* 24:563–92.
———. 1983. "Security Regimes." In *International Regimes,* edited by Stephen D. Krasner. Ithaca: Cornell University Press.
———. 1985. "From Balance to Concert: A Study of International Security Cooperation." *World Politics* 38:58–79.
———. 1986. "From Balance to Concert: A Study of Security Cooperation." In *Cooperation Under Anarchy,* edited by Kenneth A. Oye. Princeton: Princeton University Press.

———. 1988. "Realism, Game Theory, and Cooperation." *World Politics* 40: 317–49.

———. 1992. "A Political Science Perspective on the Balance of Power and the Concert." *American Historical Review* 97:716–24.

Jeshurun, Chandran, ed. 1994. *China, India, Japan.* Singapore: Institute of Southeast Asian Studies.

Ji Guoxing. 1994. "The Japanese-U.S. Alliance: Uncertain Future." *Pac Net* 9 (18 March), CSIS Pacific Forum newssheet.

Job, Brian L. 1992a. "The Insecurity Dilemma: National, Regime, and State Securities in the Third World." In *The Insecurity Dilemma: National Security of Third World States,* edited by Brian L. Job. Boulder, Colo.: Lynne Rienner.

———, ed. 1992b. *The Insecurity Dilemma: National Security of Third World States.* Boulder, Colo.: Lynne Rienner.

Johnson, Chalmers. 1982. *MITI and the Japanese Miracle.* Stanford: Stanford University Press.

———. 1992. "Japan in Search of a 'Normal' Role." Policy paper no. 3. San Diego: Institute on Global Conflict and Cooperation, University of California, San Diego.

Johnson, Teresa Pelton, and Steven E. Miller, eds. 1994. *Russian Security After the Cold War: Seven Views from Moscow.* Washington, D.C.: Brassey's.

Johnston, Alastair Iain. 1990. "China and Arms Control in the Asia-Pacific Region." In *Superpower Maritime Strategy in the Pacific,* edited by Frank C. Langdon and Douglas A. Ross. London: Routledge.

Jorgensen-Dahl, Arnfinn. 1982. *Regional Organization and Order in South-East Asia.* Hong Kong: Macmillan.

Kahler, Miles. 1991. "Beyond the Cold War in the Pacific." In *Beyond the Cold War in the Pacific,* edited by Miles Kahler. San Diego: Institute on Global Conflict and Cooperation, University of California, San Diego.

———. 1993. "Multilateralism Within Small and Large Numbers." In *Multilateralism Matters: The Theory and Praxis of an Institutional Form,* edited by John Ruggie. New York: Columbia University Press.

———. 1994. "Institution-Building in the Pacific." In *Pacific Cooperation: Building Economic and Security Regimes in the Asia-Pacific Region,* edited by Andrew Mack and John Ravenhill. London: Allen & Unwin.

Kaiser, Karl. 1968. "The Interaction of Regional Subsystems: Some Preliminary Notes on Recurrent Patterns and the Role of Superpowers." *World Politics* 21:84–107.

Kalb, Madeline. 1982. *Congo Cables.* New York: Macmillan.

Kallab, Valeriana, and Richard E. Feinberg, eds. 1989. *Fragile Coalitions: The Politics of Economic Adjustment.* New Brunswick, N.J.: Transaction Publishers.

Kanet, Roger E., and Edward A. Kolodziej, eds. 1991. *The Cold War as Cooperation.* Baltimore: Johns Hopkins University Press.

Kaplan, Stephen. 1975. "United States Aid and Regime Maintenance in Jordan, 1957–1973." *Public Policy* 23:189–217.

Karawan, Ibrahim. 1994. "Arab Dilemmas in the 1990s: Breaking the Taboos and Searching for Signposts." *Middle East Journal* 48:433–54.

Karsh, Efraim. 1988. *The Soviet Union and Syria: The Asad Years.* London: Routledge, for RIIA.

———. 1991. *Soviet Policy Towards Syria Since 1967.* London: Macmillan.

Kaser, Michael. 1967. *Comecon: Integration Problems of the Planned Economies.* 2d ed. London: Royal Institute of International Affairs.

Katzenstein, Peter J. 1993. "Regions in Competition: Comparative Advantages of America, Europe, and Asia." In *America and Europe in an Era of Change,* edited by Helga Haftendorn and Christian Tuschhoff. Boulder, Colo.: Westview Press.

Kaufman, Robert R. 1989. "Domestic Determinants of Stabilization and Adjustment Choices." In *Choices in World Politics: Sovereignty and Interdependence,* edited by B. Russett, H. Starr, and R. Stoll. New York: W. H. Freeman.

Kaufmann, Chaim D. [1988] 1994. *U.S. Mediation in the Falklands/Malvinas Crisis.* Pew Case Studies in International Affairs, no. 431. Washington, D.C.: Georgetown University Press.

Kaysen, Carl. 1990. "Is War Obsolete?" *International Security* 14:42–64.

Kaysen, Carl, Robert A. Pastor, and Laura W. Reed, eds. 1994. *Collective Responses to Regional Problems: The Case of Latin America and the Caribbean.* Cambridge, Mass.: American Academy of Arts and Sciences.

Keal, Paul. 1983. *Unspoken Rules and Superpower Dominance.* New York: St. Martin's Press.

Keddie, Nikki. 1992. "The End of the Cold War in the Middle East." *Diplomatic History* 16:95–103.

Keegan, John, and Andrew Wheatcroft. 1986. *Zones of Conflict: An Atlas of Future Wars.* New York: Simon & Schuster.

Keller, Edmond J. 1992. "Drought, War, and the Politics of Famine in Ethiopia and Eritrea." *Journal of Modern African Studies* 30 (4): 609–24.

Kelly, Philip. 1986. "Escalation of Regional Conflict: Testing the Shatterbelt Concept." *Political Geography Quarterly* 5:161–80.

Kemp, Geoffrey. 1973. "The Prospects for Arms Control in Latin America." In *Military Rule in Latin America,* edited by Philippe C. Schmitter. Beverly Hills, Calif.: Sage Publications.

Kennan, George. 1951. *Realities of American Foreign Policy.* New York: New American Library.

———. 1967a. *American Diplomacy, 1900–1950.* New York: New American Library.

———. 1967b. *Memoirs, 1925–1950.* Boston: Little, Brown.

Kennedy, Paul. 1981. "Strategy Versus Finance in Twentieth-Century Britain." *International History Review* 3:45–61.

———, ed. 1991. *Grand Strategies in War and Peace.* New Haven: Yale University Press.

Kent, John. 1993. *British Imperial Strategy and the Origins of the Cold War: 1944–1949.* London: Leicester University Press.

Keohane, Robert O. 1971. "The Big Influence of Small Allies." *Foreign Policy* 2: 161–82.

———. 1984. *After Hegemony: Cooperation and Discord in the World Political Economy.* Princeton: Princeton University Press.

———. 1986. "Reciprocity in International Relations." *International Organization* 40 (winter): 1–28.

———. 1990. "Multilateralism: An Agenda for Research." *International Journal* 45 (4): 731–64.

———. 1993. "Institutional Theory and the Realist Challenge After the Cold War."

In *Neorealism and Neoliberalism: The Contemporary Debate,* edited by David Baldwin. New York: Columbia University Press.

Keohane, Robert O., and Joseph S. Nye. 1977. *Power and Interdependence: World Politics in Transition.* Boston: Little, Brown.

———. 1989. *Power and Interdependence: World Politics in Transition.* 2d ed. Glenview, Ill.: Scott, Foresman.

Kerr, Malcolm. 1971. *The Arab Cold War: Gamal 'Abdal-Nasir and his Rivals, 1958–1970.* London: Oxford University Press.

Khaddam, Abd-al-Halim. 1995. "Khaddam Addresses Rally." Syrian Arab Television, 8 March, Damascus, as translated in Foreign Broadcast Information Service–NES-95-046, 9 March, 34–38.

Khadduri, Majid. 1988. *The Gulf War: The Origins and Implications of the Iraq-Iran Conflict.* New York: Oxford University Press.

Khalidi, Ahmed, and Hussein Agha. 1991. "The Syrian Doctrine of Strategic Parity." In *The Middle East in Global Perspective,* edited by Judith Kipper and Harold Saunders. Boulder, Colo.: Westview Press.

Khashan, Hilal. 1994. "Are the Arabs Ready for Peace with Israel?" *Middle East Quarterly* 1 (1): 19–28.

Khong, Yuen Foong. 1994. "ASEAN and the Idea of a Security Community." Paper presented at the American Political Science Association annual meeting (1–4 September), New York.

———. 1995a. "ASEAN's Post-Ministerial Conference and Regional Forum: A Convergence of Post–Cold War Security Strategies." In *United States-Japan Relations and International Institutions After the Cold War,* edited by Peter Gourevitch, Takashi Inoguchi, and Courtney Purrington. La Jolla: University of California Graduate School of International Relations and Pacific Studies.

———. 1995b. "Southeast Asia's Emerging Security and Economic Institutions." In *Southeast Asian Affairs, 1995.* Singapore: Institute of Southeast Asian Studies.

Khouri, Fred. 1966. "The Policy of Retaliation in Arab-Israeli Relations." *Middle East Journal* 20:435–55.

Kim, Sung Ho. 1987. "The Issues of International Law, Morality, and Prudence." In *Reagan and the Sandinistas,* edited by Thomas W. Walker. Boulder, Colo.: Westview Press.

Kindleberger, Charles P. 1986. "International Public Goods Without International Government." *American Economic Review* 76:1–13.

King, Gary, Robert O. Keohane, and Sidney Verba. 1994. *Designing Social Inquiry: Scientific Inference in Qualitative Research.* Princeton: Princeton University Press.

Kissinger, Henry. 1979. *White House Years.* Boston: Little, Brown.

Knight, Jonathan. 1975. "American Statecraft and the 1946 Black Sea Straits Controversy." *Political Science Quarterly* 90:451–75.

Knorr, Klaus, and Patrick M. Morgan. 1983. *Strategic Military Surprise: Incentives and Opportunities.* New Brunswick, N.J.: Transaction Publishers.

Kolodziej, Edward A., and I. William Zartman. 1996. "Coping with Conflict: A Global Approach." In *Coping with Conflict After the Cold War,* edited by Edward A. Kolodziej and Roger E. Kanet. Baltimore: Johns Hopkins University Press.

Korany, Bahgat. 1988. "The Dialectics of Inter-Arab Relations, 1967–1987." In *The*

Arab-Israeli Conflict: Two Decades of Change, edited by Yehudah Lukacs and Abdallah Battah. Boulder, Colo.: Westview Press.

Korany, Bahgat, and Ali E. Hillal Dessouki. 1991. "The Global System and Arab Foreign Policies: The Primacy of Constraints." In *The Foreign Policies of Arab States,* 2d ed., edited by Bahgat Korany and Ali E. Hillal Dessouki. Boulder, Colo.: Westview Press.

Kraehe, Enno. 1992. "A Bipolar Balance of Power." *American Historical Review* 97: 707–15.

Krasner, Stephen D. 1976. "State Power and the Structure of International Trade." *World Politics* 28:317–47.

———. 1978. *Defending the National Interest: Raw Materials Investments and U.S. Foreign Policy.* Princeton: Princeton University Press.

———, ed. 1983. *International Regimes.* Ithaca: Cornell University Press.

———. 1988. "Sovereignty: An Institutional Perspective." *Comparative Political Studies* 21 (1): 66–94.

———. 1991. "Global Communications and National Power: Life on the Pareto Frontier." *World Politics* 43:336–66.

———. 1995–96. "Compromising Westphalia." *International Security* 20:115–51.

Kratochwil, Friedrich. 1993. "Norms Versus Numbers: Multilateralism and the Rationalists and Reflexivist Approaches to Institutions: A Unilateral Plea for Communicative Rationality." In *Multilateralism Matters: The Theory and Praxis of an Institutional Form,* edited by John Ruggie. New York: Columbia University Press.

Krugman, Paul R. 1991. *Geography and Trade.* Cambridge, Mass.: MIT Press.

Kuniholm, Bruce. 1980. *The Origins of the Cold War in the Near East: Great Power Conflict and Diplomacy in Iran, Turkey, and Greece.* Princeton: Princeton University Press.

Kupchan, Charles A., and Clifford A. Kupchan. 1991. "Concerts, Collective Security, and the Future of Europe." *International Security* 16 (1): 114–61.

Kuran, Timur. 1995. "Fundamentalist Economics and the Economic Roots of Fundamentalism: Policy Prescriptions for a Liberal Society." In *Fundamentalism and Public Policy,* edited by Martin E. Marty and R. Scott Appleby. Chicago: University of Chicago Press.

LaFeber, Walter. 1975. "Roosevelt, Churchill, and Indochina, 1942–45." *American Historical Review* 80:1277–95.

———. 1989. *The American Age: United States Foreign Policy at Home and Abroad Since 1750.* New York: W. W. Norton.

———. 1993. *America, Russia, and the Cold War, 1945–1992.* 7th ed. New York: McGraw-Hill.

———. 1994. *The American Age: U.S. Foreign Policy at Home and Abroad, 1750 to the Present.* 2d ed. New York: W. W. Norton.

Laidi, Zaki. 1990. *The Superpowers and Africa: The Constraints of a Rivalry, 1960–1990.* Chicago: University of Chicago Press.

Laitin, David D., and Said S. Samatar. 1987. *Somalia: Nation in Search of a State.* Boulder, Colo.: Westview Press.

Lake, David A. 1992. "Powerful Pacifists: Democratic States and War." *American Political Science Review* 86 (1): 24–37.

———. 1993. "Leadership, Hegemony, and the International Economy: Naked Emperor or Tattered Monarch with Potential?" *International Studies Quarterly* 37: 459–89.

Lake, David A., and Robert Powell. 1995. "Strategic Choice and International Relations." Paper presented at the annual meeting of the American Political Science Association (31 August–3 September), Chicago.

Lamborn, Alan C. 1983. "Power and the Politics of Extraction." *International Studies Quarterly* 27:125–46.

———. 1985. "Risk and Foreign Policy Choice." *International Studies Quarterly* 29:385–410.

———. 1991. *The Price of Power: Risk and Foreign Policy in Britain, France, and Germany.* Boston: Unwin Hyman.

Lane, Frederic C. 1979. *Profits from Power.* Albany: State University of New York Press.

Lau, Teik Soon. 1974. "Conflict Resolution in ASEAN: The Sabah Issue." Occasional paper no. 5, Department of Political Science, University of Singapore.

Lebow, Richard N., and Janice Stein. 1994. *We All Lost the Cold War.* Princeton: Princeton University Press.

Leffler, Melvyn. 1985. "Strategy, Diplomacy, and the Cold War: The United States, Turkey, and NATO, 1945–1952." *Journal of American History* 71:807–25.

———. 1992. *A Preponderance of Power: National Security, the Truman Administration, and the Cold War.* Stanford: Stanford University Press.

Leifer, Michael. 1989. *ASEAN and the Security of South-East Asia.* London: Routledge.

Lerner, Daniel. 1958. *The Passing of Traditional Society: Modernizing the Middle East.* Glencoe, Ill.: Free Press.

Levy, Jack S. 1981. "Alliance Formation and War Behavior: An Analysis of the Great Powers, 1495–1975." *Journal of Conflict Resolution* 25 (4): 581–614.

Levy, Jack S., and Lily I. Vakili. 1992. "Diversionary Action by Authoritarian Regimes: Argentina in the Falklands/Malvinas Case." In *The Internationalization of Communal Strife,* edited by Manus I. Midlarsky. London: Routledge.

Lewis, Bernard. 1992. "Rethinking the Middle East." *Foreign Affairs* 71 (4): 99–119.

Lieven, Anatol. 1995. "Russian Opposition to NATO Expansion." *World Today* 51: 196–99.

Lindberg, Leon, and Stuart Scheingold, eds. 1971. *Regional Integration: Theory and Research.* Cambridge, Mass.: Harvard University Press.

Lipset, Seymour Martin. 1959. "Some Social Requisites of Democracy." *American Political Science Review* 53:69–105.

———. 1960. *Political Man.* Garden City, N.Y.: Doubleday.

Lipson, Charles. 1994. "Is the Future of Collective Security Like the Past?" In *Collective Security Beyond the Cold War,* edited by George Downs. Ann Arbor: University of Michigan Press.

Lizee, Pierre, and Sorpong Peou. 1993. *Cooperative Security and the Emerging Security Agenda in Southeast Asia: The Challenges and Opportunities of Peace in Cambodia.* YCISS occasional paper no. 21. Toronto: York University Centre for International and Strategic Studies.

Lobell, Steven E. n.d. "Managing Hegemonic Decline: Dilemmas of Strategy and Finance." Ph.D. diss., University of California, Los Angeles.

Lohmann, Susanne. 1997. "Linkage Politics." *Journal of Conflict Resolution* 41: 38–67.
Lomborg, Bjorn. 1996. "Nucleus and Shield: The Evolution of Social Structure in the Iterated Prisoner's Dilemma." *American Sociological Review* 61:278–307.
Lorenz, Joseph P. 1992. "Collective Security After the Cold War." In *Resolving Third World Conflict: Challenges for a New Era,* edited by Sheryl J. Brown and Kimber M. Schraub. Washington, D.C.: U.S. Institute of Peace.
Lough, John. 1993. "Defining Russia's Relations with Neighboring States." *RFE/RL Research Report* 2 (14 May): 53–60.
Louis, Roger. 1977. *Imperialism at Bay: The United States and the Decolonization of the British Empire, 1941–1945.* New York: Oxford University Press.
Lowenthal, Abraham F. 1972. *The Dominican Intervention.* Cambridge, Mass.: Harvard University Press.
Luard, Evan. 1986. *War in International Society: A Study in International Sociology.* New Haven: Yale University Press.
Luttwak, Edward. 1983. *The Grand Strategy of the Soviet Union.* New York: St. Martin's Press.
Lynn-Jones, Sean, ed. 1991. *The Cold War and After.* Cambridge, Mass.: MIT Press.
MacFarlane, S. Neil, and Thomas G. Weiss. 1992. "Regional Organizations and Regional Security." *Security Studies* 2 (1): 6–37.
———. 1994. "The United Nations, Regional Organizations, and Human Security: Building Theory in Central America." *Third World Quarterly* 15 (2): 277–95.
Mackie, J. A. 1974. *Konfrontasi: The Indonesian-Malaysian Dispute, 1963–66.* Kuala Lumpur: Oxford University Press.
Mackinder, Halford J. 1904. "The Geographical Pivot of History." *Geographical Journal* 23:421–44.
Maddy-Weitzman, Bruce. 1993. "A New Arab Order: Regional Security After the Gulf War." *Orient* 34:221–30.
Malik, Hafeez, ed. 1994. *Central Asia: Its Strategic Importance and Future Prospects.* New York: St. Martin's Press.
Mancall, Mark. 1989. *China at the Center: 300 Years of Foreign Policy.* New York: Free Press.
Mandelbaum, Michael, ed. 1994. *The Politics of the Strategic Quadrangle: The United States, Russia, Japan, and China in East Asia.* New York: Council on Foreign Relations Press.
Mansbach, Richard W., and John A. Vasquez. 1981. *In Search of Theory.* New York: Columbia University Press.
Mansfield, Edward. 1993. "Effects of International Politics on Regionalism in International Trade." In *Regional Integration and Global Trading System,* edited by Kym Anderson and Richard Blackhurst. New York: St. Martin's Press.
Mansfield, Edward, and Helen V. Milner. 1997. *The Political Economy of Regionalism.* New York: Columbia University Press.
Mansfield, Edward, and Jack Snyder. 1995. "Democratization and War." *Foreign Affairs* 74 (3): 79–97.
Maoz, Zeev. 1989. "Joining the Club of Nations: Political Development and International Conflict, 1816–1976." *International Studies Quarterly* 33:199–231.
Mares, David R. 1988. "Middle Powers Under Regional Hegemony: To Challenge or Acquiesce in Hegemonic Enforcement." *International Studies Quarterly* 32: 453–71.

———. 1995. "La guerra fría en los conflictos latinoamericanos: Mitos y realidades." *Fuerzas Armadas y Sociedad* 10 (2): 19–25.

———. 1996a. "Equilibrios estratégicos y medidas de confianza mutua: La utilidad histórica de conceptos ambiguos." In *Balance estratégico y medidas de confianza mutua,* edited by Francisco Rojas Aravena. Santiago, Chile: FLACSO.

———. 1996b. "Violent Peace: Conflict Management in Latin America." Manuscript, University of California, San Diego.

Margolis, Howard. 1982. *Selfishness, Altruism, and Rationality.* Chicago: University of Chicago Press.

Martin, Lisa. 1993. "The Rational State Choice of Multilateralism." In *Multilateralism Matters: The Theory and Praxis of an Institutional Form,* edited by John Ruggie. New York: Columbia University Press.

Masoa, Okonogi. 1977. "Domestic Roots of the Korean War." In *The Origins of the Cold War in Asia,* edited by Yonosuke Nagai and Akira Iriye. New York: Columbia University Press.

Mastanduno, Michael, David A. Lake, and G. John Ikenberry. 1989. "Toward a Realist Theory of State Action." *International Studies Quarterly* 33:457–74.

Masterson, Daniel M. 1991. *Militarism and Politics in Latin America.* New York: Greenwood Press.

Maxfield, Sylvia. 1990. *Governing Capital: International Finance and Mexican Politics.* Ithaca: Cornell University Press.

May, Ernest R. 1975. *The Making of the Monroe Doctrine.* Cambridge, Mass.: Harvard University Press.

May, Michael. 1993–94. "Correspondence: Japan as a Superpower?" *International Security* 18 (3): 82–187.

Mayer, Ann E. 1991. "The Fundamentalist Impact on Law, Politics, and Constitutions in Iran, Pakistan, and the Sudan." In *Fundamentalisms Observed,* edited by Martin E. Marty and R. Scott Appleby. Chicago: University of Chicago Press.

Mayhew, David R. 1974. *Congress: The Electoral Connection.* New Haven: Yale University Press.

Maynes, Charles William. 1993–94. "A Workable Clinton Doctrine." *Foreign Policy* 93:3–20.

McDougall, Walter A. 1993. *Let the Sea Make a Noise: . . . A History of the North Pacific from Magellan to MacArthur.* New York: Basic Books.

McMahon, Robert. 1988. "The Cold War in Asia: Toward a New Synthesis." *Diplomatic History* 12:307–27.

Mearsheimer, John J. 1983. *Conventional Deterrence.* Ithaca: Cornell University Press.

———. 1990. "Back to the Future: Instability in Europe After the Cold War." *International Security* 15:5–56.

———. 1991. "Back to the Future: Instability in Europe After the Cold War." In *The Cold War and After,* edited by Sean Lynn-Jones. Cambridge, Mass.: MIT Press.

———. 1994. "The False Promise of International Institutions." *International Security* 19 (3): 5–49.

Mecham, J. Lloyd. 1962. *The United States and Inter-American Security, 1889–1960.* Austin: University of Texas Press.

———. 1965. *A Survey of United States-Latin American Relations.* Boston: Houghton Mifflin.

Meibar, Bashir. 1982. *Political Culture, Foreign Policy, and Conflict: The Palestine Area Conflict System*. Westport, Conn.: Greenwood Press.

Miasnikov, V. S. 1992. "Russia in the New Concert of East Asian Powers." In *The Changing World Order: Prospects for Korea in the Asia Pacific Era,* edited by Bum-Joon Lee and Song-Chul Yang. Seoul: Korean Association of International Studies.

Miller, Aaron David. 1988. "Changing Arab Attitudes Toward Israel." *Orbis* 32 (1): 69–81.

Miller, Benjamin. 1990. "Perspectives on Superpower Crisis Management and Conflict Resolution in the Arab-Israeli Conflict." In *Soviet Strategy in the Middle East,* edited by George Breslauer. London: Unwin Hyman.

———. 1995a. "Explaining Military Intervention: The Sources of U.S. Engagement in Post–Cold War Regional Crises." Paper prepared for the annual meeting of the International Studies Association, Chicago, 21–25 February.

———. 1995b. "Great Powers and Regional Peacemaking: Patterns During the Cold War and Beyond." Paper prepared for the annual meeting of the International Studies Association, Chicago, 21–25 February.

Miller, Lynn H. 1973. "The Prospects for Order Through Regional Security." In *Regional Politics and World Order,* edited by Richard Falk and Saul Mendlovitz. San Francisco: W. H. Freeman.

Milner, Helen V. 1988. "Trading Places: Industries for Free Trade." *World Politics* 40:350–76.

Moltz, James Clay. 1996. "The Russian Economic Crisis: Implications for Asian-Pacific Policy and Security." In *Power and Prosperity: Economics and Security Linkages in Asia-Pacific,* edited by Susan L. Shirk and Christopher P. Twomey. New Brunswick, N.J.: Transaction Publishers.

Mor, Ben D. 1991. "Nasser's Decision Making in the 1967 Middle East Crisis: A Rational-Choice Explanation." *Journal of Peace Research*. 28:359–75.

Morgan, Patrick M. 1988. "Security in International Politics: Lessons from the Twentieth Century." Belgian Center for Defense Studies, Monograph Series, Brussels (fall).

———. 1993. "Multilateralism and Security: Prospects in Europe." In *Multilateralism Matters: The Theory and Praxis of an Institutional Form,* edited by John Ruggie. New York: Columbia University Press.

———. 1994. "Comparing the European and East Asian Regional Security Systems." Unpublished paper, Department of Politics and Society, University of California, Irvine.

Morgenthau, Hans J. 1960. *Politics Among Nations: The Struggle for Power and Peace.* 3d ed. New York: Knopf.

Morris, Benny. 1993. *Israel's Border Wars.* New York: Oxford University Press.

Morris, Michael A., and Victor Millan. 1990. *Conflicts in Latin America: Democratic Alternatives in the 1990s.* Conflict Studies, no. 20. London: Research Institute for the Study of Conflict and Terrorism.

Morrison, John. 1993. "Pereyaslav and After: The Russian-Ukrainian Relationship." *International Affairs* 69:677–703.

Mubarak, Hosni. 1995. "Mubarak Interviewed on Local, Regional Issues." *Al-Akhbar,* 1 January, 3–6, as translated by Foreign Broadcast Information Service–NES-95-002, 4 January, 21–28.

Mueller, Dennis C. 1989. *Public Choice II.* New York: Cambridge University Press.
Mueller, John. 1989–90. "A New Concert of Europe." *Foreign Policy* 77:3–16.
———. 1994. *Policy and Opinion in the Gulf War.* Chicago: University of Chicago Press.
Munoz, Heraldo. 1984. "Beyond the Malvinas Crisis: Perspectives on Inter-American Relations" *Latin American Research Review* 19 (1): 158–72.
Munro, Dana G. 1964. *Intervention and Dollar Diplomacy in the Caribbean, 1900–1921.* Princeton: Princeton University Press.
Muslih, Muhammed. 1993. "The Golan: Israel, Syria, and Strategic Calculations." *Middle East Journal* 47:612–32.
Myers, David J. 1991a. "Threat Perception and Strategic Response of the Regional Hegemons: A Conceptual Overview." In *Regional Hegemons: Threat Perception and Strategic Response,* edited by David J. Myers. Boulder, Colo.: Westview Press.
———, ed. 1991b. *Regional Hegemons: Threat Perception and Strategic Response.* Boulder, Colo.: Westview Press.
Nafi', Ibrahim. 1995. "Role of the Arab League in the Future." *Al-Ahram al-Duwali,* 27 January, 5, as translated in Foreign Broadcast Information Service–NES-95-052, 17 March, 5–7.
Nahas, Maridi. 1985. "State-Systems and Revolutionary Challenge: Nasser, Khomeini, and the Middle East." *International Journal of Middle East Studies* 17: 507–27.
Nahhas, Mona el-. 1995. "Storm over Israel's Fair Presence." *Al-Ahram Weekly,* 30 March–6 April, 2.
Nassar, Galal. 1995. "Out of Balance." *Al-Ahram Weekly,* 19–25 January.
Nelson, Daniel N. 1991. "Security After Hegemony." *Bulletin of Peace Proposals* 22 (3): 335–52.
Neuman, Stephanie. 1984. "International Stratification and Third World Military Industries." *International Organization* 1:167–97.
———. 1986. *Military Assistance in Recent Wars: The Dominance of the Superpowers.* New York: Praeger.
Niou, Emerson, Peter Ordershook, and Gregory Rose. 1989. *The Balance of Power: Stability in International Systems.* Cambridge: Cambridge University Press.
Noble, Paul. 1991. "The Arab System: Pressures, Constraints, and Opportunities." In *The Foreign Policies of Arab States,* 2d ed., edited by Bahgat Korany and Ali E. Hillal Dessouki. Boulder, Colo.: Westview Press.
Noer, Thomas. 1981. "'Non-Benign Neglect': The United States and Black Africa in the Twentieth Century." In *American Foreign Relations: A Historiographical Review,* edited by Gerald Haines and Samuel Walker. Westport, Conn.: Greenwood Press.
North, Douglass. 1981. *Structure and Change in Economic History.* New York: W. W. Norton.
Norton, Augustus Richard. 1993. "The Future of Civil Society in the Middle East." *Middle East Journal* 47:205–17.
Norton, Augustus Richard, and Robin Wright. 1994–95. "The Post-Peace Crisis in the Middle East." *Survival* 36 (4): 7–20.
Nye, Joseph P., ed. 1968. *International Regionalism.* Boston: Little, Brown.

Olcott, Martha Brill. 1994. "The Asian Interior: The Myth of 'Tsentral'naia Aziia.'" *Orbis* 38:549–65.

Olson, Mancur. 1965. *The Logic of Collective Action.* Cambridge, Mass.: Harvard University Press.

Olson, Mancur, and Richard Zeckhauser. 1966. "An Economic Theory of Alliances." *Review of Economics and Statistics* 48:266–79.

Orbell, John, Robyn Dawes, and Alphons van de Kragt. 1990. "The Limits of Multilateral Promising." *Ethics* 100:616–27.

Oren, Michael. 1992. *Origins of the Second Arab-Israel War: Egypt, Israel, and the Great Powers, 1952–1956.* London: Frank Cass.

Oren, Nissan. 1984. "An Image: Israel as the 'Holder' of the Regional Balance." In *Images and Reality in International Politics,* edited by Nissan Oren. New York: St. Martin's Press.

Organization of African Unity (OAU). 1993. "Declaration of the Assembly of Heads of State and Government on the Establishment Within the OAU of a Mechanism for Conflict Prevention, Management, and Resolution." Twenty-Ninth Ordinary Session, Assembly of Heads of State and Government, 28–30 June, Cairo, Egypt.

Organization of American States (OAS). 1992. "Hemispheric Security-Arms Proliferation." OEA/Ser.P/AG.doc.2838/92 add.3/ 12 May.

———. 1993. "Hemispheric Permanent Council of the Organization of American States, Special Committee on Hemisphere Security, Support for a New Concept of Hemisphere Security: Cooperative Security." Paper drafted by Argentine Ambassador. OEA/Ser.G CE/SH-12/93.rev. 1, 17 May.

Organski, A.F.K., and Jacek Kugler. 1980. *The War Ledger.* Chicago: University of Chicago Press.

Oye, Kenneth A., ed. 1986. *Cooperation Under Anarchy.* Princeton: Princeton University Press.

Packenham, Robert. 1973. *Liberal America and the Third World: Political Development and Ideas in Foreign Aid and Economic Social Science.* Princeton: Princeton University Press.

Page, Stephen. 1994. "The Creation of a Sphere of Influence: Russia and Central Asia." *International Journal* 49:788–813.

Pala, Major Antonio L., U.S. Air Force. 1995. Interview, Washington, D.C., March.

Papayoanou, Paul A. 1996. "Interdependence, Institutions, and the Balance of Power: Britain, Germany, and World War I." *International Security* 20 (4): 42–76.

———. 1997. "Economic Interdependence and the Balance of Power." *International Studies Quarterly* 41 (1): 113–40.

———. n.d. *Economic Interdependence and the Balance of Power.* Ann Arbor: University of Michigan Press (forthcoming).

Pappe, Ilan. 1994. *The Making of the Arab-Israeli Conflict, 1947–1951.* London: I. B. Tauris.

Paribatra, Sukhumbhand, and Chai-Anan Samudavanya. 1986. "Internal Dimensions of Regional Security in Southeast Asia." In *Regional Security in the Third World: Case Studies from Southeast Asia and the Middle East,* edited by Mohammed Ayoob. London: Croom Helm.

Parker, Richard. 1993. *The Politics of Miscalculation in the Middle East.* Bloomington: Indiana University Press.

Pastor, Robert. 1992. "The Latin American Option." *Foreign Policy* 88:107–25.
Peres, Shimon. 1993. *The New Middle East.* New York: Henry Holt.
Peri, Yoram. 1984. "Coexistence or Hegemony? Shifts in the Israeli Security Concept." In *The Roots of Begin's Success: The 1981 Israeli Elections,* edited by Dan Caspi, Abraham Diskin, and Emanuel Gutman. London: Croom Helm.
Perkins, Dexter. 1965. *A History of the Monroe Doctrine.* Boston: Little, Brown.
Perthes, Volker. 1993. "Incremental Change in Syria." *Current History* 92:23–26.
Peru, Government of. 1993–94. *Peru: Compendio Estadístico.* Vol. 30. Lima: Instituto Nacional de Estadística e Informatica.
Pervin, David J. 1994–95. "Why Israel's Nuclear Weapons Are Good for the Arabs." In "The Case for a Nuclear Israel," by Mohamed Sid-Ahmed, *Al-Ahram Weekly,* 29 December–4 January, 10.
———. 1995. "Al-Aslaha al-Nuawia wa al-salaam al-Arab al-Israeli" (Nuclear weapons and Arab-Israeli peace). *Al-Siassa Al-Dawlya* (International Politics) (Cairo) 120:96–106.
Peters, Joel. 1994. *Building Bridges: The Arab-Israeli Multilateral Talks.* London: Royal Institute of International Affairs.
Pickering, Jeffrey, and William R. Thompson. n.d. "The Use of Force in a Fragmenting International System: Interstate Intervention, 1946–1988." Manuscript.
Pike, Frederick B. n.d. *The Modern History of Peru.* New York: Praeger.
Pollack, Jonathan. 1995. "Designing a New American Strategy for Asia." Working paper, Council on Foreign Relations Asia Project, New York.
Pollins, Brian. 1989a. "Conflict, Cooperation, and Commerce: The Effect of International Political Interactions on Bilateral Trade Flows." *American Journal of Political Science* 33:737–61.
———. 1989b. "Does Trade Still Follow the Flag?" *American Political Science Review* 83:465–80.
Porter, Bruce D. 1984. *The USSR in Third World Conflicts.* Cambridge: Cambridge University Press.
Porter, Bruce D., and Carol R. Saivetz. 1994. "The Once and Future Empire: Russia and the 'Near Abroad.'" *Washington Quarterly* 17:75–90.
Posen, Barry R. 1984. *The Sources of Military Doctrine.* Ithaca: Cornell University Press.
———. 1993. "The Security Dilemma and Ethnic Conflict." *Survival* 35:27–47.
Powell, Robert. 1994. "Anarchy in International Relations Theory: The Neorealist-Neoliberal Debate." *International Organization* 48:313–44.
PRO (see U.K. Public Record Office).
Przeworski, Adam. 1991. *Democracy and the Market: Political and Economic Reforms in Eastern Europe and Latin America.* Cambridge: Cambridge University Press.
———. 1992. "The Neoliberal Fallacy." *Journal of Democracy* 3 (3): 45–59.
Przeworski, Adam, and Henry Teune. 1970. *The Logic of Comparative Social Inquiry.* New York: Wiley.
Pushkov, Alexei K. 1993. "Letter from Eurasia: Russia and America: The Honeymoon's Over." *Foreign Policy* 93:76–90.
Quandt, William. 1977. *Decade of Decisions: American Policy Toward the Arab-Israeli Conflict.* Berkeley and Los Angeles: University of California Press.
———. 1986. *Camp David.* Washington, D.C.: Brookings Institution.

Rabin, Yitzhak. 1993. "Deterrence in an Israeli Security Context." In *Deterrence in the Middle East: Where Theory and Practice Converge,* edited by Aharon Kleiman and Ariel Levite. Tel Aviv: Jaffee Center for Strategic Studies.

Rabinovich, Itamar. 1984. *The War for Lebanon.* Ithaca: Cornell University Press.

———. 1991. *The Road Not Taken: Early Arab-Israeli Negotiations.* New York: Oxford University Press.

Redick, John R. 1981. "The Tlatelolco Regime and Nonproliferation in Latin America." *International Organization* 35 (1): 103–34.

Reed, Laura W., and Carl Kaysen, eds. 1993. *Emerging Norms of Justified Intervention* Cambridge, Mass.: American Academy of Arts and Sciences.

Reich, Bernard, Meyrav Wurmser, and Noah Dropkin. 1995. "Playing Politics in Moscow and Jerusalem: Soviet Jewish Immigrants and the 1992 Knesset Elections." In *Israel at the Polls, 1992,* edited by Daniel Elazar and Shmuel Sandler. London: Rowman & Littlefield.

Reich, Robert. 1991. *The Work of Nations.* New York: Knopf.

Reinhart, Carmen, and Peter Wickham. 1994. "Commodity Prices: Cyclical Weakness or Secular Decline?" *IMF Staff Papers,* June.

Resis, Albert. 1978. "The Churchill-Stalin Secret 'Percentages' Agreement on the Balkans, Moscow, October 1944." *American Historical Review* 85:368–87.

Richards, Alan. 1993. "Economic Imperatives and Political Systems." *Middle East Journal* 47:217–27.

Robins, Philip. 1993. "Between Sentiment and Self-Interest: Turkey's Policy Toward Azerbaijan and the Central Asian States." *Middle East Journal* 47:593–610.

Rosecrance, Richard. 1963. *Action and Reaction in World Politics.* Boston: Little, Brown.

———. 1986. *Rise of the Trading State.* New York: Basic Books.

———. 1991. "Regionalism and the Post–Cold War Era." *International Journal* 46: 373–93.

———, ed. 1992a. "Cooperation in a World Without Enemies: Solving the Public Goods Problem in International Relations." Working paper no. 2, Center for International Relations, University of California, Los Angeles.

———. 1992b. "A New Concert of Powers." *Foreign Affairs* 71 (2): 64–82.

Rosecrance, Richard, and Chih-cheng Lo. 1996. "Balancing, Stability, and War: The Mysterious Case of the Napoleonic International System." *International Studies Quarterly* 40:479–500.

Rosecrance, Richard, and Arthur A. Stein, eds. 1993. *The Domestic Bases of Grand Strategy.* Ithaca: Cornell University Press.

Rosecrance, Richard, and Jennifer Taw. 1990. "Japan and the Theory of International Leadership." *World Politics* 42:184–209.

Rostow, Walt. 1960. *The Stages of Economic Growth.* Cambridge: Cambridge University Press.

Rothchild, Donald. 1996. Conclusion to *Africa in the New International Order,* edited by Edmond J. Keller and Donald Rothchild. Boulder, Colo.: Lynn Rienner.

Rothstein, Robert L. 1977. *The Weak in the World of the Strong: The Developing Countries in the International System.* New York: Columbia University Press.

Rotter, Andrew. 1987. *The Path to Vietnam: Origins of the American Commitment to Southeast Asia.* Ithaca: Cornell University Press.

Rubin, Barry. 1988. "The Soviet and U.S. Record on Arab-Israeli Wars." In *The So-*

viet American Competition in the Middle East, edited by Steven Spiegel, Mark Heller, and Jacob Goldberg. Lexington, Mass.: Lexington Books.

Rubinstein, Alvin Z. 1994. "The Asian Interior: The Geopolitical Pull on Russia." *Orbis* 38:567–83.

Ruggie, John Gerard. 1986. "Continuity and Transformation in the World Polity: Toward a Neorealist Synthesis." In *Neorealism and Its Critics,* edited by Robert O. Keohane. New York: Columbia University Press.

———. 1993. "The Anatomy of an Institution." In *Multilateralism Matters: The Theory and Praxis of an Institutional Form,* edited by John Gerard Ruggie. New York: Columbia University Press.

———. 1996. *Winning the Peace: America and World Order in the New Era.* New York: Columbia University Press.

Rumer, Boris Z. 1993. "The Gathering Storm in Central Asia." *Orbis* 37:89–105.

Rumer, Eugene. 1994. "Eurasia Letter: Will Ukraine Return to Russia?" *Foreign Policy* 96:129–44.

Russett, Bruce M. 1967. *International Regions and the International System: A Study in Political Ecology.* Chicago: Rand McNally.

Rustow, Dankwart. 1989. "Safety in Numbers: Reflections on the Middle Eastern Balance of Power." In *The Islamic World: From Classical to Modern Times,* edited by C. E. Bosworth, Charles Issawi, Roger Savory, and A. C. Udovitch. Princeton: Darwin Press.

Sadowski, Yahya. 1987. "Patronage and the Bath: Corruption and Control in Contemporary Syria." *Arab Studies Quarterly* 9:442–61.

Safran, Nadav. 1981. *Israel the Embattled Ally.* Cambridge, Mass.: Harvard University Press.

Sagan, Scott D., and Kenneth N. Waltz. 1995. *The Spread of Nuclear Weapons: A Debate.* New York: W. W. Norton.

Salame, Ghassan. 1994. "The Middle East: Elusive Security, Indefensible Region." *Security Dialogue* 25:17–35.

Samuelson, Paul. 1976. *Economics.* 10th ed. New York: McGraw-Hill.

Sandler, Todd. 1992. *Collective Action: Theory and Applications.* Ann Arbor: University of Michigan Press.

Satloff, Robert. 1992. "Jordan's Great Gamble: Economic Crisis and Political Reform." In *The Politics of Economic Reform in the Middle East,* edited by Henri Barkey. New York: St. Martin's Press.

Saunders, Harold. 1988. "Regulating Soviet-U.S. Competition and Cooperation in the Arab-Israeli Arena, 1967–86." In *U.S.-Soviet Security Cooperation,* edited by Alexander George, Philip Farley, and Alexander Dallin. Oxford: Oxford University Press.

Sayigh, Yezid. 1993. "Middle Eastern Stability and the Proliferation of Weapons of Mass Destruction." In *Non-Conventional Weapons Proliferation in the Middle East,* edited by Efraim Karsh, Martin Navias, and Philip Sabin. Oxford: Clarendon Press.

Sayyid, Mustapha K. al-. 1991. "Slow Thaw in the Arab World." *World Policy Journal* 8:711–37.

Scalapino, Robert. 1988. Introduction to *Asian Security Issues: Regional and Global,* edited by Robert Scalapino, Seizaburo Sato, Jusuf Wanandi, and Sung-joo Han. Berkeley and Los Angeles: University of California Press.

———. 1991–92. "The United States and Asia: Future Prospects." *Foreign Affairs* 70 (5): 19–40.
Schaller, Michael. 1982. "Securing the Great Crescent: Occupied Japan and the Origins of Containment in Southeast Asia." *Journal of American History* 69: 392–414.
———. 1985. *The American Occupation of Japan: The Origin of the Cold War in Asia.* New York: Oxford University Press.
Schelling, Thomas C. 1978. *Micromotives and Macrobehavior.* New York: W. W. Norton.
Scherer, F. M. 1980. *Industrial Market Structure and Economic Performance.* Chicago: Rand McNally.
Schmidt, Dana Adams. 1960. "Middle East Tense but War Is Unlikely." *New York Times,* 7 February, sec. IV, 4.
———. 1974. *Armageddon in the Middle East.* New York: John Day.
Schroeder, Paul W. 1976. "Alliances, 1815–1945: Weapons of Power and Tools of Management." In *Historical Dimensions of National Security Problems,* edited by Klaus Knorr. Lawrence: University Press of Kansas.
———. 1986. "The 19th-Century International System: Changes in the Structure." *World Politics* 39: 1–25.
———. 1989. "The Nineteenth-Century System: Balance of Power or Political Equilibrium?" *Review of International Studies* 15 (2): 135–53.
———. 1992. "Did the Vienna Settlement Rest on a Balance of Power?" *American Historical Review* 97: 683–706.
———. 1995. "History vs. Neo-Realism: A Second Look." *International Security* 20: 193–95.
Schumpeter, Joseph A. 1955. *Imperialism and Social Classes.* New York: Meridian.
Schwarz, Adam. 1994. *A Nation in Waiting: Indonesia in the 1990s.* St. Leonards, New South Wales: Allen & Unwin.
Sciolino, Elaine. 1995. "Arafat Pledges to Prosecute Terrorists, but Faults Israel." *New York Times,* 11 March, A5.
Sciolino, Elaine, with Thomas Friedman. 1994. "Amid Debt, Doubt, and Secrecy, Hussein and Rabin Made Peace." *New York Times,* 31 July, A1.
Scott Palmer, David. 1995. "Peru's 1995 Elections: A Second Look." *LASA Forum* 26 (2): 17–20.
Seale, Patrick. 1988. *Asad of Syria: The Struggle for the Middle East.* London: I. B. Tauris.
Seelye, Katherine. 1995. "Relocating Embassy in Israel: A Move That Could Backfire." *New York Times,* 18 May, A1.
Segal, Gerald. 1996. "East Asia and the 'Constrainment' of China." *International Security* 20 (4): 107–35.
Serbin, Andres. 1988. "Percepciónes de amenaza y equipamento militar en Venezuela." In *Estudio estrategico de America Latina.* Vol. 2. Santiago: Ediciones Chile América.
Sestanovich, Stephen, ed. 1994. *Rethinking Russia's National Interest.* Washington, D.C.: Center for Strategic and International Studies.
Shachar, Ron, and Michal Shamir. 1995. "Modelling Victory in the 1992 Election." In *The Elections in Israel, 1992,* edited by Asher Arian and Michal Shamir. Albany: State University of New York Press.

Shamir, Shimon. 1981. "The Arab World Between Pragmatism and Radicalism." In *Middle East Perspectives,* edited by George Wise and Charles Issawi. Princeton: Darwin Press.

Shar, Faruq al-. 1994. "Al-Shar' Grants Jerusalem TV Interview." Israel Television, Jerusalem, as translated in Foreign Broadcast Information Service–NES-94-196, 11 October, 1–3.

Sheehan, Michael. 1989. "The Place of the Balancer in Balance of Power Theory." *Review of International Studies* 15:123–34.

Shepherd, Gordon. 1960. "The Sinai Riddle." *Reporter,* 31 March, 26–31.

Shimshoni, Jonathan. 1988. *Israel and Conventional Deterrence: Border Warfare from 1953 to 1970.* Ithaca: Cornell University Press.

Shlaim, Avi. 1990. *The Politics of Partition: King Abdullah, the Zionists, and Palestine, 1921–1951.* New York: Columbia University Press.

Shlaim, Avi, and Raymond Tanter. 1978. "Decision Process, Choice, and Consequences: Israel's Deep-Penetration Bombing in Egypt, 1970." *World Politics* 30: 483–515.

Shukrallah, Hani. 1994–95. "Yes to Pluralism, No to Violence." *Al-Ahram Weekly,* 29 December–4 January, 1.

Shumaker, David. 1993. "The Origins and Development of Central European Cooperation, 1989–1992." *East European Quarterly* 27:351–73.

Sid-Ahmed, Mohamed. 1976. *After the Guns Fall Silent: Peace or Armageddon in the Middle East.* New York: St. Martin's Press.

———. 1995. "When Israelis Speak Arabic." *Al-Ahram Weekly,* 30 March–6 April, 8.

Simmons, Beth. 1993. "Why Innovate." *World Politics* 45:361–405.

Simon, Sheldon. 1982. *The ASEAN States and Regional Security.* Stanford: Hoover Institution Press.

———. 1992. "The Regionalization of Defence in Southeast Asia." *Pacific Review* 5:112–24.

Singh, Anita Inder. 1995. "India's Relations with Russia and Central Asia." *International Affairs* 71:69–81.

Skålnes, Lars. 1993. "Allies and Rivals: Politics, Markets, and Grand Strategy." Ph.D. diss., University of California, Los Angeles.

Slater, Jerome. 1990–91. "The Superpowers and an Arab-Israeli Political Settlement: The Cold War Years." *Political Science Quarterly* 105:557–77.

Smith, Anthony. 1985. "State-Making and Nation-Building." In *States in History,* edited by John Hall. Oxford: Basil Blackwell.

Smock, David, ed. 1993. *Making War and Waging Peace: Foreign Intervention in Africa.* Washington, D.C.: U.S. Institute of Peace.

Smyth, Frank. 1994. "The Horror—Rwanda: A History Lesson." *New Republic,* 20 June, 19.

Sneider, Richard, and Mark Borthwick. 1983. "Institutions for Pacific Regional Cooperation." *Asian Survey* 23:1245–53.

Snidal, Duncan. 1985. "The Limits of Hegemonic Stability Theory." *International Organization* 39:579–614.

———. 1991. "Relative Gains and the Pattern of International Cooperation." *American Political Science Review* 85:701–26.

Snyder, Glenn. 1984. "The Security Dilemma in Alliance Politics." *World Politics* 36:461–95.

Snyder, Glenn, and Paul Diesing. 1977. *Conflict Among Nations: Bargaining, Decision Making, and System Structure in International Crises.* Princeton: Princeton University Press.

Snyder, Jack. 1984. *The Ideology of the Offensive: Military Decision Making and the Disasters of 1914.* Ithaca: Cornell University Press.

———. 1989. "International Leverage on Soviet Domestic Change." *World Politics* 42:1–30.

———. 1990. "Averting Anarchy in the New Europe." *International Security* 14 (4): 5–41.

———. 1991. *Myths of Empire: Domestic Politics and International Ambition.* Ithaca: Cornell University Press.

Solchanyk, Roman. 1993. "Ukraine's Search for Security." *RFE/RL Research Report* 2 (21 May): 1–6.

Solidum, Estrella. 1974. *Towards a Southeast Asian Community.* Quezon City: University of Philippines Press.

———. 1982. *Bilateral Summitry in ASEAN.* Manila: Foreign Service Institute.

Solingen, Etel. 1994a. "The Domestic Sources of Regional Regimes: The Evolution of Nuclear Ambiguity in the Middle East." *International Studies Quarterly* 38: 305–38.

———. 1994b. "The Political Economy of Nuclear Restraint." *International Security* 19 (2): 126–69.

———. 1996a. "Democracy, Economic Reform, and Regional Cooperation." *Journal of Theoretical Politics* 8 (1): 79–114.

———. 1996b. "Democratization in the Middle East: Quandaries of the Peace Process." *Journal of Democracy* 7 (3): 139–53.

———. 1997. "Emerging Regional Orders." Manuscript, University of California, Irvine.

Spiegel, Steven, and David J. Pervin, eds. 1995a. *Practical Peacemaking in the Middle East: Arms Control and Regional Security.* New York: Garland Publishing.

———, eds. 1995b. *Practical Peacemaking in the Middle East: The Environment, Economic Cooperation and Development, Water, and Refugees.* New York: Garland Publishing.

Spulbar, Nicolas. 1968. "East-West Trade and the Paradox of the Strategic Embargo." In *International Trade and Central Planning,* edited by Alan Brown and Egon Neugerger. Berkeley and Los Angeles: University of California Press.

Stallings, Barbara. 1992. "International Influence on Economic Policy: Debt, Stabilization, and Structural Reform." In *The Politics of Economic Adjustment,* edited Stephan Haggard and Robert R. Kaufman. Princeton: Princeton University Press.

Stavrianos, L. S. 1952. *Greece: American Dilemma and Opportunity.* Chicago: Henry Regnery.

Stein, Arthur A. 1990. *Why Nations Cooperate.* Ithaca: Cornell University Press.

———. n.d. "Blood and Power." Manuscript, University of California, Los Angeles.

Stein, Janice Gross. 1993. "The Political Economy of Security Agreements: The Linked Costs of Failure at Camp David." In *Double-Edged Diplomacy: International Bargaining and Domestic Politics,* edited by Peter B. Evans, Harold K.

Jacobson, and Robert D. Putnam. Berkeley and Los Angeles: University of California Press.

St. John, Ronald Bruce. 1992. *The Foreign Policy of Peru.* Boulder, Colo.: Lynne Rienner.

Strange, Susan. 1992. "States, Firms, and Diplomacy." *International Affairs* 68: 2–16.

Stremlau, John. 1991. "The New Global System and Its Implications for Peace and Security in Africa." U.S. Department of State Dispatch, September.

Sukrasep, Vinita. 1989. *ASEAN in International Relations.* Bangkok: Institute of Security and International Studies.

Sundhaussen, Ulf. 1982. *The Road to Power: Indonesian Military Politics, 1945–1967.* Kuala Lumpur: Oxford University Press.

Sunley, Johnathan. 1994. "The Moldovan Syndrome." *World Policy Journal* 11: 87–91.

Susser, Asher. 1990. *In Through the Out Door: Jordan's Disengagement and the Middle East Peace Process.* Washington, D.C.: Washington Institute for Near East Policy.

Tantawi, Mohamed Hussein. 1995a. "Defense Minister Explains Military Policy to Assembly." MENA, Cairo, 15 January, as translated in Foreign Broadcast Information Service–NES-95-011, 18 January, 25–27.

———. 1995b. "Regional Imbalance Rejected." *Al-Ahram Weekly,* 19–25 January, 2.

Taylor, Alan. 1982. *The Arab Balance of Power.* Syracuse, N.Y.: Syracuse University Press.

Telhami, Shibley. 1992. "Israeli Foreign Policy After the Cold War." In *The Arab-Israeli Search for Peace,* edited by Steven Spiegel. Boulder, Colo.: Lynne Rienner.

Tetreault, Mary A. 1980. "Measuring Interdependence." *International Organization* 34:429–43.

Thompson, William R. 1973. "The Regional Subsystem: A Conceptual Explication and a Propositional Inventory." *International Studies Quarterly* 17:89–117.

Thongswadi, Tarnthong. 1979. "ASEAN After the Vietnam War: Stability and Development Through Regional Cooperation." Ph.D. diss., Claremont Graduate School, Claremont, Calif.

Thorndike, Terry. 1989. "Grenada." In *Intervention in the 1980s: U.S. Foreign Policy in the Third World,* edited by Peter Schraeder. Boulder, Colo.: Lynne Rienner.

Tilly, Charles. 1989. "War Making and State Making as Organized Crime." In *Bringing the State Back In,* edited by Peter B. Evans, Dietrich Rueschemeyer, and Theda Skocpol. Cambridge: Cambridge University Press.

———. 1994. "States and Nationalism in Europe, 1492–1992." *Theory and Society* 23:131–46.

Tirole, Jean. 1988. *The Theory of Industrial Organization.* Cambridge, Mass.: MIT Press.

Tolz, Vera. 1993. "The Burden of the Imperial Legacy." *RFE/RL Research Report* 2 (14 May): 41–46.

Tompkins, Pauline. 1949. *American-Russian Relations in the Far East.* New York: Macmillan.

Toukan, Abdullah. 1995. "The Middle East Peace Process, Arms Control, and Regional Security." In *Practical Peacemaking in the Middle East: Arms Control and*

Regional Security, edited by Steven Spiegel and David J. Pervin. New York: Garland Publishing.

Touval, Saadia. 1994. "Why the UN Fails." *Foreign Affairs* 73 (5): 44–57.

Tow, William T. 1991. *Encountering the Dominant Player: U.S. Extended Deterrence Strategy in the Asia-Pacific.* New York: Columbia University Press.

Trachtenberg, Marc. 1993. "Intervention in Historical Perspective." In *Emerging Norms of Justified Intervention,* edited by Laura W. Reed and Carl Kaysen. Cambridge, Mass.: American Academy of Arts and Sciences.

Triska, Jan, ed. 1986. *Dominant Powers and Subordinate States: The United States in Latin America and the Soviet Union in Eastern Europe.* Durham, N.C.: Duke University Press.

Tsebelis, George. 1990. *Nested Games.* Berkeley and Los Angeles: University of California Press.

U.K. Public Record Office (PRO). 1907. Foreign Office, Pew Gardens, London. Haggard to Sir Earl Grey, 14 December.

U.S. Arms Control and Disarmament Agency (ACDA). 1975. *World Military Expenditures and Arms Transfers, 1963–1973.* Washington, D.C.: U.S. GPO.

———. 1979. *World Military Expenditures and Arms Transfers, 1968–77.* Washington, D.C.: U.S. GPO.

———. 1986. *World Military Expenditures and Arms Transfers, 1985.* Washington, D.C.: U.S. GPO.

———. 1988. *World Military Expenditures and Arms Transfers, 1987.* Washington, D.C.: U.S. GPO.

———. 1989. *World Military Expenditures and Arms Transfers, 1988.* Washington, D.C.: U.S. GPO.

———. 1990. *World Military Expenditures and Arms Transfers, 1989.* Washington, D.C.: U.S. GPO.

———. 1994. *World Military Expenditures and Arms Transfers, 1991–92.* Washington, D.C.: U.S. GPO.

U.S. Central Intelligence Agency. 1995. *World Factbook, 1995.* Washington: U.S. GPO.

U.S. Department of Defense (DOD). 1990. *A Strategic Framework for the Asian Pacific Rim: Looking Forward to the 21st Century.* Washington, D.C.: DOD, Office of International Security Affairs.

———. 1995a. *United States Security Strategy for the Americas.* Washington, D.C.: DOD, Office of International Security Affairs.

———. 1995b. *United States Security Strategy for the East Asia–Pacific Region.* Washington, D.C.: DOD, Office of International Security Affairs.

U.S. House. 1976. Committee on International Relations. *Hearings on United States National Security Policy Vis-à-Vis Eastern Europe.* 94th Cong., 2d sess.

———. 1994. "Report to Accompany H.R. 4541: African Conflict Resolution Act." 103d Cong., 2d sess. Report 103-723.

U.S. Pacific Command. 1993. "Posture Statement 1993." Honolulu: USPACOM.

VanDeMark, Brian. 1991. *Into the Quagmire: Lyndon Johnson and the Escalation of the Vietnam War.* New York: Oxford University Press.

Van Evera, Stephen. 1984. "The Cult of the Offensive and the Origins of the First World War." *International Security* 9:58–107.

———. 1989. "Why Europe Matters, Why the Third World Doesn't: American Grand Strategy After the Cold War." *Journal of Strategic Studies* 13:1–51.
———. 1991. "Primed for Peace: Europe After the Cold War." In *The Cold War and After,* edited by Sean Lynn-Jones. Cambridge, Mass.: MIT Press.
Vasquez, John. 1993. *The War Puzzle.* Cambridge: Cambridge University Press.
Vatikiotis, Michael. 1994. *Indonesian Politics Under Suharto.* London: Routledge.
Vayrynen, Raimo. 1979. "Economic and Military Position of Regional Power Centers." *Journal of Peace Research* 16:349–69.
———. 1984. "Regional Conflict Formations: An Intractable Problem of International Relations." *Journal of Peace Research* 21: 337–59.
Velit, Juan. 1993. "El contexto político-estrategico del Peru." In *Percepciónes de amenaza y políticas de defensa en America Latina,* edited by Cruz Johnson, Vice Admiral Rigoberto, and Augusto Varas Fernandez. Santiago: FLACSO.
Viner, Jacob. 1939. "International Finance and Balance of Power Diplomacy, 1880–1914." *Southwestern Political and Social Science Quarterly* 9:49–85.
Waever, Ole. 1992. "Nordic Nostalgia: Northern Europe After the Cold War." *International Affairs* 68:77–102.
Wagner, Robert Harrison. 1993. "The Causes of Peace." In *Stopping the Killing: How Civil Wars End,* edited by Roy Licklider. New York: New York University Press.
Walker, Martin. 1994. "Russia and the West: What Is to Be Done Now." *World Policy Journal* 11:1–10.
Walker, Thomas W., ed. 1987. *Reagan and the Sandinistas.* Boulder, Colo.: Westview Press.
Wallander, Celeste. 1992. "Opportunity, Incrementalism, and Learning in the Extension and Retraction of Soviet Global Commitments." *Security Studies* 1: 514–42.
Wallensteen, Peter, and Karin Axell. 1993. "Armed Conflict at the End of the Cold War, 1989–92." *Journal of Peace Research* 30 (3): 331–46.
Wallensteen, Peter, and Margareta Sollenberg. 1995. "After the Cold War: Emerging Patterns of Armed Conflict, 1989–1994." *Journal of Peace Research* 32: 345–60.
Walt, Stephen M. 1987. *The Origins of Alliances.* Ithaca: Cornell University Press.
———. 1989. "The Case for Finite Containment: Analyzing U.S. Grand Strategy." *International Security* 10:5–49.
———. 1992. "Revolution and War." *World Politics* 44:321–68.
Waltz, Kenneth N. 1959. *Man, the State, and War: A Theoretical Analysis.* New York: Columbia University Press.
———. 1967. "International Structure, National Force, and the Balance of World Power." *Journal of International Affairs* 21:215–31.
———. 1979. *Theory of International Politics.* Reading, Mass.: Addison-Wesley.
———. 1986. "Reflections on *Theory of International Politics*: A Response to My Critics." In *Neorealism and Its Critics,* edited by Robert O. Keohane. New York: Columbia University Press.
Weatherbee, Donald. 1984. "ASEAN Regionalism: The Salient Dimension." In *ASEAN Security and Economic Development,* edited by Karl D. Jackson and Hadi Soesastro. Berkeley: Institute of East Asian Studies.

———, ed. 1985. *Southeast Asia Divided: The ASEAN-Indochina Crisis.* Boulder, Colo.: Westview Press.

Weber, Katja. 1992. "Hierarchy Amidst Anarchy: Transaction Costs and International Cooperation." Ph.D. diss., University of California, Los Angeles.

———. 1997. "Hierarchy Amidst Anarchy: A Transaction Costs Approach to International Security Cooperation." *International Studies Quarterly* (forthcoming).

Weber, Steve. 1991. *Cooperation and Discord in U.S.-Soviet Arms Control.* Princeton: Princeton University Press.

———. 1993. "Shaping the Postwar Balance of Power: Multilateralism in NATO." In *Multilateralism Matters: The Theory and Praxis of an Institutional Form,* edited by John Ruggie. New York: Columbia University Press.

Weiner, Myron. 1992. "Peoples and States in a New Ethnic Order." *Third World Quarterly* 13 (2): 317–33.

Weinstein, Franklin. 1969. *Indonesia Abandons Confrontation.* Ithaca: Cornell University, Southeast Asia Program.

Weiss, Thomas G., and James Blight. 1992. *The Suffering Grass: Superpowers and Regional Conflict in Southern Africa and the Caribbean.* Boulder, Colo.: Lynne Rienner.

Weiss, Thomas G., and Meryl A. Kessler. 1991. "The United Nations and Third World Security in the 1990s." In *Third World Security in the Post–Cold War Era,* edited by Thomas G. Weiss and Meryl A. Kessler. Boulder, Colo.: Lynne Rienner.

Wendt, Alexander. 1987. "The Agent-Structure Problem in International Relations." *International Organization* 41: 335–70.

———. 1992. "Anarchy Is What States Make of It: The Social Construction of Power Politics." *International Organization* 46: 391–25.

———. 1994. "Collective Identity Formation and the International State." *American Political Science Review* 88 (2): 384–96.

Whitaker, Arthur P. 1954. *The Western Hemisphere Idea.* Ithaca: Cornell University Press.

Williamson, Oliver. 1985. *The Economic Institutions of Capitalism.* New York: Free Press.

Wolfowitz, Paul D. 1994. "Clinton's First Year." *Foreign Affairs* 73 (1): 28–43.

Wood, Adrian. 1994. *North-South Trade, Employment, and Inequality: Changing Fortunes in a Skill-Driven World.* Oxford: Clarendon Press.

Wood, Bryce. 1961. *The Making of the Good Neighbor Policy.* New York: Columbia University Press.

———. 1966. *The United States and Latin American Wars, 1932–1942.* New York: Columbia University Press.

Woodward, Ralph Lee, Jr. 1976. *Central America.* New York: Oxford University Press.

Ya'ari, Ehud. 1987. *Peace by Piece: A Decade of Egyptian Policy Toward Israel.* Washington, D.C.: Washington Institute for Near East Policy.

Yalem, Ronald. 1973. "Theories of Regionalism." In *Regional Politics and World Order,* edited by Richard Falk and Saul Mendlovitz. San Francisco: W. H. Freeman.

Yaniv, Avner. 1987a. *Deterrence Without the Bomb: The Politics of Israeli Strategy.* Lexington, Mass.: D. C. Heath.

———. 1987b. *Dilemmas of Security: Politics, Strategy, and the Israeli Experience in Lebanon.* New York: Oxford University Press.

Yarbrough, Beth V., and Robert M. Yarbrough. 1992. *Cooperation and Governance in International Trade: The Strategic Organizational Approach.* Princeton: Princeton University Press.

Yorke, Valerie. 1988. *Domestic Politics and Regional Security: Jordan, Syria, and Israel.* Aldershot: Gower.

Young, Crawford. 1988. "The African Colonial State and Its Political Legacy." In *The Precarious Balance: State and Society in Africa,* edited by Donald Rothchild and Naomi Chazan. Boulder, Colo.: Westview Press.

Young, Marilyn. 1991. *The Vietnam Wars, 1945–1990.* New York: HarperCollins.

Young, Oran. 1968. *A Systemic Approach to International Relations.* Research monograph no. 33. Princeton: Center for International Studies, Princeton University.

Zartman, William. 1967. "Africa as a Subordinate State System in International Relations." *International Organization* 21:545–64.

———. 1989. *Ripe for Resolution: Conflict and Intervention in Africa.* New York, Oxford University Press.

Ziemke, Caroline F. 1992. "Peace Without Strings? Interwar Naval Arms Control Revisited." *Washington Quarterly* 15 (4): 87–106.

Zimmerman, William. 1972. "Hierarchical Regional Systems and the Politics of System Boundaries." *International Organization* 26:18–36.

Zisser, Eyal. 1994. "Asad Inches Toward Peace." *Middle East Quarterly* 1 (3): 37–44.

About the Editors and Contributors

BRIAN L. JOB is professor of political science and director of the Institute of International Relations at the University of British Columbia. His recent work focuses on the evolving international security order of the Asia-Pacific.

EDMOND J. KELLER is professor of political science and director of the James S. Coleman African Studies Center at the University of California, Los Angeles. Among his recent publications are *Revolutionary Ethiopia: From Empire to People's Republic* and *Africa in the New International Order: Rethinking State Sovereignty and Regional Security* (with Don Rothchild).

YUEN FOONG KHONG is a fellow of Nuffield College, Oxford University. He is the author of *Analogies at War: Korea, Munich, Dien Bien Phu, and the Vietnam Decisions of 1965*. He is completing a study funded by the Social Science Research Council–MacArthur Foundation Program on International Peace and Security and the United States Institute of Peace on the sources of security cooperation in Southeast Asia.

DAVID A. LAKE is professor of political science at the University of Caliornia, San Diego, and coeditor of *International Organization* (with Peter Gourevitch). During the preparation of this volume, he served as research director for international relations at the University of California Institute on Global Conflict and Cooperation. Lake has authored *Power, Protection, and Free Trade: International Sources of American Commercial Strategy, 1887– 1939;* edited *The International Political Economy of Trade;* and coedited *The State and American Foreign Economic Policy* (with G. John Ikenberry and Michael Mastanduno), *International Political Economy: Perspectives on Global Power and Wealth* (with Jeffry A. Frieden), *The International Spread of Ethnic Conflict* (with Donald Rothchild), and *Strategic Choice and International Relations* (with Robert Powell). He is now completing *Entangling Relations: American Foreign Policy in Its Century.*

STEVEN E. LOBELL is a doctoral candidate in political science at the University of California, Los Angeles. He is now completing his dissertation, "Managing Hegemonic Decline: Dilemmas of Strategy and Finance."

DAVID R. MARES is associate professor of political science at the University of California, San Diego. He authored *Penetrating International Markets: Theoretical Considerations and a Mexican Agricultural Case Study.* His most recent works include *Violent Peace: Lessons from Latin America* and an edited volume, *Civil-Military Relations: Democracy and Regional Security in Latin America, Southern Asia, and Central Europe.*

PATRICK M. MORGAN holds the Thomas and Elizabeth Tierney Chair in Peace and Conflict Studies and directs the Global Peace and Conflict Studies Program at the University of California, Irvine, and is on the faculty of the College of Europe, Bruges, Belgium. He is a former vice-president of the International Studies Association and past Washington, D.C., Wilson Center Fellow, Fulbright Teaching Fellow, and American Council on Education Fellow. Morgan authored *Deterrence: A Conceptual Analysis* and *Theories and Approaches to International Politics* and coedited *Strategic Military Surprise* (with Klaus Knorr) and *Security and Arms Control* (with Edward Kolodziej).

PAUL A. PAPAYOANOU is assistant professor of political science at the University of California, San Diego. He has authored the forthcoming *Economic Interdependence and the Balance of Power,* and his articles have appeared in *International Security, International Studies Quarterly,* and the *Journal of Conflict Resolution.*

DAVID J. PERVIN is a Ph.D. candidate in political science at the University of California, Los Angeles. He holds his M.A. from the Johns Hopkins School of Advanced International Studies. Pervin, with Steven L. Spiegel, coedited *Practical Peacemaking in the Middle East* and *At Issue: Politics in the World Arena.*

PHILIP G. ROEDER is associate professor of political science at the University of California, San Diego. He is the author of *Red Sunset: The Failure of Soviet Politics* and articles that have appeared in *American Political Science Review, World Politics,* and *International Studies Quarterly.* He is currently completing a book manuscript entitled "Ethnicity in the State: Negotiating Post-Soviet Constitutions."

RICHARD ROSECRANCE is professor of political science, director of the Institute of International Relations and Policy, and associate dean of International Studies and Overseas Programs at the University of California, Los Angeles. He authored *America's Economic Resurgence: A Bold New Strategy* and coedited *The Domestic Bases of Grand Strategy.* He is now at work on a study of the balance of power in modern history.

PETER SCHOTT is a graduate student in political science at the University of California, Los Angeles. His major interests include international trade and finance.

SUSAN L. SHIRK is a professor in the political science department and the Graduate School of International Relations and Pacific Studies at the University of California, San Diego, and director of the University of California Institute on Global Conflict and Cooperation. Her recent books include *The Political Logic of Economic Reform in China, Power and Prosperity: Economics and Security Linkages in Asia-Pacific* (coedited, with Christopher Twomey), and *How China Opened Its Door: The Political Success of the PRC's Foreign Trade and Investment Reforms.*

ETEL SOLINGEN is associate professor of political science at the University of California, Irvine, and a recipient of a 1995–96 MacArthur Foundation grant on peace and international cooperation. She is the author of *Industrial Policy, Technology, and International Bargaining: Designing Nuclear Industries in Argentina and Brazil,* editor of *Scientists and the State: Domestic Structures and the International Context,* and has published in *International Organization, Comparative Politics, International Studies Quarterly, International Security, Journal of Theoretical Politics,* and *Journal of Democracy.*

ARTHUR A. STEIN is professor of political science at the University of California, Los Angeles, and Senior Fellow, University of California, Institute on Global Conflict and Cooperation, 1996–97. He is the author of *The Nation at War* and *Why Nations Cooperate,* and coeditor of *The Domestic Bases of Grand Strategy.*

Index

Page numbers in italics refer to illustrations.